Globalization

Myth, Miracle, Mirage

Rolf Hackmann

UNIVERSITY PRESS OF AMERICA,® INC.
Lanham • Boulder • New York • Toronto • Oxford

9713966

GIFT
3/22/06

Copyright © 2005 by
University Press of America,® Inc.
4501 Forbes Boulevard
Suite 200
Lanham, Maryland 20706
UPA Acquisitions Department (301) 459-3366

PO Box 317
Oxford
OX2 9RU, UK

Library of Congress Control Number: 2004116504
ISBN 0-7618-3010-3 (paperback : alk. ppr.)

∞™ The paper used in this publication meets the minimum
requirements of American National Standard for Information
Sciences—Permanence of Paper for Printed Library Materials,
ANSI Z39.48—1992

Contents

Preface

The end of the second millennium ushered in a time of fundamental changes for all of mankind that in magnitude of impact and time to run its course can only be compared to the renaissance period rising out of the declining dark ages. Roughly beginning with the end of World War II and the following cold war period, it quickly led to the union of the free world under the umbrella of the U.S., the UN, and other international agencies in a broad-based effort to end armed conflict in the world, defuse hostile confrontations between political ideologies, and begin the construction of a peaceful world community.

In time, the handy acronym "globalization" entered the world's vocabulary to capture the meaning of this historic transformation. At first, it denoted the evolutionary process merely in economic terms, but since has morphed to cover practically all aspects of human life, political, humanitarian, legal, health, environmental, and other issues. Its main importance came from the vision of a "New Era" being born to sweep humanity quickly to a "borderless society," where everybody is sharing in the bounty of freedom and material progress.

This initial euphoria has given way to more sober expectations in light of actual changes taking place in the first 50 years of establishing a homogenized but happy mankind. Yes, tangible advances have been made in trade, travel, and communications as well as the consumption of global goods and services including entertainment, the widespread adoption of English as the global lingua franca, etc. All of them are touching the convenience of human life, areas where a compatibility with the local way of life is easily established. The same cannot yet be found for more sensitive, and thus carefully guarded, aspects of diverse human cultures developed over thousands of years.

Seen realistically, the door for a globalization process has been opened. But in a very limited way, which does not unleash a rushing torrent of change, only step-by-step adjustments most likely to take centuries rather than decades to reach its final point of fulfillment. The world is still just too complex, psychologically and culturally, to expect otherwise.

It is easy to address human creature comforts across the globe by merely creating an abundance of material things for the satisfaction of physical needs shared by most people, pleasing the body so to speak. All it takes is a determined effort, good planning, and a sufficient application of resources to generate the necessary economic means in terms of employment, income, production, commercial activities, investment, and the consumption flowing from them.

It is a lot more difficult to address the needs of the human mind, which are as diverse as ever and less prone to yield to outside influences than may have been expected by the engineers of globalization.

Their development model is thus beset with basic flaws by attaching too much weight to material forces driving the process, too little to human psychology, and a general impatience in pushing the agenda. Their blueprint for progress collides head-on with deeply ingrained and culturally conditioned beliefs, traditions, customs, instincts, drives, attitudes, prejudices, and habits. Expectations of turning an undifferentiated mankind into homogenized citizens of the new world by simply changing their economic conditions will be hard to fulfill in short order.

The best example for this is set by the European integration process. 50 years in the making, not even all EU members have accepted the common currency, the Euro, nor have they followed a cohesive foreign policy with regard to the U.S. intervention in Iraq, and they have yet to adopt a common European constitution. These are countries with a long history together, they know each other and may even feel a common bond in being Europeans. If their attempt at regionalization is beset with so many obstacles, how can one realistically expect smoother sailing for the globalization effort addressed at even more diverse cultures, unless it is imposed by force of course.

Two schools of thought have formed around the globalization issue. Proponents approve it ecstatically as a miracle formula for the advancement of humanity through generous sharing of wealth, resources, and technology between the affluent and the needy in an altruistic atmosphere of mutual cooperation. A world governed by the common interests of all for the benefit of all, under the auspices of an enlightened world government. It is an almost religious vision of the new world order.

Detractors see it as a clever disguise for the inevitable establishment of a crushing power elite eager for world dominance and universal exploitation of weaker and subservient elements of a global society be they nations or human masses. The ultimate outcome is a global super state, a ghetto, amounting to nothing less than a continuation of history, but on a totally different scale. This group is responsible for the growing numbers of organized and often militant protests against globalization during annual meetings of the World Bank and IMF, for example, which they consider responsible for the growing dislocation of industries, unemployment, and impoverishment in the industrial world, exploitation of unorganized labor in the developing world, and corruption of government officials worldwide. In their opinion it is a step backward from the proud and civilized achievements of the developed world with high standards of material living, education, health and social protection programs, and a general respect for all human beings.

Arguments for or against either position can be found depending on the psychological disposition of the observer. But, reality is much too complex to be painted merely in terms of black and white, gain or loss, moral or criminal, materialistic greed or altruism. Fortunately, half a century of globalization in progress permit some generalizations to be drawn from it. They are presented in three separate sections of analysis.

The first addresses the economic effect of private sector industries from all nations on the development, expressed in terms of foreign direct investments (FDI), the capital side, and its effect on the global generation of gross domestic product, the output of value added, the development of international trade, the flow of profits, and the development of global employment, all common and familiar measurements of economic progress.

Such a discussion provides details for the last two decades of the 20th century, which prove the whole globalization effect from this angle to be of only moderate proportions despite the huge commitments of human and financial resources. (Chapters 1–9).

This results from the fact that 80% of direct investments went to already developed nations, where they had more of a replacement effect on already existing local competitors with unclear real advantages for the macro-economic welfare of the recipient nations. For developing nations, the picture is decidedly more favorable for local economic development, because foreign direct investments opened production, trading, and employment opportunities where few or none had existed before. All told, the net penetration of global output of goods and services due to direct investment firms does not exceed about 10–12% at the beginning of the 21st century.

International trade, though, is the real winner because FDI activities helped it to expand tremendously. The importance of FDI for global trade is underscored by the observation that 80% of this trade is generated by FDI enterprises, be it in the form of trade going on between parent and affiliates, affiliates among themselves, or all of them with independent customers or suppliers.

A second field of investigation deals with more generalized aspects of globalization. Here, a global economy in transition emerges. Global trade is expanding strongly, but totally free trade is still a dream after 50 years of lip service to the principle and strenuous efforts by GATT, the WTO, and regular G-7 summits. The use of massive currency interventions by practically all countries, including the conservative Swiss, to better their export chances in a world of industrial overcapacity and deflationary pressures confirms that view. Demographic changes also play a role. Saturated life styles, low reproductive rates, aging, slow economic growth due to or accompanied by industrial relocation, sticky unemployment, reliance on immigrant labor, ever-growing government and related tax burdens, characterize maturing consumer societies for most developed economies.

Such a picture is in sharp contrast to the emerging economies with an age pyramid resting on a solid and expanding base of young, well educated, and ambitious producers and consumers. The size and development potential of these markets, both of which are larger than all the developed markets put together, attracts growing investment capital for industries serving the internal as well as export demand from developed nations, which is the key to financing their high rate of growth.

The rapid evolution of this part of the world is already causing a significant shift in the economic center of gravity away from the developed to the developing nations, with substantial advances in output and trade favoring the latter, and questionable benefits for employments, income levels, and standard of living for the former. Developed nations are not competitive with these countries, if free trade and investment is upheld at all costs. The present solution of relocating production capacity from the high cost countries to developing nations with their inherent cost advantages makes matters worse over the long run. It deprives these countries of investment capital, employment opportunities, and the income to continue funding of their social programs at present levels.

The more vigorous wealth creation in the emerging markets, on the other hand, totally reverses the economic, political, and military power constellation we see in place at this moment. If globalization appears as a typical Western phenomenon now, it could very well be replaced by similar processes spawned in those power houses of the future to come back like a boomerang here. These countries are developing their industries at a fast pace with the help of

Western technology. They have most of the world's energy resources in hand, and are increasingly setting the terms of global trade. Their increasing self-assurance is palpable in product and financial markets. The bold move by Islamic nations to re-introduce the gold Dinar in a world that abolished the use of monetary gold is making a statement whose impact cannot be grasped as yet. But if it means that oil and other raw materials could be billed in gold rather than paper dollars, it would certainly have catastrophic consequences for today's world used to the convenience of the dollar. (Chapter 10)

The last point to make is the impact of America's decided foreign policy re-orientation from an apparent willingness to be part of, and constructive contributor to, an emerging world community to a declared total independence in setting its foreign relations objectives. The lone-ranger mentality stated officially by the neo-conservatives under the New American Century banner, serves exclusive American interests in the pursuit of world dominance.

It is clearly directed at American leadership, independence, and dominance in world affairs. Questioning this policy will not be a privilege of other nations. They are expected to follow American demands and expectations under a constellation of clear hierarchy of command and shared financial responsibility. A spirit or actions of independence will not be tolerated, be it by friends or potential foes. Its first application is visible in the Gulf War and again in Afghanistan and Iraq.

It serves as a demonstration of the adopted principle of pre-emptive American military strikes against anybody posing only an assumed threat to America's drive towards world hegemony laid down in the "Bush Doctrine." This makes it a purely military alternative, where the perceived superiority of American values as a society, political form, economy, and military might are joined to form an overpowering and awe inspiring behemoth ready to crush any appearance of insubordination. Any misunderstanding of this point could indeed be very detrimental.

The world is faced with a very old frame of mind in a new guise. If it succeeds globalization in the broadest application of its meaning will have come to its conclusion. If it fails it will deepen the division of the world rather than leading to its unification as promised by the inspiring concept of the UN. For the moment it is a very real, dead serious attempt at globalization not as a society of equals, but a master race dominating the submissive and compliant masses of the world. How it will unfold cannot be predicted, but it will be very interesting to observe.

I want to express my gratitude, often felt but perhaps not always adequately shown, to all those who have enabled my work, my life, and the happiness flowing from both. My special gratitude is dedicated to my parents for providing the safe harbor of a good family, and sharing the principles and guidance for a meaningful life. It goes equally to my wife who accepted the often trying schedules and changes of a business career, and shouldering more than her share of raising our own family, yet find the time to encourage and support my interests. Also, to our children, who turned into adults with careers and families to be proud of, the next generation to uphold the traditions and values that have served their predecessors so well. Finally, my special thanks go out to all other fellow humans that have enriched my experiences, insights, and appreciation of life in their own ways.

Chapter One

The Background of Globalization

INTRODUCTION

Any attempt at describing globalization faces a series of obstacles starting with the definition of the term itself, which is open to so many different interpretations judging by available literature on the subject. A further drawback is the volumes of politicized opinions and attitudes on the symptoms, but little on the substance. The only point that all seem to agree on is to portray it as a phenomenon with serious implications for the world's economic, political, and cultural environment.

Some see this as a natural and inevitable consequence of mankind's progress to its final destiny. Others suspect a sinister conspiracy of interest groups aiming at world hegemony, cultural imperialism, and exploitation. Given such broad range of topics, viewpoints, and attitudes the student of globalization does well to tackle one at a time rather than all at once. As economic aspects of the process seem to dominate all discussions, they will be the focus for the ensuing analysis, a decision which offers the added advantage of keeping it within familiar, measurable, and factual economic dimensions.

It links globalization to the existing world economy, which it is expected to "globalize" by unleashing forces changing the historic context of human society. The world economy has existed since time immemorial, even though in a very fragmented constellation. It has turned into a measurable dimension as far as size and speed of expansion are concerned within the last hundred years, or so, with the emergence of scientific curiosity to describe, measure, and weigh everything. Even though it represents a developing organism, it is rather viewed as a static monument of such huge dimensions too hard to see and understand completely. Adding to the problem is the realization that despite its familiar concept, the world or global economy is not a homogeneous entity, but rather a complex mesh of different cultures, geographies, and economic development levels.

It is against this background that globalization is to be measured, regardless of whether it is a political, economic, cultural, or social force, or a combination of all of these. But unfortunately, globalization cannot be neatly measured and described like the global economy, because no standard measure has been found yet to make this process, this dynamic force comprised of so many different elements, visible in its entirety, and relate it to the familiar world economy.

The different natures of the global economy concept and the globalization force's internal impact on its development and appearance can be best explained by the two approaches economists take to describe the world of economics. On one hand they look at the sum total results of all economic endeavors undertaken by man, which they call macro-economics, and apply it to total national, regional, and even global economic structures. Here we find data on population, people employed, international trade, and gross domestic product (GDP) of goods and services measured in terms of value added, income or compensation of the labor force, or also final consumption expenditures.

On the other they try to measure the contributions of individuals, firms, and industries to the overall result, calling this the micro-economic activities contributing to the overall picture of macro-economics. Globalization efforts definitely put them into the realm of micro-economics, which are nothing but business activities instrumental in the generation of macro-economic. This distinction is important insofar as both are part of the same economic entity but measured in different terms, which makes a direct reconciliation somewhat problematic. It is similar to describing an ant hill and, simultaneously, the confluent activities of ants in shaping it.

A further distinction between the two economic magnitudes set down above is vital for the understanding of what is being measured and evaluated. The world economy, as a handy abstraction of reality, is actually a composite of many nations, that have and are proud of very different histories, cultures, ambitions, and thus strong feelings about their sovereign integrity and independence. Beyond that, their economic life may be subject to political ideologies, which for simplicity's sake may be categorized as capitalism, socialism, and totalitarian communism which are part of their cultural heritage, but potential sources of conflict with globalization forces of a different color.

What is essential to the discussion here of global economics and globalization in the following, is to understand that all macro-economic statistics are quantitative representations of national economies. This is a historic fact that provides fairly accurate still pictures for economic growth and development of individual economies, or even the global economy in the aggregate, in the mind of the beholder, yet is only poorly suited for a descriptive explanation of global integration forces added together under the term globalization. One is a static concept, the other dynamic, and both need to be linked in a meaningful way in order to gauge the impact of globalization on economies, national, regional, or global, if there is any.

This is to say, that by simply portraying the global economy in the traditional sense would miss the essence of globalization, which may be seen as the intrusion and entrenchment of one national business interest into the economy of another. Such a view would turn the output of GDP within nationally defined, political territories as constituting a truly "national" achievement or ownership of this product into a gross misrepresentation. With the robust development of foreign direct investments, and a practically totally free international trading system crossing national boundaries, the traditional view of what is national output of goods and services becomes untenable.

In the traditional scheme of things, for instance, foreign subsidiaries in the US are treated as bona fide US companies, as if they had lost their nationality by establishing themselves on American territory. Or conversely, subsidiaries of US parents becoming French, British, or Japanese entities, which are now treated as an integral part of the host country of their choice.

The concept of globalization does not necessarily question the legitimacy of political boundaries and nation states. But it demands the recognition of foreign ownership of productive resources within these national boundaries which, in turn, automatically expands the concept of national economic power to include its projection into markets beyond the original national territory. In other words, the traditional definition of a national economy based on the principle of territory, should give way to a new one based on national ownership and control over capital invested anywhere on this globe. This applies equally to capital control over production, national distribution, and international trade.

Defining globalization as the re-distribution of national shares in the global economy on the principle of capital control, does not judge the implications of this process beyond its immediate purpose for the investigation here, its economic impact. It cannot claim to let the world economy grow faster, or produce only positive economic consequences. It is, however, a basic challenge to existing traditions and norms, and by promising to be an even more prominent factor for cultural diffusion and osmosis, it clashes directly and perhaps even purposefully with jealously guarded feelings of national sovereignty, cultural elements of education, living and working conditions, consumption and communication patterns, and the politico-legal environment. It paves the road for the visionary "borderless society" of the future, the homogenized human plantation that may look at the present period of gradual exfoliation of traditional cultures as the medieval ages of all mankind.

THE SIZE AND GEOGRAPHIC DISTRIBUTION OF THE GLOBAL ECONOMY

Trying to get to the substance of globalization requires a search for quantitative information and clues from many different sources. There just are no publications dealing with the specific topic as such. The problem is compounded by the quality, limited availability, comparability, and reliability of statistical details despite the best efforts of many and diverse sources like the UN, the European Union, the OECD, the IMF, the World Bank, and governments themselves.

Most often there is no information at all, and where it becomes available in bits and pieces it may be lacking in a desirable degree of standardization and uniformity. A list of major contributors to the problems encountered is also presented by the multitudes of national currencies with ever-fluctuating exchange rates, the lack of a uniform nomenclature for industries and trade categories, different accounting standards for financial information, lack of annually updated time series, mixtures of preliminary estimates and final data, and many others.

The use of the U.S. dollar as the international standard of measurements guarantees U.S. economic data to be reported in a reliable and consistent way. But it can add to grave uncertainties and outright distortions of economic facts and trends expressed in foreign currencies, for instance, which may actually show economic trends going in opposite directions after translation into the dollar standard.

Another element is the changing methodology in defining a country's GDP. The Bureau of Economic Analysis (BEA) in the American Department of Commerce, for example, introduced a radically new way of calculation for computer-related output of value added in 1995 as explained by its own website:

> *"The new quality-adjusted semiconductor price indexes are calculated using different methodologies for memory chips and for microprocessor chips. . . . the price index for microprocessor chips is quality-adjusted using a 'matched-model' approach . . . some price data are estimated using hedonic regressions that link chip prices to various performance*

characteristics; this methodology is similar to BEA's methodology for estimating computer prices." (Source: www.bea.doc.gov/).

What this elegant phraseology says is that instead of measuring value-added in terms output costs or revenues accruing to the factors of production, as commonly done, the statistics now factor in performance increases of the merchandise produced. The significance of the switch becomes clearer when relating it to Moore's Law, a widely accepted observation stating that semi-conductor speed and processing power, their performance measure, double every 18 months, with no increase in price. Conversely, every 18 months progress in manufacturing technology cuts the cost for the same level of performance in half. (Mohr, J., 2001).

Substitution of performance for value added in traditional financial terms tends to mask realistic productivity increases of the economy by overstating them and, conversely, understating the development of the consumer price index (CPI) at the same time. It has, no doubt, contributed to the admired and also envied productivity increases documented by official American statistics. Other countries fell behind, simply because they had not yet reached this level of statistical sophistication.

Thanks to the UN, the World Bank, and the OECD a much needed and useful outline of the world economy expressed in terms of gross domestic product (GDP) emerges in Table 1.1. The original data have been grouped into six separate areas: a world total, the U.S., Europe, Japan, and an OECD aggregate as representing the industrialized or developed world, and the "all others" category referring to the developing world.

The U.S. share in this traditional view of the world market is substantial but quite changeable, with a historic range between 24–32% over a period of three decades. Yet, it has basically maintained its overall share despite all these fluctuations and rapid economic progress in other parts of the world. In the 1970s the U.S. share accounted for 27% of the global GDP volume, 30% in the 1980s, and 28% in the 1990s. The fluctuations around these averages are mainly attributable to adjustments in the dollar's exchange value due to economic and political developments like OPEC in the early and late seventies, a recession in the late eighties and early nineties, the collapse of the Soviet Union, the near-collapse of the Asian economies, etc. The currency's relative stability over the period is remarkable in view of the nation's large and growing perennial trade deficits. Theoretically, they should have undermined the dollar over a period of three decades had it not been for its reserve status vis-a-vis other currencies, the safe haven image of the country in case of international crisis, and the willingness of foreigner dollar holders to invest their surplus receipts in American real estate, bonds, and equities.

While America essentially maintained its place, Western Europe did gain share until it fell back behind the U.S. in 2000/1. This fact may have spurred a competitive development aiming at the enlargement of the European Union (EU) to embrace central European countries, and NAFTA's evolution into the Free Trade Area of the Americas (FTAA) to eventually encompass all of North, South, and Central America.

Japan's progress against the U.S. as well as Europe is phenomenal and fully confirms the competitive image of that nation. From a global GDP share of 6% in 1970 the country has risen to a peak of 18.3% in 1993, before settling back dramatically to 13% in 2001. Expressed differently, Japan has been able to advance from 20% to 49% of the U.S. output of value added between 1970 and 2000, and turn in a similar performance vis-a-vis Europe by advancing from 25% to 56%.

Table 1.1. World Gross Domestic Product—($billion)

Year	Total	U.S.A.	%	Europe	%	Japan	%	OECD	%	Other	%
1970	3,190	1,009	31.6	828	26.0	204	6.4	2,211	69.3	979	30.7
1971	3,499	1,096	31.3	938	26.8	231	6.6	2,455	70.2	1,044	29.9
1972	4,022	1,206	30.0	1,126	28.0	305	7.6	2,854	71.0	1,168	29.1
1973	4,977	1,348	27.1	1,430	28.7	414	8.3	3,463	69.6	1,514	30.5
1974	5,554	1,458	26.3	1,609	29.0	460	8.3	3,859	69.5	1,695	30.5
1975	6,211	1,586	25.5	1,880	30.3	500	8.1	4,337	69.8	1,874	30.2
1976	6,709	1,771	26.4	1,961	29.3	562	8.4	4,707	70.2	2,002	29.9
1977	7,564	1,974	26.1	2,219	29.3	691	9.1	5,294	70.0	2,270	30.1r
1978	8,985	2,229	24.8	2,724	30.3	971	10.8	6,382	71.0	2,603	29.0
1979	10,305	2,488	24.2	3,315	32.2	1,011	9.8	7,348	71.3	2,957	28.7
70-79	61,016	16,165	26.5	18,032	29.6	5,349	8.8	42,910	70.3	18,106	29.7
1980	10,830	2,772	25.6	3,806	35.1	1,059	9.8	8,360	77.1	2,470	22.8
1981	11,254	3,105	27.6	3,371	30.0	1,170	10.4	8,494	75.5	2,760	24.5
1982	11,130	3,229	29.0	3,240	29.1	1,086	9.8	8,324	74.8	2,806	25.2
1983	11,389	3,502	30.7	3,148	27.6	1,186	10.4	8,612	75.6	2,777	24.4
1984	11,895	3,897	32.8	3,023	25.4	1,265	10.6	9,025	75.9	2,870	24.1
1985	12,335	4,175	33.8	3,125	25.3	1,343	10.9	9,480	76.8	2,855	23.1
1986	14,319	4,412	30.8	4,270	29.8	1,991	13.9	11,492	80.2	2,827	19.7
1987	16,172	4,699	29.1	5,278	32.6	2,418	15.0	13,349	82.6	2,823	17.5
1988	18,159	5,062	27.9	5,861	32.2	2,918	16.1	15,013	82.7	3,146	17.3
1989	19,073	5,439	28.5	5,957	31.2	2,899	15.2	15,633	82.0	3,440	18.0
80-89	136,556	40,292	29.5	41,079	30.1	17,335	12.7	107,782	78.9	28,774	21.1
1990	21,020	5,751	27.4	7,388	35.1	3,052	14.5	17,636	83.8	3,384	16.2
1991	21,850	5,931	27.1	7,656	35.0	3,483	15.9	18,628	84.9	3,222	15.1
1992	23,210	6,262	27.0	8,336	35.9	3,802	16.4	20,003	86.3	3,207	13.7
1993	23,720	6,583	27.8	7,617	32.1	4,375	18.5	20,228	85.3	3,492	14.7
1994	25,414	6,993	27.5	8,038	31.6	4,612	18.2	21,620	85.0	3,794	15.0
1995	29,076	7,338	25.2	9,244	31.8	5,292	18.2	23,666	81.4	5,410	18.6
1996	29,846	7,751	26.0	9,425	31.5	4,696	15.8	23,812	79.9	6,034	20.1
1997	29,697	8,257	27.8	8,865	29.8	4,313	14.5	23,424	78.8	6,237	21.2
1998	29,430	8,720	29.7	9,162	31.0	3,951	13.4	23,594	80.2	5,836	19.8
1999	30,876	9,207	29.8	9,150	29.5	4,494	14.6	24,844	80.3	6,032	19.7
90-99	264,139	72,793	27.6	84,881	32.1	42,070	15.9	217,455	82.3	46,684	17.7
2000	31,493	9,810	31.1	8,466	26.9	4,765	15.1	25,213	80.0	6,280	20.0
2001	31,284	10,143	32.3	8,761	28.0	4,141	13.2	25,196	80.5	6,088	19.5

GDP at current prices and current exchange rates. (Sources: World Bank: World Tables, 1995, pp. 28/9. World Development Indicators, Section 4.2, various issues. http://www.worldbank.org. *UN, Trends in International Distribution of Gross World Product. Special Issue,* United Nations. 1993, pp. 20/1. OECD. National Accounts, Vol. I various issues. http://www.oecd.org/std/gdp.htm). LEXIS-NEXIS Statistical Universe Document, various issues: http://web.lexis-nexis.com/statuniv/document

Table 1.2. OECD GDP at Current Prices and Current PPPs ($billion)

Year	Total	U.S.A	%	Europe	%	EU-15	%	Japan	%
1990	15,900	5,751	36.2	6,239	39.2	5,752	36.2	2,263	14.2
1991	16,651	5,931	35.6	6,557	39.4	6,047	36.3	2,431	14.6
1992	17,654	6,262	35.5	6,987	39.6	6,438	36.5	2,559	14.5
1993	18,262	6,583	35.3	7,075	38.7	6,483	35.5	2,640	14.5
1994	19,231	6,993	36.3	7,407	38.5	6,817	35.4	2,724	14.2
1995	20,434	7,338	35.9	7,898	38.7	7,262	35.5	2,929	14.3
1996	21,415	7,751	36.2	8,180	38.2	7,508	35.0	3,084	14.3
1997	22,761	8,257	36.2	8,733	38.4	7,999	35.1	3,201	14.1
1998	23,524	8,720	37.1	9,087	38.6	8,349	35.5	3,096	13.2
1999	24,656	9,207	37.3˙	9,472	38.4	8,737	35.4	3,159	12.8
2000	26,178	9,810	37.5	10,024	38.2	9,233	35.3	3,296	12.6

PPP = purchasing power parity. (Source: OECD, National Accounts, Vol. I, 2002, pp. 332/323).

A painful conclusion to be drawn from Table 1.1 is the undeniable decline of the developing nations in the output of the world's GDP. Non-OECD economies failed to keep up with the 12-fold economic growth generated in the OECD area between1970 and 2000. By expanding their GDP output only 6-fold, they actually suffered a severe erosion of the 30% position they once enjoyed in the seventies down to around 20% at the end of the millennium. The majority of mankind has obviously not shared equally in the supposed benefits of globalization as a stimulus of economic development.

Information collected in Table 1.1 is based on data for 29 OECD countries and on current prices and exchange rates of national currencies to the U.S. dollar, and here lies the crux of such international statistics. A strong dollar like the one seen in the mid-eighties and again in the later nineties boosts America's position vis-a-vis all other countries or regions, while painting a technically weaker picture in case of a dollar decline at other times. Attempts have been made by OECD statisticians to overcome such inherent distortion, which led to the development of the purchasing power parity (PPP) concept. Now economic size is measured in terms of purchasing power equivalence of currencies rather than official exchange rates, thereby overcoming many of the problems.

Much can be learned from the implementation of the new yardstick about comparable economic dimensions of countries and regions, and also about the competitive strength of the main contenders in the race for leadership positions in the world economy. While Table 1.2 does not provide a worldwide context, it establishes the U.S. and Western European as staying within a very narrow percentage range over a decade. At the same time, the EU and Japan both do not display evidence of a convincing competitive strength, not to mention a marked superiority in comparison to the U.S.

NATIONAL OWNERSHIP OF THE GLOBAL MARKET

If a person from the remotest place on earth were asked where Coca Cola comes from, chances are that 99 times out of 100 the response would correctly identify America. The respondent correctly associated the brand with its national origin, and identified the product with the nationality of its owner. Quite surprisingly, official statistics published by governments and international organizations so far have been unable to assimilate the simple logic demonstrated by our hypothetical native. Publications referring to international economics and trade still adhere closely to the conventional concept of a AnationalA economy. That is to say, the geographical rationale determines the nationality of economic activities, a historic relic from the pre-Adam Smith epoch of mercantilism. Useful but not realistic, if one takes a closer look at the owners and drivers of economic activities in today's global market.

It is not geography, but capital and entrepreneurs coming from various national origins and operating in locations of their choice throughout the international arena. If the nationality of capital, location and economic activity coincide, as in the case of Swiss nationals pursuing business matters at home, the concept fits. But what if the same Swiss businesspeople take their money, know how, products and business plans to foreign countries for local production and related trading activities? Have they now turned into non-Swiss, foreign businesses just because they changed their locale? Or reversing the thought, are foreign businesses operating in Switzerland all of a sudden turning into Swiss-owned enterprises and thus Swiss nationals?

This view does not make much sense, anymore, at a time when huge relocations of national companies and industries across the globe are the order of the day. Recognition of this reality points to the need for a fundamental reorientation, a basic change the perception and definition of what national ownership of economic processes is, or ought to be, and what it means for the distribution of "national" shares in the world economy.

Understanding this view offers the key to understanding the globalization phenomenon as what it is: the diffusion and distribution of national shares in the world economy.

It is thus suggested here to forthwith work with capital ownership of productive resources rather than the more conventional approach of the past. The national origin and ownership of capital and management control determines the nationality of business enterprises, and not their legal domicile within a politically defined piece of real estate. Identification of a company's national origin thus establishes its kinship with a national economy regardless of its geographical position.

By taking this step the size and shape of what is now considered a national economy will change, and often dramatically. It will become apparent that now a national economy can become larger or smaller than what conventional "national" statistics indicate. It is largely determined by the relative size of national business interests operating outside its boundaries versus foreign interests operating within. Their respective output of sales, value-added, trade volume, etc. is now no longer an integral part of the political economy where they operate, but is rightfully ascribed to the nationality of the capital owner.

This is not a useless exercise in semantics. On the contrary, it helps to bring into focus the true impact of national economic activities in the global context. It helps to define national shares in the global output of goods and services, employment, as well as foreign trade, which identifies the drivers of globalization plus their rate of success in the global tug-of-war for market shares.

Unfortunately, this type of information is not readily available, which by necessity leaves much of the research dependent on inference and creative analogy. The ideal statistical framework should provide detailed financial and operational data for international companies structured, and measured in a directly comparable format. In addition, there is a general lack of uniform reporting standards on things related to FDI operations, often leading to grave distortions for information supposed to cover the same subject matter.

Taking, for instance, statistics for direct investment volumes from the capital exporting country and linking it to those available from the recipient country may uncover discrepancies going into the millions and even billions of dollars. Different measuring and valuation techniques, definitions, and distortions from currency fluctuations among many other reasons play a role here. Japan, for example, measured its foreign direct investment position by establishing it on the basis of cumulative capital flows approved by the Japanese Ministry of Finance. No adjustments were made for reinvestments, currency fluctuations, normal valuation gains and losses stemming from business performance, or depreciation. As a consequence Japanese data reached levels over the course of several decades far beyond what country data showed where the investments had taken place. Which information is now correct? Which needs to be adjusted and by how much?

A common pitfall for researchers is the assumption that macro-economic aggregates for foreign direct investment flows and position estimates, which are available from international organizations, can be used as a proxy for missing economic performance of the underlying organizations. In many cases, where such relationships could be checked, that assumption proved to be erroneous. It is, therefore, always prudent to approach any data with a good measure of skepticism.

Reliable performance information for FDI industries can only come from micro-economic operating data for these enterprises, such as sales, gross product, exports and imports, employment, etc. They alone permit the generation of useful, realistic, reliable, and distortion-free information on the subject. They also have the advantage that they may be directly linked to a country's macro-economic data for these same categories. But the U.S. is practically the only country which provides relevant time series in this area, with France and Germany providing only fragmentary information.

The situation is improving, though, with national governments and international organizations turning out ever more statistical information in this area. Besides furnishing more quantitative and qualitative information, it is also published increasingly in a standardized format thanks mainly to the guiding efforts of the major international organizations such as the OECD, UNCTAD, IMF, and World Bank among others. Such efforts obviously and greatly benefit the quality of national statistics. A clear sign of changing attitudes and perceptions brought about by the progressive international outlook of governments, politicians, and businesspeople.

Foreign business activities by individuals, corporations, and even public enterprises all help to shape a nation's share in the world economy. Their efforts obviously have material consequences for the home country and foreign nations, evidence of which is provided by a range of very valuable information maintained by all nations in their balance-of-payments (BOP) statistics: foreign trade, capital flows, investments, and related income flows, for instance. They are vital indicators of the globalization process, and the balances in all these accounts attest to a nation's competitiveness in the traditional sense, but do not furnish evidence as to the true nationality of such business transactions from the capital ownership point-of-view.

In other words, to fully understand the true role of economic globalization, more details about the national ownership of global economic processes are needed than are presently available. As will be seen later on, American subsidiaries are responsible for an export volume equal to or even exceeding that of the U.S. itself. On the other hand, U.S. imports are strongly influenced by foreign affiliates operating in the country which, incidentally, also help to produce the nation's persistent trade deficits.

Foreign economic activities in their broadest sense are invariably linked to either trade in the dual form of exports and imports, or investment in its direct or the portfolio form. For practical reasons, portfolio investments will be de-emphasized in the following as they serve purposes very much different from those of foreign direct investments.

CHARACTERISTICS OF NATIONAL COMPETITIVENESS

The subject deserves to receive more attention than it has so far, because globalization is a competitive process. With global business activities gathering momentum, interest in which national competitors are gaining ground, maintain their position, or fall behind in the global economy will undoubtedly intensify. Judging by the still relatively small, yet expanding volume of institutional and individual research dealing specifically with the topic of national competitiveness, this field of inquiry is just beginning to open up.

Characteristically for the very early stage of such research endeavors, there is a wide variety of approaches and definitions employed in tackling the subject indicating a lack of consensus on how to authoritatively define and measure national competitiveness. This in turn leads to a quilt of information, sometimes in the form of well developed statistical time series, still pictures in others, or strictly theoretical treatises.

The existence of only fragmented analysis and lack of an overarching, systematic approach to tackling the subject is surprising in view of pertinent information already available from a variety of sources. Unquestionably, major barriers to exploring these sources have resulted from their availability in different languages until recently, and the lack of standardized collection and maintenance procedures of cross-national databases. Both are being overcome with the help of international organizations, which translate the various background materials into a common business and research language accessible to all students of the field, and the assistance they provide in establishing uniform statistical reporting standards.

Their best efforts in creating a solid statistical foundation for all kinds of research work has yet to result in getting a firm grip on the concept of competitiveness, its definition and meaningful measurement. The idea itself is not unfamiliar, but demonstrating its tangible aspects is still a key problem. The problem arises from attempting to represent a qualitative and fluid property in quantitative terms. This being the case, competitive measurements are not always of the direct and objective kind, Actually, work in this area is often forced to resort to indirect indicators, some of them tangible, some not, in order to define the invisible quality of competitiveness.

Broadly speaking all published efforts to tackle the subject fall under two related, yet distinctly separate headings: macro-economic and micro-economic information. Both are legitimate fields of investigation and particularly useful in this context, even if they may not directly demonstrate any competitive qualities per se. But they contain the essence of competitiveness, which needs to be filtered out with proper analytical methods.

Microeconomic measuring devices employed for individual firms include sales data, separated by domestic and international customers, market shares, employment data, related growth rates, research and product development efforts (patents), and profits derived from domestic and international marketing activities, etc.

Macro-economic competitiveness is usually measured by data about national industries in comparison to each other, like the U.S. manufacturing industry against the Japanese, French, or any other national manufacturing aggregate. Specific measuring sticks are plentiful in number. Capital invested in plant, equipment, R&D, manpower development, hourly wages and output, sales and revenues, all the above in total or on a per worker, or per employee basis (productivity), or relative to GDP, to just mention a few. Other indicators refer to national leadership positions in high-tech industries, output in physical or monetary units, number of patents registered compared to other countries, etc. Attempts to cope with assessments of national competitiveness can thus be grouped under three separate categories:

a.) micro-economic approaches covering individual firms
b.) macro-economic approaches covering industrial sectors or whole economies
c.) generalized research approaches (Michael Porter, 1990, IMD, 1998).

All of them are invaluable, legitimate, and yet fragmented inputs, which in essence fall short of our declared goal of measuring true national competitiveness, the globalization issue as defined below in terms of capital ownership. The explanation is easy to find in the fact, that most comparisons between national industries in the traditional, geographic sense do not make any distinction between domestic and foreign companies. But this flaw can be easily overcome by introducing statistical refinements that capture the true identity, ownership, and control over national economies separately for domestic and foreign enterprises. The same method can then be extended in a step-wise fashion to regions and, ultimately, the global economy.

Identifying individual companies by nationality is too cumbersome to apply considering the vast number of companies involved. Their figures go into the tens of thousands, plus they fluctuate constantly either by changing their nationality through merger or acquisition, or simply entering or leaving the economic picture for a variety of reasons. The prohibitive costs of tracking such developments are the principal reason, why no such comprehensive database on the subject is published anywhere.

The solution to the problem lies in the combination of two data sources available for most countries. One is the presentation of the so-called national accounts by practically all nations on an annual basis. It is the macro-economic abstract of national economies complete with details for population aggregates, economic activity and output by the public and private sector, income distribution for both, financial and foreign trade developments, and many other details. This part of the national economic x-ray makes no distinction between activities of domestic and foreign enterprises in the private sector, which is solely of interest here, because foreign business interests are usually prevented from pursuing public sector activities.

Information on foreign elements actively engaged in national economies is, however, not totally lacking in most cases. But one has to look for it in a totally different set of statistics maintained by governments for the purpose of closely monitoring the external economic ties of their nations. It is the Balance of Payments (BOP) set of books, that keep track of imports and exports, capital inflows and outflows, income flows in both directions, plus their surplus or deficit balances. The part concerning capital flows is of special interest to governments, especially as far as so-called foreign direct investments are concerned. That is exactly the part of the economy where foreign enterprises are becoming active. Reason enough to subject them to special registration and reporting requirements. Depending on the country, such statistics on the foreign elements are more or less well developed, but usually there is enough information to fill in missing data with careful estimates where necessary.

Research into national competitiveness has also been approached from other angles. The advantage of such efforts lies in the expansion and enrichment of the discussion by including non-economic factors that unquestionably contribute to national competitiveness. Yet, that advantage turns into the information's main disadvantage at the very same time.

Identification of factors contributing to the competitiveness of national industries in this manner is not the same as measuring competitiveness in precise and concrete commercial terms directly. In addition, this type of insight does not take into account that in the age of globalization the nationality of competitive advantage can change overnight. Actually, globalization thrives on the acquisition of or merging with the owners of such competitive advantage.

Porter's contribution to the field, for instance, rests on his exposure of background factors leading to the remarkable competitiveness of national industries in the traditional sense, even though they may not be blessed with an abundance of resources, his demonstration of the "diamond." But what he calls national industry may actually be a hybrid phenomenon that cannot serve the purpose of this investigation.

Similar in scope is IMD's research into determinants of national competitiveness. Their model approach to measuring the world's competitiveness scans eight "input factors" for each economy comprised of: 1. the domestic economy, 2. internationalization, 3. government, 4. finance, 5. infrastructure, 6. management, 7. science and technology, and 8. people. These eight categories are subdivided by a total of 259 criteria, reflecting a most comprehensive evaluation of each country. The results are followed on an annual basis in their publication "The World Competitiveness Yearbook." A most interesting research endeavor that results in the production of an eye-opening ranking scoreboard.

Recognizing the fundamental importance of the subject for national prosperity and survival, the United States seem to be the only nation that has established semi-official and permanent body of investigation into the competitive developments affecting American business. The Council on Competitiveness in Washington, D.C., which is a "non-partisan forum of 150 corporate chief executives, university presidents, and labor leaders working together to set a national action agenda to strengthen U.S. competitiveness. The Council defines competitiveness as our nation's capacity to produce goods and services that succeed in international markets while maintaining or boosting the real incomes of U.S. citizens. Savings, investment, and productivity are the essential building blocks of U.S. economic competitiveness. Saving provides the pool of resources upon which we draw to invest in plant and equipment to improve the efficiency of U.S. workers. These additions to net capital stock, together with investments in research, product development and education, increase the value of the economy's output per hour worked. Gains in productivity generate growth, give U.S. products a competitive edge in world markets and allow wages to be raised without causing inflation." (September 11, 1998).

A similar organization is the Conference Board, a New York based research group, that has provided excellent studies profiling these and related subjects.

Other nations are following the American example of monitoring competitive activities and developments in the well circumscribed area of FDI. As the ultimate expression of direct competition by national industries in international markets it has no equal. Neither portfolio investments, nor trade information come even close. FDI is measurable in terms of physical or financial output, employment, income, investment in plant and equipment, domestic and foreign trade, market shares, growth rates among others but, above all, embodies the essence of competitive spirit propelling foreign nationals into a given market, the globalization force proper.

Notable examples of research in this area are presented by the OECD, UNCTAD, the IMF, the UN, the World Bank with financial databases expressed in dollars, and the statistical services of single countries like France and Germany offering similar information in their respective currencies plus non-financial data of interest. France, in particular, takes great efforts in monitoring and regularly reporting on the foreign penetration of her manufacturing industries, and related foreign trade, but so far has been able to document only one single year for her outward FDI efforts in a very broad outline. These publications clearly separate data by nationality of companies as intended by the project at hand, and will surface in the following pages.

For the purpose of this investigation, the terms "competitive" and "national" need to be clarified. Competitiveness is strictly seen and used as a business or economic term, and thus measured along three familiar and well accepted performance dimensions:

1. Position maintenance, showing neither a gain nor loss compared to a defined standard.
2. Position gain or improved performance against whatever standard of comparison chosen, a positive indicator of competitive quality and, finally,
3. Position loss, indicating a poor or inferior competitive performance

Very similar to the market share concept, but in addition to sales commonly employed for this purpose, such parameters as GDP, GNP, employment, trade statistics, capital and income flows, licensing arrangements and related payment flows, etc. will be looked at, because of their ready availability from official sources and convenient standardization for research work, plus they come in time series that stretch out over long periods of time, are or can be expressed in terms of one uniform monetary standard, the dollar, are directly comparable for past periods and will continue to be even more so with constant refinements in the future.

The "national" component of competitiveness is addressed in the familiar, non-traditional manner discussed above. The principle of geography in attributing nationality is abandoned in favor of national capital ownership and control over global business activities. This is to say that General Motors is a U.S. national, British Petroleum is British, and Sony is Japanese. The legitimacy of this view was beautifully illustrated by the recent decision of the executive board of the S&P 500 Index to remove the Chrysler Corporation from the index, because after its acquisition by Mercedes Benz it ceased to be an American company which alone is admitted to the measuring standard.

In full agreement with this decision, FDI companies complete with all overseas offshoots are treated as an integral part of the national economy of their origin. In turn, all inward FDI organizations cannot be treated as part of a domestic industry. They are and remain foreign property.

Practically speaking, it leads to a revision of national accounting in the following manner. National economies will be identified by adjusting published statistics for their foreign elements. This is to say, that the gross domestic output of goods and services as published now will be cut back by subtracting its GDP component produced by foreign-owned enterprises, wherever this is possible considering the rather limited database materials. (See Table 1.3)

On the other hand, the gross product of subsidiaries with an identifiable national origin in foreign markets will be credited to the GDP of their home country. In a similar fashion, the foreign trade of that nation will undergo like adjustments. A country's trade data as published now should be reduced by trade generated through foreign FDI affiliates active in that national territory, but increased by that nation's affiliates trading from off-shore locations.

Table 1.3.   Output of Global GDP Controlled by U.S. Capital ($billion)

Year	World	U.S.A*	%	Outward FDI	%	Inward FDI	%	U.S.A**	%
1985	12,335	4,175	33.8	220.1	1.5	134.9	1.1	4,260	34.5
1986	14,319	4,412	30.8	231.6	1.6	142.1	0.9	4,502	31.4
1987	16,172	4,699	29.1	269.7	1.7	157.9	1.0	4,811	29.8
1988	18,159	5,062	27.9	297.6	1.7	146.4	0.8	5,214	28.7
1989	19,073	5,439	28.5	320.0	1.7	168.5	0.9	5,590	29.3
1990	21,020	5,751	27.4	356.0	1.7	190.5	0.9	5,916	28.1
1991	21,850	5,931	27.1	356.0	1.6	207.1	0.9	6,080	27.8
1992	23,210	6,262	27.0	361.5	1.6	214.8	0.9	6,409	27.6
1993	23,720	6,583	27.8	359.2	1.5	223.0	0.9	6,719	28.3
1994	25,414	6,993	27.5	403.7	1.6	244.7	1.0	7,152	28.1
1995	29,076	7,338	25.2	465.6	1.6	254.9	0.9	7,549	26.0
1996	29,846	7,751	26.0	498.3	1.7	283.4	0.9	7,966	26.7
1997	29,697	8,257	27.8	520.9	1.8	313.7	1.1	8,464	28.5
1998	29,430	8,720	29.7	506.3	1.7	353.9	1.2	8,872	30.1
1999	30,876	9,207	29.8	561.2	1.8	397.3	1.3	9,371	30.3

*U.S.-controlled GDP in the traditional sense. **U.S.-controlled GDP after adjustment for the FDI factor. FDI data cover majority-owned affiliates only. See Table 5.1.

While following an acceptable logic, the approach presently suffers from two major drawbacks. One comes in the form of fluctuating exchange rates mentioned before, which may distort database inputs and their growth rates. A rather common problem affecting all databases expressed in terms of the U.S. dollar. It can be overcome by resorting to national currency data, but at the expense of information transparency and comparability. The second problem refers to the lack of detailed information in many cases, which will be handled by the use of analogies and reasonable assumptions substituting for the lack of actual data.

Table 1.3 illustrates the practical application of the proposed measuring mechanism in the case of the U.S. economy. It shows the "global" share of the American economy to be fractionally larger than its economy measured in the traditional sense. It also shows how this competitive profile is changing under the impact of the two rival forces, outward and inward FDI. The existence of outward FDI adds to the "national" economy, while inward FDI has exactly the opposite effect. At the same time, the relative changes in both positions clearly reference the competitive strength in this tug-of-war.

Chapter Two

OECD—A Surrogate Global Economy

Dealing with the world economy sketched out in Table 1.1 is helpful for the purpose of gauging the impact of globalization forces only up to a point, because many nations do not have the level of statistical sophistication needed to judge their economic affairs beyond the GDP estimates shown. Surprisingly, this applies equally to developed and developing economies. Ample evidence of the often only very fragmented or totally missing information is furnished by the international time series for OECD members used here.

Ideally, information should be available beyond general financial and employment data as customarily furnished in national account statistics for the domestic economy and flow items in the balance-of payments (BOP) for a country's external economic affairs. What is needed here is specific accounting for outward and inward foreign direct investment activities for each nation, the amount of funds invested, the number of enterprises involved by industry and location, employment, sales, assets, exports and imports, gross product, and profits produced. So far, only one country comes close to meeting these minimum requirements, the U.S.

The gap between the ideal and reality is an inescapable fact that has to be accepted as such. But it does not deter from efforts to do more with whatever auxiliary information is available. In other words, borrowing from the knowledge of economic facts and relationships on a broader scale, allows the reconstruction of missing links additional knowledge about national weight and importance in a global context.

Without question, the most useful body of information covering the above list of topics comes from the Organization for Economic Cooperation and Development, or OECD for short. It can be supplemented with research data developed by other international institutions like the UN, UNCTAD, the IMF, the World Bank, the European Union, and individual countries themselves. For all practical purposes, the OECD appears like a de-facto economic union from the amount and detail of statistical information it publishes with great regularity for each member country.

Over the years it has not only expanded the number of its members, but is has been quite successful in introducing standardized national accounting systems and procedures for all of them. Noteworthy is the organization's effort to increase the transparency of such information by converting unadjusted national output data to PPP-adjusted (PPP = purchasing power parities) series, which substantially reduces the vexing problems introduced by constantly fluctuating exchange rates.

In addition to its valuable statistical services, the organization has also been instrumental in the reduction of trade barriers, in providing mutual aid and assistance in economic planning and development in conjunction with other international development agencies. Under its auspices, regular economic summits of the G8 members are convened to chart the future course of members and associated countries. Lately, it has taken first steps to collect more specific data for FDI activities in individual economies along the lines laid down above.

Despite its only semi-official character and general lack of public appreciation of its importance, OECD's economic and geo-political role is underscored by the following facts. Its 29 members (2000) constitute the so-called developed or industrialized world clustered in the Triad countries of North America (NAFTA), Western Europe with the 15-member European Union at its core, or the more expanded European Economic Àrea (EEA) with its 18 members, and Japan. Other members are Korea, Australia, New Zealand, and the latest entries consisting of the Czech Republic, Hungary, and Poland. With a total population of around 1 billion people OECD comprises 15% of the world population, accounts for two thirds of global trade, provides 94% of all foreign direct investment funds, derives 89% of the income flowing from them, and generates in excess of 80% of global GDP, a beautiful demonstration of the 80/20 rule.

Given its size and weight in the world economy, plus the scope and quality of statistical information available, the OECD is a natural surrogate for the world economy. This is in no way intended to be a disrespectful judgment over the remaining majority of mankind it is just the lack of pertinent and specific information that isolates this most promising economic potential for the future from being getting adequate representation and recognition here.

Its most valuable aspect for the project at hand is the organization's pool of accessible, detailed, and comparable macro-economic measures accumulated over decades. While not always totally standardized or complete, as indicated by the latest and sweeping revisions of its National Accounts Statistics, it has no equal for quantitative and qualitative coverage of a broad range of national economic details.

Conversion of national currency information into dollar-denominated time series is especially gratifying for the researcher grappling with problems of transparency and comparability. Specific areas of interest here, as they relate directly to the assessment of national contributions to the globalization process, are the output of aggregate and sectoral value added or GDP, employment in total and by industrial sector, per-capita benchmarks derived from both, balance-of-payments (BOP) information relating to foreign trade, capital and income flows, specifically those linked to foreign direct investment activities, etc. As information concerning the public sector is considered secondary for this study, because it rarely engages in FDI activities, care has been taken to focus predominantly on the analysis of industrial sectors in national economies, the central source of their global competitiveness. Where needed, information from other international agencies mentioned earlier was drawn upon to complement the picture.

ECONOMIC MARKET DENOMINATORS

The information displayed in Tables 1.1 and 1.2 requires some clarification. All data appearing here refer to gross domestic product (GDP), which has become the most widely used standard for measuring and comparing national economies, and their groupings. It's convenience rests in the fact, that it allows establishment of reliable comparisons and rank orders by size and growth rates, as well as per-capita benchmarks expressed in terms of the U.S. dollar, wherever applicable.

Often GDP is carelessly equated with markets, as if the two terms were synonymous. A practice, which has to be questioned vigorously as it is technically incorrect and can lead to very distorted conclusions. A typical example is the frequent comparison between sales by large companies and output of GDP by countries found in many international business texts.

GDP measures output resulting from the combination of resources in production processes, and the value added by such economic activities. The term was coined by economists to capture a variety of factors contributing to the processing and upgrading of raw materials to the final product, plus the value created by the distribution to the same to the final consumer or user. This is accomplished via three different measuring devices with essentially equal results: a. the final expenditures at purchaser prices, b. the employee income approach and c. the output of gross values added by resident producers. This latter one is used here. It has a decided focus on the supply side of the economy, and parallels the value-added tax in many respects.

The practical difficulty arising here for the researcher is the simple fact that FDI activities, the drivers of globalization, are not measured in those macro-economic terms. Thus they require an analytical detour to portray their role in a global context.

FDI is undertaken by individual firms. This puts them automatically into the realm of micro-economics, more specifically markets, places for commercial transactions, where supply and demand meet. Markets are not measured in terms of GDP but sales, which are related with each other, yet totally different in their dimensions.

A national economy expressed in terms of sales, would be much larger than GDP data indicate. More precisely, between 3–4 times larger for the developed world, or conversely, GDP amounts to 25–30% of corresponding sales. Some narrow variability is common for individual industries and even whole economies, a fact that is handy to remember when only one input is available, which can be used to make a reasonable estimate of the other. It should be emphasized, that this applies to the industrial sectors as differentiated from the public domain, which is driven by different mechanisms of value creation (taxation).

Once understood, and in spite of their conceptual and practical differences, both measures lend themselves ideally for the analysis of competitive national achievements, rankings, and trends. For the specific purpose of measuring globalization developments, macro-economic employment and GDP data will be related to micro-economic gross product (GP) and employment data of inward and outward FDI companies. Where available, they offer the advantage of being useful indicators for national penetration rates into national economies, or even the world economy for that matter. Wherever possible, such indicators can be supplemented with data on assets, sales, income, foreign trade, or other proxies of competitive significance.

Another important point to make about all information contained in the following concerns the composition of national GDPs, and its significance for the discussion of globalization. Official GDP as an aggregate economic measure can be broken down in various ways like the private and public sector, for instance. The former includes households and industries, which are commonly subdivided into primary, manufacturing, and service industries. All of them are legitimate and useful portrayals of an economy's physiology, but with significant differences in their contribution to the globalization process. While public sectors are without doubt the chief engineers of political globalization, the private sector is the chief driver of economic globalization, as will be demonstrated in the following.

Governments are helpful for economic planning, running basic industries, providing development funds as well as the legal framework for growth of the domestic economy, and can stimulate business with financial, monetary, and tax strategies. But as far as any active participation in the economic sphere of globalization is concerned, governments play virtually only a facilitator role in developed nations, with perhaps a more entrepreneurial engagement in developing nations.

As the embodiment of national sovereignty, the public sector is, neither an active nor passive partner for FDI ventures. Economic globalization forces thus can only assert themselves in national industrial sectors open to global competition, which essentially eliminates the public sectors from further discussion here.

Speaking of industrial sectors, it should be pointed out that national and international statistical institutions, including the OECD and European sources, use the term "industry" in two very different ways. In some publications it refers specifically to the manufacturing industry, in others it is inclusive to cover the primary, manufacturing, and service sector, plus an all other category, thus following the American model.

In this maze of different definitions and national accounting practices, statistical services of international organizations are invaluable, simply because they are collected and published in a standard format, which assures a level of accuracy, reliability, and comparability that would be hard to match by converting individual national data from their original currency.

The short summary presented here is only the tip of the proverbial iceberg. It is a basic scenario, which sets the stage for the next steps of the inquiry into global competitiveness as briefly outlined in the introduction. In essence, it requires the establishment of clearly defined measures for national capital control over economic processes around the world. America's GDP, for example, now changes from the traditional geographic interpretation of having been produced within the territorial confines of the country to include the gross product (GP) produced by majority-owned U.S. subsidiaries (Mofas) in foreign countries less the GP produced by foreign affiliates located in the U.S. The results of this formula were shown in Table 1.2.

It is a legitimate reorientation of traditional views. The nationality of FDI companies changes at the border of the parent company's home country in a legal sense, but definitely not from a capital ownership and control point-of view. It is not a radically new concept, as may appear at first glance. Just taking a look at the carefully separated records covering inward and outward FDI by practically all countries, one can see the concept at work, even though it is not carried through to the same conclusion proposed here.

Put into a nutshell, all further discussions of the economic globalization will dwell on the roles of nationally defined corporations or industries in the world economy regardless of their geographical location. As pointed out earlier this puts the spotlight on FDI activities more than portfolio investments, which do not display the same degree of competitiveness in a technical sense. The ultimate outcome of such investigation will be a sort of American, Swiss, Japanese or other shares of the global market and trade for that matter, which can be substantially different from any impression created by the traditional geographical interpretation of their role.

THE ECONOMIC PROFILE OF OECD

A. The Industrial GDP

Recognizing the variety of national and regional economies, and their accounting practices, is important for the discussion of forces driving globalization, which reside in the private sector as per our definition.

Integral parts of this sector are the three industry branches of primary, manufacturing, and services. Primary industries in the OECD definition of national accounting normally include agriculture, forestry, hunting and fishery. In some publications from the same organization mining and other extractive (energy related) activities may be included. Manufacturing comprises all activities dealing with the transformation of raw materials from the primary sector into physical and tangible products for use or consumption. Major segments are mechanical and electric machinery, chemicals, metal working, automotive, food, besides many smaller ones. Services, on the other hand, cover all activities dealing with the production of intangibles for immediate consumption. They normally include trade, wholesale and retail, financial and business services, construction, transportation, utilities, etc.

For reasons of convenience, GDP or value added by these distinctly different branches of industrial has become the commonly employed international denominator for macro-economic performance. Past differences in the way GDP was defined and measured, or the ways in which industries were classified, have now been mostly eliminated for OECD countries, such that the data used in the following display a high degree of homogeneity and comparability.

One significant disturbance factor in the portrayal of national GDPs, and one which can not be totally eliminated ever, is posed by the existence of different national currencies with freely fluctuating exchange rates. In extreme cases, as has been indicated before, this can cause data movements expressed in a standard currency like the U.S. dollar to give a totally different picture from the same movements visible in the underlying national currency data. The introduction of the Euro at the beginning of 1999 goes a long way towards relieving this predicament for a large part of the global economy, because it puts the 15 members of the EU on a directly comparable statistical footing. Yet, even here, it does not free these statistics from distortions once they are translated into the U.S. dollar, as both currencies have undergone substantial valuation swings against each other. The fact that only eleven of these members have voted to adopt the Euro as their national currency starting in 2001, however, has little or no bearing on the generation of a common statistical standard for all members of the European Economic Area (EEA). Ten other nations from Eastern Europe will join the Euro bloc on May 1, 2004, adding even more transparency to economic developments in that part of the world.

It is by no means so, that the economic profiles of nations measured in terms of sector stratification, are very similar. For OECD as a whole, government accounted for 21% of GDP output, industry for 79%, manufacturing for 21%, services for 56%, and primary for 2% in 1998. For the U.S., the public sector accounted for 20%, industry for 80%, manufacturing for 20%; and services for 52%. Japan, by comparison, displayed the following ratios: government 29%, manufacturing 26%, and services 48%. Taking France as a model for a more socialized and thus top-heavy administrative sector, we find a split of 24% for the public sector, 21% for manufacturing, and services 56% illustrating the different structures of national economies. With some exceptions the structure of the industrial sectors in OECD countries is very similar in that services are in a solid lead position, followed by manufacturing and a trailing primary sector.

Table 2.1. OECD GDP by Industry*—$million

Year	Total	Industrial	%	Manufacturing	%	Services	%	Primary	%
1982	8,338	7,054	84.6	1,793	21.5	4,828	57.9	434	5.2
1983	8,627	7,324	84.9	1,846	21.4	5,099	59.1	380	4.4
1984	9,043	7,424	82.1	1,944	21.5	5,064	56.0	416	4.6
1985	9,502	8,048	84.7	2,090	22.0	5,540	58.3	418	4.4
1986	11,525	9,520	82.6	2,501	21.7	6,408	55.6	611	5.3
1987	13,392	11,035	82.4	3,013	22.5	7,459	55.7	562	4.2
1988	15,076	12,377	82.1	3,618	24.0	8,367	55.5	392	2.6
1989	15,708	12,896	82.1	3,723	23.7	8,796	56.0	425	2.7
1990	17,636	14,338	81.3	4,092	23.2	9,612	54.5	635	3.6
1991	18,628	14,902	80.0	4,284	23.0	10,022	53.8	596	3.2
1992	20,003	15,942	79.7	4,441	22.2	10,862	54.3	640	3.2
1993	20,228	15,919	78.7	4,389	21.7	10,943	54.1	587	2.9
1994	21,620	17,210	79.6	4,670	21.6	11,934	55.2	605	2.8
1995	23,666	18,436	77.9	5,207	22.0	12,590	53.2	639	2.7
1996	23,812	18,550	77.9	5,072	21.3	12,620	53.0	857	3.6
1997	23,424	18,599	79.4	4,896	20.9	13,094	55.9	609	2.6
1998	23,504	18,710	79.3	4,860	20.6	13,307	56.4	543	2.3
1999	24,844	19,751	79.5	5,043	20.3	14,136	56.9	571	2.3

*all data exclude Czech Republic, Hungary, and Poland. Values are quoted at current prices and exchange rates. Source: OECD, National Accounts, Volume II, Detailed Tables, various issues.

All nations keep meticulously track of foreign intrusions into their industrial infrastructure via FDI. But predominantly only in the form of financial data referring to monetary inflows versus outflows, or accumulated stock positions. Much more limited, if not totally absent, are vital details on industrial operating details like assets, employment, sales, costs, gross product, income and taxes, imports and exports, etc. The general lack of, or the only very sketchy nature of such details does not, however, preclude meaningful deductions, estimates, and conclusions to be drawn about the general course globalization is taking.

B. OECD Employment

Another broad and useful indicator of economic activity exists in the number of people employed by national economies. Employment statistics are actually more useful and reliable than GDP figures in making sound judgments about a nation's economic strength. This is, because employment figures are not prone to the omni-present distortion potential stemming from the currency factor. If separate labor data are reported for people employed by domestic and foreign-owned enterprises within a country, or by a country's industries in foreign economies for that matter, they provide another reliable insight into the foreign role within a national economy or, conversely, of that nation's role in global employment outside its own political boundaries.

Employment data should more or less evidence a reasonable relationship to the size and trend of GDP statistics for the same industry. That is to say, that inward FDI companies employing 5% of the national labor force, should also reach about 5% in the nation's output of value added. This one-on-one relationship does not exist in reality, however. Actually, one should expect the GDP percentage to be above the employment level, simply because foreign companies operating in a foreign environment are there because of their superior capabilities in management, production, and marketing.

Information about employment and related output of GDP leads to another commonly employed and most useful economic indicator, the per capita output. Where reliable and differentiated information for sufficient numbers of industries is furnished, it can be used to pinpoint pockets of competitive strength or weakness for a nation as a predictor of its likely performance in the globalization process.

Quite often such competencies are not directly measurable. The superior quality and appeal of Italian styling and design, for instance, is widely accepted, and yet as a component of an intangible service function cannot be accorded a precise valuation. This is different from national competitiveness in the machinery sector, for example, where the measurable output differences combined with prestige for precision and quality determine the industry's competitive advantage.

If OECD labor statistics can be faulted for any reason, it may be their present lack of detail with regard to the "alien" component of a nation's labor pool. Not even a handful of OECD members maintain statistics on the number of people employed by foreign companies in general or in specific industries. But this is changing, with a recent publication, the first of its kind, by OECD statisticians. Once these data are furnished on a regular and complete basis, the degree and trend of foreign participation by economic sector will become more transparent. In combination with similar information for the outward FDI employment of the same country, a national economy can be identified as a winner or loser in the global race for a bigger share in the global economy.

The industrial sector provides slightly less than 70% of all OECD jobs, and is apparently in a long-term decline shared also by manufacturing and services. For manufacturing the trend may accelerate judging by the sizable relocation of OECD companies in Asia and other areas. Even services may eventually follow suit, if the example of American banks, insurance, tele-

Table 2.2.   OECD Employment by Industry*—000

Year	Total	Industrial	%	Manufacturing	%	Services	%	Primary	%
1982	268,841	208,976	77.7	65,931	24.5	134,445	50.0	8,600	3.2
1983	270,435	209,704	77.6	64,646	23.9	136,530	50.5	8,528	3.2
1984	276,252	214,568	77.7	65,432	23.7	140,832	51.0	8,304	3.0
1985	280,854	218,223	77.7	65,353	23.3	144,612	51.5	8,258	2.9
1986	286,257	224,843	78.7	65,647	22.9	150,672	52.6	8,524	3.0
1987	291,308	229,156	78.6	65,436	22.5	155,293	53.3	8,427	2.9
1988	333,009	265,984	79.8	71,942	21.6	178,266	53.5	15,776	4.7
1989	338,832	272,265	80.3	72,758	21.5	184,279	54.4	15,228	4.5
1990	346,728	253,336	73.0	81,072	23.4	175,928	50.7	13,336	3.8
1991	368,918	256,320	69.5	81,449	22.1	161,059	43.7	13,812	3.7
1992	369,720	265,052	71.7	79,777	21.6	162,899	44.1	13,376	3.6
1993	371,570	256,658	69.1	78,912	21.2	164,543	44.3	13,203	3.6
1994	375,161	258,166	68.8	77,477	20.7	168,017	44.8	12,672	3.4
1995	381,767	261,047	68.3	76,615	20.1	171,725	45.0	12,707	3.3
1996	384,422	264,771	68.9	77,484	20.2	174,639	45.4	12,648	3.3
1997	392,315	268,930	68.5	77,774	19.8	178,801	45.6	12,355	3.2
1998	397,590	272,407	68.5	77,539	19.5	182,429	45.9	12,439	3.1
1999	402,877	277,110	68.8	77,540	19.2	187,183	46.5	12,387	3.1

*all data exclude Korea, Czech Republic, Hungary, and Poland. Employees only. Source: see Table 2.1.

com and other industries is being followed by European and Japanese firms. If the present migration rate to China, India, and other areas is sustained, serious consequences for investment, employment, production, and foreign trade balances for the still so-called developed world will be inevitable. It could very well lead first to loss of leadership in R&D, then economic decline and, lastly, living standards in general.

For the time being, the diversity in industrial structures noted for the output of GDP is replicated in the employment picture of individual nations. In the U.S., industrial employment account for 67% of the total national labor force. For the U.K an even higher 80% is recorded. Lower shares are found in Japan with 65%, France 62%, and Sweden 59%. The picture changes when measuring the shares held by manufacturing in the overall industrial employment. Italy leads with a 39% share, followed by 36% in Japan, 34% in Germany, 28% in France, and a low 22% in the U.S.

C. OECD in World Trade

The final area for measuring OECD's stature in the world economy is offered by its global trade figures. On either side of the merchandise trade ledger OECD accounts for a steady two thirds of the global volume.

Noteworthy is the fact that the trade balance for OECD is slightly negative for almost all years shown, mainly under the influence of the U.S. trade imbalance, which has been worsening practically every year for almost three decades now. Europe's trade is more balanced in total volume with years of deficits alternating with years of surplus. Japan, the third major component in the OECD picture on the other hand, has always shown favorable trade balances, the hallmark of the country's position in international trade.

Table 2.3. World Merchandise Exports—$billion

Year	World	OECD	%	U.S.A.	%	W. Europe	%	Japan	%
1980	1,931.7	1,265.1	65.5	225.6	11.7	809.4	41.9	130.4	6.7
1981	1,924.4	1,243.9	64.7	238.7	12.4	748.3	38.8	157.5	8.2
1982	1,777.2	1,177.2	66.2	216.4	12.2	720.0	40.5	138.4	7.8
1983	1,736.0	1,162.7	67.0	205.6	11.8	702.6	40.5	147.0	8.5
1984	1,840.8	1,240.5	67.4	223.9	12.2	722.4	39.2	168.7	9.2
1985	1,875.8	1,282.8	68.4	218.8	11.7	760.7	40.6	177.2	9.4
1986	2,048.5	1,485.0	72.5	227.2	11.1	931.6	45.5	210.8	10.3
1987	2,419.0	1,736.2	71.8	254.1	10.5	1,118.7	46.3	231.3	9.6
1988	2,765.2	1,986.5	71.9	322.4	11.7	1,239.7	44.8	264.9	9.6
1989	3,008.5	2,127.9	70.7	363.8	12.1	1,322.2	43.9	273.9	9.1
1990	3,423.4	2,453.9	71.7	393.6	11.5	1,595.4	46.6	287.6	8.4
1991	3,498.5	2,502.2	71.5	421.7	12.1	1,588.1	45.4	314.8	9.0
1992	3,713.9	2,650.9	71.4	448.2	12.1	1,674.0	45.1	339.9	9.2
1993	3,752.3	2,596.5	69.9	464.8	12.4	1,566.7	41.8	362.2	9.6
1994	4,266.0	2,914.1	68.3	512.6	12.0	1,782.6	41.8	397.0	9.3
1995	5,099.8	3,469.8	68.0	584.7	11.5	2,184.4	42.8	443.1	8.7
1996	5,267.6	3,515.2	66.7	625.1	11.9	2,182.9	41.4	410.9	7.8
1997	5,497.4	3,640.9	66.2	688.7	12.5	2,239.8	40.7	421.0	7.7
1998	5,405.8	3,665.6	67.8	682.1	12.6	2,307.7	42.7	387.9	7.2
1999	5,554.4	3,722.5	67.0	702.1	12.6	2,288.4	41.2	419.4	7.6

Table 2.4.   OECD Merchandise Imports—$billion

Year	World	OECD	%	U.S.A.	%	Europe	%	Japan	%
1980	2,001.2	1,400.4	70.0	257.0	12.8	911.6	45.6	141.3	7.1
1981	1,981.9	1,328.8	67.1	273.4	13.8	810.7	40.9	142.9	7.2
1982	1,865.9	1,249.4	66.9	254.9	13.7	771.0	41.3	131.5	7.1
1983	1,804.0	1,224.8	67.9	269.9	15.0	737.4	40.9	126.4	7.0
1984	1,925.7	1,340.2	69.6	346.4	18.0	747.3	38.8	136.2	7.1
1985	1,952.3	1,374.7	70.4	352.5	18.1	778.7	39.9	130.5	6.7
1986	2,131.0	1,545.5	72.5	382.3	18.0	920.5	43.2	127.6	6.0
1987	2,499.2	1,829.9	73.2	426.4	17.1	1,124.9	45.0	151.0	6.0
1988	2,862.6	2,069.3	72.2	459.5	16.1	1,264.7	44.2	187.4	6.5
1989	3,098.2	2,239.7	72.3	492.9	15.9	1,362.7	44.0	209.7	6.8
1990	3,516.0	2,575.3	73.2	517.0	14.7	1,656.0	46.9	235.4	6.7
1991	3,626.5	2,593.1	71.5	508.4	14.0	1,681.1	46.3	237.0	6.5
1992	3,850.1	2,706.9	70.3	553.9	14.4	1,745.4	45.3	233.2	6.1
1993	3,804.3	2,558.6	67.3	603.4	15.9	1,631.3	42.9	241.6	6.4
1994	4,323.4	2,902.0	67.1	689.2	15.9	1,842.9	42.6	275.2	6.4
1995	5,159.5	3,432.0	66.5	770.9	14.9	2,237.1	43.4	335.9	6.5
1996	5,371.0	3,512.6	65.4	822.0	15.3	2,239.0	41.7	349.2	6.5
1997	5,587.6	3,631.9	65.0	899.0	16.1	2,112.9	37.8	338.8	6.1
1998	5,519.3	3,725.8	67.5	944.4	17.1	2,217.4	40.2	280.5	5.1
1999	5,732.9	3,907.5	68.2	1,059.4	18.5	2,208.7	38.5	311.3	5.4

Sources: *IMF, International Financial Statistics, Yearbook 2000, pp. 128/9, 132/3.*

Putting these data side-by-side with those developed for OECD's role in the global production of GDP and employment makes it clear, just how much of the world economy is concentrated in the industrialized nations, despite the fact that they represent only a 15% minority of the world's total population.

The top-heavy relationship in favor of OECD lends credence to the argument to use the economic area as a legitimate surrogate for the global economy. Its concentrated market potential, investment and income volumes, plus a highly stable political and predictable environment make it the top attraction for business from developed and developing nations alike.

Putting it differently, continued expansion of the number of OECD members, and their deepening inward and outward integration, is the key to an accelerated development of the rest of the world. Its high standard of living can and will be shared with all nations willing to open their borders and share their resources in an equitable manner.

Chapter Three

Foreign Direct Investment—A Fundamental Globalization Strategy

INTRODUCTION

International business is conducted in only two basic ways, through trade and investments, including portfolio and direct investments. Licensing, franchising, strategic alliances, etc. are part of the latter investment type displaying similarities with trade, insofar as they do not require major capital commitments. Trade has existed for centuries, has operated in pretty much the same fashion all along, and was never perceived as a "globalization" factor until recently. So, what has changed that deserves a flashy new acronym for staid, historic international business relationships?

It is a result of a profound re-orientation. In the past, people understood international economics merely in terms of trade relations, disregarding the fact that foreign direct investments on a smaller scale co-existed as well. But, playing only a subordinated role to trade in magnitude, they were all but ignored by economic theoreticians until recently. Their benign neglect stood in sharp contrast to the attention paid to its existence by politicians that saw direct investments as potential encroachment on national sovereignty and thus in need of tight regulation.

Today's emphasis on a new world order has brought a palpable shift in national policies. Demands for the complete liberalization and protection of international business relations include the removal of the last bulwark of traditional nationalism, political independence. Its declared vision and mission is to share the benefits of economic, scientific, technological, educational, and cultural advances with all mankind. A messianic message that promises to shift the interests of a few to the welfare of all, local to global thinking, and selfish attitudes to altruism. Powerful and persuasive in sentiment and political appeal it receives enthusiastic lip service from politicians of different colors, and is visibly enshrined in powerful supra-national organizations.

The change in people's perception of the world will be helped by their understanding of the forces driving them progressively in that direction. Developed nations as the spearhead of the new order have turned their private sectors into the motor of globalization. Here lies the source of capital, technology, managerial know-how, and entrepreneurial spirit to tackle the task in the most effective and efficient way. Thriving on a minimum of bureaucratic interference, as evidenced by the demand for liberal trade and capital transfer policies, the sector's preferred modus operandi has shifted from trade to FDI as the principal development strategy in a significant break with traditional thinking about international economics.

Trade has been, and actually still is, the central issue of academic as well as political attention from the time of the mercantilists, through Adam Smith and David Ricardo to the present day. Visible proof is the detailed trade records kept by practically all nations for centuries in order to assess surplus or deficit situations affecting national fortunes. In sharp contrast to this historic focus, direct investments are only now beginning to be noticed judging by the obvious absence of comprehensive documentation, except for only a handful of nations. That attention deficit is a direct outcome of the mercantilist preoccupation with balance-of-payment flows, where capital flows are still dwarfed by trade statistics, thereby creating a false impression of economic realities.

Actually, meager capital flows and the economic activities they support over time have led to a gradual role reversal for trade and direct investments over time. To understand this process helps to understand the globalization phenomenon. Originally, trade took place from ship to shore without the need of much direct investment support. From there it advanced to strictly commercial transactions among foreigners involving some physical support (FDI) structures like warehouses, harbor facilities, banks, etc. The important step forward in the gradual progression from mere trading activities to the present stage of international integration came with the addition of full-fledged production facilities in foreign countries to complement strictly commercial activities before. In other words, by being able to freely move the three basic elements of business, investment, production, and trade across the globe, business enterprises with diverse national backgrounds have metamorphosed from local producers with trade link to other nations to truly global operators, thereby globalizing the business environment.

The following investigation will make it clear how this transition has affected the historic trade-direct investment relationship by completely reversing their traditional roles, and delegating foreign trade into a service function for FDI in the process. It will be shown, how national exports are dominated by outward investments, while imports are influenced to a large extent by inward FDI, if the U.S. and French experience discussed below can be generalized. A reality which demonstrates the close interdependence between direct investments and trade as inseparable twin strategies for global market penetration and development.

Japan furnishes a prime example illustrating such relationship. Their original trading operations, whose success has been faulted for producing sizable and permanent trade deficits for the U.S. and Europe, are now complemented by a vast global network of production enterprises, FDI proper. In both cases Japan was practically forced into these investments in order to reduce the trade imbalances of their host nations, and thus protect their own global business interests. In the process, Japanese trade competition changed into local competition, which is politically more acceptable as it supports local employment, an expanded tax base, and relief for the BOP, even though it did intensify, not reduce, competition for local industries. It is doubtful, that Japan's trading base could have been maintained intact or even expanded without the FDI strategy, which is same as saying that FDI has become the primary key success factor with a logical, but secondary role left for trade. This view is supported by the fact that FDI business results measured in conventional terms of sales or GDP is much larger than related exports, as reported in the following.

The leading role of FDI in penetrating the global market depends solely on one key attribute not found in its trading alternative: full control over all foreign business activities from being physically present in target markets. It assures greater strategic flexibility vis-a-vis changing market conditions, adds to the company's learning process, helps to reduce distribution costs, opens otherwise closed markets, and permits trading with third markets in addition to parent trade from the domestic base among others.

FDI is the logistical infrastructure for the penetration of external markets by national firms, which can be built in two distinctly different ways.

a. by establishment of foreign footholds in the form of brick and mortar structures, hiring and training of employees, transfer of working capital, and implantation of suitable management practices to exploit opportunities of selected target markets. This avenue, often referred to as green field investment, is normally pursued by companies with ample financial resources, and superior marketing strategies developed for their domestic market and deemed suitable also for foreign markets.

b. by acquisition of, or fusion with, existing organizations. This is different, inasmuch as the primary purpose of this strategy may be to overcome the lack of any proprietary superiority, and gaining a competitive advantage by investing in existing technology, market access, financial resources, or management skills. It is more economical than the first strategy, mainly because the investment is in something that is in place already, offers an advanced stage on the learning curve, and permits a better assessment of profitability before the investment is undertaken. The recent global merger mania is a prime example of this approach.

The importance of FDI for individual companies is underscored by the annual financial statements of large numbers of multinationals. A review of this source makes it quickly clear how important international business is for their aggregate sales and profits. In many cases it amounts to more than 50%. A typical example is furnished by the giant Swiss companies, which would not even be known worldwide, if it were not for their FDI activities. The home market is just too small to give them the global visibility and weight for which they are known. Citing the U.S. situation once more, in 1997 Mofas generated a gross product reaching 33% of their parents domestic output, and employed an equal 33% share of the number employed by their parents. In terms of sales and net income they even reached a substantially higher 41% of their respective parent levels. (SOCB, July 1999)

What is more important for assessing the real role of FDI for development of global business is indicated by comparing U.S. parent merchandise exports of $434 billion for the same year to Mofa sales of $1,983 billion. Both represent sales to foreign markets by related companies. There is no way that the parents in this case could have duplicated the affiliate business volume through exports alone, if FDI had not taken place. A similar picture appears for Germany. Again for 1997, sales by German subsidiaries reached DM 1,276 billion compared to total German merchandise exports of DM 512.4 billion. Assuming that 60% of that volume is accounted for by FDI parents, like in the U.S. example, this would result in DM 310 billion of parent exports. In other words, American parent companies sell 4–5 times more through their subsidiaries than they export, and German parent organizations do likewise with 4 times their estimated merchandise export volume. Obviously, a good part of parent exports actually go to affiliate organizations, which helps to accentuate their role in the total globalization picture.

An interesting question arising in this context would be to find out whether the gains of FDI enterprises be equated with similar beneficial effects for the economies where they are active? This cannot be answered with certainty, as the FDI effect is likely to be quite different for developed and developing economies. In developed countries, for instance, inward FDI has more of a displacement than additive effect. That is to say, local competitors may be faced with vital consequences more so than the economy in general. In developing nations with little or no local industrial infrastructure, by contrast, the appearance of FDI has a net expansionary effect for the economy as such. Common to both though, is the undeniable and potentially negative effect on the country's BOP through growing outflows of repatriated capital and income, which affects developing countries more so than mature economies.

Once in place, FDI begins to dominate a country's foreign trade activities. Today by far the largest portion of world trade is solidly in the hands of direct investment interests. In the U.S. case it can be demonstrated that 85–90% of her exports are handled by FDI companies, both outward and inward, and so are between 60–70% of her imports. This covers trade between U.S. parent organizations with third party customers as well as intra-company transactions. Extending the U.S. experience to the global scene, which appears to be totally justifiable at this point, identifies foreign trade as one key link in the value chain of FDI enterprises. It is not a stand-alone, independent phenomenon, as the prominence of foreign trade statistics without any mention of the FDI relationship may suggest.

FDI as the physical and highly visible projection of national business interests into foreign markets is well understood by all host nations, and they are anxious to monitor such development as closely as possible. Unfortunately, their efforts rarely go beyond financial measurements of capital inflows and outflows, and development of related investment stocks. Also, as different accounting procedures are still rather common among nations, this results in global statistics of highly variable informational value, and prompting a great deal of uncertainty on the researcher's part.

The most useful aspect of national time series developed on the subject of FDI is the fact, that inward and outward statistics are established on the basis of identical accounting processes and, also importantly, in the same currency. Whether the results are 100 percent compatible or comparable internationally, especially after they have been subject to often grave distortions following their conversion into a standard currency like the dollar, is of secondary importance for the moment. What counts is the possibility to measure and assess the trends underlying the relative growth of outward against inward investments. That is to say, we are looking at an opportunity to directly gauge a nation's shifting foothold in the world economy in terms of its own currency standard.

Borrowing from the market share concept, economic weight defined by national capital control over FDI operations leads to one logical conclusion: as long as outward FDI is larger and grows faster than inward investments, the country must expand its influence and position in the global market. Its industrial base is competitively superior, and thus contributes positively to the globalization process. In the reverse case a country's share of the global market is declining.

It is no longer meaningful or justified to say America's, Europe's, or Japan's share in the world economy is amply documented by the volume of their respective domestic GDPs, or foreign trade volumes relative to that of other nations similarly defined by geographic or political terms. As will be demonstrated in the following discussion, sizable parts of the U.S. industry and her foreign trade are controlled by foreign capital interests. The same goes for Europe, to a lesser degree also Japan, and many other important economies.

In the previous chapter dealing with America's position in the OECD output of value added, industrial employment, and external trade, it was pointed out, how the economic importance of her FDI presence abroad outweighs that of her domestic foreign trade. Particularly so when the foreign role in her own trade picture is taken into account. Again it must be stressed, that trade and FDI are intimately tied together in a complementary relationship, but FDI activities are, or are fast becoming, the leading variable in this constellation with trade playing only a dependent role, and not the other way around.

In this conceptual vein, the investigation into America's position in the global economy needs to be coupled with observations about inward FDI's impact on the U.S. national ownership of economic processes and resources, in order to balance the assessment of the American economic role in the world. In other words the focus changes from the country's national economy in geographic terms to the proposed global view defined by capital control.

Opening the discussion of FDI's leadership role in the globalization of the world economy may be best handled by a review of the best documented evidence concerning the existence and development trends of FDI, the huge sums of money devoted to this particular market penetration strategy. Customarily, it is measured in two different ways by entries in a country's BOP: as capital flows among nations on one side, and stock or position estimates of capital accumulated, outward and inward, over a period of time on the other.

Both sources indicate that literally trillions of dollars worth have been poured into this particular investment form, which excludes portfolio commitments for the reasons given. In-depth analysis of these sources of strictly financial aspects should address at least two questions: what net effect has this investment spending had for both the developed and developing parts of the global economy, the globalization bonus, and can it be helpful in identifying the winners or losers in the race for a share in that market?

FDI CAPITAL FLOWS

At first glance the information collected in Tables 3.1 and 3.2 appear quite uninspiring. Compared to world trade flows at easily ten times the levels for capital movements per annum, the latter look anemic. But capital flows to the tune of hundreds of billion dollars per year are funds adding to an already existing investment base, and thus reflect a serious commitment to the maintenance and expansion of global businesses.

Capital consists essentially of three different fund types: 1. equity or ownership funds, 2. inter-company debt or loans, and 3. reinvestments. The division has legal as well as practical perspectives. Income on equity capital is paid as dividends, loans require payments of interests, but reinvested funds do not form a separate category of capital nor do they draw distinct income payments like the other two. All funds ultimately flow into one common pool to be used as investment or working capital.

The data presented create perplexing impressions stemming from the wide differences in the volumes reported for both out flowing and inflowing funds for two investment partners. Theoretically, they should represent identical mirror images for each other, once reported as outflows from the investor country, and then reported by the recipient nation. It is difficult to reconcile the discrepancies in evidence with a simple explanation.

One major contributing factor in the divergence, besides normal time lapses involved in funds leaving one country and arriving in another, lies in the use of different accounting methods. Some capital exporting countries measure only actual funds leaving their borders, while others include reinvested funds, which are treated as virtual fund outflows. Japan for years accepted capital transfers authorized by the Ministry of Finance as actual capital exports, but apparently never tracked reinvestments.

The practical difficulties arising from this double accounting standard for the recipient nation can be readily appreciated. Its own BOP entry system is designed to register only actual fund inflows. In addition, reinvestments by FDI organizations are often not even monitored as a separate statistic for the purpose of calculating a nation's internal new capital formation. They are viewed as normal capital expenditures by a domestic company. A wonderful illustra-

Table 3.1. World Foreign Direct Investment Outflows*—$6 billion

Year	Total	U. S. A.	W. Europe	Japan	OECD	Other
1980	58.4	19.2	20.9	1.8	53.6	4.8
1981	55.0	9.6	24.3	4.2	48.5	6.5
1982	23.7	1.1	17.2	4.1	25.6	-1.9
1983	42.1	6.7	22.1	3.6	34.9	7.2
1984	54.1	11.6	25.8	5.9	48.3	5.8
1985	62.9	12.7	32.3	6.5	56.6	6.3
1986	99.2	17.7	50.6	14.5	89.8	9.4
1987	137.0	29.0	73.6	19.5	133.9	3.1
1988	168.5	17.9	103.1	34.2	161.6	6.8
1989	222.9	37.6	124.1	44.1	211.6	11.3
1980-89	923.8	163.1	494.0	138.4	864.4	59.3
1990	238.3	31.0	144.1	48.0	227.4	10.9
1991	192.7	32.7	113.5	30.7	185.7	7.1
1992	195.2	42.6	115.6	17.4	182.7	12.5
1993	223.5	77.2	107.1	13.8	207.9	15.6
1994	264.3	73.3	134.3	18.1	246.4	17.9
1995	333.8	98.8	175.9	22.5	312.3	21.5
1996	368.8	91.9	203.7	23.4	340.7	28.1
1997	442.7	104.8	243.5	26.1	404.8	37.9
1998	681.9	142.6	434.1	24.6	639.7	42.2
1999	1,027.1	188.9	774.4	22.3	978.0	49.1
1990-99	3,968.3	883.8	2,446.2	246.9	3,725.6	242.7
2000	1,375.6	178.3	1,016.2	31.5	1,279.3	96.3
2001	620.9	127.8	367.9	38.5	581.7	39.2

*includes partial coverage for reinvestments. (Sources: U.S. data: SOCB, August 1991, p. 85. August 1992, p. 122. August 1994, p. 133. August 1991, p. 85. August 1992, p. 122. October 1998, p. 127. September 2002, p. 74. All other data: UNCTAD: World Investment Report 1998, p. 367. IMF: Balance of Payments Statistics Yearbook, Part 2, various issues. OECD: International Direct Investment Statistics Yearbook, various issues).

tion of the different perspectives offered by analysis defined on the principle of territory versus capital ownership.

A third disturbance factor comes from fluctuating exchange rates. All national BOPs are maintained in their national currencies. The U.S. reports dollar outflows, for instance, but the beneficiaries will acknowledge fund inflows in their own currency, and both are subject to changing exchange values, unless they are tied to each other in a fixed relationship. Considering the fact that hundreds of currencies may be involved in FDI activities at any given moment, all fluctuating against each other, makes the potential for considerable distortions quite clear.

There is more to consider. Reinvestments do not represent international capital flows by traditional definition. They stay in the economy that produced the earnings from which they are derived in the first place. But what happens, if income earned abroad is not reinvested in the country of origin, but ends up in a third country. For the FDI company it is clearly a reinvestment of funds, for the capital exporting country it becomes a bona-fide FDI outflow, as well as a regular FDI inflow for the recipient country, perhaps identified by the nation of export or possibly, if the BOP system is sophisticated enough, by the nationality of the ultimate beneficial owner in American accounting lingo. A further complication may arise, if the funds flow through tax havens on their way to the ultimate destination for whatever reason. One single flow from the exporter's perspective now turns into two with the potential additive effect of double-counting.

Reinvestments are practically handled in the following manner by American BOP accounting standards. Funds earned abroad, which are not flowing back to the parent organization in the form of dividends or interests, are still counted as income flowing through the U.S. BOP's current account. As a BOP is a double entry system, which always balances a positive flow with a simultaneous negative flow, the hypothetical income entry (+) is neutralized by a fund outflow of equal size in the capital account (-). It leads here, just as on the income side to the impression of larger fund flows than really take place.

The difficulty in comparing such global transactions follows from the fact, that this practice has not been adopted uniformly by all countries. As mentioned, Japan had its own measuring system which did not include reinvestments in their calculations of inward or outward FDI statistics until 1995 when it was changed to conform to OECD and IMF standards.

Another point to make concerns the huge flows in the trillions of dollars over the course of years, which lead to the impression of vast amounts of productive capacity being generated by those fund movements. But by taking into account the global inflation since the first oil crisis in the early seventies and the second inflation push at the end of the decade, again related to OPEC, can only lead to the realistic conclusion that the amounts shown for the eighties and nineties suffer from a serious erosion of purchasing power. If one were to accept a conservative estimate of price levels having risen 5–6 times since the mid-seventies, all those impressive numbers appear in a totally different light.

It would lead to the convincing argument that effective investment levels have not really risen substantially between the seventies and the mid-nineties. In other words the economic impact of all these super funds flowing across national borders plus the related changes in investment stocks they have caused, as discussed next, may not be what they pretend to be. Support for this hypothesis will come from the discussion of FDI income flows and output shares in national or global GDP at a later point.

Concerning this latter point, it should be noted that the disposition of the transferred funds has a significance all of its own. Equity funds are quite different from inter-company debt, inasmuch as the former indicate business expansion, while the latter amount to business support activities ranging from facilities upgrading to shortfalls in cash flow, in the extreme case amounting to the coverage of potential losses.

The discussion of FDI flows would not be complete without mentioning two important observations. The first pertains to the rapidly rising fund flows in the 1999/2000 period in contrast to the sharp fall in 2001 and beyond, which is real even though final data are not yet available. An ominous indicator for the weakening world economy so strongly visible in the OECD countries, and political uncertainties lurking all of a sudden everywhere. It is not the end of globalization, but definitely the beginning of a protracted cooling period.

The second point concerns the geographic origin or destination of such transactions over time. In the 1980s, the U.S. generated 18% of all FDI outflows. During the 1990s it was closer to 22% with wide variations for individual years. Europe's share went from 53% to 62%, and Japan fell from 15% to 6% respectively. Looking back to comments on variable accounting

Table 3.2.   World Foreign Direct Investment Inflows—$billion

Year	Total	U. S. A.	W. Europe	Japan	OECD	Other
1980	55.2	13.0	15.8	0.2	46.4	8.8
1981	59.1	21.6	13.8	0.2	41.0	18.1
1982	52.8	12.6	13.2	0.4	30.4	22.4
1983	51.3	11.9	16.1	0.4	30.8	20.5
1984	59.4	25.5	9.8	nil	41.0	18.4
1985	56.3	19.0	18.1	0.6	43.1	13.2
1986	86.6	35.6	25.5	1.3	70.2	16.4
1987	126.9	59.6	41.6	1.2	113.2	13.7
1988	156.9	58.6	60.3	-0.5	132.1	24.8
1989	194.8	69.0	88.5	-1.1	166.5	28.4
1980-89	899.4	326.4	302.7	2.7	714.7	184.7
1990	201.2	48.4	109.7	1.8	169.6	31.6
1991	154.4	22.8	82.3	1.4	113.7	40.7
1992	166.5	19.2	85.8	2.8	117.6	48.9
1993	218.6	50.7	83.9	0.2	143.3	75.3
1994	244.6	45.1	78.9	0.9	141.6	102.9
1995	327.9	57.8	122.7	-	205.5	122.4
1996	373.0	86.5	121.8	0.2	226.5	146.5
1997	461.4	105.6	140.8	3.2	272.3	189.1
1998	690.4	179.0	274.3	3.3	486.5	203.9
1999	1,076.7	289.4	511.5	12.3	844.8	231.9
1990-99	3,914.7	904.5	1,611.7	26.1	2,721.4	1,193.3
2000	1,489.8	307.7	844.8	8.2	1,241.5	248.3
2001	729.2	130.8	343.3	6.2	513.8	215.4

(Sources: U.S. revised data: SOCB, August 1991, p. 51. August 1992, p. 92. August 1994, p. 103. August 1995, p. 58. September 2002, p. 44. UNCTAD: World Investment Report, 1998, p. 361. IMF: Balance of Payments Statistics Yearbook, Part 2, various issues. International Financial Statistics Yearbook 1998. OECD: International Direct Investment Statistics Yearbook, various issues).

practices involved here, it may be said that U.S. flow data have always included reinvestments, while Western Europe's data have a patchy history for many member states and still exclude them for Belgium-Luxembourg, Denmark, Greece and Spain through 1999, and Japan excluded them until 1995.OECD countries lead global capital exports with 94% for the whole period.

On the capital import side, America plays a different role. During the eighties 36% of globally reported inflows went to the States, but only 23% in the nineties. Europe's 33% share for the eighties was second behind the U.S., but increased to 41% in the nineties. Japan's respective shares of 0.3% and 0.7% are hardly worth mentioning, yet they confirm the country's resistance to encroachment from the outside, and not selectively from the U.S. alone, as has been claimed by anxious American interests.

As far as the developing countries are concerned, their role as capital exporters is small with 6% for the almost two decades covered, as could be expected. As beneficiaries of global capital exports, however, their role is totally reversed with a share growth from 21% to 30% over the period, almost matching Europe's level for the nineties. The significance of this development is underscored by the fact that, while global FDI capital inflows quadrupled for the world as a whole decade to decade, they increased six-fold for these countries. Considering their relative development stage, such fund flows must have provided an incredible development push for their economies and more importantly, there is no letdown in sight. While capital transfers among the OECD countries are considerably down in 2001, the developing nations enjoy the same level of inflows as before.

FDI POSITIONS

Information on FDI stocks, also called positions, measures the accumulated value resulting from all investment activities, combining actual fund flows in and out of a country, reinvestments, but also funds stemming from local capital sources. As long as there is a positive flow of investment capital out of a nation or, conversely into a national economy, the investment stock or position has the tendency to grow. It may only be reduced under the influence of three factors: the investor liquidates the holdings and repatriates the funds, the value of the investment shrinks because of negative business developments or exchange rate fluctuations, or the investment is expropriated by government fiat.

The body of information on FDI stock developments is quite well developed and yet again is affected by different accounting practices in place, similar to the situation mentioned for flow data. This becomes visible by a comparison between the global inward and outward positions depicted in Tables 3.3 and 3.4.

Position statistics involve incredibly large sums of capital owned by or owed to global investors. Overall they approach 12% of the worldwide GDP, that is partially produced with the help of such investments. But it is not only the sheer volume of investments that impresses. Equally astounding is the fact that these positions are expanding with breathtaking speed in monetary terms. During the first half of the 1980s outward FDI stocks grew by 15%, in the second half they effectively more than doubled, and during the 1990s they almost quadrupled, despite their already high starting point.

It must be admitted that the growth figures are somewhat affected by the fact that a complete set of data for many nations was not available for the 1980s. But it may be assumed that similar expansion rates also applied to non-reporters. The heady integration pace of the world economy intimated by these figures may not continue for two reasons.

For one, the world economy is already showing signs of a significant slowdown in the industrialized zone. Overcapacity and market saturation, stiffening competition and price deflation, slowing demand by the consumer and business sectors, ballooning credit and debt loads, and the lack of new industries are a powerful combination of factors that prove impervious to frantic demand stimulation measures. Japan has seen its domestic economy stall out since 1989. The U.S. and Europe are just beginning to go into a downward spiral that may last for more than a decade. The threat of war in the sensitive energy belt leads to further erosion of consumer and investor confidence. It could very well lead to larger confrontations with a tremendous disruptive potential for everybody. The only exceptions seem to be China and India where economic activity is bursting at the seams, for the moment.

The second reason is the indisputable backlash of large segments of the world against economic, cultural, and military encroachment by Western interests. Globalization in its broader connotation is seen here as a serious threat for their cultural integrity and economic independence, which has to be resisted or even totally rejected. The emergence of a totally new front between the West and these countries is not only a question of economic and military superiority, which may not be a convincing insurance against the spread of terrorism. It may actually foreshadow possible and un-

Table 3.3.   Global Outward Foreign Direct Investment Position—$million

Year	Total*	U. S. A**	W. Europe*	EU*	Japan	OECD*	Other*
1980	521,486	215,375	237,694	215,582	19,612	499,428	22,058
1981	557,472	228,348	247,760	227,418	24,506	534,039	23,433
1982	552,022	207,752	250,111	230,224	28,969	524,221	27,801
1983	568,098	207,203	251,812	232,890	32,178	539,202	28,896
1984	600,320	211,480	264,251	245,674	37,921	568,326	31,994
1985	691,745	230,250	321,972	295,727	43,974	656,276	35,469
1986	835,264	259,800	407,451	371,554	58,071	794,400	40,864
1987	1,047,434	314,307	522,019	474,225	77,022	1,000,544	46,890
1988	1,194,574	335,893	584,959	532,024	110,780	1,149,011	45,563
1989	1,411,608	381,781	691,870	632,086	154,367	1,340,349	71,259
1990	1,721,462	430,521	875,571	798,525	201,441	1,630,443	91,019
1991	1,925,170	467,844	987,482	899,342	231,791	1,820,784	104,386
1992	2,007,232	502,063	993,674	907,335	248,058	1,874,462	132,770
1993	2,200,158	564,283	1,063,160	958,837	259,795	2,027,394	172,764
1994	2,511,836	612,893	1,238,471	1,107,976	275,837	2,288,096	223,740
1995	2,854,853	699,015	1,457,253	1,292,043	238,45225	2,577,550	277,303
1996	3,170,554	795,195	1,575,886	1,408,550	8,618	2,845,068	325,486
1997	3,455,779	871,316	1,699,395	1,505,649	271,894	3,074,471	381,308
1998	4,150,994	1,000,703	2,125,761	1,909,431	270,052	3,658,301	492,693
1999	4,909,695	1,173,122	2,584,040	2,351,978	248,786	4,248,783	660,912
2000	6,086,428	1,293,431	3,421,542	3,148,830	278,438	5,316,292	770,136
2001	6,552,011	1,381,674	3,721,228	3,440,890	N/A	5,751,947	800,064

*UNCTAD data. **US data. (Sources: UNCTAD, World Investment Report, http://stats.unctad.org/fdi/eng/TableViewer/wdsview/print.asp. OECD: International Direct Investment Yearbook, various issues)

Table 3.4.   Global Inward Foreign Direct Investment Position—$million

Year	Total*	U. S. A.	W. Europe*	EU*	Japan	OECD*	Other*
1980	635,534	83,048	232,081	216,840	3,270	389,715	245,819
1981	687,642	108,714	228,569	211,808	3,915	419,823	267,919
1982	738,877	124,677	224,935	208,512	3,998	443,487	295,390
1983	775,620	137,061	226,897	210,717	4,364	462,920	312,700
1984	817,072	164,583	225,490	209,579	4,458	489,654	327,418
1985	913,182	184,616	285,544	267,618	4,743	568,670	344,512
1986	1,053,289	220,415	356,637	329,112	6,514	688,921	364,368
1987	1,251,522	263,394	455,018	419,556	9,018	856,924	394,598
1988	1,411,473	314,754	502,274	467,762	10,416	991,044	420,429
1989	1,627,114	368,924	612,193	576,079	15,655	1,174,361	452,753
1990	1,871,594	394,911	780,813	733,303	18,432	1,382,978	488,616
1991	2,053,730	419,108	876,285	822,919	22,771	1,515,821	537,909
1992	2,090,119	423,130	855,395	807,665	26,855	1,494,686	595,433
1993	2,242,453	467,412	877,420	823,904	29,933	1,571,700	670,753
1994	2,533,763	480,667	1,032,548	966,261	34,088	1,768,532	765,231
1995	2,911,725	535,553	1,192,427	1,115,081	-	2,021,303	890,422
1996	3,238,145	598,021	1,275,056	1,198,344	29,936	2,195,533	1,042,612
1997	3,515,063	681,842	1,309,658	1,255,507	27,076	2,295,841	1,219,222
1998	4,262,298	778,418	1,702,533	1,602,543	26,066	2,800,598	1,461,700
1999	5,110,655	955,726	1,877,998	1,769,328	46,117	3,216,854	1,893,801
2000	6,258,263	1,214,254	2,498,247	2,381,954	50,322	4,124,261	2,134,002
2001	6,845,723	1,321,063	2,776,627	2,648,651	N/A	4,504,122	2,341,601

*UNCTAD data (Sources: see Table 3.3).

expected realignments of present alliances. Both of the scenarios in combination could very well spell the end of globalization as has been seen for the last fifty years.

There are solid reasons behind the general preference shown by international investor for concentrating their attention on developed markets, the OECD countries. Political stability, high levels of income, converging standards of living and demand, a growing commonality of legal and business practices, all make them more attractive than potentially large footholds in areas with higher perceived risks. These are, by the way, all key factors driving globalization. The result is obvious. Even though the developing world represents roughly 20% of the world economy at this moment, and 85% of the world's population, OECD investors allocate no more than 22% of their funds here. (Table 3.5)

The encouraging aspect of information given in Tables 3.3 and 3.4 is the fact, that economies of the developing world are expanding, and actually to a point enabling them to become capital exporters in their own right. While the outward FDI stock of OECD grew eight-fold between 1980 and 1999, developing countries expanded their outward FDI base thirty-fold. (Table 3.3). As a consequence, they were able to expand their share in the global outward FDI position from 4% to a respectable 13% for those years.

FDI is undertaken by private enterprises that see the possibility of recovering their investments and making a profit despite the many perceived risks associated with international business. This is a positive aspect for both parties involved. But still, there can be no doubt that the developing countries are falling deeper and deeper into a net debtor status when also considering development loans extended by international credit institutions. For many countries the point has been reached, where repayment of a crushing debt burden becomes questionable. One suggested solution has

Table 3.5. Geographical Distribution Estimates for Outward FDI by Major OECD Members—1999 Percentages

From\To	OECD	USA	NAFTA	Europe	Japan	L.America	Asia	M. E./Africa	Other
OECD	77.8	23.8	27.8	50.0	1.1	9.6	7.5	2.5	1.5
USA	72.8	-	12.7	52.0	4.4	16.6	7.4	2.2	4.7
Canada	73.7	50.2	51.4	20.9	1.5	16.7	4.4	0.9	4.2
W. Europe									
France	86.4	26.6	27.7	56.4	1.9	4.5	1.3	2.3	5.9
Germany	90.4	27.9	30.3	58.2	1.7	3.8	3.7	1.0	1.3
Italy	78.1	11.0	N/A	95.9	1.1	3.8	N/A	N/A	N/A
Netherlands	88.1	23.2	25.5	61.8	0.5	4.4	4.4	1.6	1.8
Switzerland	77.9	22.0	24.3	51.1	1.8	13.1	7.3	1.6	0.8
UK	88.8	46.8	48.6	38.2	0.8	3.6	3.3	2.2	3.3
Japan	74.9	47.5	49.7	19.9	-	6.3	16.9	7.0	0.2

(Source: OECD: International Direct Investment Statistics Yearbook, 2001)

been debt forgiveness on a large scale, which is tantamount to large-scale destruction of capital and possibly a serious backlash in investor readiness to continue lending here. If it comes to that, the impetus for a unified world may become even more focused on the developed world, with the consequence of seriously slowing down the globalization process proper.

Interesting to observe is the way investors gauge the geographical attractiveness for their investment funds. Of all OECD investments worldwide 78% remain in the OECD itself. U.S. business parked 52% of its outward FDI in Europe, Japan only 20%. European investors prefer to keep about 60% of their capital in their own area, which is next door and familiar, and put less than 30% into the U.S., which in economic terms is more or less equal to their own market. A striking exception here is furnished by the UK, which keeps less than 40% of its investment total in Europe, most likely due to its strong position in the energy sector. In percentage terms Switzerland invests three times as much in Latin America as do other European nations. Japan's primary investment focus is on the U.S. The 48% commitment there is over twice the level devoted to Europe, which for all practical purposes offers them an equal market potential. Do Japanese investors consider the Europeans to be more formidable competitors, or have American trade concerns forced them into these investment allocations?

NET FDI POSITIONS-INDICATORS OF RELATIVE GLOBAL COMPETITIVENESS

The statement referring to the discrepancy between aggregate inward and outward investment stocks being due in some degree to the influence of different accounting techniques employed by national statisticians does, of course, not necessarily apply in the same manner to national or regional statistics. Actually, discrepancies here must be expected and are quite normal, because there is no way they can balance out when countries export consistently more capital than they receive, or the opposite.

Looking at OECD statistics quickly leads to the realization that even among developed nations there are two distinct categories of countries: net exporters and net importers of FDI capital. Even though not shown, it may be fair to assume that most, if not all, developing countries are net importers. A minus sign in front of a country's or region's net FDI position identifies that position as a bona-fide FDI debtor. As aggregate inward positions are larger than like outward positions (Tables 3.3 & 3.4) we have a ready explanation for the minus signs appearing in front of the global net position and that of the developing nations shown in the table below.

According to the basic premise advocated here, a country's true national share of the world economy is determined by its output of goods and services from domestic industries, augmented by the nation's capital control over productive resources and processes in other nations, but reduced by foreign control over that nation's domestic economy, leading to their respective net FDI positions.

A country's categorization as a net FDI capital importer or exporter leads to a first and very useful conclusion about a country's competitiveness in the global market. It is thus correct to assume that net exporters own a larger share of the world market than indicated by the size of their national economy alone, as conventionally measured at the present. Conversely, net importers of FDI capital can by definition hold only a smaller share in the world economy than indicated by their national GDP statistics, simply because foreigners control a bigger piece of their national economy than they hold in foreign markets.

Table 3.6 summarizes the net positions for major OECD members. It shows how the U.S. came dangerously close to losing their international competitive position in 1989 due to the erosive influence of inward FDI. Europe started from a very weak competitive position, but now ranks as the uncontested number one, outflanking the U.S. and Japan by a factor of 3:1. Japan's performance is very impressive, as repeatedly noted before. Not only is its outward position practically equal to that of the U.S., but it has a virtually unbroken record of advancing against all competitors until 1995, when Japan ceased to use its traditional accounting system and adopted the international standard.

The aggregate data appearing here help to create a somewhat erroneous impression of a positive outward investment balance for all OECD members. On closer inspection this picture needs to be adjusted. Actually, of all 29 OECD countries only 12 show a clearly positive investment balance, which allows the conclusion that their position in the world economy is stronger than suggested by their domestic economic indicators like employment, GDP, and foreign trade in relation to other countries or OECD as a whole.

Relative positional strength as indicative of relative competitive superiority will later be corroborated by similar information on relative income streams generated by FDI business activities flowing into and out of these specific economies. While it is true that relative positions never remain the same for many different reasons, it is fair to say, that a country's changing competitiveness may be a major, if not actually the major reason behind growth or decline of its global market share.

Which leads to another conclusion that can be legitimately drawn from observable trends in inward and outward investment positions. The relative speed at which they move against each other, decides whether a nation is gaining in the race for global market share, holding its ground, or falling behind.

Such conclusions seem paradox in some way, because the argument could be made that a net inflow of FDI capital is beneficial for the recipient, whereas a net outflow could have the opposite effect on a national economy. Both arguments have their validity, especially for developing economies, but we are not concerned with the internal effect of capital flows on a

Table 3.6.   Net Foreign Direct Investment Position—$million

Year	World	U. S. A.	W. Europe	EU	Japan	OECD	Other
1980	-114,048	132,327	5,613	-1,258	16,342	109,713	-223,761
1981	-130,170	119,634	19,191	15,610	20,591	114,216	-244,486
1982	-186,855	83,075	25,176	21,712	24,971	80,734	-267,589
1983	-207,522	70,142	24,915	22,173	27,814	76,282	-283,804
1984	-216,752	46,897	38,761	36,095	33,463	78,672	-295,424
1985	-221,437	45,634	36,428	28,109	39,231	87,606	-309,043
1986	-218,025	39,385	50,814	42,442	51,557	105,479	-323,504
1987	-204,088	50,913	67,001	54,669	68,004	143,620	-347,708
1988	-216,899	21,139	82,685	64,262	100,364	157,967	-374,866
1989	-215,506	12,857	79,677	56,007	138,712	165,988	-381,494
1990	-150,132	35,610	94,758	65,222	183,009	247,465	-397,597
1991	-128,560	48,736	111,197	76,423	209,020	304,963	-433,523
1992	-82,887	78,933	138,279	99,670	221,203	379,776	-462,663
1993	-42,295	96,871	185,740	134,933	229,862	455,694	-497,989
1994	-21,927	132,226	205,923	141,715	241,749	519,564	-541,491
1995	-56,872	163,462	264,826	176,962	-	556,247	-613,119
1996	-67,591	197,174	300,830	210,206	228,682	649,535	-717,126
1997	-59,284	189,474	389,737	250,142	244,818	778,630	-837,914
1998	-111,304	222,285	423,228	306,888	243,986	857,703	-969,007
1999	-200,960	207,490	706,042	582,650	202,669	1,031,921	-1,232,881
2000	-171,835	79,177	923,295	766,876	228,116	1,192,031	-1,363,866
2001	-293,712	60,611	944,601	792,239	N/A	1,247,825	-1,541,537

Outward FDI position (+) less inward FDI (−) position.

specific economy, we are looking for ways to measure the development of a country's absolute share in the global economy.

Table 3.5 in conjunction with in-depth information on America's FDI activities presented further on emphasizes the positive effect of outward direct investments for a national economy, but also the offsetting consequences of growing inward direct investments.

Statistics on worldwide FDI and related aspects are, unfortunately, not as abundant and detailed as those for the U.S. This holds also true for position data, which are now available for most developed countries due to the best efforts of the OECD. Yet the data are not fully compatible due to the different definitions and collection methods still being employed as mentioned before. For this and other reasons they are notoriously unsuitable to draw inferences about their actual economic impact, because operational statistics like sales, gross product (GP), costs, employment and related compensation, income, and foreign trade connected with FDI, are particularly scarce, which makes direct comparisons and valid observations about national progress or lack thereof very difficult.

Quite annoying is also the distorting influence of exchange rate fluctuations on financial data. A look at this type of information in terms of the national currency may give the impression of positive developments, which can immediately be contradicted by the same data after their conversion into U.S. dollars. Students of the subject are thoroughly familiar with the problem and hence become very cautious when interpreting and evaluating comparative findings. It is sometimes hard to attribute these breaks in trends to underlying economic or business changes, or entirely to currency factors, which normally occur together, and in very variable constellations.

There are, however, avenues that may lead to surrogate information of admittedly lesser, but still reasonable usefulness and validity. Next to a nation's internal and external FDI stock positions and related developments there are BOP statistics measuring the net flow of services, and here in particular streams of FDI related inward versus outward income, the development of trade balances in general and, where available, FDI generated trade flows in particular. The trouble with these pieces of financial information again is that they may show a development which is out of synchrony with actual market developments, and thus do not permit actual share estimates as far as employment, sales, imports/exports, etc. are concerned. Such divergence can be produced by business strategies of corporate management, which at an advanced stage of its network of subsidiaries can easily shift from one source of supply to another as dictated by cost, profit, or political considerations.

An additional caveat concerns the lack of uniform and standardized procedures for measuring some FDI information. The U.S. estimate of inward and outward FDI positions is a combination of investment flows, reinvestments, valuation adjustments, and periodic benchmark surveys to check the actual status of the FDI position proper and making adjustments where necessary. Japan at the other end did use only cumulative net investment flows derived from approvals by the Ministry of Finance to establish both FDI positions until 1995. Reinvestments were completely disregarded, and surveys helpful in adjusting these estimates have not been furnished.

Other countries fall somewhere in between. The Netherlands, for example, do not make it mandatory for companies to report their foreign ventures, at all. If they do, it is entirely voluntary. What this leads to is illustrated by data allegedly covering the same subject: Japan's FDI stock in the U.S. for 1994 amounts to $194 billion according to Japanese data, but only $105 billion according to the American side. (OECD1997).

Other information points in exactly in the same direction. There are no data, for instance, on Japan's inward position either by country or in total for 1995. 1996 figures return to a more detailed presentation of country statistics, but now expressed totally in yen, whereas they used to be furnished in dollars before. All of this indicates that Japan has harmonized its reporting system with OECD and IMF reporting standards resulting in a sharp downward revision of both positions.

However constructed, position estimates are better to work with than the more variable fund flows, because they offer more consistent development patterns over time. Given all this, there is a need for other sources of relevant information to bolster a researcher's comfort level. FDI related income flows might serve as an indicator of trends supporting facts unearthed about positions. Yet again they often produce similarly baffling discrepancies resulting from different national accounting practices. In the American way of handling FDI income, it is derived from actual disbursements of dividends, net interest payments, and reinvestments all combined under FDI income in the BOP income (current) account. When trying to link this information to a country's reported outflow of income to the U.S. one will find that the figures may be totally different. This stems from the fact mentioned, already, that the country in question counts only actual flow volumes, which by definition exclude reinvestments. The information may be further influenced by the fact that U.S. parent companies may cause their earnings to flow out of a foreign country, but not necessarily immediately into their domestic bank accounts. If this money is deposited in a third nation, like a tax haven, the exporting country correctly notes the outflow to that nation and not the U.S. as the ultimate owner of the cash.

None of these reported financial indicators come even close to measuring FDI's true economic impact for a given nation in terms of sales, employment, gross product, trade, etc. which could be directly linked to macro-economic statistics maintained and furnished by practically all developed and many developing nations, if it were available. For the moment such information is pitifully underdeveloped.

OECD'S DISTRIBUTION OF FDI POSITIONS BY MEMBER COUNTRY

Being the world' most important source of direct investment capital begs the question, how major OECD members either contribute to the investment pool, or themselves share in it. Europe leads in both fields as the major source of funds and the main beneficiary of global capital exports. Table 3.5 shows 78% of OECD capital exports to flow right back into other OECD member economies.

The U.S. ranks in second place as both recipient and investor. In neither function, it displays a clear and consistent growth pattern, that would result in significant share gains. As an investment target it had a flurry of popularity in the mid-eighties, but saw its OECD investment share decline from 34% in 1984 to less than 30% throughout the 1990s, despite huge capital inflows. The lower level is actually in line with America's overall share in the global economy, indicative of a tough competitive environment facing foreign investors here, and also the capital needs required for establishing a solid foothold in this huge market. (Table 3.7)

As a source of capital the U.S. is clearly playing a declining role, dropping from over 40% in the early eighties to under 30% at the present. In the beginning, that is to say the early 1980s, American and European outward positions were practically equal, as they should be. But then a period of relaxing attention by U.S. investors to the outside world, indicated by the fairly stagnant levels of capital stocks reported from the late eighties through the early 1990s, initiated a steady relative decline in the U.S. position. Compared to the European growth performance, which is generated by a world area of practically equal economic weight, this is a remarkable contraction. (Table 3.8)

Two reasons may be given for the trend reversals between both areas. U.S. industries, in general, do not depend on foreign markets to the same degree that Europeans have to for business growth. This holds particularly true for smaller and medium sized American companies, which are less well financed and perceive foreign ventures as beset with risks they would rather avoid. Then there is the impetus created by Europe's integration, which undoubtedly challenged all European industries to invest in increased productivity and readiness for the invigorated competitive environment expected from the disappearing trade and political barriers, plus the cost/price transparencies created by the Euro.

Available information indicates that Europeans account for more than 60% of Europe's inward FDI stock, a fact that is confirmed by the 55–60% of their outward stock being concentrated there, compared to only 20 in the U.S. (Table 3.5).

Japan stands out among all OECD countries. Not only because of its huge outside FDI stock, but equally for its almost insignificant inward position. Japan's emphasis on outward FDI as its key global expansion strategy is readily explained by the country's almost total lack of natural resources and thus total dependence on overseas markets for survival. At the same time, nothing could better illustrate the importance of FDI as a key political instrument for main-

Table 3.7. Distribution of OECD's Inward FDI Position by Major Member—$million

Year	OECD	USA	%	W. Europe	%	Canada	%	Australia	%	Japan	%	Other	%
1980	389,715	83,048	21.3	232,081	59.6	51,596	13.2	24,291	6.2	3,270	0.8	-4,571	-
1981	419,823	108,714	25.9	228,569	54.4	56,069	13.3	28,617	6.8	3,915	0.9	-6,061	-
1982	443,487	124,677	28.1	224,935	50.7	55,991	12.6	27,379	6.2	3,998	0.9	6,507	1.5
1983	462,920	137,061	29.6	226,897	49.0	64,023	12.9	25,652	5.6	4,364	0.9	4,923	1.1
1984	489,654	164,583	33.6	225,490	46.1	65,070	13.3	27,454	5.5	4,458	0.9	2,599	0.5
1985	568,670	184,616	32.5	285,544	50.2	64,657	11.4	24,482	4.3	4,743	0.8	4,628	0.8
1986	688,921	220,415	32.0	356,637	51.8	69,579	10.1	27,586	4.0	6,514	0.9	8,190	1.2
1987	856,924	263,394	30.7	455,018	53.1	81,983	9.6	39,568	4.6	9,018	1.1	7,943	0.9
1988	991,044	314,754	31.8	502,274	50.7	96,305	9.7	52,442	5.3	10,416	1.1	14,853	1.5
1989	1,174,361	368,924	31.4	612,193	52.1	105,928	9.0	67,808	5.8	15,655	1.3	3,853	0.3
1990	1,382,978	394,911	28.6	780,813	56.5	112,872	8.2	74,300	5.4	18,432	1.3	1,650	0.1
1991	1,515,821	419,108	27.6	876,285	57.8	116,984	7.7	77,410	5.1	22,771	1.5	3,263	0.2
1992	1,494,686	423,130	28.3	855,395	57.2	108,511	7.3	72,112	4.8	26,855	1.8	8,683	0.6
1993	1,571,700	467,412	29.7	877,420	55.8	106,868	6.8	78,917	5.0	29,953	1.9	11,150	0.7
1994	1,768,532	480,667	27.2	1,032,548	58.4	110,188	6.2	94,254	5.3	34,088	1.9	16,787	0.9
1995	2,021,303	535,553	26.5	1,192,427	59.0	123,199	6.1	95,898	4.7	-	-	NMF	1.3
1996	2,195,533	598,021	27.3	1,275,056	58.1	132,939	6.1	111,555	5.1	29,936	1.4	48,026	2.2
1997	2,295,841	681,842	29.7	1,309,658	57.0	138,727	6.0	98,515	4.3	27,076	1.2	40,023	1.7
1998	2,800,598	778,418	27.8	1,702,533	60.8	144,867	5.2	99,476	3.6	26,066	0.9	49,238	1.8
1999	3,216,854	965,632	30.0	1,877,998	58.4	171,019	5.3	115,977	3.6	46,117	1.4	40,111	1.2

(Source: See Table 3.4. OECD, International Direct Investment Statistics Yearbook, various issues).

Table 3.8. Distribution of OECD's Outward FDI Position by Major Member—$million

Year	OECD	U.S.A.	%	W. Europe	%	Canada	%	Japan	%	Other	%
1980	499,428	215,375	43.1	237,694	47.6	21,639	4.4	19,612	3.9	5,108	1.0
1981	534,039	228,348	42.7	247,760	46.4	27,470	5.1	24,506	4.6	5,955	1.1
1982	524,221	207,752	39.7	250,111	47.7	27,818	5.3	28,969	5.5	9,571	1.8
1983	539,202	207,203	38.4	251,812	46.8	32,064	5.9	32,178	6.0	15,945	2.9
1984	568,326	211,480	37.1	264,251	46.5	37,908	6.7	37,921	6.7	16,766	3.0
1985	656,276	230,250	35.1	321,972	49.1	40,947	6.2	43,974	6.7	19,133	2.9
1986	794,400	259,800	32.7	407,451	51.3	44,548	5.6	58,071	7.3	24,530	3.1
1987	1,000,544	314,307	31.4	522,019	52.2	54,118	5.4	77,022	7.7	33,078	3.3
1988	1,140,011	335,893	29.5	584,959	51.3	63,782	5.6	110,780	9.7	44,597	3.9
1989	1,340,349	381,781	28.5	691,870	51.6	72,850	5.4	154,367	11.5	39,481	2.9
1990	1,630,443	430,521	26.4	875,571	51.6	84,808	5.2	201,441	12.3	38,102	2.3
1991	1,820,784	467,844	25.7	987,482	54.2	94,382	5.2	231,791	12.7	39,285	2.2
1992	1,874,462	502,063	26.8	993,674	53.0	87,870	4.7	248,058	13.2	42,797	2.3
1993	2,027,394	564,283	27.8	1,063,160	52.4	92,468	4.6	259,795	12.8	47,688	2.4
1994	2,288,096	612,893	26.8	1,238,471	54.1	104,267	4.5	275,837	12.1	56,628	2.5
1995	2,577,550	699,015	27.1	1,457,253	56.5	118,122	4.6	238,452	9.2	64,708	2.5
1996	2,845,068	795,195	27.9	1,575,886	55.3	132,291	4.6	258,618	9.1	83,078	2.9
1997	3,074,471	871,316	28.3	1,699,395	55.3	149,463	4.8	271,894	8.8	82,403	2.7
1998	3,658,301	1,000,703	27.4	2,125,761	58.1	167,090	4.6	270,052	7.4	94,695	2.6
1999	4,248,783	1,173,122	27.6	2,584,040	60.8	187,236	4.4	248,786	5.9	55,599	1.3

(Source: See Table 3.7)

taining national independence, and growing economic influence in the outside world at the same time, than this totally disparate FDI picture for Japan.

A final comment concerns the Triad's contribution to the development of the non-OECD world. The data for 1999 show a U.S. position of $321 billion, Japan $186 billion, and Europe an estimated $388 billion in developing economies. Their aggregate total of $895 billion thus accounts for a surprisingly low 47% of the inward position estimate for that area in that same year furnished by UNCTAD. (Table 3.4)

FDI POSITIONS OF MAJOR OECD INDUSTRIES

Three major industrial categories have been established for the uniform collection of pertinent statistics concerning the development of inward and outward investment stocks by OECD researchers: primary, manufacturing, and services industries with many specific sub-categories in each.

Table 3.9 and 3.10 do not cover all OECD countries, but allow the general observation that primary industries are not only the smallest part of the outward investment picture, with under 10% of the total, and a somewhat more important 11% share on the inward side. In both cases, they also seem to be losing ground as investment objects in percentage terms judging by their declining shares.

FDI positions in the primary sector consisting of agriculture, mining , and energy related extraction and processing activities are dominated by energy (oil & gas) data for some countries,

Table 3.9.   Industry Share of OECD Outward FDI Position—$million

Year	Total	Primary	%	Manufacturing	%	Services	%
1990	1,630,443	158,352	9.7	645,868	39.6	819,020	50.2
1995	2,577,550	215,946	8.4	1,014,392	39.3	1,348,255	52.2
1999	4,248,783	314,164	7.4	1,421,192	33.4	2,518,709	59.3

Table 3.10.   Industry Share of OECD Inward FDI Position—$million

Year	Total	Primary	%	Manufacturing	%	Services	%
1990	1,382,978	168,726	12.2	524,157	37.9	604,371	43.7
1995	2,021,303	141,491	7.0	703,412	34.8	1,115,758	55.2
1999	3,216,854	128,680	4.0	1,132,331	35.2	1,888,320	58.7

Note: data are pro-rated on basis of reporting countries, estimated to represent 80% of the inward position.

which are prominent in that sector like Australia, the US., UK, France, Norway, and Canada. The other sectors normally play only a small role for FDI interests. Important is the fact that the outward position expressed in actual dollar terms is growing vigorously, while the inward position is stagnant. A clear indication that investments in extractive industries are primarily going to non-OECD destinations.

Manufacturing as the second ranking investment volume, shares the fate of the primary sector in that both inward and outward investment categories of that industry are losing share in the overall investment picture. Even though still on an upward trend in actual dollar terms that share has fallen from over 40% in 1990 to only 36% four years later, in a parallel development to the primary sector.

Outward OECD investments are growing strongly while inward positions are moving at a slower pace suggesting a saturation level has been reached here with new funds spilling over into newly developing economies.

Leading is the services industry with a share of over 50% of total fund commitments, and clearly expanding its share in both the inward and outward categories. Again, similar to the manufacturing situation, the outward part of that industry is growing faster than the inward stock, permitting the conclusion that non-OECD destinations are more attractive to investors than their traditional targets.

But looking at these totals is seeing only the proverbial tip of the iceberg, which is clearly visible, but reveals little about structures under the surface. Going beyond industrial aggregates, affords unobstructed insights into the lively behavior and changing patterns of industries as components of overall FDI positions in OECD member nations. The position mix is in a constant flux. Existing positions suddenly grow after periods of stagnation, get smaller, or disappear altogether. At times, new stocks move into place, either in existing or new industries, quickening, slowing, or ending these changes in position patterns. After all, individual industry positions are not growing in a linear fashion as perhaps suggested by the overall data presented. Investments may be acquired, but also abandoned, even merged on occasion, which may change the nationality of these partnership components.

All these movements can be linked to specific nations, both in their capacity as capital exporters or importers, and the respective ebbs and flows become true indicators of national competitive advantages. Companies with superior technology, marketing and management skills, access to capital markets, and the entrepreneurial spirit to venture out into foreign markets make decisions that cause the fluctuations in positions. It is like a giant chess game with very similar strategic advances and retrenchments.

As far as national share differences in each major industrial investment category are concerned, here is a quick overview of the main players in OECD:

a. Primary Industry in 1994
    Inward: UK: 33.3%; U.S.A.: 29.9%; Canada: 14.4%; Australia: 10.0%; Norway: 4.4% for a combined total of 92.0%
    Outward: U.S.A. : 36.2%; UK: 26.8%; Japan: 11.1%; Canada: 11.0%; France: 7.8%. Their combined total reaches 92.9%
b. Manufacturing Industry in 1994
    Inward: U.S.A.: 34.5%; UK: 11.7%; Canada: 10.7%; Netherlands: 8.4%; France: 7.9%; Germany: 7.0% for a combined total of 80.2%

Outward: U.S.A.: 24.7%; Japan: 15.1%; UK: 12.8; Netherlands: 8.6%; Germany: 8.2%; France: 6.9%; Switzerland: 6.4% for a combined total of 82.7%

c. Services Industry in 1994

Inward: U.S. A: 33.2%; Germany: 16.2%; UK: 11.3%; France: 10.1%; Netherlands: 7.1%; Australia: 5.1% for a combined total of 83.0%.

Outward: U.S.A.: 27.6%; Japan: 23.7%; Germany: 11.0%; UK: 9.5%; France: 6.9%; the Netherlands: 5.8% for a cumulative 84.5% share of the grand total.

The dominance of the US in practically all categories will be of great importance for later discussions of actual national positions in the world market as a reliable indicator of the globalization process. This is so, because of the country's obvious weight in international investments on one hand, and the quantity and quality of the FDI documentation produced for decades on the other. In that respect, American research and statistical coverage of her FDI activities is far beyond that of any other nation, regardless of whether the inward or outward positions are concerned. The only country coming close to the American fastidiousness with record keeping is Germany, with France in third place on the basis of a fairly complete inward FDI database for her manufacturing industry, but none of the others. Realizing the enormous gap in knowledge resulting from neglect in this vital area is finally stirring the OECD research apparatus into activity at the end of the twentieth century. The organization's 1999 publication "Measuring Globalization, the Role of Multinational in OECD Economies" is certainly a welcome initiative in this regard.

Chapter Four

The Economic Dimensions of U.S. Outward FDI

INTRODUCTION

FDI is undertaken for different reasons. Opening new markets, protection of existing business at home or overseas, securing vital raw material supplies, bowing to political pressures, cost reduction through increased sales volume, development of the critical mass needed to be a world player, assured amortization of large investments in R&D, acquisition of existing technology in preference over self-development, engaging in strategic alliances, and many more. Their common bond is the expected increase in profits to assure survival and growth of the business. FDI is almost exclusively undertaken in the private industrial sectors of national economies. Where it touches the public sector, it is more the exception than the rule, and is usually confined to the energy and primary industry sector of developing nations.

After looking at the billions and even trillions of FDI dollars in the previous sections, it is legitimate to wonder what tangible consequences these enormous efforts have brought for the global economy, and also the investors, whether seen on a national, industrial, or individual company basis. FDI is the extension of national industries into the global market and, more importantly, manifests direct national capital control over productive resources beyond the investor's home economy. It is a force that expands the national economy's size, scope, and market share in the global context.

But, it must at all times be remembered that FDI is not a one-way street. Outward expansion of one country's industry can and normally is being offset to some degree by like expansions of other national industries into its own domain, the inward FDI aspect for the original outward investor nation. In the discussion of inward versus outward FDI positions of a nation it was claimed that nations with larger and faster expanding investment stock abroad, compared to their inward positions held by foreigners, are the true winners in the race for global market share, or in the opposite case the losers.

All FDI activities result in measurable benchmarks like assets, sales, employment, output of value added, income, imports and exports, to mention only the most common ones, which can be directly related to macro-economic data regularly published by all nations in detail. In other words, if FDI data could be found for these categories they would be ideally suited for evaluation of the economic weight of FDI operations in the domestic part of national economies or, by extension, the global economy itself. Similar information could also be generated for the impact of nationally defined FDI involvement in a given nation's foreign trade, or world trade itself.

More concretely spoken, the American FDI position, or for that matter the position of any other nation, produces economic output that should be credited to the capital owners of the productive resources, rather than disappear in the national statistics of the investment's location. Thus, a nation's economy is larger than its domestic economy in the presence of measurable outward FDI positions. Such enlargement, on the other hand, can be neutralized, or even reversed, by inward FDI positions within the geographical boundaries of the country. As stated before, depending on the relative volumes of both positions, and the speed of development against each other, a country's weight in the global economy is enhanced, unaffected, or diminished.

Unfortunately, separate and comprehensive FDI statistics beyond capital flows and position estimates are very rare. The most valuable contribution to the field comes from the US, which publishes well developed time series for inward and outward FDI positions, capital flows, sales, employment, value-added, foreign trade, etc. Germany and France do offer similar, but only partial insights in this regard.

Even though a complete picture cannot be derived from the scarce data bases, the fact that the US outward FDI account for roughly 27% of the world's aggregate FDI position allows certain cross-references and estimates to be made based on available FDI data for other nations. In addition, the fact that US inward FDI data are similarly detailed and often account for a substantial share in the total outward FDI position of other nations allows further analogies and assumptions to be drawn.

OECD researchers recently have laid a useful foundation for the discussion at hand, by estimating the overall scope of all FDI activities as expressed by the investment stock, assets, employment, sales, and gross product for several nations' manufacturing industries. This complements very well the format of the investigation into America's FDI, which follows a very similar pattern. The close correspondence of the approaches reveals how American and OECD researchers have developed a common research standard by borrowing liberally from each other.

As a first step in the FDI impact on the global economy, America's development in OECD's industrial GDP and employment is presented. All references to the public sector of individual economies are excluded, as U.S. FDI is undertaken only by and in the private sector.

THE DEVELOPMENT OF MAJORITY-OWNED AFFILIATE GROSS PRODUCT

Data on this subject has been collected with consistency and great detail practically from 1989 forward. They concern value-added information for majority-owned affiliates (Mofas) only, which means it refers to economic achievements that are truly American owned and managed. This is what was previously referred to as the extension of American industry into the global economy. It has the great advantage that it can be directly linked and compared to national GDP data that are regularly published by all OECD nations. In view of the advanced harmonization of OECD statistical procedures and data output, the following observations on the U.S. role in individual, regional, and global OECD industries must be considered highly compatible.

Table 4.1.   Global U.S. FDI Gross Product by Geographical Area—$million Year Total Europe % EU % Japan % OECD % Other %

Year	Total	Europe	%	EU	%	Japan	%	OECD	%	Other	%
1977	161,136	69,360	43.1	63,162	39.2	3,065	1.9	108,220	67.2	52,916	32.8
1982	223,717	112,577	50.3	104,787	46.8	4,587	2.1	165,429	73.9	58,288	26.1
1983	216,683										
1984	220,331										
1985	220,074										
1986	231,644										
1987	269,734										
1988	297,556										
1989	319,994	179,758	56.2	170,025	53.1	14,940	4.7	266,582	83.3	53,412	16.7
1990	356,033	213,419	59.9	201,415	56.6	14,565	4.1	299,696	84.2	56,337	15.8
1991	355,963	217,355	61.1	204,829	57.5	16,547	4.6	303,206	85.2	52,757	14.8
1992	361,524	217,652	60.2	206,973	57.3	15,747	4.3	302,044	83.5	59,480	16.5
1993	359,179	206,967	57.6	196,012	54.6	17,603	4.9	291,635	81.2	67,544	18.8
1994	403,696	235,432	58.3	222,828	55.2	21,752	5.4	331,418	82.1	72,278	17.9
1995	465,576	279,298	60.0	264,144	56.7	24,331	5.2	379,750	81.6	85,826	18.4
1996	498,310	91,732	58.5	273,633	54.9	25,677	5.1	391,189	78.5	107,121	21.5
1997	520,867	297,441	57.1	279,000	53.6	26,578	5.1	414,274	79.5	106,593	20.5
1998	506,269	302,248	59.7	282,129	55.7	23,776	4.7	412,656	81.5	93,613	18.5
1999	561,158	321,581	57.3	299,119	53.3	30,761	5.5	454,611	81.0	106,547	19.0

Note: majority-owned non-bank affiliates only.

Table 4.1 traces the development of U.S. FDI gross product in total and by major world region. In general the data show a distribution broadly similar to the one observed for the related investment volumes discussed in Chapter 3. In addition, it also contrasts the sharp differences in U.S. output levels in Europe, where 50% of America's FDI is invested, but delivers a much higher 60% of total affiliate gross product. A second impression concerns Japan, which is the second largest national economy with a GDP reaching more than 60% of that of the U.S., and about 50% of the European output. (Table1.1)

In view of the vast potential Japan offers, America's participation in that market definitely is not what it could or should be. But this is not surprising. The lack of success here only accentuates the difficulties encountered by all foreigners trying to enter the Japanese market. Without the well-known entry barriers, the U.S. performance in Japan should reach closer to half the American level reached in Europe, yielding to a substantially different distribution picture for America's FDI affiliates in the process. Yet, despite the weak picture in Japan, over 80% of Mofa gross product is derived from OECD markets, thus following the global GDP pattern found in Table 1.1. A point worth noting in this respect is OECD's strengthening position between 1982 and 1992, and the subsequent emergence of non-OECD economies in the general direction of their historic high levels of more than 30% in the 1970s, based on a turnaround from their low of 17.4% in 1992. There can be no doubt, that the developing nations are moving forward.

Another view of America's FDI relates to its distribution by industry, which is presented in an unusual four-way breakdown compared to the customary three major industrial divisions employed by international agencies and countries: manufacturing, services, and primary industries. The reason for a different American classification is the secrecy shrouding the oil industry. Usually, extraction of crude oil, natural gas, and coal are covered under primary industry data, while processing is covered under manufacturing, and wholesaling operations for oil products should appear under the services category. It is difficult to disentangle this petroleum mix by country, as the needed details are not furnished, with the exception of the benchmark years 1982, 1989, and 1994.

The all other category presents similar difficulties as it covers primary industries like agriculture, forestry and mining together with typical service industries like construction, communication, transportation, utilities, and retail trade. Their dis-aggregation again is possible only for the above-mentioned benchmark years.

Significant changes have taken place in the geographic distribution of U.S. FDI gross product by industry over the period, even though the reasons are not be immediately clear. For instance, there is no direct correlation between investment and GP shares by world area, proving an inexplicable disjuncture between investment intent and operational results. As a prime example, Western Europe's share in gross product generation by all U.S. FDI operations significantly exceeds its share in the accumulated investment stock. (Table 3.5 and 4.3).Yet, for the OECD as a whole output of value-added is below affiliate investment levels. A number of factors are at work here producing the enigmatic results. Thus, investment levels and relative positions are anchored in historic capital flows, which are only marginally affected by such short-term events like exchange rate fluctuations, business cycles, cost and price changes, etc. In the case of value-added calculations, results are at all times and immediately affected by just such changes in the business environment. In addition, being tied to foreign currencies, the valuation of commercial output in the form of sales, value-added, and profits tends to go in the opposite direction of the ever-shifting dollar rates.

Table 4.2.   Global U.S. FDI Gross Product by Industry—$million

Year	Total	Manufacturing	%	Petroleum	%	Services	%	Other	%
1977	161,136	71,609	44.4	62,010	38.5	24,200	15.0	3,317	2.1
1982	223,717	99,756	44.6	85,608	38.3	28,598	12.8	9,755	4.4
1983	216,683								
1984	220,331								
1985	220,074								
1986	231,644								
1987	269,734								
1988	297,556								
1989	319,994	172,008	53.8	77,195	24.1	55,998	17.5	14,793	4.6
1990	356,033	187,573	52.7	86,987	24.4	62,960	17.7	18,513	5.2
1991	355,963	182,082	51.1	88,775	24.9	63,829	17.9	21,277	6.0
1992	361,524	181,927	50.3	92,526	25.6	65,561	18.1	21,511	5.9
1993	359,179	177,745	49.5	91,506	25.5	71,304	19.9	18,623	5.2
1994	403,696	205,208	50.8	94,005	23.3	83,992	20.8	20,491	5.1
1995	465,576	238,901	51.3	99,683	21.4	101,676	21.8	25,316	5.4
1996	498,310	250,351	50.2	109,870	22.1	109,472	22.0	28,617	5.8
1997	520,867	254,623	48.9	111,838	21.5	125,493	24.1	28,913	5.5
1998	506,269	246,991	48.8	94,847	18.7	129,469	25.6	34,960	6.9
1999	561,158	312,419	55.7	40,910	7.3	163,268	29.1	44,561	7.9

Table 4.3.   Geographical Dispersion of U.S. FDI Gross Product by Industry—$million

Year	Grand Total	%	Manufacture	%	Petroleum	%	Services	%	Other	%
Total U.S. FDI										
1982	223,717	100	99,756	100	85,608	100	28,598	100	9,755	100
1998	506,269	100	246,991	100	94,847	100	129,469	100	34,960	100
Canada										
1982	34,017	15	16,413	16	10,998	13	3,231	11	3,375	35
1998	53,502	11	26,076	11	7,842	8	11,691	9	7,893	22
Europe										
1982	112,577	50	54,727	55	38,413	46	17,450	61	1,987	20
1998	302,248	60	151,619	61	57,685	61	80,820	62	12,124	35
Japan										
1982	4,587	2	2,178	2	N/A	-	967	3	N/A	-
1998	23,776	5	7,925	3	N/A	-	10,335	8	N/A	-
Australia & New Zealand										
1982	10,687	5	4,576	5	3,558	4	1,368	5	1,185	12
1998	19,212	4	7,693	3	3,703	4	5,040	4	2,205	6
OECD*										
1982	161,868	72	77,894	78	52,969	62	23,016	80	7,989	67
1998	398,738	79	192,253	78	69,230	73	107,886	83	28,326	81
Latin American Republics										
1982	25,285	11	17,280	17	3,897	5	2,668	9	1,617	16
1998	52,259	10	34,589	14	4,840	5	5,143	4	6,687	19
Caribbean Islands										
1982	2,654	1	251	-	2,076	2	138	-	189	2
1998	7,246	2	613	-	845	2	5,109	2	679	2
Asia**										
1982	22,338	10	2,799	3	N/A	-	1,211	4	N/A	-
1998	36,087	7	16,350	7	12,950	14	8,712	7	N/A	-
Middle East										
1982	8,112	4	187	-	6,548	8	901	3	476	5
1998	3,687	1	773	-	1,935	2	659	1	320	1
Africa										
1982	10,055	5	1,345	1	7,861	9	664	2	185	2
1998	6,763	1	1,354	1	3,952	4	959	1	498	1

*excludes Korea and Mexico. **excludes Japan, Australia, and N. Zealand.

Table 4.4. Geographical Dispersion of U.S. FDI Manufacturing Gross Product—$million

Total U.S. FDI												
1982	99,756	100	8,884	100	16,429	100	17,619	100	18,055	100	38,769	100
1998	246,991	100	26,623	100	52,133	100	35,078	100	41,291	100	91,865	100
Canada												
1982	16,413	16	1,448	16	2,303	14	2,002	11	4,123	23	6,537	17
1998	26,076	11	2,514	9	3,642	7	2,243	6	8,406	20	9,271	10
Europe												
1982	54,727	55	4,267	48	7,892	48	11,956	68	9,462 ·	52	21,149	54
1998	151,619	61	14,488	54	32,942	63	23,465	67	24,159	59	56,565	62
Japan												
1982	2,178	2	140	2	497	3	N/A	-	1	-	N/A	-
1998	7,925	3	1,232	5	3,012	6	577	2	63	-	3,041	3
Australia & New Zealand												
1982	4,576	5	445	5	1,096	7	364	2	1,209	7	1,462	4
1998	7,693	3	1,103	4	1,628	3	392	1	1,139	3	3,431	5
OECD*												
1982	77,894	78	6,300	71	11,788	72	14,322	81	14,795	82	29148	75
1998	193,313	78	18,679	70	41,224	79	26,677	76	33,767	82	72,966	79
Latin American Republics												
1982	17,280	17	2,168	24	3,770	23	1,723	10	2,647	15	6,972	18
1998	34,589	14	6,181	23	7,858	15	2,171	6	7,168	17	11,211	12
Caribbean Islands												
1982	251	-	21	-	137	1	0	-	0	-	93	-
1998	613	-	33	-	180	3	1	-	0	-	264	-
Asia**												
1982	2,799	3	159	2	463	3	N/A	-	379	2	N/A	-
1998	16,350	7	800	3	2,386	5	6,094	17	292	1	6,778	7
Middle East												
1982	187	-	7	-	49	-	N/A	-	0	-	N/A	-
1998	773	-	107	-	61	-	30	-	0	-	575	1
Africa												
1982	1,345	1	229	3	222	1	N/A	-	232	1	N/A	-
1998	1,354	1	164	1	424	1	104	-	63	-	599	2

*excludes Korea and Mexico. **excludes Japan, Australia, and N. Zealand.

THE ROLE OF US OUTWARD FDI FOR THE GENERATION OF OECD GDP

All the billions invested in overseas ventures have reaped rather variable positions for American firms in OECD economies as measured by the shares they have produced in major industries of all member states. (Table 4.5) At first glance, the U.S. share in the group's output of GDP produces several surprises. The U.S. share in the overall industrial output is only fairly modest with individual shares well below 10% except for two countries: Canada and Ireland. Shares in the manufacturing industries, on the other hand, are quite impressive with levels of 25% or even higher in Canada and Ireland. The surprise does not come so much from the levels achieved, but the fact that manufacturing in the U.S. has been viewed as a mature sector worthy more of neglect than active interest for a long time. Now, all of a sudden, America's participation in overseas manufacturing ventures demonstrates an unusual vitality. While the strong position of U.S. firms in this sector rests mainly on outright establishment of subsidiary companies in other parts of the world, Europe must be excepted as FDI here has a strong leaning towards acquisition of already existing enterprises. A policy which blends local production and marketing skills with established market access, implying less risk for the American investor.

Even more astounding is the American participation in OECD's services industries, with unusually weak levels considering the emphasis this sector has received in the home market. It has been pointed out on many occasions that America's economy has become a service economy providing the engine for the country's economic growth. Very little of this attention is obviously filtering through into foreign markets, where levels exceeding 2% are exciting news. Table 4.5 provides a quick overview of the U.S. share development in major OECD industries.

This condensed overview hides share performance for many individual OECD economies. U.S. FDI data actually confirm that, with the sole exception of Iceland, all countries have been investment targets. In Europe, America's share has held quite steady overall, but may display a renewed tendency to grow as of late. Canada is falling from its former place of importance, as may be Australia.

Definite growth shows up in Mexico, particularly in the manufacturing sector, a trend that

Table 4.5.   U.S. FDI Share in GDP Produced by Major OECD Industries—$million

Year	All OECD Industries	U.S. FDI	%	Manu-facturing	U.S FDI	%	Services	U.S. FDI	%	Primary	U.S. FDI	%
1982	4,120	165.6	4.0	1,161	80.9	7.0	2,501	23.5	0.9	458	61.2	13.4
1983	4,165			1,166			2,535			464		
1984	4,209			1,190			2,563			456		
1985	4,450			1,288			2,807			355		
1986	6,044			1,733			4,007			304		
1987	7,426			2,078			4,992			356		
1988	7,819			2,615			4,696			508		
1989	7,991	267.3	3.3	2,678	147.7	5.5	4,801	50.2	1.1	512	69.4	13.6
1990	9,328	300.6	3.2	3,051	162.9	5.3	5,642	58.9	1.0	415	78.8	19.0
1991	9,771	304.2	3.1	3,240	159.7	4.9	5,934	58.6	1.0	396	85.9	21.7
1992	10,506	303.1	2.9	3,387	155.0	4.6	6,517	60.2	0.9	403	87.9	21.8
1993	10,361	292.8	2.8	3,286	148.0	4.5	6,494	62.0	1.0	385	82.8	21.5
1994	11,060	332.9	3.0	3,477	172.7	5.0	6,972	72.5	1.0	402	87.7	21.8
1995	12,146	381.7	3.1	3,928	199.1	5.1	7,585	87.1	1.1	427	95.5	22.4
1996	11,934	403.8	3.4	3,816	207.5	5.4	7,449	92.8	1.2	426	103.5	24.3
1997	11,350	416.6	3.7	3,592	204.6	5.7	7,130	125.3	1.8	379	86.7	22.9
1998	11,002	413.6	3.8	3,422	206.4	6.0	6,983	139.5	2.0	363	67.7	18.7
1999	11,711	454.6	3.9	3,589	270.3	7.5	7,530	165.8	3.1	355	18.5	5.2

OECD data exclude: U.S.A., Czech Republic, Hungary, Poland.

may be connected with Canada's decline as an investment target in the aftermath of NAFTA. Mexico stands out in America's FDI history as the only major oil producer where American interests have never been able to establish a foothold of any consequence. It will be interesting to see, for how long Mexico's policy of national exclusivity can be maintained under the NAFTA agreement.

The true weight of America's involvement in the world economy can be viewed from a different angle by comparing its overall outward FDI dimensions with national economies. Its present output of gross product in the vicinity of $500 billion puts it on a similar footing with Canada, Spain, Korea, or Australia. Even a comparison with the industrial output of larger OECD economies confirms a substantial weight for America's overseas investments. It is thus close to reaching 50% of Italy's, 40% of France's, 26% of Germany's, and 11% of Japan's.

U.S. FDI SHARE IN INDUSTRIAL EMPLOYMENT OF OECD COUNTRIES

The second most popular measure of economic relevance is the number of people employed by a nation, industry, or company. These data can be directly related to each other, thus establishing reliable and comparable benchmarks of economic scope and weight.

For the American side employment figures cover all employees of Mofas. There are also data for all employees including minority-owned enterprises. But they are less useful for two reasons. First, they cannot be matched with output of gross product, which is only reported for Mofas, and second, minority-held operations do not meet the criterion of capital control.

In a fashion similar to one used for value-added information concerning U.S. companies operating abroad, employment may be shown for two separate sets of information: employment by major geographical area (Table 4.6) and also by industry (Table 4.7). Both then can

Table 4.6.   Global U.S. FDI Employment by Geographical Area—000

Year	Total	W. Europe	%	EU	%	Japan	%	OECD	%	Other	%
1977	5,369	2,532	47.2	2,245	41.8	66	1.2	3,735	69.6	1,634	30.4
1982	5,022	2,249	44.8	1,993	39.7	82	1.6	3,585	71.4	1,437	28.6
1983	4,854	2,143	44.1								
1984	4,841	2,140	44.2								
1985	4,810	2,143	44.6								
1986	4,723	2,084	44.2								
1987	4,664	2,058	44.1								
1988	4,769	2,103	44.2								
1989	5,114	2,306	45.1	2,186	42.7	132	2.6	3,885	76.0	1,229	24.0
1990	5,356	2,534	47.3	2,381	44.5	142	2.6	4,142	77.3	1,214	22.7
1991	5,387	2.565	47.6	2,405	44.6	147	2.7	4,204	78.0	1,183	22.0
1992	5,282	2,478	46.9	2,315	43.8	153	2.9	4,089	77.4	1,193	22.6
1993	5,223	2,419	46.3	2,236	42.8	157	3.0	4,014	76.9	1,209	23.1
1994	5,707	2,493	43.7	2,412	42.3	165	2.9	4,200	73.6	1,507	26.4
1995	5,924	2,585	43.6	2,500	42.2	168	2.8	4,322	73.0	1,602	27.0
1996	6,077	2,794	46.0	2,567	42.6	167	2.8	4,556	75.0	1,521	25.0
1997	6,480	2,969	45.8	2,732	42.2	179	2.8	4,791	73.9	1,689	26.1
1998	6,773	3,082	45.5	2,778	41.0	192	2.8	5,043	74.5	1,730	25.5
1999	7,471	3,419	45.8	3,101	41.5	212	2.8	5,629	75.4	1,842	24.6

Note: majority-owned foreign affiliates (Mofas). OECD includes Mexico.

Table 4.7.   Global U.S. FDI Employment by Industry—000.

Year	Total	Manufacturing	%	Petroleum	%	Services	%	Other	%
1977	5,369	3,773	70.2	288	5.4	977	18.2	331	6.2
1982	5,022	3,358	66.9	356	7.1	792	15.7	516	10.3
1983	4,854	3,201	65.9	326	6.7	768	15.8	559	11.5
1984	4,841	3,228	66.7	311	6.4	770	15.9	532	11.0
1985	4,810	3,202	66.6	284	5.9	760	15.8	564	11.7
1986	4,723	3,104	65.7	251	5.3	811	17.2	557	11.8
1987	4,664	3,031	65.0	242	5.2	846	18.2	545	11.7
1988	4,769	3,064	62.2	253	5.3	888	18.6	564	11.8
1989	5,114	3,247	63.5	242	4.7	1,020	19.9	606	11.9
1990	5,356	3,377	63.1	191	3.6	1,055	19.7	733	13.7
1991	5,387	3,300	61.3	183	3.4	1,101	20.4	803	14.9
1992	5,282	3,269	61.9	179	3.4	1,096	20.7	738	14.0
1993	5,223	3,226	61.8	183	3.5	1,115	21.3	699	13.4
1994	5,707	3,516	61.6	173	3.0	1,277	22.4	741	13.0
1995	5,924	3,606	60.9	170	2.9	1,333	22.5	815	13.8
1996	6,077	3,668	60.4	175	2.9	1,408	23.2	826	13.6
1997	6,480	3,853	59.5	177	2.8	1,602	24.5	848	13.3
1998	6,773	3,921	57.9	174	2.6	1,699	25.1	991	14.6
1999	7,471	4,245	56.8	206	2.8	1,529	20.5	1,491	20.0

Note: majority-owned affiliates (Mofas).

be compared to national data for industrial employment for individual countries or major OECD areas.

America's employment share in the developed economies represented by OECD rose between 1982 and 1993, but has returned to approximately the 1982 level as of now. It has never really dropped below 70% of total. Western Europe's overall share represents the bulk of America's overseas employment and shows a fairly steady position. But the EU's share is clearly gaining, indicating a growing concentration of U.S. investments in that area and a shift away from the smaller European economies. Japan is a clear gainer, but the levels attained are very modest for an economy its size, reaffirming the previous impression of entry difficulties for outsiders.

Between 1977 and 1993 Mofa employment stagnated with periods of actual decline. A decided expansion in numbers did not start until 1994, but then showed a growth of 31% by 1999, as if to make up for the previous years of sluggishness. The same picture is more or less visible for the whole OECD area, where the bulk of Mofa employment is concentrated, and most of the impetus for growth comes from. With total employment growing by 39% between 1977 and 1999, the OECD area increased by 51%, Europe only by 35%, and Japan by an astounding 221%.

Comparing the OECD figure with the 13% growth in employment for the non-OECD countries confirms the distribution of capital resources invested by American businesses in the past. But it seems that renewed interest in the developing nations has helped to overcome the stagnant employment situation there, and opened a new phase of expansion for the time being.

The fairly vigorous expansion in FDI employment here makes economic sense, which may be not be so obvious when looking at the dispersion of employment and value added alone. While 75% of Mofa employees (Table 4.6) working in the OECD area produced an impressive 81% of value added in 1998 for U.S. FDI (Table 4.1), they were contributing only 73% of related net income for the year. That means that, even though the remaining 25% of Mofa employees in other countries generated only 19% of total FDI gross product, they still contributed 27% of net income.

Besides the numbers shown and their relative trends, one cannot overlook the fact that the future of American FDI interests in the developing countries is going to depend more on political than economic developments in an exact reversal of the situation encountered in the industrialized part of the world.

Shifting the focus to employment by major industrial categories reveals other interesting aspects. Manufacturing employment dominates the U.S. FDI scene with 60% of total, clearly increasing by number of employees, but a decreasing its share of total.

Petroleum affiliates are not only defying the upward trend in overall employment, they surprise by a sharp drop in actual numbers of employees as well as share beginning with the early eighties. (Table 4.7). The development was ushered in when U.S. companies lost their concessions in Saudi Arabia in 1980. (Hackmann, 1997, p.145)

The absolute decline in employment numbers is remarkable in view of the affiliates' comparatively high and sustained 20% plus share in the overall output of gross product, a clear indication of the firm position commanded by the U.S. in this oligopolistic industry, and its high operational efficiency. Without the oil affiliates the American share of the global GDP would be substantially lower. Being a capital-intensive industry its absence would, of course, be of little effect on the U.S. share in global employment. (Table 4.7) Employment in the services and other industries is clearly gaining in absolute numbers as well as percentage share

Such allocation of resources is probably not sustainable over the long run for economic reasons. This is more or less supported by the fact that affiliate gross product in the developing economies has been slipping for most of the years under review as a percentage of total. Even now with an upward trend visible since 1991 it is still far under the 32% and 26% levels it enjoyed in 1977 and 1982 respectively. (Table 4.1)

The information outlined above raises the question, how the U.S. ranks as an employer in the various OECD economies. According to the output of GDP data America's overseas industry has attained quite respectable shares in individual countries and, in general, employment statistics should reflect pretty much the same picture. The evidence accumulated in the next table is noteworthy for two different aspects.

For one, U.S. affiliates show lower employment shares than GDP shares for all of OECD, which reflects a common observation for most FDI situations: since only the most productive companies engage in FDI, they need only proportionately smaller number of employees than less productive domestic industries to produce the same output. From their starting advantage, they then are capable of continuing or even expanding the gap to the point where they require a diminishing share of the national labor force as a consequence of going down their learning curve. But while this is true for overall and manufacturing MOFA employment, it does not seem to apply to the service and primary industry sectors, where employment is disproportionately high in comparison to output shares. (Tables 4.3 and 4.9)

The other point is the confirmation of the previously observed fact of the relatively high American share in OECD's manufacturing sector, compared to a rather disappointing record in the employment of the area's services industry. Again it must be stressed that the high ranking position for U.S. companies in the manufacturing sector is owed to the unique position of the petroleum affiliates. Not too many developed countries have this kind of benefit with an industry that is very concentrated in the hands of companies from the U.S., England, France, and the Netherlands. (Table 4.8)

Table 4.8.   U.S. FDI Share* In Employment of Major OECD Industries—000

Year	All Industries	U.S. FDI	%	Manu-facturing*	U.S. FDI	%	Services	U.S. FDI	%	Primary	U.S. FDI	%
1982	191,929	3,599	1.9	64,669	2,661	4.1	87,893	938	1.1	38,793	-	-
1983	193,253			62,160			91,970			38,458		
1984	191,308			63,700			89,027			37,940		
1985	191,451			64,596			88,748			37,513		
1986	197,065			58,111			101,589			36,623		
1987	196,764			58,438			101,289			36,248		
1988	205,554			58,625			110,291			36,027		
1989	209,811	3,911	1.9	60,059	2,573	4.3	113,660	1,339	1.2	35,357	-	-
1990	218,053	4,169	1.9	65,362	N/A		118,013	N/A		34,678	N/A	
1991	237,648	4,231	1.8	67,244	N/A		136,469	N/A		33,935	N/A	
1992	237,590	4,116	1.7	65,323	N/A		139,046	N/A		33,221	N/A	
1993	233,659	4,040	1.7	62,738	2,435	3.9	138,221	1,562	1.1	32,660	43	0.1
1994	224,015	4,229	1.9	61,643	2,589	4.2	129,788	1,626	1.3	32,584	14	-
1995	230,414	4,354	1.9	61,370	2,238	3.6	137,574	1,739	1.3	31,470	377	1.1
1996	241,568	4,589	1.9	61,113	2,695	4.4	149,352	1,817	1.2	31,103	77	0.2
1997	242,354	4,787	2.0	59,904	2,837	4.7	151,762	1,986	1.3	30,688	36	0.1
1998	243,564	5,042	2.1	60,646	2,868	4.7	152,172	2,106	1.4	30,746	68	0.2
1999	245,500	5,630	2.3	60,345	3,136	5.2	154,676	2,450	1.6	30,479	44	0.1

Note: *Based on Mofas. **include manufacturing and petroleum affiliates. OECD data exclude: U.S.A., Czech Republic, Hungary, Poland (Source: Tables 2.2).

The visible drop in shares here between 1977 and 1988 is partly owed to the data bank available, which is admittedly less than complete for the earlier years. If all country data were available for those years that were furnished later on, the U.S. employment shares would certainly show lower levels between the above mentioned years. Despite these shortcomings it may be safely assumed that the U.S. share in OCED employment has fallen by roughly one percentage point between 1977 and 1993, which in and by itself is not a negative development. Quite the contrary the increasing output of gross product per employee suggests consistently growing productivity gains. In 1977 one MOFA employee produced $30,000 compared to $80,900 in 1996. (Tables 4.1 & 4.6)

U.S. OUTWARD FDI COMPARED TO THE U.S. ECONOMY

The above discussion started with the question about the impact of the vast FDI funds spent by all countries, and the U.S. in particular, on the world economy. A partial answer can be given

Table 4.9. Geographical Dispersion of U.S. FDI Mofa Employment by Industry—000

Year	Grand Total	%	Manufacturing	%	Petroleum	%	Services	%	Other	%
Total U.S. FDI										
1982	5,022.4	100	3,357.6	100	356.0	100	793.0	100	515.8	100
1998	6,773.1	100	3,921.9	100	174.6	100	1,698.7	100	978.5	100
Canada										
1982	780.6	13	454.6	15	49.7	14	118.3	15	158.0	31
1998	850.5	13	370.2	9	18.4	11	187.5	11	274.5	28
Europe										
1982	2,248.5	45	1,627.7	48	96.4	27	422.5	53	101.9	20
1998	3,081.8	46	1,777.8	45	48.6	28	973.4	57	282.0	29
Japan										
1982	82.2	2	47.5	1	2.9	1	30.1	4	1.8	-
1998	192.2	3	66.5	2	N/A	-	109.0	6	N/A	-
Australia & New Zealand										
1982	215.5	4	128.5	4	12.8	4	39.0	5	74.3	14
1998	261.4	4	116.0	3	N/A	-	78.5	5	N/A	-
OECD*										
1982	3,326.8	66	2,258.3	67	161.8	46	609.9	77	336.0	65
1998	4,385.9	65	2,330.5	59	67.0	38	1,348.4	79	640.0	65
Latin American Republics										
1982	949.1	19	709.6	21	30.4	9	83.7	11	125.3	24
1998	1,345.1	20	906.3	23	30.6	18	177.7	10	230.4	24
Caribbean Islands										
1982	44.8	1	14.5	-	10.0	3	15.7	2	4.7	1
1998	37.6	1	17.3	-	30.4	17	11.2	1	6.1	1
Asia**										
1982	397.1	8	287.5	9	29.3	8	40.8	5	39.5	8
1998	836.7	12	593.0	15	36.9	21	115.9	7	90.9	9
Middle East										
1982	111.0	2	7.1	-	72.6	27	17.0	2	14.3	3
1998	49.5	1	15.7	-	7.2	4	22.5	1	3.7	-
Africa										
1982	75.3	1	23.8	1	19.1	5	9.8	1	22.5	4
1998	109.1	2	59.2	2	17.8	10	23.1	1	9.0	1

*excludes Korea and Mexico. **excludes Japan, Australia & New Zealand

Table 4.10. Geographical Dispersion of U.S. FDI Manufacturing Employment—000

Year	Total	%	Food & related	%	Chemicals	%	Industrial Machinery	%	Transport equipment	%	Other	%
Total U.S. FDI												
1982	3,357.6	100	355.2	100	486.7	100	440.8	100	578.6	100	1,496.2	100
1998	3,921.9	100	439.2	100	530.9	100	550.8	100	637.7	100	1,763.3	100
Canada												
1982	454.6	14	43.8	12	59.2	12	45.2	10	102.5	18	204.0	14
1998	370.2	9	37.9	9	39.4	7	33.7	6	103.8	16	156.5	9
Europe												
1982	1,627.7	48	134.8	38	209.0	43	291.6	66	319.0	55	673.3	45
1998	1,777.8	45	159.3	36	252.0	47	295.2	54	319.4	50	751.9	43
Japan												
1982	47.5	1	2.2	1	16.3	3	17.8	4	.1	-	4.5	-
1998	66.5	2	3.2	1	23.1	4	7.1	1	1.1	-	31.9	2
Australia & New Zealand												
1982	128.5	4	13.3	4	24.9	5	10.8	2	40.8	7	38.7	3
1998	116.0	3	24.7	6	19.6	4	8.9	2	20.1	3	42.7	2
OECD*												
1982	2,258.3	67	194.1	55	309.4	64	365.4	83	462.4	80	920.5	62
1998	2,330.5	59	225.1	51	334.1	63	344.9	63	444.4	70	983.0	56
Latin American Republics												
1982	709.6	21	111.7	32	130.4	27	53.7	12	95.6	17	318.2	21
1998	906.3	23	171.6	39	124.1	23	53.5	10	173.9	27	383.2	22
Caribbean Islands												
1982	14.5	-	1.0	-	4.0	1	0	-	0	-	9.4	1
1998	17.3	-	1.4	-	2.6	-	N/A	-	0	-	15.6	1
Asia**												
1982	287.5	9	31.6	9	30.7	6	14.7	3	7.2	1	203.3	14
1998	593.0	15	39.7	9	55.0	10	147.4	27	16.9	3	334.0	19
Middle East												
1982	7.1	-	.2	-	1.6	-	N/A	-	0	-	N/A	-
1998	15.7	-	3.6	-	1.1	-	0.8	-	0	-	10.2	1
Africa												
1982	80.6	2	15.5	4	10.6	2	6.4	1	13.5	2	34.6	2
1998	59.2	2	5.2	1	14.0	3	4.3	1	2.4	-	33.3	2

*excludes Korea and Mexico. **excludes Japan, Australia & New Zealand

at this point for the U.S. direct investment efforts during a period of well over two decades. Most of the investments have taken place in OECD countries, where 73% of American funds were parked in 1999 in competition for a share of the most concentrated economic potential of the world at the moment.

According to the evidence accumulated the U.S., which account for an estimated 25% of the world economy, held a 3% share of the OECD output of industrial GDP, exclusive of the American economy, in the mid-nineties. This share was down from almost 6% in the late seventies and early eighties. (Table 4.5) A similarly unconvincing development is visible in the industrial employment of OECD, again exclusive of the U.S., with the U.S. share practically unchanged for two decades. (Table 4.8)

Such modest performance for America's direct investment efforts in the world economy comes totally unexpected, considering the high respect accorded American entrepreneurship, economic power, and managerial talent among all competitors in the world. The actual situation could, however, be even worse considering that a growing number of formerly truly bona-fide, that is capital-controlled, American firms are being taken over by foreign business interests. In addition, according to official sources cited earlier, about 15% of what are statistically listed as U.S. outward direct investors, are in reality already foreign-owned American subsidiaries.

But the impression gains credibility to some extent by a set of information depicting U.S. outward FDI in relation to the U.S. business economy itself. After all, here is a major motor for the world economy, which has spawned its own FDI effort, and it is interesting to observe how this parent-child relationship has prospered. Again there is little encouraging development visible for an important player in the globalization process. Measuring Mofa growth performance against the overall U.S. industrial development since 1977 along the two parameters of gross product and employment, deepens the impression that the more than $1 trillion held in FDI stock abroad have barely allowed Mofas to keep up with the pace of the American economy itself.

In both areas, Mofas are developing only as fast, at best, or even slower than their domestic peers, so to speak. (Table 4.11) But, in line with the proposed novel way of measuring national ownership shares, the actual Mofa shares should be higher in this case, because of the reduction in size of what could be called the true American domestic economy after adjustment for its foreign-held portion. (See Chapter 5 for details). The net effect would be to raise the Mofa shares slightly by 5–6% against the level shown, but without much effect on the downward trend.

If Mofas had only held on to their 1977 shares here, their gross product would stand at $755 billion in 1999, a plus of 35% over actual levels reached, and their employment at 8.70 million, a 16% increase.

Table 4.11.   The Size of Outward FDI Relative to U.S. Economy

Year	U.S. Industrial* GDP $billion	Nonbank Mofa GP $billion	%	U.S. Industrial* Employment 000	Mofa Employment 000	%
1977	1,738	161.1	9.3	67,344	5,369	8.0
1982	2,794	223.7	8.0	73,707	5,022	6.8
1989	4,735	319.9	6.8	90,105	5,114	5.7
1990	4,997	356.0	7.1	91,098	5,356	5.9
1991	5,129	356.0	6.9	89,847	5,387	6.0
1992	5,425	361.5	6.7	89,956	5,282	5.9
1993	5,718	359.2	6.3	91,872	5,223	5.7
1994	6,097	403.7	6.6	95,035	5,707	6.0
1995	6,411	465.6	7.3	97,886	5,924	6.1
1996	6,793	498.3	7.3	100,189	6,007	6.0
1997	7,254	520.9	7.2	103,132	6,480	6.3
1998	7,678	506.3	6.6	106,042	6,773	6.4
1999	8,117	561.2	6.9	108,710	7,471	6.9

*excludes agriculture. (Sources: U.S. data: Economic Report of the President, February 2002, Tables B-12 & B-46. Mofa employment: Table 4.6. Mofa GP: Table 4.1. See also Table 5.7C).

CONCLUSIONS

The above analysis is searching for benchmarks that allow realistic measurements of FDI's role in national, regional, and global economies to be taken. These are believed to be furnished handily by macro-economic indicators, here specifically output of GDP and employment. Even though different from market share calculations in terms of dollar or unit sales used for companies or industries, they allow a pretty good assessment of economic and commercial results flowing from FDI endeavors undertaken by individual national industries. In that respect they even become an indicator of a nation's industrial and commercial competitiveness. The overall results furnished here can easily be expanded to individual industries in practically all countries that keep adequate statistical records like OECD members, which make this analytical approach very versatile and useful. The most immediate conclusions to be drawn from this discussion can be summarized as follows.

FDI is undertaken to either protect or gain market shares. This is no different from investments in a domestic market setting.

FDI activities are conventionally measured in strictly financial terms: capital flows, position or stock aggregates, etc. They are built on historic fund flows, usually without adjustments for exchange rate changes, capital consumption and other valuation changes affecting assets, inventories, operating expenses, or the role of non-FDI capital. Reinvestments as an important source of equity funds are not recognized in many cases, a fact that prevents a clearer assessment of the real investment volumes involved.

Investments made do not automatically relate to business success. This is where the general lack of operating details, like number of employees, sales, expenses, gross profits, foreign trade data, etc. for both outward and inward FDI is a serious handicap, because it reduces any efforts to correctly assess the economic impact of FDI operations in an economy to guesswork, even though it may be educated. Availability of such information would be more helpful in assessing the true impact of investments made on national production, commerce, and related market share gains or losses.

FDI has been generally neglected as a valuable information tool for national penetration levels of the world market in total and individual nations in particular. Because of the unwieldy nature of financial information produced, the cause is measured, but not the effect.

Information concerning FDI comes in several and not always complete or comparable packages, even after years of painstaking efforts to harmonize and standardize relevant national inputs by international organizations, like the UN, OECD, IMF, World Bank, and the EU. In the case of U.S. statistics it is possible to differentiate between total investments and operational details for all affiliates and Mofas separately with the sole exception of total affiliate gross product which is not available. Hopefully, this type of information will be furnished routinely for other countries as well in the future.

Mofas are ideally suited to demonstrate the level of a nation's industrial competitiveness, as they are owned, operated, and managed by clearly identifiable national enterprises.

The present focus on FDI data in the form of capital flows and positions widely accessible from international sources mentioned above can easily mislead the uninitiated reader. All those millions and even billions of dollars spent and accumulated over years create the quick and superficial impression of enormous and expanding economic power overwhelming all competition where it is encountered.

This is not the case at all. There is no direct correlation between these funds and market shares as evidenced by the American example. Actually, despite dynamically huge investments over time America's market position in OECD countries, their main competitors, has not grown as might be expected. Indications are that it has held its own at best. This holds true also for non-OECD countries where America's position seems to have gone from 2.3% in 1977 to 1.7% in 1999. (Tables 1.1 and 4.1)

Attention is drawn to the data compiled in Table 4.12, which fully support the conclusions reached in the previous statement. What the huge American capital flows plus reinvested funds have achieved can be summed up as follows. In the late seventies and early eighties each dollar of investment stock produced roughly one dollar of Mofa gross product. By the late nineties the same dollar invested yields only $0.50 of GDP. In a different vein, about $3 in assets were needed for the output of $1 in gross product in the early period compared to between $7–8 at the end. Income on the investment dollar in the same time period went from 14% to 9%. Clearly, more money is needed today to make a dollar. The productivity of capital is clearly subject to the law of diminishing return. This is true despite the fact that nominal employee productivity is on the upswing. Mofa gross product per employee went from $29,987 in 1977 to $75,090 in 1999, but it took an increase in assets from $68,100/capita for all employees to $519,591/employee to accomplish it.

FDI information of the sort developed here is a much better indicator for a nation's economic rank, weight, and position in the world than the traditionally employed national GDP or foreign trade statistics. Two reasons make this plausible. First, ranks are affected by foreign capital interests working in that country. Any inward FDI position in national economies is de-facto owned by foreigners. In no case known, do politically or geographically defined data reveal anything about this important aspect of true national ownership. Second, as will become clearer in future discussions, foreign trade figures, which are commonly employed as a valid measure for the economic importance of a national economy in the international community, are actually rather meaningless for the same reason.

A practical example will help to make this point. In 1999 all U.S. overseas affiliates generated sales of $2.6 trillion. This dwarfs total U.S. merchandise exports of $696 billion for the same year by a factor of 3:1, not adjusted for exports by foreign businesses operating in the U.S. Both are directly comparable pieces of information, because they measure actual sales volumes. Adjusting U.S. exports for the foreign ownership aspect reduces true American exports to an estimated $540 billion. (Table 6.1) It is quite doubtful that this export volume from U.S. shores could have been expanded to the $2.6 trillion sales level of U.S. affiliates recorded in that year, if these affiliates did not exist. Nor could U.S. exports have yielded the $112 billion in additional net income for the U.S. generated by the American FDI in the same year.

Table 4.12. Summary Aspects of Total U.S. Outward FDI—($billion)

Year	Position	Employment 000	Sales	Gross Product*	Total Capital Outflows	Reinvested Earnings	Equity/Debt Outflows	Income**	Assets
1977	145.9	7,196	647.9	161.1	11.9	N/A	N/A	19.7	490
1978	162.7	N/A	N/A	N/A	16.1	N/A	N/A	25.5	N/A
1979	187.9	N/A	N/A	N/A	25.2	N/A	N/A	38.2	N/A
1980	215.4	N/A	N/A	N/A	19.2	N/A	N/A	37.1	N/A
1981	228.3	N/A	N/A	N/A	9.6	N/A	N/A	32.5	N/A
1982	207.8	6,640	935.8	223.7	1.1	4.8	-3.7	21.4	752
1983	207.2	6,383	886.3	216.7	6.7	13.5	-6.8	20.5	751
1984	211.5	6,418	898.6	220.3	11.6	17.3	-5.6	21.2	760
1985	230.3	6,419	895.5	220.1	12.7	13.7	-.9	28.3	835
1986	259.8	6,250	928.9	231.6	17.7	9.0	8.7	30.9	931
1987	314.3	6,270	1,052.8	269.7	29.0	17.7	11.3	38.5	1,111
1988	372.4	6,404	1,194.7	297.6	17.9	13.3	4.6	50.4	1,206
1989	381.8	6,622	1,284.9	319.9	37.6	12.7	24.9	53.9	1,330
1990	430.5	6,834	1,493.4	356.0	31.0	21.4	9.6	58.0	1,559
1991	467.8	6,878	1,541.6	356.0	32.7	18.2	14.5	52.1	1,678
1992	502.1	6,660	1,574.1	361.5	42.6	16.3	26.3	50.6	1,762
1993	564.3	6,685	1,570.6	359.2	77.2	30.0	47.2	59.4	2,047
1994	612.9	7,105	1,757.4	403.7	73.3	24.1	49.2	69.0	2,207
1995	699.0	7,345	2,040.7	465.6	92.1	47.2	44.9	87.3	2,826
1996	795.2	7,544	2,233.7	498.3	84.4	47.2	37.2	93.6	3,092
1997	871.3	7,973	2,350.9	520.9	95.8	49.0	46.8	104.8	3,416
1998	1,000.7	8,184	2,369.9	506.3	131.0	32.5	98.4	90.7	3,921
1999	1,173.1	8,907	2,587.3	561.2	174.6	61.2	113.4	112.4	4,628

*Mofa Data. **BOP flows. (Sources: Position, Income, and Capital Flows: SOCB: August 1991, p. 85. August 1992, p. 122. October 1998, p. 127. September 2002, p. 74. Gross Product: SOCB: February 1994, p. 44. December 1996, p. 12. October 1997, p. 67. October 1998, pp. 72/3. March 2002, p. 25. Assets: Benchmark Surveys: 1977, p. 110. 1982, p. 88. 1989, p. M-25. SOCB: September 1986, p. 33. June 1987, p. 33. June 1988, p. 90. June 1990, p. 36. August 1992, p. 72. July 1993, p. 52. June 1994, pp. 43, 54. June 1995, p. 43. December 1996, p. 31. October 1997, p. 62. July 1999, p. 29. July 2000, p. 39. March 2002, p. 48. Sales: Benchmark Surveys: 1977, p. 138. 1982, p. 109. 1989, p. M-25. SOCB: June 1987, p. 33. June 1988, p. 90. June 1989, p. 32. June 1990, p. 36. October 1991, p. 29. August 1992, p. 72. July 1993, p. 52. June 1994, p. 54. August 1994, pp. 154. 174/5. June 1995, p. 43. December 1996, p. 31. October 1997, p. 62. July 1999, p. 29. July 2000, p. 39. July 2000, p. 39. March 2002, p. 48. Employment: SOCB: February 1982, p. 41. March 2002, p.25).

Chapter Five

FDI Impact on National Economies

I. THE UNITED STATES

A convincing illustration of how FDI has the capacity to tilt national ownership shares of the world economy by means of capital control is given in Table 5.1. It is not so much the amounts of money shown, but the shift in the ratios of invested capital and their operational impact relative to each other, which becomes a reliable indicator for the changing balance of economic power among national competitors. The size and development of U.S. outward versus inward FDI, exclusive of foreign trade data, show inward FDI catching up fast with outward FDI, but still leaves the U.S. with an overall leadership position for the present. What is significant about the relative development of these numbers is their rapid convergence, which can lead only to these conclusions: foreigners are building their position in real terms and their market shares in the U.S. at a faster pace than the U.S. is abroad, and they also hold a larger share of the U.S. economy than American investments do abroad in line with the assumed 25/75% distribution of the world market. (Table 1.1)

Expressing it another way, foreign business interests operating in the U.S. have expanded their capital base measured in terms of their inward FDI stock volume as a percentage of the like U.S. stock position abroad from 24% in 1977 to 82% in 1999. Similar advances are registered for employment from 17% to 68%, sales from 30% to 93%, gross product from 22% to 82%, income from 20% to 41%, and assets from 29% to 107% for the same years. The vigorous advance of FDI in the U.S. began in the eighties, at a time when U.S. outward FDI activities slowed after three decades of rapid expansion. This investment hiatus is the main reason for allowing foreigners to catch up with their American competitors. Their penetration of U.S. industries was most pronounced in the manufacturing sector which, at that time, was downplayed by such pejorative terms as "smokestack or rust-belt industries" by the U.S. business community and public. American domestic investment interests centered on service industries with higher and thus more promising growth rates, creating a vacuum in manufacturing that aggressive foreigners recognized and exploited readily.

Table 5.1 reveals even more about America's situation in those years. Allowing foreigners to take over large parts of America's industry in a relatively short period was certainly influenced by resignation over dwindling domestic margins, the need to upgrade aging factories,

Table 5.1. Comparative Aspects of U.S. Outward vs. Inward FDI—$billion

Year	Position		Employment*		Sales*		Gross Product		Income		Assets*	
	Out	In	Out	In	Out	In	Out**	In*	Out	In	Out	In
1977	145.9	34.6	7,196	1,219	647.9	193.9	161.1	35.2	19.7	4.0	490	144
1978	162.7	42.5	N/A	1,430	/A	241.5	N/A	42.9	25.5	4.8	N/A	181
1979	187.9	54.5	N/A	1,753	N/A	327.9	N/A	55.4	38.2	7.3	N/A	229
1980	215.4	83.0	N/A	2,034	N/A	412.4	N/A	70.9	37.1	8.8	N/A	291
1981	228.3	108.7	N/A	2,417	N/A	510.2	N/A	98.8	32.5	11.2	N/A	407
1982	207.8	124.7	6,640	2,448	935.8	518.1	223.7	103.5	21.4	3.8	752	476
1983	207.2	137.1	6,383	2,547	886.3	536.6	N/A	111.5	20.5	5.6	751	532
1984	211.5	164.6	6,418	2,714	898.6	596.0	N/A	128.8	21.2	9.6	760	603
1985	230.3	184.6	6,419	2,862	895.5	632.9	N/A	134.9	28.3	5.4	835	741
1986	259.8	220.4	6,250	2,938	928.9	672.0	N/A	142.1	30.9	2.5	931	838
1987	314.3	263.4	6,269	3,224	1,052.8	744.6	N/A	157.9	38.5	7.8	1,111	944
1988	372.4	314.8	6,404	3,844	1,194.7	886.4	N/A	190.4	50.4	12.0	1,206	1,201
1989	381.8	368.9	6,622	4,412	1,284.9	1,058.6	319.9	223.4	53.9	9.3	1,330	1,431
1990	430.5	394.9	6,834	4,735	1,493.4	1,175.9	356.0	239.3	58.0	-4.5	1,559	1,550
1991	467.8	419.1	6,878	4,872	1,541.6	1,185.9	356.0	257.6	52.1	-11.0	1,678	1,753
1992	502.1	423.1	6,660	4,715	1,574.1	1,231.9	361.57	266.3	50.6	1.4	1,762	1,825
1993	564.3	467.4	6,685	4,766	1,570.6	1,329.4	359.2	285.7	59.4	7.1	2,047	2,066
1994	612.9	480.7	7,105	4,841	1,757.4	1,443.5	403.7	313.0	69.0	20.9	2,207	2,207
1995	699.0	535.6	7,345	4,942	2,040.7	1,544.6	465.6	322.6	87.3	30.9	2,826	2,389
1996	795.2	598.0	7,544	5,105	2,233.7	1,667.6	498.4	358.1	93.6	30.4	3,092	2,682
1997	871.3	681.8	7,973	5,202	2,350.9	1,726.3	520.9	389.4	104.8	39.9	3,416	3,071
1998	1,000.7	778.4	8,184	5,646	2,443.4	1,881.9	506.3	419.8	90.7	32.4	4,001	3,526
1999	1,173.1	955.7	9,220	6,028	2,611.8	2,044.4	566.4	457.7	112.4	46.4	3,921	4,177
2000	1,293.4	1,214.3	9,607	6,525	2,891.5	2,334.7	605.9	516.2	135.1	52.5	4,628	4,847

*All Nonbank Affiliates. **Mofa data. (Sources: OUTWARD U.S. FDI: Position: SOCB: August 1983. p. 35. July 1999. p. 35. July 2002, p. 50. July 2002, p. 21. Employment, Sales. Gross Product. Net Income. Assets: SOCB. August 1999, p. 25. August 2000. p. 25. August 2000, pp. 141–158. August 2002, pp. 149–166. September 202. pp. 38–67). INWARD FDI: Position: SOCB. August 1983, p. 35. July 1999, p. 50. July 2002, p. 21. Employment, Sales. Gross Product. Net Income. Assets: SOCB. August 1999, p. 25. August 2000, pp. 141–158. August 2002, pp. 149–166. September 202. pp. 38–67).

escape from powerful unions at the time, search for lower production costs, the lure of higher profits in less mature markets, and other reasons. But letting outsiders come in and thrive in exactly the same environment that American business was willing to abandon, may have resulted from poor judgment by hindsight. How can a crumbling home base support a strong competitive stance abroad? As a minimum, it amounted to a gross underestimation of the competitive strength of the outsiders. After years of overwhelming technological, managerial, and capital strength displayed by American FDI in overseas markets, here was a sort of competitive backlash by foreigners, who had learned so much from their U.S. counterparts after World War II, improved upon it, and now became a formidable challenge.

A curious aspect of the changing situation is reflected in these facts. U.S. outward FDI employment has risen about 24% in twenty years, which accommodates an investment volume eight times larger plus more than triple the sales generated in 1977. The faster growth in the investment position and assets over the period thus led to a rapidly increasing capital intensity per employee. But, the trend in capital buildup is even more pronounced for inward investors, such that in 1999 US outward FDI concentrated $44,022 in assets per employee compared to $69,293 per employee for US inward FDI, a 57% difference. It must be assumed that a good part of this represented investments in the most modern productivity-enhancing equipment. (Table 5.1)

Sales output per employee displays similar variations. 1999 sales of $246,400 per outward employee face $339,100 for each inward employee, a spread of 38%. The economic implications of the 57% higher capital investment yielding only a 38% higher sales output per employee for foreign investors in the States are difficult to explain without further studies.

Another statistic worth mentioning is the identical margin for the output of value added measured against sales by both investor types. Outward investment produced a 26% added-value margin on Mofa sales of $2.2 trillion in 1998 compared to a 22% margin for all inward affiliates in the States. This is a significant coincidence as the structure of gross profits generated in both world areas is considerably different. Employee compensation and profit-type components drive the inward investment results, whereas indirect business taxes and related factors predominate in the generation of the outward investment value added.

As far as income is concerned American Mofas produced a 5.1% return on sales in 1999, compared to only 2.3% for foreign business operations in the U.S. Similar profit policies by both investor types may be involved here. In order to escape the American tax bite both are aiming at maximizing their profits outside the U.S., where they can be legally sheltered in many different tax havens.

A previous comment regarding U.S. FDI made in the rest of the world should be recalled at this point. Without access to the data in Table 5.1 and others below it would be difficult to gauge the economic implications of the growth in the inward FDI position and related capital flows. The billions of dollars being shifted around might easily convey the impression that strong gains in market or industry shares have automatically taken place. An untenable notion, as demonstrated by the example of U.S. outward FDI plus the discussion below.

Money flows and position changes are merely indicators of activities and good intentions, and despite their impressive size may have relatively little impact on tangible results in a competitive situation. That is to say, they increase business volume and employment, for instance, but without necessarily commensurate developments in market shares. After all, measures of financial transactions hide a lot of different subjects. Capital flows break down into equity and debt funds serving such diverse investment purposes as new or only upgraded brick and mortar structures, repair and replacement, working capital for marketing activities, or even loss coverage. Position calculations are affected by changes in asset valuations, depreciation and amortization, accounting changes, exchange rate fluctuations. etc. All this takes place within independent market dynamics. Regardless of the impressive monetary volumes appearing in print, FDI activities are only a relatively small factor in most national economies of the developed world and even more so for outward investments of developing nations.

Inward FDI's Role in U.S. Industry

After all the foreign investment activities documented by the above benchmark statistics, how much of the U.S. economy is actually foreign-controlled? The various FDI data provided so far allow a clear expression and measurement of such influence in the national production of goods and services plus industrial employment. Similar information for foreign trade, balance-of-payment (BOP) flows, and related subjects will be dealt with later. As pointed out earlier the ideal method for establishing these relationships would be to cover majority-owned enterprises only, where the local power and authority in the decision-making process is clearly determined by the foreign element. As it turns out, the discussion has to dwell on the much broader combination of both majority and minority holdings, because the database does not always allow a clear separation of the two. Fortunately, the comprehensive nature of American statistics on the subject allows a fairly detailed insight and assessment of the development of global inward FDI in American industry since 1977.

Tables 5.2–5.4 summarize the impact of inward FDI in terms of percent share of U.S. industrial sales, employment, assets, and output of value added. In all cases foreigners are showing gains against their American competitors. They are most impressive in the manufacturing sector where shares above 10% and even 20% are not uncommon indicating a competitive edge for the foreign investors. The highest recorded shares are found in the chemical industry with figures above 30%. In the service sector the opposite holds true. Foreigners seem to have difficulties in making comparable inroads.

Shares remain under 10% of all industries surveyed in this sector and lack the general buoyancy seen in manufacturing. Actually, judging by the latest available information, further gains by foreigners may be more difficult to achieve here. The highest shares recorded were in wholesaling, insurance, and transportation. But even here none broke the 7% barrier.

A Changing Set of Competitors

Many foreign companies vie for a share of America's economy in competition with domestic American companies. In agreement with its unflagging support of free trade America maintains an open-door policy to any legitimate business that wants to set up local production either through acquisition of an existing firm or by starting from scratch. Actually, the official policy of the country is to welcome the influx of foreign capital and know-how with open arms and, as a consequence, many states offer very attractive incentives to lure foreign investors.

But establishing a foothold and surviving in the very competitive environment are two very different things, as many foreigners have found out. Once they have entered, foreign companies face a very different competitive constellation. In addition to familiar companies in their

Table 5.2.   Nonbank Foreign Affiliate Share of U.S. Business Employment

Year	Total	Manuf.	Retail	Wholesale	Finance*	Services	Communication	Insurance	Transport	R. Estate	Construct.
1977	1.7	3.2	0.9	2.9	0.3	N/A	N/A	2.3	N/A	0.8	N/A*
1980	2.7	5.4	2.4	2.7	3.0	0.6	N/A	3.5	N/A	1.5	1.0
1981	3.1										
1982	3.2										
1983	3.3										
1984	3.4										
1985	3.4										
1986	3.5										
1987	3.7	7.7	3.3	4.7	7.5	1.3	0.6	3.7	2.7	2.3	1.1
1988	4.3	8.9	3.9	4.8	9.2	1.6	0.6	5.0	3.7	2.3	1.2
1989	4.9	10.2	4.7	5.1	9.0	1.9	1.0	5.6	5.0	2.1	1.3
1990	5.1	10.9	4.2	5.7	5.2	2.3	1.3	5.8	6.2	2.5	1.5
1991	5.3	11.5	4.5	5.6	6.0	2.5	1.3	6.4	6.2	2.4	1.5
1992	5.1	11.5	4.0	5.6	6.3	2.3	1.5	6.5	5.6	2.4	1.4
1993	5.0	11.6	4.1	5.9	5.0	2.2	1.7	6.3	6.8	2.2	1.3
1994	4.9	11.7	3.9	5.8	4.9	2.1	3.6	6.1	6.5	1.9	1.2
1995	4.9	11.4	4.1	5.8	5.2	2.1	4.5	6.0	6.5	1.9	1.4
1996	5.0	11.4	4.2	5.8	5.2	2.0	6.0	6.0	5.4	2.0	1.3
1997	4.9	12.4	5.1	6.5	5.8	N/A	9.0	6.1	6.2	3.2	1.2
1998	5.2	13.4	5.0	6.7	6.2	N/A	6.6	5.2	4.4	3.4	1.3
1999	5.4	13.5	5.3	6.8	6.5	N/A	8.7	6.7	5.0	3.8	1.3
2000	5.6	13.9	4.7	7.6	7.1	N/A	9.4	6.9	6.2	3.2	1.2

*except banking

Nonbank Foreign Affiliate Share in U.S. Manufacturing Employment

Year	Chemicals	Ceramics*	Electric/ Electronic	Primary Metals	Rubber & Plastics	Food & Kindred	Instruments	Motor Vehicles	Industrial Machinery	Fabricated Metal Prod.
1977	17.0	N/A	4.7	5.2	N/A	4.6	N/A	N/A	1.9	1.2
1980	15.2	5.6	7.6	5.6	5.3	6.0	7.4	7.4	4.6	3.2
1987	26.2	14.5	12.0	12.2	6.6	8.4	7.4	6.6	5.9	4.1
1988	27.2	15.6	13.7	10.6	10.7	10.8	8.2	7.4	7.5	5.9
1989	29.4	18.7	15.7	12.6	11.3	12.3	9.9	8.9	9.9	6.9
1990	30.5	19.8	16.2	14.8	14.5	12.5	11.2	11.2	10.3	7.1
1991	31.4	19.6	17.3	15.4	14.5	12.6	12.2	12.2	10.9	8.0
1992	32.1	20.8	17.2	15.9	14.8	11.9	11.9	11.0	11.2	8.3
1993	33.0	20.7	16.9	16.6	14.3	10.9	12.5	11.7	11.2	8.5
1994	33.5	19.4	16.9	16.6	14.1	11.2	13.3	12.6	11.1	8.4
1995	30.5	20.9	17.9	15.9	14.2	10.8	13.4	13.1	11.3	7.9
1996	30.7	21.0	18.0	14.1	14.7	9.3	12.8	14.2	11.0	8.6
1997	34.8	21.2	19.4	15.2	13.7	9.6	N/A	18.5	14.2	6.8
1998	34.1	23.3	19.3	16.6	14.4	9.8	N/A	28.2	13.9	6.7
1999	33.2	23.5	22.5	16.4	13.5	8.7	N/A	28.8	15.1	6.0
2000	32.3	23.7	20.9	15.5	14.1	9.7	N/A	28.0	15.3	6.2

*stone, clay & glass products. (Sources: FDI in the U.S., Review and Analysis of Current Developments, August 1991, Tables 5–9, 5–18. Ibid., An Update, June 1993, p. 33. SOCB, May 1981, p. 46, July 1994, p. 161, May 1995, p. 66, June 1998, p. 51. SOCB, August 1999, p. 32, August 2000, p. 147. Statistical Abstract of the United States, 1979, Table 681.)

Table 5.3. Nonbank Foreign Affiliate Share of U.S. Business Gross Product

Year	Total	Manuf.	Retailing	Wholesale	Finance*	Services	Insurance	Real Estate	Other
1977	2.3	3.6	1.2	3.8	2.2	0.5	2.4	0.6	0.5
1978	2.5	3.9							
1979	2.9	4.6							
1980	3.4	5.3							
1981	4.2	7.2	2.3	5.0	4.2	0.7	4.0	2.2	1.0
1982	4.3	7.3							
1983	4.3	7.6							
1984	4.4	7.9							
1985	4.3	7.8							
1986	4.3	8.0							
1987	4.3	10.5	2.4	6.9	16.5	0.9	6.3	3.0	1.2
1988	5.0	11.4	3.0	7.0	17.7	1.3	5.4	2.9	1.6
1989	5.4	13.0	3.3	7.2	18.7	1.4	3.9	3.4	2.0
1990	5.5	13.8	3.4	7.4	6.1	1.7	5.4	3.3	2.2
1991	5.9	14.2	4.2	8.3	6.2	1.7	5.3	3.4	2.6
1992	5.8	13.9	3.5	8.8	5.6	1.8	5.3	2.6	2.3
1993	5.8	-							
1994	6.0	-							
1995	5.9	-							
1996	6.1	-							
1997	6.2	-							
1998	6.3	13.3							
1999	6.5	13.4							
2000	7.0	13.8							

*except banking (Sources: FDI in the U.S., Review and Analysis of Current Developments, August 1991, Tables 5–4, 5.–9. SOCB, June 1990, p. 46. July 1994, pp. 154, 160. June 1998, p. 39. August 1999, p. 21. August 2000, p. 141. August 2002, p. 149).

Nonbank Foreign Affiliate Share of U.S. Manufacturing Gross Product

Year	Chemicals	Ceramics*	Electric/ Electronic	Primary Metals	Rubber & Plastics	Food & Kindred	Instruments	Motor Vehicles	Industrial. Machinery	Fabricated Metal Prod.
1977	17.5	-	-	-	-	7.8	-	-	2.7	3.3
1986	32.2	-	-	-	-	8.9	-	-	-	8.0
1987	33.3	-	-	-	-	8.4	-	-	-	7.4
1990	31.9	24.8	15.6	19.3	17.6	13.8	11.9	4.9	10.3	7.9
1991	35.2	24.8	16.3	19.8	13.0	11.7	10.1	7.6	-	9.8

(Sources: SOCB: June 1990, p. 46. January 1994, p. 37. Statistical Abstract of the United States, various issues.).

Table 5.4. Nonbank Foreign Affiliate Share of U.S. Manufacturing Assets

Year	Chemicals	Ceramics*	Electric/ Electronic	Primary Metals	Rubber & Plastics	Food & Kindred	Instruments	Motor Vehicles	Industrial Machinery	Fabricated Metal Prod.
1977	15.4	7.3	5.1	6.2	.6	4.4	3.3	.6	3.7	2.8
1986	32.6	24.8	11.6	20.6	5.8	9.6	7.0	2.7	4.9	8.5
1987	31.6	34.3	10.7	19.5	13.6	12.2	8.7	2.8	6.1	9.0
1988	31.3	39.6	15.2	19.9	22.2	N/A	7.5	3.1	9.8	16.2
1989	36.0	38.2	16.2	24.9	24.0	N/A	9.1	4.2	13.1	24.7
1990	42.4	42.3	20.2	29.1	33.1	N/A	11.6	4.7	12.6	19.0
1991	40.4	43.7	21.0	31.5	28.8	N/A	13.5	4.9	13.1	18.7

Nonbank Foreign Affiliate Share of U.S. Manufacturing Sales

Year	Chemicals	Ceramics*	Electric/ Electronic	Primary Metals	Rubber & Plastics	Food & Kindred	Instruments	Motor Vehicles	Industrial Machinery	Fabricated Metal Prod.
1977	14.5	6.8	5.8	6.7	2.8	3.8	3.8	.2	3.8	1.9
1986	29.2	21.9	12.2	19.0	4.8	6.8	7.1	3.1	5.4	7.6
1987	32.0	24.6	12.6	19.3	10.4	6.7	9.1	2.6	6.7	7.0
1988	30.0	25.9	15.9	19.0	14.7	N/A	8.2	2.7	9.8	11.3
1989	33.3	29.4	16.3	23.3	15.9	N/A	8.7	4.7	13.9	17.4
1990	38.4	32.1	20.0	26.8	21.9	N/A	10.5	5.6	14.4	13.6
1991	37.4	32.9	20.7	27.7	18.7	N/A	13.9	6.1	14.1	14.5

*stone, clay & glass products. (Sources: SOCB. May 1988, p. 64. July 1989, p. 131. July 1991, p. 80. May 1992, p. 55. May 1993, p. 98.)

home market or third markets, including U.S. firms, they now face unknown local producers, channel members, financial organizations with often very unfamiliar business practices.

Which nationalities were successful in adapting themselves to their new environment and grow, because of their strategic flexibility? There are several ways in measuring the relative standing of foreign nationals over a period of time. U.S. government statisticians furnish a number of details like gross product (GP), assets, income, sales, employment, and other data by country and world area, which relate this type of information even to the country of ultimate beneficial owner. In other words it establishes the true nationality of the subsidiaries listed, exactly the identification needed for the purpose of this study.

Table 5.5 provides an impression of how companies from major countries and world areas have fared in the U.S. market by referencing their share development in the GP generated by all foreign enterprises in the U.S. While the actual volume for all has been going up steadily (Table 5.1), the country-by-country contribution has been less smooth. Variations here are a natural occurrence due to investment, or disinvestment decisions, a particular focus on industry sectors subject to business cycles different from the overall economy, competitive activities, etc. which are reflected in the contribution of companies from major countries in the production of GP by inward FDI companies between 1989 and 1997. Obviously, not all could be winners, but there are still some significant changes emerging from Table 5.5.

A typical example is Canada, a country with a still important share in the generation of GP among all foreign companies, but clearly falling behind its foreign competitors, as is confirmed also by Exhibit 1. Australia shares the same fate, with its share practically cut in half, even though at a much lower level. It remains to be seen whether Canada's position can be strengthened again in the future in view of its NAFTA membership.

The opposite development is true for European companies, whose share in total output by foreign subsidiaries rose from 58% in 1989 to 64% in 1997. Their six point rise eclipses the 2–point gain shown by Japan, which rose from 14% to 16% during the period. But measured on an individual country basis, this share puts Japan right into the second position after England, whose leadership position with the only share consistently above 20% rests in good part on its petroleum affiliates in the U.S. The same reason can be given for the strong and very steady showing of the Dutch output share of around 9%. Japan is now taking the place held for so long by Canada, followed by Germany, France, the Netherlands, and Canada in sixth place. Taken together these six nations accounted for no less than 76% of the foreign-controlled output of GDP in the U.S. in 1997. Remarkable is also the 90% plus share of the OECD countries in this picture. It is a strong reminder of the tough competitive conditions facing foreign companies in the U.S. market, which leaves very little room for competition from the developing world.

Switching from GP to employment, leaves the UK, Japan, and Germany in the first three positions, but puts Canada in fourth place followed by France and the Netherlands in 1997. Their combined share with 75% of total is essentially equal to the 76% share shown on the GP side.

Such comparisons can often become useful, when missing information needs to be filled in by analogy to similar situations found elsewhere.

The Profile of Inward FDI by Nationality and Industrial Sector

Having identified the major direct investors in the U.S. by nationality, and their development over the last decade raises the question, where specific national investors have found their

Table 5.5. Country Shares in U.S. Inward FDI Gross Product (Percentages)

	1989	1990	1991	1992	1993	1994	1995	1996	1997	1998	1999
All	100.0	100.0	100.0	100.0	100.0	100.0	100.0	100.0	100.0	100.0	100.0
Canada	16.1	16.0	15.3	12.6	14.4	13.3	10.9	9.1	8.9	9.5	9.3
Mexico	N/A	.3	.3	.4	.5	.5	.5	.5	.3	N/A	N/A
France	5.9	6.2	6.6	7.1	6.7	7.4	7.4	9.6	9.3	8.9	9.8
Germany	9.3	10.1	10.0	10.8	11.2	11.2	11.5	12.0	11.9	15.9	15.4
Italy	.5	.7	.8	.9	.9	1.0	.9	.9	.8	N/A	N/A
Netherlands	8.6	7.6	7.2	7.4	7.3	8.0	8.6	8.4	8.9	6.9	7.8
Sweden	2.2	2.1	2.0	2.6	2.1	1.7	1.7	1.8	2.1	N/A	N/A
UK	21.1	22.3	21.4	21.6	21.0	21.5	22.5	21.4	20.1	17.9	18.2
EU	50.9	50.2	48.4	53.6	52.2	54.0	56.1	57.4	56.4	N/A	N/A
Switzerland	6.5	6.1	5.9	6.4	5.9	5.5	5.8	5.8	6.8	6.7	6.9
W. Europe	58.2	58.4	58.0	60.5	58.9	60.2	62.6	64.0	63.9	63.9	65.3
Japan	13.9	14.4	15.5	16.0	15.6	15.6	15.7	16.2	16.2	15.5	14.2
Korea	N/A	.2	.2	.2	.2	.2	.3	.2	.2	N/A	N/A
Other Asia	1.9	1.1	1.3	1.4	1.4	1.7	1.8	1.5	1.5	3.3	3.6
Africa	.5	.5	.5	.5	.5	.5	.7	.7	.7	.7	.3
Lat. America	3.8	3.6	3.5	3.3	3.5	3.8	3.8	3.6	3.5	4.1	4.5
Australia	3.3	3.9	3.7	3.0	2.7	1.5	1.4	1.6	1.4	N/A	N/A
Middle East	1.9	1.3	1.5	1.3	1.6	1.9	1.5	1.8	1.9	1.1	.6
OECD	91.5	93.2	93.0	92.1	91.6	90.6	90.6	90.9	90.5	N/A	N/A

(Sources: SOCB, July 1996, p. 111. August 1999, p. 30. August 2000, p. 144. August 2002, p. 153).

competitive niche. Information of this sort nicely supplements that given for the penetration of major American industries by foreign business interests in total in Tables 5.2–5.4. Now the focus changes from the output share of all foreign firms in a given industry to the actual players by national origin. The subject requires a two-step analysis.

First, it will be shown how aggregate inward FDI is dispersed among major industrial branches as an indication where exactly foreigners have been active and successful in establishing a firm foothold in the biggest and very competitive single country market. After addressing this point by means of the information collected in Table 5.6 the focus shifts to the identification of the leading foreign enterprises by their national origin in each market segment

Table 5.6.   Distribution of Inward Nonbank FDI Gross Product by Industry of Affiliate—Percentages

INDUSTRY	1988	1989	1990	1991	1992	1993	1994	1995	1996
ALL INDUSTRIES	100.0	100.0	100.0	100.0	100.0	100.0	100.0	100.0	100.0
PRIMARY*	1.5	1.8	1.8	2.2	2.3	1.9	2.1	2.2	1.7
PETROLEUM	11.3	10.8	11.1	9.6	9.6	9.1	9.2	9.1	9.2
MANUFACTURING	47.7	48.9	50.1	48.9	50.4	49.9	50.2	48.3	46.5
Food & related	4.2	4.4	4.7	4.8	4.6	4.0	3.9	3.8	3.5
Chemicals	14.8	14.5	15.6	15.1	15.7	15.5	15.5	12.6	12.2
Metal products	5.5	7.0	6.1	5.7	5.7	5.8	5.3	5.2	5.1
Industrial machinery	4.0	4.9	4.3	4.1	3.8	3.6	4.1	4.1	4.1
Electric/onic equipm.	5.5	4.9	5.5	5.6	5.9	5.8	5.9	5.7	5.6
Rubber & plastics	1.8	1.7	2.2	1.7	2.0	2.1	2.2	2.3	2.2
Motor vehicles	.6	.7	1.1	1.2	1.0	1.3	1.8	2.3	2.0
Other manufacturing	11.3	10.8	10.6	10.7	11.7	11.8	11.5	12.3	11.7
SERVICES	39.5	38.5	37.0	39.3	37.7	39.1	39.5	41.4	42.6
Wholesale trade	11.3	10.5	10.2	11.0	11.6	11.7	11.3	12.1	11.6
Retail trade	7.3	7.3	7.1	8.3	7.5	7.3	7.0	7.3	6.9
Transportation	2.9	3.4	3.1	3.6	2.9	4.0	3.7	4.0	3.8
Communication	.6	.5	.8	.8	1.2	1.2	2.4	4.1	5.2
Finance**	10.4	9.5	6.6	6.9	5.7	5.7	5.7	5.0	6.7
Business services	5.9	5.9	7.3	7.1	7.6	8.3	7.5	6.9	7.3
Other***	1.1	1.4	1.9	1.6	1.2	.9	1.9	2.0	5.2

*includes agriculture, forestry, fishing, and mining. **includes finance, except banks, insurance, and real estate. ***mainly construction. (Sources: SOCB: July 1996, p. 109. June 1997, p. 49. June 1998, p. 47. August 1999, p. 28. August 2000, p. 145. August 2002, p. 163).

in Exhibit 1. The measuring base is gross product output by industry and by foreign entity. Foreigners with leading gross product shares in each business category are clearly the ones holding distinct competitive advantages over their foreign, but also American peers. The answer to the first question concerning the dispersion of inward FDI by target sector is given by Table 5.6, which provides an overview of inward FDI's generation of value-added for the three key industrial groupings: primary, manufacturing, and services. The last two are subdivided into some major components. Using value-added output rather than investment data was done deliberately. Financial data are affected by long-term accounting practices, which do not reflect the actual economic results achieved by the funds invested. Investment data also have another and more serious drawback against GP information, in that it cannot be linked directly to national account statistics, which makes their use rather impractical.

At any rate, while manufacturing used to be the leading source of GDP output by foreign subsidiaries, it seems to have yielded ground permanently to the service sector, such that both are now fairly equal in weight. This picture is not totally accurate. The petroleum sector, which by American accounting tradition is maintained on a separate basis, should rightfully be split into the manufacturing, and retailing components to conform to international practice. This would make sense, because foreign interests are not engaging in any extraction activities to speak of in the U.S., which would touch the primary sector in our case. Taking this step leaves manufacturing in the lead for the moment, followed by services for a combined share of more than 98%, with only a minuscule field of operation in the primary industry.

Still, after making this cosmetic adjustment, there can be little doubt, that the service field will crowd out manufacturing in the foreseeable future as the key investment object. Since 1995, services are on a clear upward trend against the rest, and it will only be a matter of time for their share to cross the 50% mark.

Generally speaking, the dispersion of inward FDI by industry output of GDP is quite steady. Notable exceptions are the motor vehicle sector in manufacturing, which is on a strong upswing, and the communications, business services, and all other category among the service industry components, with equally impressive share gains. The service area used to be thought of as the uncontested domain of American entrepreneurship, the field where American ingenuity set a shining example for the rest of the world. Clearly, the rapid inroads made here by outsiders will become a matter of concern for the future.

Addressing the second question as to the nationality of leading foreign FDI interests in America's industrial sectors is more complicated. Information on the dispersion of inward FDI by industry and major national producer is not very well developed for two reasons: only major investor countries are covered, and often actual information is suppressed to protect business interests of individual firms. It occurs mostly in sectors with oligopolistic structures, where any detailed information could lead to the disclosure of competitive intelligence not otherwise available. Notorious for its secretive behavior is the petroleum industry, where the seven sisters watch each other very closely, and government statisticians tread very carefully so as not to upset these powerful interest groups.

The British, Dutch, and to a lesser extent also the French oil companies are by all practical intents and purposes sharing the foreign investments among themselves in this sector, and their market prominence precludes details from emerging in official statistics. It also applies to Latin American interests, Mexico and Venezuela. Similar situations may be found in the automotive and chemical branches, yet they do not seem to evoke the extreme sensitivities found in the oil industry. Other industries see larger numbers of competitors, which lessens the need for such protective precaution.

The following information gives an impression of which nationalities are leaders in the production of GP among FDI companies and how their position has changed between 1990 and 1996, indicative of relative competitive strengths. Two facts seem to be noteworthy here: first, in most cases the three leading countries account for more than 50% of the value-added in a particular industry. Second, once a country has made the leadership ranks it may change its rank from year to year, but it still belongs to the front runners penetrating America's industry.

Exhibit 1.   Leading Competitors by Industry and Nationality—based on output of GDP

	Total GDP	1. Place	2. Place	3. Place
Petroleum				
1990	$26,712	UK—31%	Holland—N.A.	L. America—11%
1995	$29,252	Holland—39%e	UK—21%	L. America—19%
1996	$33,007	Holland—37%e	UK—20%	L. America—19%
Manufacturing				
1990	$119,704	UK—23%	Canada—18%	Japan—12%
1995	$155,741	UK—23%	Japan—16%	Germany—14%
1996	$166,553	UK—23%	Germany—15%	Japan—15%
Food and related products				
1990	$10,944	UK—39%	Switzerland—N.A.	Canada—16%
1995	$12,127	UK—33%	Switzerland—20%	Canada—17%
1996	$12,579	UK—31%	Switzerland—24%	Canada—16%
Chemicals				
1990	$37,387	UK—23%	Germany—18%	Canada—N.A.
1995	$40,552	UK—26%	Germany—23%	Switzerland—16%
1996	$43,771	UK—27%	Germany—25%	Switzerland—16%
Primary and Fabricated Metals				
1990	$14,623	Japan—24%	France—18%	Canada—12%
1995	$16,872	Japan—36%	Canada—N.A.	Germany—12%
1996	$18,202	Japan—27%	France—14%	Germany—13%
Industrial Machinery				
1990	$10,130	Japan—33%	UK—18%	Switzerland—N.A.
1995	$13,381	UK—24%	Japan—23%	Germany—16%
1996	$14,578	UK—28%	Japan—19%	Germany—17%
Electric/Electronic Equipment				
1990	$13,089	Canada—17%	Holland—N.A.	German—16%
1995	$18,542	Germany—17%	Japan—15%	Canada—14%
1996	$19,934	Germany—17%	Canada—17%	Japan—17%
Printing and Publishing				
1990	$5,462	Canada—51%	UK—22%	N.A
1995	$8,810	Canada—59%	UK—20%	Germany—N.A.
1996	$9,260	Canada—51%	UK—3%	Germany—N.A.
Transportation Equipment				
1990	$3,849	Japan—43%	UK—28%	France—11%
1995	$9,233	Japan—47%	UK—21%	Germany—12%
1996	$9,374	Japan—51%	Germany—15%	UK—14%

Exhibit 1. Leading Competitors by Industry and Nationality—based on output of GDP

	Total GDP	*1. Place*	*2. Place*	*3. Place*
Wholesale Trade				
1990	$24,392	Japan—43%	Germany—16%	UK—11%
1995	$38,966	Japan—42%	Germany—15%	UK—9%
1996	$41,714	Japan—47%	Germany—15%	UK—8%
Motor Vehicles & Equipment				
1990	$6,451	Japan—61%	Germany—29%	UK—2%
1995	$8,420	Japan—56%	Germany—37%	N.A.
1996	$9,697	Japan—60%	Germany—32%	N.A.
Electrical Goods				
1990	$4,154	Japan—79%	Other Asia—3%	UK—2%
1995	$6,834	Japan—84%	Other Asia—5%	France—3%
1996	$8,503	Japan—87%	France—3%	Other Asia—2%
Professional & Commercial Equipment and Supplies				
1990	$1,873	Japan—59%	UK—14%	Germany—10%
1995	$3,988	Japan—58%	Germany—10%	Holland—8%
1996	$4,003	Japan—57%	Holland—10%	Germany—9%
Retail Trade				
1990	$17,130	Canada—34%	Germany—23%	Switzerland—13%
1995	$23,518	Germany—27%	UK—17%	Japan—14%
1996	$24,770	Germany—26%	UK —17%	Japan—14%
Finance (excluding banks)				
1990	$5,014	Japan—42%	UK—18%	Canada—15%
1995	$2,925	UK—48%	Switzerland—25%	Holland—12%
1996	$6,277	Japan—49%	UK—18%	Switzerland—15%
Services				
1990	$16,690	UK—32%	Japan—16%	Switzerland—10%
1995	$22,224	UK—21%	Japan—14%	Switzerland—14%
1996	$26,230	UK—22%	Japan—14%	Canada—13%
Other Industries				
1990	$17,690	Australia—23%	UK—21%	N.A.
1995	$36,810	UK—37%	Canada—24%	N.A.
1996	$59,014	UK—37%	N.A.	Canada—10%
All Industries				
1990	$243,227	UK—22%	Canada—16%	Japan—14%
1995	$322,631	UK—22%	Japan—16%	Germany—11%
1996	$358,085	UK—22%	Japan—16%	Germany—12%
1999	$522,238	UK—21%	Japan—14%	France—11%

e = estimate. (Sources: SOCB: May 1993, p. 108; June 1998, pp. 64/5. August 1999, pp. 51/2. August 2002, p. 153).

U.S. Parent Organizations in the U.S. Economy

After exploring the development of foreign businesses in the U.S. economy, a look at what overall effect the combined inward and outward FDI activities have had on the U.S. economy in the past is quite interesting.

The foregoing discussion has shown inward FDI to account for about 6% of all U.S. business GDP and a slightly smaller 5% of business employment. Both indicators seem to have reached a solid plateau at these levels in the nineties, despite still rising investment volumes, which is once again a reminder to be careful with drawing conclusions from mere investment fund flows. But here the question is, whether this represents a natural level, which is hard to overcome, or have foreign interests decided that other opportunities in the world economy are more attractive. One compelling reason could be the low return on investments made by foreigners in relation to their American counterparts, which will have to be addressed at a later point. (Tables 5.2–5.4)

The cut-off point for new or additional international investment commitments is normally established by a balance between the perceived risks involved by venturing into foreign markets and the return premium expected to cover that risk. As long as more profit can be made than by investing in domestic opportunities, foreign investments are attractive. The higher the return difference at acceptable risk levels, the more attractive the foreign opportunity becomes.

Curiously enough, a parallel situation was uncovered for U.S. outward FDI in the previous chapter. American affiliates' share in the industrial GDP of OECD was found to have reached a firm level since the mid- eighties (Table 4.5), as well as in OECD employment (Table 4.8). Still another statistic confirms these amazing findings. A similar plateau effect appears in the case of America's outward FDI, when comparing affiliate GP and employment data with those of U.S. industry. (Tables 4.11 and 5.7C)

Again the question, is this all the globalization effect that FDI can muster, or is it only a temporary phenomenon? There is another point of interest connected with America's foreign ventures. After half a century of vigorous direct investments activities in practically all parts of the world, how has this affected the position of parent companies in the U.S. economy, and their relationship with affiliates in foreign markets?

A three-part analysis captured in Tables 5.7A, B., and C. can be summarized as follows.

A. American parent organizations show a clearly declining trend against the country's overall economic development. This is established by their shares in employment, GDP, and foreign trade between 1977 and 1997, which are down significantly for the period covered. (Table 5.7A)

Probably the data do not do full justice in describing the real situation, because it has to be remembered, that about 11% of these parents with an 8% share in overall parent gross product, are owned by foreign investors. (SOCB, July 1999, p. 11) Nothing is revealed as to the time frame during which this took place, but it definitely makes the real picture even worse than shown. As further evidence attention is drawn to the footnote to Table 5.7B referring to parent shares in U.S. foreign trade, which would be reduced by 14 and 8 percentage point on exports in 1996 and 1997 respectively, and 11% percentage points for imports in the both years. These are dramatic reductions in parent shares they once held in U.S. foreign trade.

B. American Mofas are gaining against their parents as is clearly established by their shares in GP and employment relative to their parents. Affiliate foreign trade has exceeded that of their parents for all the years where they became available. Does the information prove that

Table 5.7.A. Parent Companies' Role in U.S. Economy

Year	U.S. GDP*	Parent GP	%	U.S Employment**	Parent Employment	%	U.S. Exports of Goods	Parent Exports	%	U.S. Imports of Goods	Parent Imports	%
1977	1,738	491	28	67,344	18,885	28	120.8	93.5	77	151.9	77.8	51
1982	2,794	796	28	73,707	18,705	25	211.2	153.3	73	247.6	111.0	45
1989	4,735	1,045	22	90,105	18,765	21	359.9	223.4	62	477.6	181.1	38
1990	4,997			91,098	18,430	21	387.4	229.4	59	498.4	200.0	40
1991	5,129			89,847	17,959	20	414.1	244.8	59	491.0	199.7	41
1992	5,425			89,956	17,530	19	439.6	249.9	57	536.5	205.2	38
1993	5,718			91,872	17,537	19	456.9	256.7	56	589.4	206.4	35
1994	6,097	1,314	22	95,035	18,565	20	502.9	321.2	64	668.7	236.1	35
1995	6,411	1,365	21	97,886	18,576	19	575.2	348.8	59	749.4	263.6	35
1996	6,793	1,481	22	100,189	18,790	19	612.1	373.4	64	803.1	294.8	37
1997	7,254	1,573	22	103,132	19,878	19	678.4	407.3	59	876.5	321.6	37
1998	7,678	1,609	21	106,042	19,820	19	670.4	406.5	60	917.1	326.5	36
1999	8,117	1,809	22	108,710	21,380	20	684.6	405.4	58	1,029.9	347.1	34
2000	8,657			111,078			772.2			1,224.4		

Note: *GDP/GP for private U.S. business in $ billion. Employment figures in 000. Foreign trade data in $ billion. **Excludes agricultural and government employment. (Sources: *U.S. GDP, Employment,and Foreign Trade data*: Economic Report of the President, February 2002, Tables B-12, B-46, and B-103. *Parent exports/imports*: SOCB: July 1993, p. 45. June 1994, p. 51. June 1995, p. 39. December 1996, p. 22. October 1997, p. 50. September 1998, p. 54. July 1999, p. 14. July 2000, p. 29. March 2002, p. 39). Parent trade data are overstated as they include companies that are affiliates of foreign companies. Adjusted exports would read: $313.1 (1996), $344.3 (1997), $384.2 (1998), and $381.1 (1999) reducing actual parent trade shares to 50%, 50%, 56%, and 56% respectively. Imports now read $207.9 (1996), $227.3 (1997), $259.2 (1998), and $272.7 (1999) reducing actual parent trade shares to 26%, 26%, 28%, and 27% respectively.

Table 5.7. B.   Outward FDI Affiliates in Comparison to their Parents

Year	Parent GP	MOFA GP	%	Parent Employment	MOFA Employment	%	Parent Exports	MOFA Exports	%	Parent Imports	MOFA Imports	%
1982	796	223.7	28	18,705	5,022	27	153.3	214.2	140	111.0	120.9	109
1989	1,045	319.9	31	18,765	5,114	27	223.3	282.5	127	181.1	204.2	113
1990		356.0		18,430	5,356	29	229.4	343.1	150	200.0	242.8	122
1991		356.0		17,959	5,387	30	244.8	365.3	149	199.7	257.9	129
1992		361.5		17,530	5,282	30	249.9	382.9	153	205.2	280.1	137
1993		359.2		17,537	5,223	30	256.7	400.4	125	206.4	204.7	99
1994	1,314	403.7	31	18,565	5,707	31	321.2	424.3	132	236.1	330.1	140
1995	1,365	465.6	34	18,576	5,924	32	348.8			263.6		
1996	1,481	498.3	34	18,790	6,077	32	373.4			294.8		
1997	1,573	520.9	33	19,878	6,480	33	407.3			321.6		
1998	1,609	506.3	31	19,820	6,773	34	406.5			326.5		
1999	1,809	561.2	31	21,380	7,471	35	405.4	688.9	170	347.1	495.7	143

Note: Mofa exports consist of sales to third countries plus shipments of goods to U.S. Mofa imports are a combination of U.S. export shipments and interaffiliate sales, which amount to less than total Mofa imports. Except for Mofa trade with the U.S., which relates srictly to merchandise shipments, all other trade may include services. (Sources: Mofa employment and gross product: SOCB: March 2002, p. 25. Mofa exports: 1982 Benchmark Survey, pp. 235, 333. SOCB: October 1991, pp. 36, 40. August 1992, p. 68. June 1994, p. 51. June 1995, pp. 39/40. December 1996, pp. 24, 32/3. March 2002, pp. 38/39. Mofa imports: SOCB: June 1988, pp. 87, 96. June 1990, pp. 40/2. October 1991, pp. 36, 40. August 1992, p. 68. June 1994, p. 51. June 1995, pp. 39/40. December 1996, p. 24, 32/3. March 2002, pp. 38/39).

Table 5.7.C. Outward FDI Affiliates in Comparison to U.S. Economy

Year	U.S. GDP	MOFA GP	%	U.S Employment	MOFA Employment	%	U.S. Exports of Goods	MOFA Exports	%	U.S. Imports of Goods	MOFA Imports	%
1982	2,794	223.7	8	73,707	5,022	7	211.2	214.2	101	247.6	120.9	49
1989	4,735	319.9	7	90,105	5,114	6	359.9	282.5	78	477.7	204.2	43
1990	4,997	356.0	7	91,098	5,356	6	387.4	343.1	88	498.4	242.8	49
1991	5,129	356.0	7	89,847	5,387	6	414.1	365.3	88	491.0	257.9	53
1992	5,425	361.5	7	89,956	5,282	6	439.6	382.9	87	536.5	280.1	52
1993	5,718	359.2	6	91,872	5,223	6	456.9	400.4	88	589.4	204.7	35
1994	6,097	403.7	7	95,035	5,707	6	502.9	424.3	84	668.7	330.1	49
1995	6,411	465.6	7	97,886	5,924	6	575.2			749.4		
1996	6,793	498.3	7	100,189	6,077	6	612.1			803.1		
1997	7,254	520.9	7	103,132	6,480	6	678.4			876.5		
1998	7,678	506.3	7	106,042	6,773	6	670.4			917.1		
1999	8,117	561.2	7	108,710	7,471	7	684.6	688.9	101	1,029.9	495.7	48

(Sources: Tables 5.7.A and 5.7.B).

parents deliberately relinquish part of their own trade to their subsidiaries? (Table 5.7B).Also, is the Mofa strength responsible for the poor parent performance at home, because they invest more attention and investment funds abroad? It definitely seems that way, because domestic capital expenditures by parents in 1982 amounted to $188.3 billion versus $60 billion expended for all affiliates or 31.9% of parent investments. In 1989 that affiliate share rose to 37.2% on actual investments of $201.8 billion against $75 billion. In 1994, the share reached an even higher 41.5% on dollar volumes of $231.9 billion and $96.3 billion respectively. (SOCB, July 1999, p. 8)

Another statistic worth mentioning measures gross product per parent employee in comparison to that for affiliates. In 1997 parent employees produced an average of $79,000 in GP compared to $79,600 for Mofa employees. In 1989 these figures showed $55,700 for parents and $62,600 for affiliates. What factors were at work to achieve the convergence in later years is not known. The data do not necessarily indicate a superior performance on anybody's part, inasmuch as Mofas generally operate in countries with wide variations in the GP component as part of related economic processes.

C. Table 5.7C relates Mofa data to American industrial GDP, employment and foreign trade. Here, Mofas have a significantly higher per capita output of GP against the average American industrial employee. Again for 1997, the U.S. average stands at $67,100 compared to the $79,600 for Mofas, as mentioned above. Foreign trade levels of Mofas look impressive, especially in comparison to total American trade data. Their true significance for America's stature in world trade will be referenced in a later discussion, when all the various aspects of American industry in the global context will be pulled together.

More significant is that all Mofa indicators cannot hide the fact, that despite their wonderful growth over the years, they are only treading water in relation to the development of the U.S. economy. Their shares in employment, GDP, and even foreign trade to some degree are fairly flat. The affiliates are not making headway against the economy of their parent country, even though they work in markets comprising about 75% of the global economic potential.

Pulling all information together shows outward FDI to be a less convincing experience for the U.S. economy than might have been assumed from the surging financial indicators. America's foreign business interests have grown from modest beginnings 20 years ago, but cannot break the sound barrier of this market, as their hypothetical employment share is glued to the 6% level. The same is true on the output side, where their share in the country's industrial GDP cannot convincingly clear the 8% hurdle. (Table 5.7C)

Combining U.S. parent and inward FDI information we find that, realistically, only 25–30% of the U.S. economy are affected by FDI in one form or another. For GDP the 1997 data indicate 29% and 24% for employment. But to belabor the point made before, U.S. parent data may be overstated by up to 10%, judging from disclosures made by government researchers. (Tables 5.2, 5.3, and 5.7A)

In the foreign trade sector FDI plays a decidedly larger role. Accepting the parent data at face value, their 60% share in U.S. exports is enhanced by another 5% of exports by unaffiliated American firms trading with Mofas. On top there are the exports of inward FDI organizations, with approximately 23% of total. This establishes that between 85–90% of all U.S. merchandise exports are FDI-related.

On the import side, the FDI share can be estimated to reach 75%, broken down into 40% for outward FDI related trade plus 35% for foreign companies in the U.S. All told the FDI impact on foreign trade seems.to be three times the level that it has on the economy as such. (For more details on foreign companies active in U.S. foreign trade refer to Chapter 6).

II. FRANCE

France is one of less than a handful of countries that has produced data series on the role of FDI for its economy similar to that seen for the U.S. However, all available information is almost exclusively devoted to the coverage of inward FDI, while information on outward FDI is practically non-existent. Also, unlike the complete set of American data for all industries— primary, manufacturing, and services—the French have only produced statistical details for the manufacturing sector. In order to avoid any confusion, it should be pointed out, that the French term "l'industrie" does not cover all industries as its equivalent does in American and other national statistics. It strictly refers to manufacturing, a practice that is also followed by Eurostat, the EU's statistical service, by the way. Even though the information is not available for every year, it is sufficient to draw a picture for major facts and trends affecting the French economy.

Speaking in general terms, there are parallels between the U.S. and French economy, despite their sharp differences in size and geographical separation. France belongs to the elite of the developed nations, is a member of the EU, which is equal in economic terms to the U.S., ranks fourth in the world behind the U.S., Japan, and Germany, and is home to many world class companies. That rank is remarkable as the country's manufacturing GDP (including agriculture) amounts to only 26% of the national GDP, compared to Japan's 38%, Germany's 33%, and Italy's 31%. The French economy is thus closer to that of the U.S. (25%) and the UK (27%). (SESSI, 1998).

Like its neighbors, the UK and Spain, France enjoys preferential access to vast territories across the globe, a legacy of her colonial past. By comparison, France's population reaches 22%, total GDP 21%, and per capita output of GDP 89% of the respective U.S. levels (1996). France is a significant economy in its own right, and thus adds important insights for the study at hand.

Table 5.8. **Percentage Share of Inward FDI Companies in National Manufacturing Industries**

	Employment Share		Revenue Share	
	1980	1992	1980	1992
France	16	24	23	29
Germany	10	7	17	13
UK	16	18	20	27
Italy	14	13	17	N/A
U.S.A.	6	12	4	15
Japan	2	1	3	3

(Source: OECD, Majority-held Affiliates of Manufacturing Industries excluding agriculture and food)

The country's economic prominence is also reflected in the volume of FDI funds it has attracted. The U.S. had invested no less than 6% of its total outward FDI stock there in 1997, and Germany, the largest foreign investor in France, shows an even higher 8% level.

Much of the information available from official statistics is purposefully maintained in the French currency, which offers the advantage of economic data free of exchange rate distortions, and thus maintaining the important ratios among all indicators undisturbed. As far as possible the following tables summarize the actual numbers published, but add percentage share information comparing FDI to the overall French economy where this makes sense.

Like in the American example the information is dovetailed into overall and majority-owned FDI information. The latter amounts to around the same 80%+ level in evidence in the American statistics, proving a universal preference for full capital and management control, where FDI activities are concerned.

Unlike the American situation, inward FDI reaches a much higher level of diffusion in the French economy, where an overall foreign penetration of 30% or more in the manufacturing sector has been documented compared to only 14–15% in the U.S., and the trend still points upward. (See Tables 5.4, 5.11, and 5.12) Whatever the reason for the exclusive preoccupation with the manufacturing sector, there are much better developed foreign trade data related to FDI, especially as far as trade among FDI members operating in France and business partners in other countries is concerned.

Foreigners account for 40% of French merchandise exports in 1996, the latest year available, and between 30–35% of imports. In the U.S. case much lower levels of around 23% for exports and an almost identical 34% for imports were recorded. The limited information seems to indicate that the export share is still growing, while the foreign share of imports is declining, if two years of information (1977 and 1993) allow any valid conclusions to be drawn. What the data also suggest is that foreign companies are responsible for sizable trade deficits, just like in the U.S. case. Inward FDI's main purpose is to serve as an outlet for merchandise and services provided from many sources including, but not limited to, parent organizations. Their role as exporter to the outside world is only secondary. There is no need to compete with parent companies and other affiliates.

Concerning the foreign participation in French manufacturing, a study by the OECD provides the following perspective on comparative foreign penetration levels for several countries. The averages in the French case are based on ranges from less than 10% for many an industry's sales to 85% (office machinery). Foreign participation is particularly strong in the high-tech industries with 40% of sector sales in 1993, and even 45%, if restated, without airframe manufacturing, because the airbus is produced by a consortium of European manufacturers. (SESSI–Tresor, 1997)

These penetration data for the manufacturing sector are, of course, only one part of the foreign presence in the French economy. According to 1996 OECD statistics presented in Appendix A.3 foreign investments in the French service sector exceed those in manufacturing by 50%. Granting that the generation of gross product in the service sector is on average lower than in the manufacturing sector for each dollar sold or invested, the fact that service GDP is close to 72% of total French industrial GDP in 1996, almost three times the level of manufacturing makes a high foreign level of penetration here quite likely. Perhaps not as high a share as seen in manufacturing, but certainly not lower than 15%.

Table 5.9. Inward FDI Manufacturing Data for: France—millions of: Ffrs

Year	Annual Investment	Sales	No. of Firms	Employment*	Employee Compensation	Gross Profits	Gross Product	Merchandise Exports	Merchandise Imports
1972	9,480	134,571	1,487	846	N/A	N/A	N/A		
1973	N/A								
1974	10,502	219,980	1,600	838	27,526	24,194	61,120		
1975	10,645	225,020	1,599	823	31,972	16,610	59,248		
1976	10,551	277,393	1,599	839	36,426	20,411	71,234		
1977	10,760	276,039	1,621	818	39,552	18,907	75,077	54,969	74,717
1978	11,546	297,563	1,879	789	42,922	20,605	81,272		
1979	13,584	360,279	2,044	785	48,263	31,982	100.526	85,879	
1980	19,221	451,336	2,196	812	57,946	37,320	119,804	103,129	
1981	18,619	525,156	2,264	802	65,201	38,941	132,501	122,751	
1982	17,158	588,013	2,344	797	72,969	39,277	145,169	142,629	
1983	18,157	632,777	2,353	747	75,615	41,339	151,541	156,459	
1984	21,096	642,397	2,254	716	78,848	43,544	197,902	175,892	
1985	18,799	496,827	2,232	698	75,767	45,199	163,877	158,979	
1986	N/A								
1987	27,068	612,692	2,548	703	88,583	64,559	204,194	188,133	
1988	30,337	695,354	2,687	717	94,685	79,125	228,682	213,391	
1989	38,079	786,714	2,859	766	104,714	90,907	256,941	244,266	
1990	N/A								
1991	42,689	846,931	2,911	787	116,309	84,039	270,713	276,733	
1992	41,223	867,865	2,919	790	119,916	80,228	273,443	289,190	
1993	33,211	859,552	2,840	755	121,016	86,685	267,460	287,205	
1994	N/A								
1995	N/A								
1996	43,364	1,089,369	3,125	839	143,570	97,886	324,553	412,174	380,000

*in 000. (Sources: Ministere d l'Industrie, Direction Generale de L'Industrie—SESSI, Publication No. 10, 1977. Ibid., No. 28, 1980. Ibid., No. 52, 1984. Ministere de l'Industrie, de la Poste et des Telecommunications, SESSI, l'implantation etrangere dans l'industry au 1er janvier 1994, ed. 1997, p. 35. Ministere de l'Economie, des Finances et de l'Industrie, SESSI, Industrie francaise et mondialisation, 1998, p. 81).

Table 5.10. Majority-Owned Inward FDI Manufacturing Data for: France—millions of: Ffrs

Year	Investments	Sales	No. of Firms	Employ-ment*	Employee Compensation	Gross Profits	Gross Product	Merchandise Exports	Merchandise Imports
1972	7,390	104,528	1,209	647	N/A	N/A	N/A		
1973									
1974	9,069	189,962	1,246	684	22,684	20,393	50,883		
1975	8,981	193,551	1,257	648	25,751	14,027	48,193		
1976	8,504	239,575	1,253	664	28,808	17,102	57,456		
1977	8,657	233,253	1,284	645	31,143	15,472	59,856		
1978	8,942	250,858	1,513	625	33,948	16,831	64,768		
1979	11,085	307,911	1,657	637	39,330	26,885	82,730	71,639	
1980	16,515	388,491	1,792	662	47,376	32,125	99,492	87,040	
1981	16,023	460,057	1,852	662	53,918	32,890	110,015	106,244	
1982	14,803	513,918	1,918	651	60,146	34,259	121,402	121,889	
1983	15,461	558,162	1,936	613	62,763	36,385	127,425	136,767	
1984	17,584	560,280	1,858	592	65,698	43,276	171,918	152,721	
1985	19,799	496,827	2,232	698	75,767	45,199	163,877	158,979	
1986									
1987	24,188	546,183	2,095	610	78,010	59,097	181,734	172,072	
1988	27,139	631,678	2,213	636	85,049	72,111	206,413	199,591	
1989	33,199	711,377	2,385	679	93,547	82,186	230,520	225,932	
1990									
1991	38,357	765,840	2,564	700	103,688	74,984	241,417	251,871	
1992	37,895	802,639	2,584	717	109,401	72,827	249,197	271,985	
1993	30,943	810,051	2,618	698	112,136	81,924	248,943	271,171	
1994/5	N/A								
1996	42,654	1,066,422	2,970	815	139,577	95,817	316,282	404,988	

*in 000. (Sources: Ministere d'l'Industrie, Direction Generale de L'Industrie—SESSI, Publication No. 10, 1977. Ibid., No. 28, 1980. Ibid., No. 52, 1984. Ministère de l'Industrie, de la Poste et des Télécommunications, SESSI, l'implantation étrangère dans l'industry au 1er janvier 1994, ed. janvier 1994, ed. 1997, p. 35. Ministère de l'Economie, des Finances et de l'Industrie, SESSI, Industrie française et mondialisation, 1998, p. 81)

Table 5.11.   Inward FDI Manufacturing Data for: France—Percentages of French total

Year	Investments	Sales	No. of Firms	Employ-ment*	Employee Compensation	Gross Profits	Gross Product	Merchandise Exports	Merchandise Imports
1972	24.1	25.8	6.1	18.6			N/A		
1973									
1974	21.8	25.9	6.7	17.4	19.3	26.6	22.2		
1975	20.9	25.4	6.5	17.4	19.4	24.1	21.1		
1976	19.9	26.7	6.6	17.7	19.7	22.1	20.1		
1977	18.5	23.6	6.5	17.5	19.1	20.0	19.3	27.8	42.9
1978	17.8	24.3	7.9	17.3	18.9	19.6	18.9		
1979	17.0	25.0	8.5	17.5	19.2	22.9	20.0	26.3	
1980	19.1	26.6	9.0	18.5	20.3	24.8	21.3	28.4	
1981	18.0	27.3	9.4	19.2	21.0	24.6	21.6	28.9	
1982	15.2	27.4	9.8	19.2	20.9	23.7	21.3	29.8	
1983	15.4	27.2	9.9	18.6	20.3	21.9	20.4	29.2	
1984	16.8	25.9	9.8	18.7	20.2	22.3	22.6	28.9	
1985	24.2	25.0	9.8	19.6	21.3	32.0	23.6	28.0	
1986	N/A								
1987	25.6	26.9	11.0	21.6	23.3	30.9	25.2	29.9	
1988	25.7	27.5	11.2	22.3	24.2	29.9	25.8	30.3	
1989	28.4	28.4	11.8	23.7	25.6	30.9	27.1	31.1	
1990									
1991	29.5	29.2	11.5	24.4	26.2	33.6	28.1	33.0	
1992	31.0	29.9	11.8	25.3	26.7	34.9	28.9	33.6	
1993	32.8	31.8	12.5	26.3	28.3	37.4	30.8	35.6	32.4
1994/5	N/A								
1996	35.3	35.2	14.2	29.2	31.3	42.7	34.4	40.0	

Table 5.12.   Majority-Owned Inward FDI Manufacturing Data for: France—Percentages of French total

Year	Investments	Sales	No. of Firms	Employ-ment*	Employee Compensation	Gross Profits	Gross Product	Merchandise Exports	Merchandise Imports
1972	18.8	20.0	5.0	13.8					
1973									
1974	18.8	22.4	5.2	14.2	15.9	22.4	18.5		
1975	17.6	21.8	5.1	13.7	15.6	20.4	17.2		
1976	16.0	23.1	5.2	14.0	15.6	18.5	16.2		
1977	14.9	19.9	5.2	13.8	15.0	16.4	15.4		
1978	13.8	20.5	6.4	13.7	15.0	16.0	15.1		
1979	13.9	21.4	6.9	14.2	15,6	19.2	16.5	21.9	
1980	16.4	22.9	7.3	15.1	16.6	21.3	17.7	24.0	
1981	15.5	23.9	7.7	15.8	17.4	20.8	17.9	25.0	
1982	13.1	24.0	8.0	15.7	17.2	20.7	17.8	25.5	
1983	13.1	24.0	8.1	15.3	16.8	19.2	17.2	25.5	
1984	14.0	22.6	8.1	15.4	16.8	19.9	19.6	25.1	
1985									
1986									
1987	22.9	23.9	9.0	18.7	20.6	28.3	22.4	27.3	
1988	23.0	25.0	9.2	19.7	21.7	27.2	23.2	28.3	
1989	24.7	25.6	9.8	21.0	22.9	27.9	24.3	28.8	
1990	N/A								
1991	26.5	26.4	10.1	21.7	23.4	30.0	25.1	30.0	
1992	28.5	27.7	10.5	22.9	24.4	31.7	26.4	31.6	
1993	30.5	30.0	11.5	24.3	26.3	35.3	28.7	33.6	
1994/5	N/A								
1996	34.7	34.5	13.5	28.3	30.4	41.8	33.5	39.3	

Table 5.13. Total Manufacturing Industry Data for: France -millions of: Ffrs

Year	Investment	Sales	No. of Firms	Employ-ment*	Employ. Compens.	Gross Profits	GDP	Merch. Exports	Merch. Imports
1972	39,381	521,066	24,061	4,684	N/A	N/A	N/A		
1973									
1974	48,209	850,398	23,888	4,800	142,786	90,976	275,176		
1975	50,926	886,814	24,499	4,720	165,032	68,776	280,348		
1976	53,126	1,038,798	24,158	4,729	185,234	92,332	354,397		
1977	57,929	1,171,792	24,869	4,673	206,745	94,541	389,185	197,858	
1978	64,715	1,225,872	23,770	4,552	226,977	104,985	429,480		
1979	79,725	1,441,683	24,098	4,473	251,461	139,762	502,141	326,510	
1980	100,542	1,695,644	24,390	4,371	284,739	150,433	562,815	363,476	
1981	103,501	1,925,740	24,060	4,186	310,314	158,405	613,313	424,278	
1982	112,865	2,144,396	23,934	4,143	349,758	165,519	680,514	478,367	
1983	117,847	2,325,593	23,828	4,013	372,767	189,060	741,331	536,409	
1984	125,942	2,478,251	23,022	3,839	390,118	217,277	875,534	607,436	
1985	77,622	1,986,473	22,830	3,555	354,917	141,428	693,982	566,989	
1986	N/A								
1987	105,557	2,276,438	23,071	3,253	378,722	208,738	808,899	628,137	
1988	117,651	2,521,872	23,892	3,213	391,000	264,460	886,498	703,396	
1989	133,908	2,770,433	24,214	3,220	407,935	294,027	945,766	783,368	
1990	N/A								
1991	144,545	2,898,749	25,301	3,224	442,866	249,680	961,567	837,027	
1992	133,032	2,898,376	24,710	3,123	447,615	229,486	946,065	860,773	
1993	101,313	2,698,812	22,736	2,868	426,932	231,988	867,687	807,550	
1994/5	N/A								
1996	122,953	3,094,086	22,069	2,876	458,680	229,396	943,555	1,030,467	

(Sources: See table 5.9 above).

A further assumption, even in the absence of pertinent information, is that foreign capital interests are more likely to be concentrated in a smaller number of service sectors, because of the pervasive existence of government enterprises in the French economy, as in other European countries, which leaves less discretion for foreign participation across service industries. Good examples are utilities, transportation, postal services (savings accounts), energy/fuels, etc.

All percentage penetration figures for the French manufacturing sector (Tables 5.11 and 5.12) indicate strongly expanding inroads by inward FDI companies. Between 1972 and 1996 foreigners practically doubled their foothold here to levels reaching uniformly between 30–40% on all measures employed. Similar growth trends may be assumed for the service sector.

Moreover, as there are no comprehensive economic data on French outward FDI, at all, it is not possible to say whether France is a net winner in the globalization race. Two meager clues exist in the form of the only survey undertaken for France's outward FDI in 1994, plus some FDI position data available from OECD sources. According to the latter, there is a reassuring ratio between the global inward position of Ffrs.754 billion versus an outward position of Ffrs. 1,011 billion for 1996. While positive per se, there is no way to translate these purely financial numbers into reliable indicators of relative economic performance.

More important is statistical material collected by the 1994 survey which, once more, extends only to manufacturing subsidiaries. According to the published material, French manufacturing subsidiaries abroad employed 980,000 people in 1993, 877,000 in production plus 102,000 in sales branches. This is 34% of France's total manufacturing employment (2,902,000), and 69% of parent employment (1,414,000). With a production volume of Ffrs.770 billion, roughly equivalent to all French exports of manufactured goods, and 60% of their parents' domestic output (Ffrs 1,300 billion), they again reached one third the level of the French aggregate manufacturing output (Ffrs. 2,400 billion). These data do not exactly match the information laid down from other French sources in Table 5.13 above, but they come reasonably close.

With such figures, French outward FDI in the manufacturing sector almost matched foreign inroads into the same sector of the French economy. Inward investors employed less people, 755,000 against 980,000, but sold more, Ffrs. 860 billion against Ffrs. 770 billion. A still picture, which does not say much about the growth rates over time, and comparable to inward developments at best.

What becomes clear, though, is the fact that in comparison to U.S. inward FDI, the French industry is much more international. From the very sketchy evidence furnished, it could well be that foreigners control three to five times higher shares of France's economy than was found for the U.S., where foreigners have only reached a penetration level of 5–6% for all industries. In manufacturing, the U.S. globalization rate has reached 12–15%, against a French level in the vicinity of 35%. (Tables 5.2, 5.3, and 5.11)

As far as outward FDI in relation to parent organizations is concerned, Mofas have reached one third the size of their U.S. parents in employment and output of GP. French subsidiaries, on the other hand, do even better with 69% of parent employment, and 60% of their production output. These ratios do not surprise. They result simply from the vastly disproportionate relationships of domestic against foreign market potentials faced by both contestants.

Another significant deviation from the U.S. situation, though, is the fact that foreign control over U.S. merchandise exports reached 22% in 1996 for all industries, compared to 39% for foreign-owned enterprises in France's manufacturing industry alone. This makes it an absolute minimum figure as service businesses often engage in this kind of trade as well. More about the FDI involvement in international trade is covered in the next chapter. (SESSI, 1998, pp. 63–71)

III. GERMANY

German statistics provide a limited, but detailed, history covering more than two decades for both in- and outward FDI activities. Like in the U.S. case, and unlike the French information, these data cover all industries: primary, manufacturing, and services. Available information is presented in the original currency, where applicable, to avoid inevitable exchange complications and distortions.

The only real flaw in the statistics stems from the absence of any information concerning foreign trade and the output of GDP connected with both forms of FDI. But, as sales information is complete for the years 1976–97 for both inward and outward FDI, Germany's inward FDI GDP was estimated on a combination of information provided for overall OECD GDP by industry, data available for American Mofas operating in the OECD, including Germany and, finally, information dealing with the per capita output of GDP by inward FDI operations for selected OECD nations. As American companies accounted for 24% of all inward FDI in 1998, 28.5% of all people employed, and 26.5% of revenues of these foreign operations, their GP/Sales ratio was given special weight. (Bundesbank, May 2000).

For Germany's outward FDI, broad estimates were developed, which took into consideration the fact that the generation of gross product as a percentage of sales within Germany is higher than outside the country, plus the discrepancy of GP levels between manufacturing and services, which seem to be universal. Another consideration is Germany's geographical distribution of its direct investments. 47% are concentrated in the EU with higher GDP/sales ratios than in other parts of the world, notably the U.S., where 28% of Germany's FDI stock is found.

If the estimates are close to reality, they lead to surprising conclusions: there is a vast disparity between levels of inward versus outward GP generation per capita. Inward FDI operations show a volume of DM 219,400 per employee compared to only DM127,700 for German companies located abroad in 1998. This mimics to a certain extent the sales levels for each employee with DM 664,800 and DM 456,100 respectively. The sharp discrepancy in productivity is needed to justify foreign investments in Germany, a country known for its very high labor costs and taxes by international standards. At the same time, the relatively higher and faster growing employment figures for German affiliates abroad reveal the growing trend among German manufacturers to relocate production facilities in cost-advantaged areas outside the country. Recent examples: Daimler-Benz, Siemens, and BMW in the U.S.

Support for the oblique relationship comes from other quarters. Income flows from FDI operations in the German BOP show negative balances for most years. Not a superb record for one of the world's great economies, and considering that Germans have invested 90% more abroad than foreigners did within—DM 690 billion compared to DM 363 billion in 1998. (Tables 5.14 and 5.15)

Table 5.14.   Outward FDI Data for Germany*—DM million

Year	Position*	Sales	No. Firms	Employees**	Assets	Profits***	G. Product (1)
1976	49,081	174,200	9,059	1,204	261	1,885	48,800
1977	52,774	192,700	9,562	1,271	312	771	53,956
1978	60,767	221,600	10,336	1,473	395	2,090	62,048
1979	70,330	275,300	11,180	1,651	450	2,129	77,084
1980	84,485	325,300	12,256	1,743	552	1,645	91,084
1981	101,918	400,500	13,084	1,762	663	385	112,140
1982	109,918	417,800	13,449	1,685	712	36	116,984
1983	123,497	436,100	14,044	1,617	773	2,002	122,108
1984	145,605	522,900	14,857	1,697	885	5,362	146,412
1985	147,453	564,000	15,132	1,789	891	5,291	157,920
1986	151,546	514,500	15,458	1,788	907	6,248	144,060
1987	156,797	522,000	15,931	1,881	958	6,462	146,160
1988	185,483	612,800	16,666	1,974	1,164	4,910	171,584
1989	194,908	701,300	17,952	2,172	1,315	8,827	196,364
1990	221,794	746,000	19,631	2,337	1,494	9,759	208,888
1991	253,453	793,200	20,895	2,408	1,674	8,167	222,096
1992	275,780	830,100	22,134	2,510	1,940	5,757	232,428
1993	308,399	889,100	20,784	2,537	2,346	9,073	248,948
1994	330,907	966,400	21,424	2,645	2,643	11,433	270,592
1995	370,047	1,046,500	23,369	2,834	3,134	13,223	293,020
1996	421,725	1,185,900	24,987	3,120	3,768	21,842	332,052
1997	513,495	1,419,200	27,181	3,289	4,765	26,387	397,376
1998	588,289	1,537,700	25,062	3,396	4,628	27,337	430,556
1999(2)	767,546	920,000	25,585	3,720	3,430	13,872	257,600

*includes all investments-direct and indirect. **in 000. ***dividends, interests, reinvestments. (1) estimated at 28% of sales based on OECD averages. (2) Euro. Sources: Deutsche Bundesbank: Reihe 3, Zahlungsbilanzstatistik, Nr. 4, April 1984, p. 4. Ibid., Nr. 4, April 1991, p. 4. Ibid., Mai 1994, p. 6. Kapitalverflechtung mit dem Ausland, Statistische Sonderveröffentlichung 10, various issues).

Another interesting aspect is this. It took until 1993 for German companies in foreign countries to catch up with foreign firms operating in Germany in terms of sales generated, even though German FDI volume abroad exceeded inward funds since 1981. Comparing the relative GDP volumes of both parties reveals that expatriate German companies did not match the volume produced by foreign operations in the country until 1996. In other words, the data lead to the startling conclusion that Germany's position in the world economy, measured in global output of German-controlled GDP, was weaker than official data for the country seem to indicate until that very year.

It also proves that a closer look has to be taken at various measurements for the realistic assessment of national weight and importance in the global economy. Relying strictly on financial yardsticks can be misleading, as stated before. Leaving GDP and sales out of the equation would lead to the obvious conclusion, that in terms of funds invested and employment, Germany should have a positive and leading role in the world economy. It does, but quite feeble if measured in accordance with the principles developed here.

Startling as these revelations may appear, they are not unrealistic when looking at all the pieces of information at hand separately. It is best explained by the fact that it took German industry a very long time to overcome the aftereffects of World War II. While foreigners found it easy to enter the German market during the period of reconstruction, German business was

Table 5.15. Inward FDI Data for Germany—DM million

Year	Position	Sales	No. Firms	Employees*	Assets	Profits	G. Product**
1976	78,899	359,500	7,033	1,664	297	N/A	118,600
1977	79,205	382,300	7,561	1,700	326		126,200
1978	85,748	402,700	7,989	1,696	355		132,900
1979	91,059	471,600	8,295	1,673	391		155,600
1980	93,928	512,100	8,515	1,636	418		168,900
1981	98,931	552,200	8,680	1,637	461		182,200
1982	100,793	549,900	8,715	1,533	474		181,500
1983	109,394	577,800	9,165	1,526	495		190,700
1984	113,370	623,500	9,383	1,474	534		205,800
1985	121,787	665,400	9,739	1,484	568		219,600
1986	126,811	630,200	9,852	1,500	589		207,900
1987	137,064	617,400	10,138	1,511	596		203,700
1988	148,295	633,200	10,496	1,515	657		208,900
1989	158,289	732,700	10,664	1,674	739		241,791
1990	183,123	806,200	11,475	1,789	812		266,046
1991	207,351	886,400	12,271	1,871	906		292,512
1992	215,357	903,000	12,783	1,862	948		297,990
1993	221,992	879,000	11,741	1,758	1,020		290,070
1994	234,873	905,400	11,581	1,673	1,039		298,782
1995	257,734	965,000	11,866	1,684	1,122		318,450
1996	272,033	993,400	11,906	1,662	1,180		327,822
1997	317,359	1,086,000	12,093	1,706	1,341		358,380
1998	362,896	1,107,500	12,042	1,666	1,512		365,475

*in 000. **estimated at 33% of sales based on Appendix B.2.4. (Sources: Deutsche Bundesbank: Reihe 3, Zahlungsbilanzstatistik, Nr. 4, April 1984, p. 25. Ibid., Nr. 4, April 1991, p. 25. Ibid., May 1994, p. 48. Kapitalverflechtung mit dem Ausland, Statistische Sonderveröffentlichung 10, various issues).

taxed heavily by the twin task of rebuilding itself within, and regaining the foothold it once had in the world market. It has taken no less than five decades to get to this point.

A new period of trial for the German economy came with the country's reunification, which becomes visible in consolidated statistics beginning with 1995. They reveal a pronounced impact on the national productivity, which not only declined in total per capita output of GDP, but also to varying degrees for individual industries as documented for the post-reunion period.

Other significant insights are provided by the comparison of the number of firms and their related employment data for German and foreign companies involved. The number of German-owned firms abroad is more than double the number owned by foreigners in Germany. A similar situation exists for the number of employees. But when averaging out the number of people employed per establishment one finds that German outward firms employ about 145 people and foreign-owned businesses in Germany about 138. It reflects the basic structure of the German economy with its highly diversified number of small and medium-sized firms, which are a major asset because they assure a high degree of resilience and stability in turbulent times.

Foreign Share in Germany's Industry

To what extent is Germany's industry owned by foreigners? This key question cannot be answered without linking the information furnished so far for inward FDI to macro-economic indicators for the country. This is possible for employment and GDP figures, but with one caveat. While employment figures have been published, those for GDP by FDI organizations are strictly estimates derived from sales information, which is also available from official publications. The approach has been to take the total GDP data from Table 5.15 and allocate it by industry in line with the sales distribution. Being an estimate itself, handling the GDP calculations in this manner admittedly produces only a very crude analogy. But it may be excused with its only alternative of not having any information, at all.

Table 5.16. German Inward FDI by Industry

Year	All Industries	Manufacturing	Services	Primary
		Employment - (000)		
1990	1,789	1,241	546	2
1991	1,871	1,255	614	2
1992	1,861	1,228	632	1
1993	1,744	1,151	592	1
1994	1,673	1,104	562	7
1995	1,684	1,086	586	12
1996	1,662	1,059	592	11
1997	1,706	1,058	637	11
1998	1,666	1,007	649	10
		Sales - (DM billion)		
1990	806	464	340	2
1991	886	499	385	2
1992	903	504	397	2
1993	879	484	393	2
1994	905	496	405	4
1995	965	517	441	7
1996	993	524	461	8
1997	1,086	565	513	8
1998	1,108	564	536	8
		Gross Domestic Product* - ($billion)		
1990	164.2	94.5	69.3	0.4
1991	176.2	99.2	76.6	0.4
1992	191.0	106.6	84.0	0.4
1993	175.8	96.8	78.6	0.4
1994	184.4	101.1	82.5	0.8
1995	222.7	119.3	101.8	1.6
1996	217.1	114.6	100.8	1.7
1997	207.2	107.8	97.9	1.5
1998	207.7	105.7	100.5	1.5

*estimate. (Sources: Deutsche Bundesbank: Statistische Sonderveröffentlichung 10, p. 60/61, 1995, 1996, 2000)

Table 5.17 reveals a fairly modest penetration level with under 10% of the country's industrial workforce, and probably a declining one at that. The sharp reduction in share after 1994 can be explained with the German reunification, which raised the total number of people employed without adding likewise to the statistics for inward FDI. The former communist country just was not attractive to foreign investors.

Compared to the U.S. situation Germany appears much more internationalized. Actually, Germany's total business employment before reunification shows a foreign share of 9% against 5% for the U.S. For manufacturing the gap was not as pronounced and is shrinking to very comparable levels at around 12% after the country's merger. Both rates compare to a 30% level in the case of France. For the respective service sectors it appears that both countries face quite similar levels of penetration until 1995, when German statistics begin to incorporate the full effect of the country's reunification.

Switching the focus to GDP reveals a different picture. The foreign share of business GDP in the U.S. stands at 6% and twice that level with 11–12% for Germany. France, like all other countries surveyed, does not yet furnish this information. More pronounced are the differences for manufacturing. Here France leads with a 34% share, followed by Germany with 21%, and the U.S. with only 14%. (Tables 5.2, 5.3, 5.11 and 5.17)

Table 5.17.   Inward FDI Share in German Industries

Year	All Industries	Manufacturing	Services	Primary
Employment - %				
1990	9.0	14.5	5.0	0.4
1991	9.1	14.4	5.4	0.5
1992	9.0	14.4	5.4	0.3
1993	8.6	14.4	5.0	0.3
1994	8.5	14.6	5.0	0.7
1995	6.1	12.3	3.3	1.2
1996	6.1	12.4	3.3	1.1
Gross Domestic Product - %				
1990	12.0	18.8	8.3	1.2
1991	12.2	19.3	8.5	1.3
1992	11.6	19.1	7.9	1.2
1993	11.0	19.3	7.4	1.4
1994	10.8	19.2	7.2	3.6
1995	11.2	20.6	7.3	6.4
1996	11.5	21.2	7.6	7.0

*excludes the petroleum sector for the U.S. **German data are estimates. (Sources: Tables 4.2, 4.7, 5.18).

Which countries are the leading investors in Germany? Far ahead of everybody is the U.S. with a 25% share in the 1998 inward position, followed by the Netherlands (23%), Switzerland (11%), France (9%), and Japan (5%), for a total of 74%. Remarkable is also the engagement of all European countries here with a combined share of no less than 66%.

Germany's Share in OECD Industries

German statistics provide details for investment stocks, number of firms, employment, assets, and sales by industry for practically all countries in which German companies are domi-

Table 5.18.   German Outward FDI by Industry

Year	All Industries	Manufacturing	Services	Primary
Employment - (000)				
1990	2,337	1,647	674	16
1991	2,408	1,679	714	15
1992	2,510	1,713	783	14
1993	2,537	1,730	791	16
1994	2,645	1,810	822	13
1995	2,834	1,917	896	21
1996	3,120	2,000	1,097	23
1997	3,289	2,115	1,147	27
1998	3,731	2,402	1,306	23
Sales - (DM billion)				
1990	746	363	377	6
1991	793	396	391	6
1992	830	405	419	6
1993	889	440	442	7
1994	966	489	471	6
1995	1,047	528	512	7
1996	1,186	582	595	9
1997	1,419	694	714	11
1998	1,702	873	820	9
Gross Domestic Product - ($billion)*				
1990	128.9	62.7	65.2	1.0
1991	133.8	66.8	66.0	1.0
1992	149.0	72.7	75.2	1.1
1993	150.9	74.7	75.0	1.2
1994	167.0	84.5	81.5	1.0
1995	204.9	103.3	100.2	1.4
1996	219.9	107.9	110.3	1.7
1997	229.7	112.3	115.6	1.8
1998	270.7	138.8	130.4	1.5

*estimates. (Sources: Deutsche Bundesbank: Statistische Sonderveröffentlichung 10, p. 26/27, 1995, 1996, 2000)

ciled. Of immediate interest here are employment and sales figures, the latter of which are helpful in arriving at affiliate GDP estimates by industry, even though they may be very tentative ones. These, in turn, then can be linked to the area's overall industrial GDP for major industry groupings discussed in Chapter 2.

Such calculations result in penetration rates by foreign direct investors in a given country's or area's industry, the desired goal of this study. Unfortunately, establishment of such shares are presently only possible for two countries: the U.S. and Germany.

Germany's outward FDI share in all OECD industrial employment stands at about 1%, in manufacturing close to 3%, and in services 0.4%, once again making a strong statement about the disconnect between huge sums of moneys being invested, creating expectations of major inroads into the world economy, and the relatively inconspicuous effects on the actual economic position achieved. The data also tie in very nicely with U.S. data presented in Table 4.8 with shares of 3%, 7%, and 2%, because they reflect pretty closely the overall economic dimensions of both economies. (Tables 4.8 & 5.19)

On the GDP side more parallels become visible. Germany's shares of 1% in all industries, 2% in manufacturing, and 1% in services face U.S. shares of 3%, 10%, and 1% respectively. America's high share in the OECD manufacturing sector is due to the inclusion of the petroleum industry in the country's FDI data. If adjusted, because Germany's petroleum industry is practically no factor in this picture, America's manufacturing position in OECD is closer to 7%.

The relative shares held by each country in OECD's industries require some explanations. They look somewhat distorted because the U.S. economy weighs so heavily on OECD data. Being about equal in size to the European economy and twice that of Japan, its position as the largest economy in the world automatically dwarfs all other country economies by comparison. America's FDI operations take place in a hypothetical OECD excluding the U.S., while all other countries compete in an OECD with the huge American market added in, where the removal of their domestic economy carries little weight.

Table 5.19. German Outward FDI Share in OECD Industries

Year	All Industries	Manufacturing	Services	Primary
Employment - %				
1990	0.9	2.6	0.4	0.1
1991	1.0	2.7	0.4	0.1
1992	1.0	2.8	0.4	0.1
1993	1.0	2.9	0.4	0.1
Gross Domestic Product - %				
1990	1.0	1.9	0.7	0.2
1991	0.9	2.0	0.7	0.2
1992	1.0	2.1	0.7	0.2
1993	1.0	2.2	0.7	0.2

Note: OECD data were reduced by German economic figures. (Sources: Tables 3, 4, and 45).

Table 5.20 A Comparison of U.S. & German Outward FDI

Year	All Industries	Manufacturing*	Services	Primary
Employment - 000				
U.S.A				
1990	5,356	3,377	1,055	733
1995	5,924	3,606	1,333	815
1996	6,077	3,668	1,408	826
1997	6,525	3,880	1,597	867
Germany				
1990	2,337	1,647	674	16
1995	2,834	1,917	896	21
1996	3,120	2,000	1,097	23
1997	3,289	2,115	1,147	27
%				
1990	43.6	48.8	63.9	2.2
1995	47.8	53.2	67.2	2.6
1996	51.3	54.5	77.9	2.8
1997	50.4	54.5	71.8	3.1
Gross Domestic Product - $billion**				
U.S.A				
1990	356.0	187.6	63.0	18.5
1995	465.6	238.9	101.7	25.3
1996	498.3	250.4	109.5	28.6
1997	519.3	256.4	122.2	29.9
Germany				
1990	128.9	62.7	65.2	1.0
1995	204.9	103.3	100.2	1.4
1996	219.9	107.9	110.3	1.7
1997	229.7	112.3	115.6	1.8
%				
1990	36.2	33.4	103.5	0.5
1995	44.0	43.2	98.5	0.6
1996	44.1	43.1	100.7	0.6
1997	44.2	43.8	94.6	0.6

*excludes the petroleum sector for the U.S. ** German data are estimates. (Source: 4.2, 4.7, 5.18).

Interesting for the discussion at this point is a direct comparison between American and German FDI dimensions and their effect on the relative share calculations made above. Two surprising facts emerge from Table 5.20. Overall, Germany's outward FDI is disproportionately larger in employment and output of GDP, than suggested by the country's estimated overall industrial size of only 32% relative to the U.S. economy.

In the 1990s Germany's FDI reached employment levels of 45–51%, and GDP levels of 44–56% of those shown for U.S. affiliates. No doubt, that is a direct consequence of a higher global orientation of European nations in general, due to their limited home markets, and thus a tougher commitment to compete globally. This, at least is strongly suggested by the services sector, where Germany shows GDP and employment levels approaching those of the U.S. in absolute terms.

Chapter Six

Foreign Direct Investment's Role in the U.S. Balance of Payments

GENERAL COMMENTS

The only modest foothold of foreign enterprises in America's domestic economy belies its vastly different role in the country's foreign business transactions, commonly referred to as the balance of payments (BOP). Not only because of the volumes involved, but also the positive and negative economic and political consequences it engenders. Exploring this role in detail will be coupled with observations about the effect of America's outward FDI at the same time. The joint investigation will drive home several important points.

For one it establishes how closely a nation's trade is linked to inward and outward FDI. In the U.S. case it is almost absolute, that is to say that trade by firms not connected with either inward or outward FDI does not exceed 15% of total. It will further reveal that FDI related trade not only accounts for the dominant portion of overall merchandise exports and imports, but also produces totally opposite effects for the balance of trade, when looking at inward and outward FDI trade separately. Generally speaking, foreign subsidiaries operating in the U.S. are the main cause of its perennial, huge, and growing trade deficits, while trade associated with U.S. parent companies has always produced a surplus.

FDI's role in the U.S. balance of payments becomes even larger when the countervailing flows of income, dividends, royalties and license fees, management and technical assistance fees, etc. in the services account, or fund movements through the capital account are taken into consideration. Implicit in these data are invisible policy decisions affecting the accounting practices behind those documented transactions like inter-company pricing, the use of tax havens, sourcing and changes in the finishing status of materials shipped among parents and subsidiaries, and others.

The influence of fluctuating exchange rates and their distortion potential on reported values and volumes of individual country statistics cannot be overestimated. As the dollar is the accounting currency for all international economic and trade statistics produced by the IMF, its wide swings since 1971 introduce an element of volatility of its own, which is not reflected in like series of individual countries or areas, when expressed in their own currencies. Recognition of this grave inadequacy for establishing reliable international comparisons has led to the introduction of statistics based on purchasing power parities (PPPs) by international organizations such as the OECD which, however, are only used for the purpose of comparing national GDPs and not trade.

Accounts relevant to the BOP discussion are the current account, harboring data for the trade of goods (merchandise) and services, and the capital account. Trade, of course, always implies imports as well as exports of merchandise, which may be presented either in the form of physical volume, value, or both. Value data are being used exclusively here as the most valuable reference point for any discussion of FDI. The same holds true for all non-merchandise trade related information referring to the in- and outflow of services, the so-called invisibles, and capital.

Despite the best efforts of international organizations, it is probably correct to say that most BOP statistics cannot be assumed to follow a totally standardized accounting system. It is a peculiarity of the American system, not necessarily shared by other nations, to include reinvestments as part of their BOP income and capital flow accounts, even though, by definition, they do not cross international borders, like all real flows appearing in national BOPs.

Recognizing this fact, U.S. government statisticians responsible for monthly or annual BOP information use a double entry to effectively neutralize the BOP effect of the information provided. Practically speaking, this is handled in the following manner.

In the case of U.S. outward FDI, reinvestments appear as fund inflows under the income section of the services account (with a +sign in front of the dollar amount), and again as a fund outflow in the same amount in the capital account (this time with a −sign in front). While technically off-setting each other, they lead to artificial account value inflation. When stripped away, this often leads to very sizable readjustments in account volumes and related balances. If not, international flow comparisons tend to become biased for countries that do not follow this accounting practice. Data on inward FDI are presented in exactly the same format, but with reversed value signs. Unawareness of this practice can lead a researcher to face inexplicable and irreconcilable differences in the same transactions reported by the U.S. and other countries. This phenomenon was actually brought up before, in conjunction with the discussion of FDI capital flows in Chapter 3.

Another point to keep in mind about international BOP statistics is that accounts can be maintained in terms of actual and separate transaction values, or in their net form. The trade account, for instance, shows imports and exports in actual dollar volumes, while the trade balance indicates the net effect of these transactions running counter to each other. The same can be accomplished in the services and capital accounts. Since this may not be explicitly mentioned in official publications, it is always helpful to be sure, which of the data one is looking at.

When talking about goods and services in these BOP accounts, one should also keep in mind the intricate nature of all merchandise transactions, which invariably contain a service component, like shipping and handling charges for instance, that is inconvenient to measure, and thus not reported separately for this reason.

I: FDI AND THE U.S. BALANCE OF TRADE

After these general observations, Table 6.1 introduces the overall FDI effect on the U.S. trade account. On the export side inward and outward FDI account for more than 85% of all shipments of goods on average, which leaves less than 15% of such trade in the hands of non-FDI related third parties. On the import side both together maintain a somewhat lower trade share of about 70%, leaving double the share of trade to businesses unrelated to FDI.

Table 6.1. FDI Involvement in U.S. Foreign Trade—$billion

	1980	1981	1982	1983	1984	1985	1986	1987	1988	1989
U.S. Merchandise Exports										
Total**	224.3	237.0	211.2	201.8	219.9	215.9	223.3	250.2	320.2	362.1
Out FDI*	N.A	N.A.	163.4	154.4	168.7	171.9	171.0	178.9	215.2	236.4
%	-	-	77.4	76.5	76.7	79.6	76.6	71.6	67.3	65.3
In FDI	52.2	64.1	60.2	53.9	58.2	56.4	49.6	48.1	69.5	86.3
%	23.3	27.0	28.5	26.7	26.5	26.1	22.2	19.2	21.7	23.8
All FDI	N.A.	N.A.	223.6	208.3	226.9	228.3	220.6	227.0	284.7	322.7
%	-	-	NMF	NMF	NMF	NMF	98.8	90.8	89.0	89.1
U.S. Merchandise Imports ($ billion)										
Total**	249.8	265.1	247.6	268.9	332.4	338.1	368.4	409.8	447.2	477.4
Out FDI*	N.A	N.A	120.8	124.7	141.0	153.6	147.1	166.4	180.9	201.2
%	-	-	48.8	46.4	42.5	45.4	40.0	40.6	40.5	42.1
In FDI	75.8	82.3	84.3	81.5	100.5	113.3	125.7	143.5	155.5	171.8
%	30.3	31.0	34.0	30.3	30.3	33.5	34.2	35.0	34.8	36.0
All FDI	N.A	N.A	205.1	206.2	241.5	266.9	272.8	309.9	336.4	373.0
%	-	-	82.8	76.7	72.7	79.0	74.1	75.6	75.3	78.2

	1990	1991	1992	1993	1994	1995	1996	1997	1998	1999
U.S. Merchandise Exports										
Total**	389.3	416.9	440.4	456.8	502.4	575.8	612.1	679.7	670.3	695.8
Out FDI*	241.3	257.9	265.9	274.7	344.5	374.0	407.4	441.3	438.3	440.9
%	61.9	61.9	60.5	60.2	68.7	64.9	66.5	64.9	65.4	63.4
In FDI	92.3	96.9	103.9	106.6	120.7	135.2	140.9	141.3	150.8	153.6
%	23.7	23.2	23.6	23.3	24.0	23.1	22.5	20.5	22.1	22.1
All FDI	333.6	354.8	369.8	381.3	465.2	499.3	544.0	582.6	589.1	594.5
%	85.8	85.1	84.0	83.5	92.6	86.6	88.9	85.7	87.9	85.4
U.S. Merchandise Imports										
Total**	498.3	490.9	536.5	589.4	668.6	749.6	803.3	876.4	917.2	1,024.6
Out FDI*	213.4	212.6	219.7	231.1	256.8	289.9	321.0	350.8	354.0	377.1
%	42.9	43.3	41.0	39.2	38.4	39.0	40.3	40.3	38.8	36.8
In FDI	182.9	178.7	184.5	200.6	232.4	250.8	268.7	264.9	289.7	325.0
%	36.7	36.5	34.4	34.1	34.7	33.7	31.8	30.5	31.8	31.7
All FDI	396.3	391.3	404.2	431.7	489.2	543.2	574.0	615.7	643.7	702.1
%	79.5	79.6	75.2	73.3	73.1	72.4	71.5	70.3	70.2	68.5

*includes all outward FDI related shipments of goods: exports combine parent shipments to foreign affiliates, their foreign parent groups and other foreigners plus shipments by other U.S. persons to foreign affiliates. Imports consist of affiliate and other foreign shipments to parents as well as affiliate shipments to other American customers. **excludes military. (Sources: U.S. trade data: SOCB: July 2000, pp.88/9. **Outward FDI**: SOCB: September 1986, p. 28. June 1988, p. 87. June 1990, p. 42. October 1991, p. 36. July 1993, p. 45. June 1994, p. 51. June 1995, p. 39. December 1996, p. 21. October 1997, p. 51. September 1998, p. 54. July 2000, p. 29. March 2002, p. 39. **Inward FDI**: SOCB: August 2000, p. 151. August 2002, p. 163).

Outward FDI is responsible for about two thirds of all U.S. export shipments, and inward FDI for another 20–25%. This relationship is to be expected, as the principal purpose of outward FDI is twofold: expand the marketing efforts of the parent companies in overseas markets, and feed subsidiary marketing divisions with semi-finished, or even ready-to-sell merchandise, while inward FDI companies are counted on to complement their parent organizations' marketing strategies to a lesser and only absolutely necessary extent. (For details about parent/affiliate trade roles see chapter 7).

On the import side their roles are reversed. Here, inward FDI subsidiaries account for a more elevated one-third of all U.S. imports. Not only is this roughly equal to the import volume of outward FDI, but in view of the vastly larger U.S. import volume translates into double their level of exports, the main reason behind their contribution to the American trade deficit documented below. Not unlike in the US case they serve as the principal export channels for raw material, semi-finished, or finished products from their parents, which supply more than 70% of their imports, while taking less than 50% of their exports. (Table 7.5)

The surprising fact that U.S. outward affiliate exports reach or exceed total official U.S. domestic exports as shown in Table 5.7C may be explained by two factors. Government researchers may not have made the necessary adjustments for the fact that companies labeled "American parents," continued to be included in outward FDI statistics, even after their acquisition by foreign principals. This made some double-counting unavoidable. The first mention of this problem appeared in the SOCB of June 1995, p. 39.

Also, affiliate data are not strictly reported as shipments of merchandise, which would make them directly compatible with official trade statistics, but represent a blend of shipments and sales including also service transactions

A summary illustration of the roles played by inward and outward FDI organizations in U.S. trade is furnished by Table 6.1. On the export side companies related to outward FDI, either parents, or unrelated U.S. suppliers to U.S. parent subsidiaries abroad, account for three times the level reached by companies representing inward FDI. On the import side, which in the U.S. case is vastly larger than exports, and the cause of the deficit situation, the roles of both FDI are more closely matched, with U.S. companies only slightly ahead of their foreign competitors.

It has to be realized that U.S. parent companies accounted for 30% of all GDP produced by private business in the U.S. in the benchmark survey year of 1982 and 23% in 1997, which is 4 times higher than that shown for inward FDI competitors in Table 5.7.

In view of their economic weight per se and relative to that of foreign FDI companies American parents are comparatively minor importers, yet their trade shares are very steady. A noteworthy development with regard to foreign companies operating in the U.S. is their declining import share, which could only be explained by a trend towards increased local sourcing, or falling import prices of goods in general, aided also by the strong dollar, whether for upgraded or raw materials. (Table 6.1)

This cross-purpose of FDI organizations as trading conduits is of importance insofar as both FDI forms contribute to a country's BOP in exactly opposite ways. In the U.S. case it can be demonstrated how trade connected with outward FDI companies always shows a trade surplus, while inward companies produce consistent and sizable deficits for the two decades covered. Actually, they can be identified as major contributors to the country's

Table 6.2.   FDI Contribution to the American Trade Deficit—$ billion

	Total Deficit	In-FDI	%	Out-FDI	%	Other	%
1977	$-31.1	$-19.0	61.1	$15.1	positive	$-27.2	87.5
1978	-33.9	-24.4	72.0	N/A	N/A	N/A	-
1979	-27.6	-18.7	67.8	N/A	N/A	N/A	-
1980	-25.5	-23.6	92.5	N.A.	N.A	N.A.	-
1981	-28.0	-18.2	65.0	N.A.	N.A.	N.A.	-
1982	-36.5	-24.1	66.0	42.6	positive	-55.0	150.1
1983	-67.1	-27.6	41.1	29.7		-69.2	103.1
1984	-112.5	-42.3	37.6	27.7		-97.9	87.0
1985	-122.2	-56.9	46.6	18.3		-83.6	68.4
1986	-145.1	-76.1	52.4	23.9		-92.9	64.0
1987	-159.6	-95.4	59.8	12.5		-76.7	48.1
1988	-127.0	-86.0	67.7	34.3		-75.3	59.3
1989	-115.2	-85.5	74.3	35.2		-64.9	56.3
1990	-109.0	-90.6	83.1	27.9		-46.3	42.5
1991	-74.1	-116.8	157.6	45.3		-114.9	155.1
1992	-96.1	-80.6	83.8	46.2		-61.7	64.2
1993	-132.6	-94.0	70.7	43.6		-82.2	62.0
1994	-166.2	-111.7	67.2	87.7		-142.2	85.6
1995	-158.8	-118.2	74.4	74.3		-114.9	72.4
1996	-170.2	-127.8	75.1	86.4		-128.8	75.8
1997	-180.5	-123.6	68.5	90.5		-147.4	81.7
1998	-229.8	-138.9	60.4	84.1		-175.0	76.2
1999	-345.6	-171.4	52.1	63.8		-238.0	67.3

overall trade deficits existing since 1980, alternating in that role with non-FDI related U.S. companies as shown in Table 6.2. Combining the two pieces of information provided for U.S. parent shares in the country's trade and output of national GDP above, suggests a causal link with the progress made by foreign companies in the U.S. and the weakening parent positions in both. While the figures cannot be matched one-by-one, they may point to a competitive imbalance at work, as also suggested by the growing takeovers of American companies by foreigners.

II: FDI AND THE U.S. BALANCE OF SERVICES

Just like for merchandise trade, both outward and inward FDI play important roles in America's services account. Three entries are summarizing relevant transactions.

The first one, income, consists basically of corporate earnings after taxes which is broken down further into two separate parts: distributed and reinvested earnings. The distributed portion of these earnings, in turn, breaks down again into dividends paid on equity capital plus interest earned on inter-company debt capital, both adjusted for withholding taxes paid where applicable. This is the actual cash flowing into parent pockets. Income data are reported in two different ways for the U.S. Figures appearing in Table 6.3 are adjusted for payment of withholding taxes, while figures reported in official BOP transaction tables are before those taxes, which makes them invariably slightly higher.

Earlier references to U.S. BOP accounting practices mentioned the fact that reinvestments are part of the income stream, which may not be included in BOP tables published by other nations. The size of these reinvested earnings can be seen from data given under the discussion of the U.S. capital account in the next section. Looking at their enormous size makes one appreciate their impact on the services account. If they were removed from official statistics, because technically speaking they are not true trans-border flows, they would wipe out the surplus in the account for many of the years covered. In other words, the U.S. would be running another deficit on top of the trade deficits shown.

The second entry, royalties and license fees, refers to income derived from sharing industrial property rights like patents, trademarks, know-how, etc. held by U.S. owners with parties abroad, which could be affiliated organizations, but also unrelated foreigners. Again the data shown here are actual flows after the deduction of withholding taxes at the time of payment, unlike in the official BOP statistics which represent values before deduction of these taxes. According to official sources parent companies are the principal beneficiaries of these flows. In 1996, for instance, U.S. parent organizations accounted for 68% of all these fund inflows, which can be assumed to reflect the typical level. Since such parent income can come from affiliated payers (subsidiaries), but also third-party foreigners, it becomes clear that, by not having an active FDI program in place, parents would most likely not enjoy the same levels of income derived from licensing arrangements.

The third entry, income reported in the "other services" account, consists of service charges like consulting, technical assistance, and management fees, and rentals for tangible property, as well as film and television tape rentals. It is interesting to see that only in this account foreign companies operating in the U.S. register a net inflow of funds. Most likely this is directly related to the heavy engagement of Japanese investors in Hollywood studios, and other investors in the printing and publishing sector.

Two points of great influence on the American balance of international transactions stand out. Outward FDI contributes between 40–50% of the very large annual receipts of charges for services. The account dwarfs like fund outflows by a considerable margin. But again, there is a question of whether these American parents may to some degree be affected by foreign ownership alluded to before.

America's payments to the world are relatively low by comparison to the overall inflow of like funds, the reason for a big and growing American surplus in this account. For the time being this favorable situation exists merely, because of the low volume and share of inward FDI

Table 6.3. FDI Flows in U.S. Services Account—$million

	1980	1981	1982	1983	1984	1985	1986	1987	1988	1989
U.S. Receipts on Services										
Total BOP Receipts	47,584	57,354	64,079	64,307	71,168	73,155	86,689	98,861	110,919	127,087
Outward FDI Receipts net	37,146	32,549	29,469	31,750	35,325	35,410	36,938	46,288	58,445	61,981
Income	37,146	32,549	24,828	26,813	30,046	27,858	29,927	38,523	50,429	53,929
Royalties & License Fees	3,693	3,658	3,507	3,597	3,921	4,096	5,412	6,889	8,333	10,014
Other Fees	2,087	2,136	1,816	2,532	2,483	2,490	3,024	2,446	3,091	4,333
%	90.2	66.9	47.0	51.2	51.2	45.8	44.5	48.5	55.7	53.7
U.S. Payments on Services										
Total BOP Payments	-41,491	-45,503	-51,749	-54,973	-67,748	-72,862	-80,147	-90,787	-98,526	-102,470
Inward FDI Payments net	9,063	7,259	3,096	5,103	9,556	7,318	6,751	9,025	13,597	8,690
Income	-8,635	-6,898	-2,114	-4,120	-8,443	-6,945	-6,856	-7,676	-12,150	-7,045
Royalties & License Fees	378	413	325	405	597	466	602	896	1,001	1,249
Other Fees	50	-52	-403	-471	-478	-696	-1,284	-530	-178	-50
%	21.8	16.0	6.0	9.3	14.1	10.0	8.3	9.9	13.6	8.3
Balance on Services Account										
Total	6,093	11,852	12,329	9,335	3,419	294	6,543	7,874	12,393	24,607
FDI	33,863	31,084	27,055	27,839	26,894	27,126	31,612	38,833	48,256	59,586
%	555.8	262.3	219.4	298.2	786.6	922.7	705.9	625.9	436.4	259.6

(continued)

Table 6.3. FDI Flows in U.S. Services Account—$million (continued)

	1990	1991	1992	1993	1994	1995	1996	1997	1998	1999
U.S. Receipts on Services										
Total BOP Receipts	147,832	164,261	176,916	185,941	201,031	219,229	240,007	257,235	262,653	271,884
Outward FDI Receipts net*	74,201	69,491	69,698	78,530	93,656	113,297	121,491	133,684	119,808	139,220
Income	58,004	52,087	50,565	59,381	68,987	87,346	93,594	104,794	90,676	112,359
Royalties & License Fees	11,998	12,689	14,000	13,968	17,893	19,777	20,864	20,614	21,413	21,834
Other Fees	4,199	4,715	5,124	5,181	6,776	6,174	7,033	8,276	7,719	5,027
%	50.2	42.2	39.4	42.2	46.6	51.7	50.6	51.9	45.6	51.2
U.S. Payments on Services										
Total BOP Payments	-117,659	-118,459	-116,476	-122,281	-131,878	-141,447	-150,850	-166,502	-182,697	-191,296
Inward FDI Payments net	-4,131	850	-1,695	-8,399	-22,618	-33,277	-32,708	-42,578	-36,102	-52,204
Income	2,938	-2,856	1,401	7,071	20,880	30,931	30,407	39,945	32,402	46,385
Royalties & License Fees	1,499	2,098	2,353	2,284	2,338	3,023	2,649	3,840	4,718	6,095
Other Fees (-) signifies net receipt	-306	-92	-2,059	-956	-600	-677	-348	-1,207	-1,018	-276
%	3.5	NMF	1.5	6.9	17.1	23.6	21.7	25.6	19.8	27.3
Balance on Services Account										
Total	30,173	45,802	60,440	63,660	69,153	77,782	89,157	90,733	79,956	80,588
FDI	70,070	70,341	68,003	70,131	71,038	80,020	88,783	91,106	83,706	87,016
%	232.2	153.6	112.5	110.2	102.7	102.9	99.5	100.4	104.7	107.9

*net refers to parent receipts less parent payments net of withholding taxes. (Sources: BOP data: SOCB July 2000, pp. 88/9, April 2001, pp. 38,50. Outward FDI data: SOCB: August 1991, p. 85. August 1992, p. 123. September 1997, p. 125. October 1998, p. 127. September 2000, p. 67. September 2002. p. 74. Inward FDI data: SOCB: August 1991, p. 51. August 1992. p. 92. August 1995, p. 58. September 1997, p. 83. September 1998, p. 81. September 2000, p. 37. September 2002. p. 44).

transfers to their parents. But there can be no doubt, that with the aggressive foreign engagement in U.S. industry during the last few years these outflows will continue to rise rapidly. Thus American inflows could very well be subject to erosion in the future, signs of which appear, already, in Table 6.3. It all depends on the relative speed at which outward and inward FDI develop in response to growth opportunities in the U.S. versus the outside world economy.

Less obvious, but of tremendous consequences with both positive and negative potential are also the fluctuations of the dollar's exchange value. Its wide swings in the past have left very clear imprints in the U.S. BOP, and their effect can be summarized as follows. A rising dollar is detrimental to the current account in two ways. In the trade account it can lead to lower exports and rising imports of goods, which exacerbates the perennial problem of America's trade deficit.

In the services account it causes depressed income flows, because foreign earnings are generated in foreign currencies which become weaker as the dollar gains. The best that may be said about the stronger dollar, or any other currency for that matter, is that it encourages capital outflows as foreign investment objects now look cheaper and more attractive. Expansion of the investment base, in turn, leads to long-term growth in market shares, income flows, and trade.

A weaker dollar, on the other hand, has exactly the opposite effect. With the pronounced export orientation of American officials and policy makers, little intervention is to be expected from Washington if the currency turns down, whereas a major upturn will create a flurry of activity. That is exactly what happened during the crisis in Asia, where all currencies, and with them the purchasing power of the afflicted nations, dropped dramatically against the dollar. American exports to that area effectively vanished, while U.S. imports from there virtually exploded. It will be some time before the sudden exchange disequilibrium precipitated by currency speculators can make the dollar attractive enough to serve as an export motor there, despite the heavy mobilization of international credit packages through the IMF and other organizations.

III: FDI AND THE U.S. CAPITAL ACCOUNT

FDI capital flows, as opposed to portfolio investments, into and out of the U.S. are much smaller in dollar volume than similar FDI-related movements in the current account, yet considerably larger than similar flows registered in the services account (Tables 6.1, 6.3, and 6.4).

Yet, regardless of their size, capital flows exert a strong technical influence over the fund flows discussed under the above headings. As shown in Table 6.4 capital flows are made up of three components: equity, reinvestments, and debt flows. Equity investments and reinvestments lead to the payment of dividend income in the services account, while debt capital is serviced through interest payments. Another aspect worth considering is, that capital flows affect the capital stock held abroad as measured by the investment position encountered before. The flows can have positive or negative effects on the position, depending of whether capital is exported or repatriated. At any rate, they have a long-term effect, which is not seen for the other flows discussed here.

How are these various flows to be interpreted? According to the mercantilist model, money flows out of the country are considered patently unfavorable for the economy and any inflows

Table 6.4. FDI Flows in U.S. Capital Account

	1980	1981	1982	1983	1984	1985	1986	1987	1988	1989
U.S. Capital Flows to Foreign Countries ($ million)										
Total BOP Outflows	86,967	114,147	122,335	61,573	36,313	39,889	106,753	72,617	100,221	168,744
Outward FDI Flows	19,222	9,624	1,078	6,686	11,649	12,724	17,706	28,980	17,871	37,604
Equity Capital	-	-	9,708	4,903	1,347	-2,210	551	4,635	-6,112	6,395
Reinvestments	-	-	4,806	13,453	17,276	13,665	9,048	17,650	13,319	12,697
Inter-company Debt	-	-	-13,436	-11,669	-6,973	1,269	8,106	6,696	10,665	18,512
%	22.1	8.4	0.9	10.9	32.0	31.8	16.6	39.9	17.9	22.3
Foreign Capital Flows into the U.S. ($ million)										
Total BOP Inflows	62,612	86,232	96,418	88,780	118,032	146,383	230,211	248,383	246,065	224,390
Inward FDI Flows	16,918	25,195	13,810	11,518	25,567	20,490	36,145	59,581	58,571	69,010
Equity Capital	9,027	14,795	9,723	8,699	15,044	15,214	25,086	34,319	45,046	51,776
Reinvestments	5,177	2,945	-2,361	-340	3,105	90	-239	579	1,963	-7,390
Inter-company Debt	2,713	7,455	6,448	3,159	7,418	5,186	11,298	24,683	11,562	24,624
%	26.9	29.2	14.3	13.0	21.7	14.0	24.7	24.0	23.8	30.8
Balance on Capital Account ($ million)										
Total Net Flows	24,355	27,915	-25,917	27,207	81,819	106,494	123,458	175,766	145,844	55,646
FDI	-2,304	15,571	12,732	4,832	13,918	7,766	18,439	30,601	40,700	31,406
%	9.5	positive	positive	17.6	17.0	7.4	14.9	17.4	27.9	56.5

	1990	1991	1992	1993	1994	1995	1996	1997	1998	1999
U.S. Capital Flows to Foreign Countries ($ million)										
Total BOP Outflows	-81,234	-64,388	-74,410	-200,562	-178,056	-352,376	-413,923	-488,940	-335,436	-430,187
Outward FDI Flows:	30,982	32,696	42,647	77,247	73,252	92,074	84,428	95,769	134,083	136,510
Equity Capital	8,739	17,682	14,647	24,565	33,659	40,485	27,533	40,792	73,332	52,093
Reinvestments	21,436	18,327	16,294	30,014	24,088	47,233	47,233	48,978	35,651	57,250
Inter-company Debt	807	-3,313	11,705	22,668	15,505	4,357	9,661	5,999	25,100	29,167
%	38.2	50.8	57.3	38.5	41.1	26.1	20.4	19.6	40.0	31.7
Foreign Capital Flows into the U.S. ($ million)										
Total BOP Inflows	141,571	110,806	170,663	282,040	305,989	465,684	571,796	756,962	482,235	753,564
Inward FDI Flows: (-)outflows	48,422	22,799	19,222	50,663	45,095	58,772	84,455	103,398	174,434	283,376
Equity Capital	56,239	45,811	31,635	29,674	37,210	47,890	63,734	59,498	147,091	221,562
Reinvestments	-14,156	-18,684	-12,212	-7,761	3,857	9,422	6,459	12,764	-1,769	-1,940
Inter-company Debt	6,339	-4,328	-202	28,750	4,027	1,461	14,262	31,136	29,112	63,754
%	34.1	20.5	11.2	18.0	14.7	12.6	14.8	13.7	37.8	35.9
Balance on Capital Account ($ million)										
Total Net Flows (-)outflows	60,337	46,418	96,253	81,478	127,933	113,308	157,873	268,022	146,799	323,377
FDI	17,440	-9,897	-23,425	-26,584	-28,157	-33,302	27	17,629	40,351	146,866
%	28.9	NMF	NMF	NMF	NMF	NMF	nil	6.5	27.5	45.4

(Sources: *BOP data:* SOCB July 2000. p. 89. Outward FDI data: SOCB: August 1991. p. 85. August 1992. p. 122. September 1997. p. 125. October 1998. p. 127. September 2000. p. 67. September 2002. p. 74. Inward FDI data: SOCB: August 1991. p. 51. August 1992. p. 92. August 1995. p. 58. September 1998. p. 81. September 2000. p. 37. September 2002. p. 44).

favorable. To this day their thinking prevails in the accounting practices employed in all national BOPs: money inflows are credited with the +sign, and money outflows with the −sign.
Their absolute views on money flows were perfectly correct for their times, but have to be
looked at in a more differentiated manner today. Money outflows in exchange for imports
(consumption) have completely different economic consequences than money outflows for
capital projects (investments).

Foreign capital inflows, be it for portfolio or direct investment purposes, according to the
above view should be welcomed. Short-term, it benefits the domestic economy by increasing
demand for financial assets, manpower, and other resources. Yet at the same time, FDI in particular, inevitably entails increasing foreign influence over productive resources in the host
country and, long-term, causes growing outflows of funds connected with remittances of profits in the form of dividends, interests, royalty & license fees, etc. As evidenced by the American experience, it can also lead to large and lasting trade deficits. None of the implied positive
consequences of annual capital inflows are thus necessarily favorable long-term for a country's
BOP, as well as the economic and perhaps political independence of a nation. That was under-
standably overlooked by mercantilist doctrine, because in their days foreign investments were
not a particularly noteworthy phenomenon.

On the other hand, outflows of capital in any form carry a negative connotation according
to the traditionalists. It is commonly associated with loss of funds for domestic investment
purposes, a reduction in demand for domestic assets, resources, employment, and a potential
cause of economic decline through neglect of productivity-enhancing measures. Yet, there is
the positive side, with exactly the reverse consequences discussed for the current account discussed above. In other words the capital drain should produce potentially increasing inflows of
earnings, improve the country's exports with a potentially more favorable balance in the trade
account, market expansion and diversification with its positive effects on costs and gains in
competitive know-how, etc. under normal circumstances.

Obviously, there is a trade-off. In line with proposed evaluation criteria for national competitiveness made earlier, FDI capital outflows signify maintenance or even growth in global
market shares, while increasing inflows have the opposite effect. They help to erode a country's foreign economic base. This race between inward and outward FDI stock becomes a useful measure of a country's relative competitive strengths and a predictor of its future share in
the global economy.

CONCLUSIONS

According to all statistical evidence presented here, the U.S. has clearly been a winner in the
race towards economic globalization, even though it may go in fits and spurts. Prior to 1980
the U.S. expanded its share of the world economy at a faster pace than foreigners did in the
U.S. But since then, foreign pressure on America's global position has become intense. The
balances in the FDI capital account show foreigners investing much faster in America than
American business did overseas during the 1981–90 period, and again starting with 1996 after
a brief reversal in the American role from 1991– 96. Starting with 1996, foreign investors have
targeted the U.S. market with a veritable investment blitz. Inward and outward commitments
were equal in 1996, but then foreigners escalated their U.S. investments sharply in subsequent

years such that by 1999 they invested exactly double the amount America's industry invested abroad. This establishes ominous signs for the country's future in the world economy, if the situation persists for any length of time.

The official data warrant closer scrutiny, though. As mentioned earlier, reinvestments do not represent bona-fide BOP flows. When removed from inward and outward FDI data it can be shown that foreigners invest at a much faster pace through actual capital transfers to the U.S. than the U.S. does abroad, which again does not forebode well for America's future market share. Bringing this trend into sharper focus are restated 1990–99 capital flow data with and without reinvestments.

Including the latter, the U.S. shows a cumulative FDI outflow of $800 billion against $886 billion coming in. Removing reinvestments reduces actual U.S. net outflows to only $436 billion compared to $780 billion in net inflows. This difference of $344 billion is significant for several reasons. For one thing, foreigners outpaced America's direct investments by a substantial margin and they did so, in spite of net disinvestments amounting to $53.5 billion shown as negative reinvestments, or capital repatriation, in Table 6.4 above.

A second observation relates to the economic potentials of the geographical sectors of the global economy that are targeted by these fund flows. Assuming that the American economy represents roughly 25% of the global market, U.S. investors should theoretically maintain a flow volume three times larger than the comparable volume invested in the U.S. economy, in order to achieve a similar impact in the outside world. But, none of the figure quoted above is anywhere near that ratio. Perhaps this is an utopian thought, but it still serves as a practical reminder of what vast amounts of capital it takes when trying to build or even maintain global market shares.

Also, looking at investment flows and related financial data alone plus their development over time is not the best way to judge a nation's progress in the globalization process. Information of this sort is in ample supply, but does not permit valid conclusions about the true economic impact generated by all these investment activities. After all the world economy is a dynamic, moving target and it takes a lot of resources to just keep up with it and even more, if the goal is to make genuine advances. Referring back to Tables 4.5, 4.8, 5.17, and 5.19 reveals that the undeniably vigorous investment activities of the U.S. and Germany, for instance, have only led to less than spectacular market penetration gains, expressed in OECD's GDP and employment shares.

America's outward FDI position grew almost 4 times between 1980–97, employment only 23% at best, sales 2.5 times, and GDP can be assumed to have little more than doubled. Income shown in Table 6.3 is on record with a growth of about 160% indicating that international growth requires increasing commitment in financial resources which, due to environmental changes, yield only diminishing returns.

To emphasize the obvious, there is no straight correlation between investments and related macro-economic effect. America's share in the GDP and employment of foreign economies, for example, has not developed in a direct correlation to the huge U.S. capital outflows, plus reinvestments. The analysis in the previous chapter proves how this share has stagnated or even declined for many years, a clear warning to refrain from associating capital flows with automatic gains in market, employment, and output shares. In a similar vein, foreigners increased their FDI position in the U.S. more than 8 times, with the result that their employment here grew 2.5 times, sales and output of GDP about four- to fivefold, with a similar increase in income. The net effect of all these commitments in the U.S. was a gain in the nation's GDP from 2–6%, and for employment from 2–5%. More or less, a confirmation of the situation encountered with U.S. outward FDI. (Tables 5.1 and 6.3)

A striking difference in investment strategies between inward and outward U.S. FDI is the use of reinvestments. They account for 53% of all U.S. FDI capital outflows recorded in the BOP, but only 10% for foreign investors in the U.S., who rely predominantly on equity and debt capital financing to achieve their expansion goals. The fundamental difference in financing mentality can only be assumed to stem from very different factors: the rapid buildup of the U.S. position could not be fully financed from funds generated in the U.S. without unwanted consequences for domestic investment needs; there might be tax advantages connected with capital exports for the foreign investors; then perhaps also the need to safeguard domestic capital from internal and external political developments by parking it in the politically more stable U.S., especially for European businesses.

Chapter Seven

Foreign Direct Investment and Foreign Trade

INTRODUCTION

From the original proponents of free trade down to our days international trade is viewed and discussed with a reverent, ideological rigidity introduced by their teachings. Their primary focus on foreign trade based on products blessed by absolute or relative production cost advantage still overshadows academic teachings, public policy, and international relations in general. While serving a useful bridging function between the era of mercantilism and our present world at the time, their gospel has evolved little to keep pace with reality. World trade today is determined by factors which the fathers of free trade did not or could have considered. Convertible and fluctuating currencies instead of the gold standard they were familiar with, new industries and technologies, modern modes of transportation and communication, the decline of the nation state as seen in economic unions, politico/legal forces, unrestricted availability and mobility of capital, etc. render the classical arguments for free trade anchored on geographical determinants too inflexible. The days of jealously guarded national economies and protective sentiments, which spawned the classical trade doctrine as a political plea for trade liberalization, are drawing to a close.

Foreign direct investment is the visible manifestation of the changes that have taken place. Not only has it become the motor driving international trade. It actually has turned into the key determinant of a country's competitive position in the world market by preserving the nationality of the business interests behind the investments and related trade flows. It has effectively reversed the traditional sequence of trade leading to limited investment abroad, from a trade-subordinated role of FDI so to speak, to FDI as the force governing trade developments.

Among other things, free traders could never master the marketing concept that seeks to control the process of serving human needs or wants from the manufacturing stage to the final user or consumer, especially where multi-national markets are concerned. For them the production and export process stopped at the edge of the importing nation. FDI as a border-spanning production and trading process was never part of their theoretical construct, which could have helped to overcome their utterly limited notion of geography being the national determinant of production and trading processes. But that view is still very much in evidence by the way a country's output of GDP and trade is presented in official statistics.

It is time to review and modernize the concept of international economic relations, of which trade is still an important, but not the only aspect. It has to take into account the reality of national ownership of production, commercial, financing, and trading activities beyond the boundaries of geographically defined nations. The rigid adherence to geography as the defining element of national ownership of economic processes has to give way to the acceptance of capital ownership as the determining factor of "national" economies. This step will not only redefine national ownership of production, but it will lead to the recognition that international trade attributable to a national entity is much broader than envisaged by most observers of global relations. FDI, as the visible part of national ownership in foreign markets, for instance, is not designed to merely manufacture for local consumption. It is at the same time also a significant conduit for imports as well as exports, a fact that greatly expands a nation's involvement in international trade. FDI and international trade are integral parts of a closed system designed to serve global markets. The term nation, as used here, then is not a reference to the nation of domicile for the FDI enterprise, but the nation which furnishes and controls capital invested regardless of its geographical location.

FDI did exist in the days of Adam Smith and David Ricardo, already, even though its existence and importance was not recognized by the free traders. Now it is time to change its perception from a peripheral trade facilitator, at best, to a strategic, invasive market development and control function. Trade is still its integral component, but no longer its principal driver. This is confirmed by the findings outlined below, which clearly show foreign trade to be a declining factor in overall FDI business. (Table 7.6) Rather than dwelling on national trade shares in the traditional sense, which may be more misleading than helpful in establishing the true national ownership shares in the global economy, the focus of attention needs to shift to the process which builds these shares via a fivefold constellation of clearly identifiable, national forces reaching beyond their original political boundaries: investment, production, sales, imports, and exports.

This is important, because it fundamentally changes the concept and definition of international trade. Until now, such trade is assumed to bear the nationality of its geographic origin. With FDI spreading rapidly across the globe, that definition is awkward and clashes with reality. National origin and control over the capital behind such diversified business operations is more important than geographical location of production units themselves. They remain foreign-owned implants into national territories, yet retain their full "nationality" from a business point-of-view.

Awareness of the change outlined develops only slowly. Evidence is provided by the almost universal absence of statistics charting this revolution with only a handful of exceptions discussed below. The examples of the U.S. and France explore in more or less detail the role of both outward and inward FDI in the respective foreign trade of these nations. Where it is possible quantitative volume and trade shares for both will be supplemented with related qualitative aspects such as the changing ratios between finished products and semi-processed materials, and the importance of such trade for FDI-affiliated enterprises. In the absence of similar statistical evidence, it can only be assumed that some of the findings apply to other nations as well.

I. U.S. TRADE ASSOCIATED WITH OUTWARD FDI

Ia. U.S. FDI-Associated Exports to Outward Affiliates and Non-Affiliated Foreigners

A large and apparently growing part of global business is conducted by and among FDI members including parents companies, their affiliates, and unrelated business partners of the two. A major obstacle to a clear vision of their connection is that no standardized, international documentation of FDI-associated trade in goods and services has been developed, making it particularly difficult to assess its relative magnitude and rate of change over time. Full coverage for U.S. outward FDI trade relations exists four only four census years: 1966, 1977, 1982, 1989, with intermittent and partial estimates provided for the years after 1982.

A related problem exists for trade information expressed in terms of sales and shipments which are often hard to reconcile with one another, because their differences are too large to be explained with service charges, time lags between booking and shipment, fob/cif quotation differentials, etc. In order to avoid potential confusion the following discussion is narrowed down to U.S. outward FDI-associated exports, and centers on shipments of goods between all parties concerned: parent companies, their foreign affiliates, and independent trading partners of the two. This provides not only a very tangible indicator of such business relationships within the overall framework of U.S. external trade, but also a meaningful connection with global merchandise trade data.

Parent sales of goods to majority-owned affiliates (Mofas) play only a minor role with slightly more than 4% of their total sales in 1982 and 1989. But that intra-company share increases to over 40% of all parent export sales for both years, and between 31–40% of all parent export shipments for the 1966–1991 period.

Parent trade with those overseas affiliates is only one part of the U.S. trade picture. Parents also trade extensively with unrelated business partners abroad, while their overseas subsidiaries often maintain rather extensive business relations with third-party companies in the U.S. Supplying to and sourcing from those partners are naturally smaller in scope than their business with parents, but still significant. Table 7.1 offers a summary view of merchandise exports from the U.S.: parents to their subsidiaries, parents to foreigners, and unrelated U.S. businesses to American affiliates abroad. The dominant role of parents in overall U.S. exports with roughly two-thirds of the total becomes immediately visible.

Also the fact, that parent export shipments, account for 21–27% of all U.S. merchandise exports, thus establishing them as a vital export conduit for those companies as well as the U.S. economy. Their very steady export share is significant when seen against the overall parent export share in overall U.S. exports which seems to be slipping. Adding shipments by independent American suppliers to those overseas subsidiaries raises their aggregate share to a fairly consistent level between 26–30% of all U.S. merchandise exports.

Looking at the whole picture in Table 7.1, reveals that all outward FDI-related exports combining parent shipments to all foreign customers, and affiliate purchases from non-affiliated U.S. suppliers, account for more than 60% of all U.S. exports between 1966 and 1997.

This picture needs to be amended by additional information available only since 1989. Starting with that year, parent exports to foreigners are broken down to reveal exports to foreign parent groups of U.S. parents, indicating not only a sizable trade taking place between both, but also one that, technically, might also be called trade between affiliated companies. Data shown in brackets in Table 7.1 are adjusted in that sense. They have no effect on total parent exports, but alter the ratio of sales made in favor of the affiliate portion. This revelation, once again, raises the question, why foreign-owned U.S. parent organizations are still maintained as part of U.S. outward FDI statistics. It has to be assumed, that they are majority-controlled, the preferred FDI strategy, and thus introduce unnecessary bias into the picture.

Another breakdown of published information allows a comment on the changing nature that those exports have experienced over a period of about two and one-half decades. Original government data present a division of their overall export volumes into three distinct categories: merchandise ready for resale without further processing, merchandise requiring further processing, and capital goods which may be used in affiliate operations or for leasing purposes.

Exports of finished merchandise to affiliates have maintained a surprisingly steady 10–12% share of total U.S. exports for the 30–year period under review. Goods requiring further processing by affiliate organizations abroad before they can be marketed, on the other hand, are of growing importance in the trade picture. Their share has risen by a lofty 60–70% from the 9–10% level recorded in 1966, and now represents 14–17% of all U.S. merchandise exports.

Table 7.1.   U.S. FDI Merchandise Exports Shipped to Affiliates and Foreigners—$billion

Year	Total U.S. Exports	Total Parent Exports	% of U.S. Total	Parents Exports to Affiliates	% of U.S. Total	All U.S. Exports to Affiliates	% of U.S. Total	All FDI related exports	% of U.S. Total
1966	29.3	17.7	60.7	6.3M	21.5	7.7M	26.3	19.1	65.2
1977	120.8	86.7	71.8	32.4A	26.8	40.8A	33.7	95.1	78.7
				29.3M	24.3	35.8M	29.6		
1982	211.2	139.3	66.0	46.6A	22.1	56.7A	26.9	149.4	70.7
				44.3M	21.0	52.8M	25.0		
1988	320.2	198.5	62.0	81.2A	25.4	94.9A	29.7	212.2	66.3
				78.2M	24.4	90.8M	28.4		
1989	362.1	225.1	62.2	91.2A	25.2	102.6A	28.3	236.5	65.3
				86.1M	23.8	97.5M	26.9		
				(5.3)	(1.5)	(102.8)	(28.4)		

1990	389.3	223.9	57.7	94.6A	24.3	106.4A	27.4	235.7	60.5
				88.4M	22.7	100.2M	25.8		
				(7.5)	(3.9)	(107.7)	(29.7)		
1991	416.9	242.4	58.1	102.2A	24.5	115.3A	27.8	255.5	61.3
				95.7M	22.9	108.8M	26.2		
				(8.3)	(2.0)	(117.1)	(28.2)		
1992	440.4	239.9	54.5	105.3A	23.9	120.3A	27.3	254.9	57.9
				99.1M	22.5	114.1M	25.9		
				(18.7)	(8.5)	(139.2)	(34.4)		
1994	512.6	321.2	62.7	136.1A	26.6	159.5A	31.1	344.6	67.2
				132.7M	25.9	153.5M	29.9		
				(18.2)	(3.5)	(177.7)	(33.4)		
1997	689.2	407.3	59.1	186.5A	26.5	220.5A	31.3	441.3	64.0
				185.1M	26.2	212.8M	30.5		
				(23.1)	(3.0)	(243.5)	(33.3)		
1998	682.1	406.5	59.3	185.4	27.2	217.2A	31.8	438.3	64.3
				184.4	27.0	210.6M	30.8		
				(22.5)	(3.2)	(239.7)	(35.1)		
1999	695.8	405.4	58.3	173.4A	24.9	208.9A	30.0	440.9	63.3
				169.5M	24.3	202.9M	29.2		
				(24.3)	(3.5)	(233.2)	(33.5)		

A = All Affiliates; M = Mofas. *Exports to Mofas only. () Figures in brackets represent exports by U.S. parents to their foreign parent groups which are not treated officially as affiliated foreigners. (Sources: Total U.S. Exports: SOCB, June 1994, p. 94/7. Exports by Product Type: Benchmark Surveys: 1966, p. 91. 1977, p. 348. 1982, p. 275. 1989, p. 247. 1994. p. 247. U.S. FDI-associated Exports: Benchmark Surveys: 1966, pp. 83, 197. 1977, pp. 138,185, 282. 1982, pp. 111.128/9, 217, 271. 1989, p. 235. SOCB: October 1991, p. 36. August 1992, p. 68. July 1993, p. 45. October 1994, p. 51. October 1997, p. 50. July 1999, p. 14. July 2000, p. 29. March 2002, p. 39).

Table 7.2.   U.S. Exports Shipped to Outward FDI Affiliates by Type—$billion)

Year	Total U.S. Exports	U.S. to Affiliates	% of U.S.	For Direct Resale	% of U.S.	For Further Processing	% of U.S.	Capital Goods	% of U.S.
1966	29.3	7.7M	26.3	3.4T	11.6	3.1T	10.6	0.9T	3.1
				3.2P	10.9	2.5P	8.5	0.5P	1.7
1977	120.8	40.8A	33.7	20.5T	17.0	13.8T	11.4	1.6T	1.3
		35.8M	29.6	18.5P	15.3	9.6P	7.9	1.2P	1.0
1982	211.2	56.7A	26.9	21.0T	9.9	27.8T	13.2	3.2T	1.5
		52.8M	25.0	19.4P	9.2	22.4P	10.6	2.1P	1.0
1989	362.1	102.6A	28.3	38.4T	10.6	55.9T	14.3	2.4T	0.6
		97.5M	26.9	36.3P	10.0	47.7P	12.3	1.5P	0.4
1994	512.6	159.5A	31.1	62.2T	12.1	87.6T	17.1	3.2T	0.6
		153.5M	29.9	58.8P	11.5	71.7P	14.0	1.9P	0.4
1999	695.8	202.9M	29.2	59.9T	8.6	138.6T	19.9	2.2T	0.3
				55.5P	8.0	111.3P	16.0	1.2P	0.2

A = All affiliates. M = Mofas. T = Total. P = Parents. (Sources: see table 7.1)

The capital goods category has never amounted to a significant part of the FDI-related business and yet deserves a comment or two. While growing in dollar volume over the years it shows a dramatic drop in export share, which may be the result of two factors at work: the growing domination over these parent organizations by foreign investors, who would provide most of the needed equipment from their established sources, but potentially also a competitive weakness in the U.S. machinery industry. In view of the enormous 8–9–fold expansion of U.S. FDI stock in the period under investigation, investments in plant and equipment resulting from this expansion should have offered a golden opportunity for U.S. machinery and equipment manufacturers in what, after all, constitutes a captive market. But for unknown reasons that chance was missed. It may also just be the demonstration of forces playing an unavoidable role in a step-wise international market development model going from finished exports to local assembly to fully integrated foreign production.

But whatever the cause, such reorientation in the historic export structure with affiliates has produced major implications for the value chain of the U.S. economy. The growing semi-finished product category is definitely an opportunity cost for America that translates into solid gains for foreign economies.

Ib. U.S. FDI-Associated Imports from Outward Affiliates and Others

U.S. imports associated with outward FDI organizations relate to shipments from those very same affiliates which play a beneficial, but changing facilitator role for U.S. exports seen in the previous tables. Total affiliate exports to the U.S. break down into those shipped to parents and unrelated U.S. customers. As parents import also from non-associated foreigners, that part of trade needs to be added to bring the full FDI trade importance for U.S. merchandise imports to light. This is done in Table 7.3 which summarizes information for the period 1966–92. A major difference to the export side exists in the lack of data concerning the finishing status of imported materials, which could have added very useful insights for the purposes of this investigation.

The first impression here is that all outward FDI-related imports are losing ground in overall U.S. imports, but still reach 40%, which is not necessarily a bad sign in view of the perennial trade deficits of the U.S. Actually, combining the information for all trade related to America's outward FDI establishes its overall positive effect for the U.S. balance of trade.

Composite FDI-associated imports, according to official American statistics have declined from a high of 57% in 1977 to under 40% in the nineties. The net effect of these developments is the clear dominance of outward FDI on America's export side with a 66% level, but a clearly subordinated role on the import side with a less than a 40% share.

The picture is superficially correct, yet again in need of revision like in the case of exports. As stated parent imports are probably overstated by reason of some official statements which seem to modify previous accounting practices concerning shipments from affiliated companies. Since 1989 parent imports from foreigners in general are split into those from unrelated suppliers and foreign parent groups of U.S. parents. What this oblique statement seems to say again, is that U.S. outward FDI may be actually smaller than official statistics insinuate, if the measuring stick of capital control is applied. The only official reference is leading to this conclusion are found first in a brief 1995 statement, which reads *"some U.S. parents are foreign owned (15% in 1993). For those parents, a portion of their trade with "others" represents trade with their foreign parent groups. In 1993, trade between U.S. parents and their foreign parent groups accounted for 5 percent of MNC-associated U.S. merchandise exports and 15 percent of imports."* (SOCB, June 1995, p. 39/40). This is followed by another reference four years later saying in part: *"in 1997, U.S. parents that were ultimately controlled by foreign parents accounted for 11% of all U.S. parents and for 8% of their gross product."* (SOCB, July 1999, p. 11)

Both statements do not shed much light on the real situation, but they indicate a substantial foreign factor playing a role in U.S. outward FDI, whose overall dimensions thus may be overstated by as much as 10–15% for both its actual situation in the U.S. market and its external role in the global market. At any rate, given data reveal sizable shipments from foreign parent groups to U.S. parents. If counted as trade among affiliated companies, which appears totally justified, they alter the information in a significant way. Now, trade among "affiliated" FDI companies is larger than that with unrelated foreigners, the exact opposite impression conveyed by the unadjusted data. The changes were assumed to affect Mofa data only and the results are highlighted in brackets in Table 7.3.

Table 7.3. U.S. FDI Merchandise Imports Shipped by Affiliates and Foreigners—$billion

Year	Total U.S. Imports	Total Parent Imports	% of U.S. Total	Parents from Affiliates	% of U.S. Total	All Imports from Affiliates	% of U.S. Total	All FDI related imports	% of U.S. Total
1966	25.5	N/A	-	4.6M	18.0	6.3M	24.7	N/A	-
1977	151.9	77.8	51.2	32.6A 30.9M	21.4 20.3	41.5A 38.0M	27.3 25.0	86.7A 84.9M	57.1 55.9
1982	247.6	120.8	48.8	41.6A 38.5M	16.8 15.5	51.4A 46.1M	20.7 18.6	130.6A 128.4M	52.7 51.9
1989	477.4	181.1 (32.4)	37.9	77.3A 71.3M (103.7)	16.2 14.9 (21.7)	97.4A 84.3M (116.7)	20.4 17.7 (24.4)	201.2A 194.1M	42.1 40.7
1990	498.3	213.4 (36.8)	42.8	- - 75.3M (112.1)	- 15.1 (22.5)	102.2A 88.6M (125.4)	20.5 17.8 (25.2)	- 226.7M	- 45.5
1991	490.9	212.6 (35.9)	43.3	- 77.6M (113.5)	- 15.8 (23.1)	102.8A 90.5M (126.4)	20.9 18.4 (25.7)	- 225.5M	- 45.9

1992	532.7	205.2 (33.8)	38.5	93.9A 84.9M (118.6)	17.4 15.8 (22.3)	108.4A 98.0M (131.8)	20.3 18.4 (24.7)	219.7A 218.3M	41.2 41.0
1994	663.3	236.1 (43.2)	35.6	113.4A 107.2M (150.4)	17.1 16.1 (22.7)	134.2A 122.4M (165.6)	20.2 18.5 (5.0)	256.8A 245.0M	38.8 37.0
1995	743.5	263.7 (51.7)	35.5	122.3A 118.4M (170.1)	16.4 15.9 (22.9)	148.6A 136.3M (188.0)	20.0 18.3 (25.3)	290.0A 281.6M	39.0 37.9
1997	869.7	318.6 (64.0)	36.6	147.4A 145.4M (209.4)	25.7 16.6 (24.0)	178.7A 166.8M (230.8)	28.6 19.2 (26.5)	350.8A	40.2
1998	911.9	356.0 (65.7)	39.1	158.1A 154.8M (220.5)	17.3 17.0 (24.2)	187.6A 178.2M (243.9)	20.6 19.5 (27.0)	356.0A	39.0
1999	1,024.6	347.1 (?)	33.9	163.6A 158.2M (238.0)	16.0 15.4 (23.2)	193.9A 181.3M (268.3)	18.9 17.7 (26.2)	377.1A	36.8

A = All Affiliates; M = Mofas. () Figures in brackets represent imports from foreign parent groups of U.S. parents, which are not treated officially as imports from affiliated foreigners. (Sources: Total U.S. Imports: SOCB, June 1994, p. 94/7. U.S. FDI-associated Imports: *Benchmark Surveys*: 1966, pp. 198, 201, 209. 1977, pp. 189, 399. 1982, pp. 131, 133, 155. 1989, p. 116. *SOCB*: see Table 7.1)

Ic. The Role of U.S. Trade in Affiliate Business Operations

Sourcing from and supplying to the U.S. market amounted to a total trade volume of close to $400 billion for overseas U.S. subsidiaries in the late nineties. This is not an insignificant amount, especially not when compared to the U.S. trade volume proper, and even total world trade itself. It also indicates a substantial control of U.S. FDI companies over world trade beyond the territorial boundaries of the U.S., because affiliate trade with the U.S. as seen above is only one part of total affiliate-generated international trade which involves purchases and sales that do not touch U.S. territory. Without going into details at this point, it may be mentioned in passing that affiliate exports have at times exceeded total U.S. exports of goods in the past. They thus have turned into a major expatriate U.S. business entity, a second U.S. economy away from home.

Trading with affiliates is not an important part of the total business conducted by U.S. parents, as mentioned before. Exports to and imports from them taken individually do not even reach 4.0% of the $4.9 trillion in parent sales reported for 1997. This may not be the true picture in physical terms, though, because much of this intra-firm trade can be assumed to be subject to transfer pricing. Usually, this entails artificially low export prices, and import prices compared to the arms-length pricing normally found with independent customers, in order to shelter some profits in tax havens with low corporate income taxes.

For Mofas, trading is an entirely different matter. Table 7.4 provides the 30–year history of affiliate trade with four different parties: their parents, affiliates in third countries, unaffiliated business partners in the U.S., as well as third countries, excluding all domestic sales of affiliates within their markets of domicile.

As far as trade with the U.S. is concerned, Mofa imports from, as well as exports to the U.S., account for a growing share of their business. Based on actual shipments of goods, which allow a direct comparison with official U.S. merchandise trade data, Mofa exports reach 8–10% of their overall sales. If combined with the sales of services, affiliate exports grow slightly from 8.5 — 10.3% of those sales.

In turn, export sales to the U.S., amounting to $147.3 billion are less than half of the $323.9 billion in export sales to third countries in 1994. The total export volume of $471.2 now reaches 32.8% of Mofa sales, important business for the affiliates themselves, and also big business in relation to U.S. as well as global foreign trade. (1994 benchmark survey, p. 186/7).

Similar data for the Mofa import volume are available for 1977 only. So is partial information on sales among affiliate, which complement the above information concerning trade with the U.S. alone. According to the latest information on the subject, sales among affiliates, exclusive of transactions with the U.S. and inter-affiliate sales in the country of affiliate domicile, amounted to $190.0 billion in 1994. Of these $178.0 billion refer to sales of goods, leaving $12 billion for the sale of services

Whichever figure is chosen, if compared with official trade data for the U.S., American subsidiaries are trading partners of world rank. In 1994, the latest year for which this information was published, they exported almost half a trillion dollars worth of goods and services, while importing a minimum of $343 billion, not counting imports from unrelated business partners. This amounts to a 31% export share in Mofa sales, and a slightly smaller 24% sales share for imports.

The statistical evidence accumulated so far for the U.S. outward FDI situation furnishes compelling evidence for the important role of affiliate organizations in general, and for Amer-

Table 7.4. Weight of Trade in MOFA Business—$ billion

Year	Total Sales	Exports to U.S.*	%	Exports to Others**	%	Exports to Affiliates **	%	Total Exports	%
1966	$97.8	$6.3	6.4	N/A	-	N/A	-	N/A	-
1977	507.0	38.0	7.5	100.1	19.7	49.8	9.8	138.1	27.2
1982	730.2	46.1	6.3	175.5	24.0	68.2	9.3	221.6	30.3
1988	927.9	75.6	8.1	220.1	23.7	113.5	12.2	295.7	31.9
1989	1,019.9	84.3	8.3	214.7	21.0	114.2	11.2	299.0	29.3
1990	1,208.3	88.6	7.3	275.0	22.8	151.4	12.5	363.6	30.1
1991	1,242.6	90.5	7.3	292.6	23.6	158.0	12.7	383.1	30.8
1992	1,298.6	98.9	7.6	305.7	23.5	174.5	13.5	404.6	31.1
1993	1,275.8	107.9	8.5	301.4	23.6	170.6	13.4	423.8	33.2
1994	1,435.9	122.4	8.5	323.9	22.6	189.5	13.2	446.3	31.1
1995	1,693.8	136.3	8.0						
1996	1,868.6	152.3	8.1						
1997	1,972.5	167.1	8.5						
1998	1,971.9	171.8	8.7						
1999	2,195.3	181.3	8.3	507.6	23.1	292.8	13.3	688.9	31.4

Year	Total Sales	Imports From U.S.*	%	Imports from Others**	%	Imports from Affiliates**	%	Minimum Imports	%
1966	$97.8	$7.7	7.9	N/A	-	N/A	-	N/A	-
1977	507.0	35.8	7.1	66.5	13.1	46.9	9.3	102.3	20.2
1982	730.2	52.8	7.2	N/A		68.2	9.3	121.0	18.2
1988	927.9	90.9	9.8			113.5	12.2	204.4	22.0
1989	1,019.9	97.5	9.6			114.2	11.2	211.7	20.8
1990	1,208.3	100.2	8.3			151.4	12.5	251.6	20.9
1991	1,242.6	108.8	8.8			158.0	12.7	266.8	21.4
1992	1,298.6	114.1	8.8			174.5	13.4	288.6	22.2
1993	1,275.8	124.1	9.7			170.6	13.3	294.7	23.1
1994	1,435.9	153.5	10.7			189.5	13.2	343.0	23.9
1995	1,693.8	171.4	10.1						
1996	1,868.6	188.0	10.1						
1997	1,972.5	212.8	10.8						
1998	1,971.9	210.6	10.7						
1999	2,195.9	202.9	9.2			292.8	13.3	495.7	22.5

*Shipments. **Sales including services. (Sources: 1966 census, pp. 83, 197. 1977 census, pp. 319, 363. 1982 census, pp. 225, 230, 235, 268/71, 285/88, 316, 332, 335. SOCB, October 1991, pp. 36, 40. August 1992, p. 68. July 1993, pp. 45/6. June 1994, p. 51. June 1995, pp. 39, 40. December 1996, pp. 21, 24. October 1997, pp. 50, 69. September 1998, pp. 54, 69. July 1999, pp. 30/1. July 2000, pp. 40/1. March 2002, pp. 38, 49/50).

ica's foreign trade in particular. U.S. parents were found to account for about two thirds of all U.S. exports and roughly 37% of all imports, which translates into 8% of parent sales (exports) and 6.5% (imports) in 1997.

Mofas generated $2.4 trillion against parent sales of $4.9 trillion in 1997, or 49% in volume. But foreign trade not only accounted for a much higher share of their sales with 31% for exports and 24% for imports, they actually produced absolutely higher trade volumes in terms of dollars. 1994 parent exports of $321.2 billion are thus more than matched by Mofa exports of $446.3 billion. The same goes for parent imports of $236.0 billion versus the $343.0 reported by Mofas in the same year. Import figures are an absolute minimum amount, because Mofas do not report imports from unaffiliated business partners in third countries. Mofas are thus not only larger traders in absolute terms, they are actually also responsible for more than doubling the parents' share in international trade.

In strict accordance with our definition of national capital control over market and trade shares on a global scale, Mofas obviously add significantly to America's stature in global trade. Conversely, by not giving due credit in this form, America's true ownership role in international trade would never become visible. This is exactly the same situation uncovered by the discussion of America's real share in the output of global GDP. Neglecting the FDI connection in either case, would not give full credit to America's real share in the global economy.

II. U.S. TRADE ASSOCIATED WITH INWARD FDI

IIa. U.S. Exports/Imports by Inward FDI Affiliates

The role of FDI in America's foreign trade would be incomplete without information concerning trade connected with inward FDI organizations. Trading activities of American subsidiaries of foreign parents are monitored even more closely by the U.S. government than those of American-owned affiliates located abroad. This is a characteristic reaction of all nations that see the foreign element encroaching on their economy, territory, and perhaps political life. A vestige of traditional phobias about foreigners, and a curious anachronism for a time openly committed to free trade and investment. For the student in this field it proves to be a fortunate curiosity, as it means an ample documentation for a variety of data ranging from sales, assets, employment, imports, exports, etc to others. They appear with greater regularity, in greater detail, and for more years, but not necessarily in the same form as for outward FDI.

Table 7.5 allows a summary view of the trading activities of inward FDI affiliates for a great number of years. It points out several things. For one it shows foreigners contributing substantially to U.S. merchandise exports. Generally speaking foreign business interests have maintained a steady level of between 19–25% here. The short period of their exports exceeding this level between 1981–85 coincides with the period of an unusually strong dollar, which led to weakening U.S. exports overall, but affected the trade associated with those foreign affiliates to a lesser extent.

Notwithstanding their importance for U.S. exports, those foreign affiliates import consistently much more in value than they export, making them the leading cause of the monumental American trade deficits discussed in the previous chapter (Table 6.2). But again, they account for a very steady share here, which averages around 35% of total imports in the latest period observed. In real terms, these foreign companies begin to rival the U.S. import volume generated by outward FDI-associated trade, which averaged between 35–39% based on official statistics.

The data establish foreign companies as the second most important group in U.S. merchandise imports, right behind those from outward affiliates. In actuality, it is not only possible, but more than likely that trade associated with inward FDI plays a more significant role for the U.S. trade imbalance than indicated by the above numbers. Foreign parent companies and related business interests may be assumed to account for additional business in both exports and imports by also dealing with unrelated American businesses directly, a fact not visible by the way these trade data are maintained. A mirror image of the situation found for the U.S. outward FDI group.

What makes Table 7.5 noteworthy is the following. Foreign-controlled business exports from the U.S. go overwhelmingly to unaffiliated parties in third countries. Exports to affiliated

Table 7.5. Merchandise Trade by Foreign Affiliates in the U.S.—Shipments—$billion

Year	All U.S. Exports	Affiliate Exports	%	Affiliates to Parent Groups	%	All U.S. Imports	Affiliate Imports	%	Affiliates from Parent Groups	%
1974	$98.3	$24.2	24.6	N/A	N/A	103.8	30.5	29.3	N/A	N/A
1977	120.8	24.9	20.6	$11.7	9.7	151.9	43.9	28.9	$30.9	20.3
1978	142.1	32.2	22.7	16.6	11.7	176.0	56.6	32.2	39.5	22.4
1979	184.4	44.3	24.0	22.1	12.0	212.0	63.0	29.7	45.3	21.4
1980	224.3	52.2	23.4	21.0	9.4	249.8	75.8	30.3	47.0	18.8
1981	237.0	64.1	27.0	26.9	11.4	265.1	82.3	31.1	52.2	19.7
1982	211.2	60.2	28.5	25.0	11.8	247.6	84.3	34.0	51.9	20.9
1983	201.8	53.9	26.7	22.6	11.2	268.9	81.5	30.4	54.8	20.4
1984	219.9	58.2	26.5	27.1	12.3	332.4	100.5	30.2	70.5	21.2
1985	215.9	56.4	26.1	25.9	12.0	338.1	113.3	33.5	81.7	24.2
1986	223.3	49.6	22.2	21.9	9.8	368.4	125.7	34.2	93.4	25.4
1987	250.2	48.1	19.2	19.1	7.6	409.8	143.5	35.1	108.2	26.4
1988	320.2	69.5	21.7	26.4	8.3	447.2	155.5	34.9	118.4	26.5
1989	362.1	86.3	23.8	34.3	9.5	477.4	171.8	36.1	129.9	27.3
1990	389.3	92.3	23.7	37.8	9.7	498.3	182.9	36.7	137.5	27.7
1991	416.9	96.9	23.2	42.2	10.1	491.0	178.7	36.5	132.2	26.9
1992	440.4	103.9	23.6	48.8	11.0	536.5	184.5	34.5	137.8	25.7
1993	456.8	106.6	23.3	47.4	10.4	589.4	200.6	34.1	150.8	25.6

(continued)

Table 7.5. Merchandise Trade by Foreign Affiliates in the U.S.—Shipments—$billion (*continued*)

1994	502.4	120.7	24.1	51.1	10.2	668.6	232.4	34.7	174.6	26.2
1995	575.9	135.2	23.4	57.2	9.9	749.4	250.8	33.5	191.2	25.5
1996	625.1	140.9	22.6	60.8	9.8	795.3	268.7	33.8	197.7	24.9
1997	689.2	141.3	20.5	63.0	9.1	869.7	264.9	30.5	202.4	23.2
1998	682.1	151.0	22.1	57.6	8.4	911.9	292.0	31.8	203.5	22.3
1999	695.8	153.6	22.1	59.9	8.6	1,024.6	325.0	31.4	229.9	22.4

(Sources: Total U.S Trade: SOCB, July 1998, pp. 68/9. Table 7.1 Affiliate Trade Data: SOCB: May 1976, p. 43. August 2002, p. 161).

companies including parents consistently account for less than half of all their exports. Exactly the opposite is true for the import side, Here parents and affiliates furnish about 75% of all affiliate imports, thereby confirming the previously made observation, that FDI subsidiaries are primarily export channels for their parents.

IIb. The Role of Trade in Affiliate Business

Taking a look at the role of external trade in the overall business of the inward-FDI affiliates and comparing the results with the data established for their outward cousins leads to interesting insights. The first impression of data in Table 7.6 is that exports and imports account for much larger sales shares in affiliate business here than was found for outward affiliates.

In the case of exports that is true in the beginning, but then there is an unmistakable trend towards convergence of both series at the 7–8% level. On the import side, a definite discrepancy between the data is noticeable with imports for inward FDI affiliates generally running at almost double the level of that for outward affiliates. But even here there is a hint of an eventual evening-out process, as the percentages seem to be dropping ever so slowly for inward affiliates.

This is understandable when one considers the weight of automotive sales, for instance, in the whole picture. Passenger and utility vehicles used to enter the U.S. market as totally finished products in the past, but have slowly been giving way to local assembly and even fully integrated production by Japanese and European firms.

The change is well documented by the following numbers. Overall, imports ready for resale shown in Table 7.7 accounted for 78.2% of affiliate imports in 1980, then declined to 67.6% by 1997. Merchandise requiring further processing, on the other hand, is in an upward trend with shares developing from 21.2 to 31.7% during the same time span.

The same picture appears for imports from affiliate organizations alone (Table 7.8), but the speed of transformation is even more pronounced. It mimics the process seen at work for America's outward FDI. A definite, but slow conversion to more raw materials and semi-finished imports, with capital goods playing almost no role, at all.

An interesting sidelight is the possibility, that capital goods play such a small role in inward and outward trade, because American machinery is manufactured in inch standards, while foreign machines follow metric dimensions. Their employment in other countries adhering to a different standard might conceivably lead to burdensome conversion expenses, or potential disruptions of production, with undesirable effects for the bottom line.

Comparing all this information with that found for the outward FDI situation leads to the conclusion that both FDI groups use their affiliates quite differently at this moment.

Outward U.S. FDI operations are further along in the process of upgrading of their imports in foreign markets, which has negative aspects for America's industrial output and foreign trade, because it tends to lower the revenue volumes received for semi-finished products, equipment, accessories, and raw materials in comparison to potentially higher export volumes generated by exports of higher value-added products in advanced stages of finishing or even fully processed.

By comparison, foreign investors in the U.S. still prefer imports of upgraded or even fully finished goods ready to sell. At this stage their share still stands at 75% of all affiliate imports. This compares to less than 40% for all U.S. exports to affiliates. The ratios for items exported to American affiliates abroad for further processing reach 55%, versus only 25% on imports by

Table 7.6.   Weight of Trade Shares in Affiliate Business—$billion

Year	Total Sales	Total Exports	%	To Parents	%	Total Imports	%	From Parents	%
1977	193.9	24.9	12.8	11.7	6	43.9	22.6	30.9	16
1978	241.5	32.2	13.3	16.6	7	56.6	23.4	39.5	16
1979	327.8	44.3	13.5	22.1	7	63.0	19.2	45.3	14
1980	412.4	52.2	12.7	21.0	5	75.8	18.4	47.0	11
1981	510.2	64.1	12.6	26.9	5	82.3	16.1	52.2	10
1982	518.1	60.2	11.6	25.0	5	84.3	16.3	51.9	10
1983	536.6	53.9	10.0	22.6	4	81.5	15.2	54.8	10
1984	583.7	58.2	9.9	27.1	5	100.5	16.9	70.5	12
1985	632.9	56.4	8.9	25.9	4	113.3	17.9	81.7	13
1986	672.0	49.6	7.4	21.9	3	126.7	18.9	93.4	14
1987	744.6	48.1	6.5	19.1	3	143.5	19.3	108.2	15
1988	886.4	69.5	7.8	26.4	3	155.5	17.9	118.4	13
1989	1,056.6	86.3	8.2	34.3	3	171.8	16.3	129.9	12
1990	1,175.9	92.3	7.8	37.8	3	182.9	15.6	137.5	12
1991	1,185.9	96.9	8.2	42.2	4	178.7	15.1	132.2	11
1992	1,232.0	103.9	8.4	48.8	4	184.5	15.0	137.8	11
1993	1,329.4	106.6	8.0	47.4	4	200.6	15.1	150.8	11
1994	1,443.5	120.7	8.4	51.1	4	232.4	16.1	174.6	12
1995	1,544.6	135.2	8.8	57.2	4	250.8	16.2	191.2	12
1996	1,667.6	140.9	8.5	60.8	4	268.7	16.1	197.7	12
1997	1,726.3	141.3	8.2	63.0	4	264.9	15.4	202.4	12
1998	1,881.9	151.0	8.0	57.6	3	292.0	15.5	205.2	11
1999	2,044.4	153.6	7.5	59.9	3	325.0	15.9	229.9	11

(Sources: *SOCB*, August 2002, p. 161).

Table 7.7.   Total U.S. Inward FDI Imports of Goods by Finishing Status—$million

Year	ALL Imports	Capital Equipment	%	For Resale	%	For Further Processing	%
Total Imports							
1980	75,803	447	0.6	59,260	78.2	16,097	21.2
1987	143,537	N/A	-	109,408	76.2	N/A	-
1992	184,464	1,718	0.9	130,426	70.7	52,320	28.3
1997	261,482	1,631	0.6	176,851	67.6	83,001	31.7
Manufactured Goods							
1980	10,413	285	2.7	4,158	40.0	5,970	57.4
1987	24,548	N/A	-	5,526	22.6	N/A	-
1992	53,341	814	1.5	16,573	31.1	35,955	69.3
1997	99,304	720	0.7	33,490	33.7	65,093	65.6
Petroleum Goods							
1980	10,588	N/A	-	2,999	28.3	N/A	-
1987	8,971	N/A	-	2,643	29.5	N/A	-
1992	17,198	43	nil	7,214	41.9	8,941	52.0
1997	11,086	N/A	-	N/A	-	N/A	-
Wholesale Goods							
1980	54,016	107	nil	51,582	95.5	2,327	4.3
1987	107,278	N/A	-	98,823	92.0	N/A	-
1992	109,631	195	nil	103,277	94.2	6,159	5.6
1997	155,716	384	0.2	138,186	88.8	17,146	11.0
All Other							
1980	786	N/A	-	521	66.3	N/A	-
1987	2,740	N/A	-	2,416	88.2	N/A	-
1992	4,294	666	15.5	3,362	78.3	175	4.1
1997	6,462	527	8.2	5,175	80.1	762	11.8

(Sources: see Table 7.8).

Table 7.8.   U.S. Inward FDI Imports of Goods from Affiliates by Finishing Status—$ million

Year	All Imports	Capital Equipment	%	For Resale	%	For Further Processing	%
Total Imports							
1980	47,010	238	0.5	39,348	83.6	7,424	15.8
1987	108,201	N/A	-	84,317	78.7	N/A	-
1992	137,799	1,016	0.7	102,935	74.6	33,848	24.5
Manufactured Goods							
1980	7,808	123	1.6	3,507	44.9	4,178	53.6
1987	17,570	N/A	-	3,939	22.3	N/A	-
1992	37,259	612	1.6	12,002	32.1	24,644	66.0
Petroleum Goods							
1980	2,784	1	nil	N/A	-	N/A	-
1987	4,099	N/A	-	1,574	38.4	N/A	-
1992	9,672	37	nil	6,069	62.8	3,567	36.9
Wholesale Goods							
1980	36,068	91	nil	34,305	95.0	1,672	4.6
1987	85,092	N/A	-	77,591	91.2	N/A	-
1992	89,202	186	nil	83,532	93.6	5,485	6.1
All Other							
1980	324	N/A	-	N/A	-	N/A	-
1987	1,440	N/A	-	1,213	84.2	N/A	-
1992	1,666	181	10.9	1,332	80.0	152	9.1

(Sources: Foreign Direct Investment in the United States, 1980, October 1983 p. 170/1. Ibid., 1987 Benchmark Survey, Final Results, pp. 153/4. Ibid., 1992 Benchmark Survey, Final Results, September 1995, p. 153. Ibid., Review and Analysis of Current Developments, August 1991, Table 5–20. SOCB: July 1994, p. 167. July 1996, p. 108. August 1999, p. 41).

foreign affiliates in the U.S. Both strategies could follow a common logic: keeping profits of their respective FDI business outside of the U.S. In view of the dollar's potential for long-term deterioration of its exchange value, it seems a prudent course of action to take. For inward FDI companies it means avoiding exchange losses, resulting from both transaction and translation activities, in terms of their home currencies.

For American companies working abroad it offers the potential of considerable exchange rate gains, not to mention lower tax rates available from tax shelters in Europe, the Caribbean, and Asia.

The economic consequences for the U.S. are obviously equally disastrous, as both offer little incentive to employ more people for upgrading operations, and the necessity to spend unduly high prices on imports, thereby exacerbating the deficit situation.

Is a fundamental improvement of this situation in sight? That depends on many factors. If it comes, it will be slow, judging by the experience with U.S. outward FDI. Here the conversion process lasted for over three decades, and the process promises to be as protracted for inward FDI according to the above discussion, and data furnished in Tables 7.7 and 7.8. A pivotal role falls to the dollar. If the exchange value is expected to erode quickly and strongly, a possibility vis-a-vis the serious and growing deficit problem, foreigners will find little incentive to opt for more investment in productive capacity and higher U.S. domestic upgrading and content. The status quo in such case would be preferable to the real possibility of incurring major transaction and translation losses.

IIc. A Comparative Trade Profile for U.S. Outward and Inward FDI

Previous information reveals very different ways in which parent organizations use their affiliates as commercial trade channels. On the outward FDI side, parents account for 85% of all U.S. exports going to overseas affiliates in 1997, and 82% of all U.S. imports from affiliates exclusive of the business done with foreign parent groups of these parents. (Based on Tables 7.1 and 7.3)

In the case of inward FDI, foreign parents or their foreign-based subsidiaries provided only 75% of total affiliate imports during the same year, and purchased only a much lower 45% of their total exports. (Adapted from Table 7.5) No valid explanation for this skewed picture is offered by available sources.

The data in Table 7.9 also indicate how trade functions for the same product group can be handled by totally separate industries. Note the prominence of transport equipment & motor vehicle trade in both inward and outward trade. For outward-related trade the bulk of this merchandise is handled by the manufacturing industry itself. Inward-associated trade for the same product category falls mainly within the domain of wholesaling, a strong indicator of finished imports. The difference is also explained by the fact, that America's automotive sector has established many more factories abroad than foreigners have in the U.S. This will gradually change with more and more production facilities moving into the U.S. and/or foreign acquisition of American automakers The Japanese started to build plants years ago to mitigate America's trade deficits and ward off potential protectionist backlash beyond the "voluntary export quotas" imposed by Washington. They were later joined by German companies, which set up production facilities to escape the crowded industry conditions and high labor costs in Germany itself, and found the investment incentives, labor conditions and the size of the U.S. automotive market hard to ignore.

Table 7.9.   Structural Profile of FDI-Associated U.S. Trade—1994 Product Share of Total

	Exports to Outward FDI*	Inward FDI Exports	Imports from Outward FDI*	Inward FDI Imports
Total Volume	$159.5 billion	$120.7 billion	$134.2 billion	$232.4 billion
%Share	100.0%	100.0%	100.0%	100.0%
Petroleum	1.4	9.2	N/A	7.4
Manufacturing	65.8	40.9	81.7	29.4
Food & kindred	1.7	2.1	1.8	1.4
Chemicals	7.2	11.9	4.3	6.2
Industrial Machinery	9.5	5.3	16.7	4.6
Electric/Electronic	9.8	8.6	12.1	6.6
Prim./Fabr. Metals	1.5	3.3	1.9	3.3
Transp. Equipment	28.5	2.2	36.4	3.8
Other	7.5	7.9	8.6	3.7
Wholesale Trade	29.5	45.5	8.2	61.2
Motor Vehicles	-	6.8	-	21.3
Professional Equip.	-	1.1	-	6.6
Metals & Minerals	-	12.7	-	5.3
Electric Goods	-	3.2	-	13.3
Machinery	-	6.5	-	4.5
Farm Product, raw	-	13.3	-	6.8
Retail Trade	0.9	1.2	nil	1.4
All Other	2.4	7.9	N/A	3.3

*U.S. outward FDI-related trade covers all affiliates, their parents, and un-affiliated U.S. businesses. (Sources: 1994 Benchmark Survey, p. 64. SOCB: June 1997, p. 62.)

While information for outward FDI-associated trade is not complete, the data for inward FDI affiliates allow pinpointing the major product categories, which help to generate the huge trade deficits and, at the same time, indicating product groups of particular foreign competitive strength. In the lead are motor vehicles and transport equipment with a $47.4 billion shortfall, followed by electrical goods with $32.0, professional and commercial equipment $13.8, and machinery and equipment $6.8 billion. In combination these groups account for 90% of the affiliate trade deficit of $111.7 billion in 1994, and as such for 54% of the overall U.S. deficit.

The information contained in Table 7.9 neatly contrasts the respective trade volumes produced by outward and inward FDI members. It should be remembered, though, that outward FDI data may be inflated by the fact that government accountants still count U.S. parent companies owned by foreign direct investors as part of the American outward FDI position. It is not clear whether this understates the inward FDI data, or whether there is even some double-counting involved.

IId. The Global Scope of FDI Trade

Without going into lengthy discussions of the matter, it can be stated that databases used in compiling the above picture reveal the globe-spanning trade engaged in by foreign affiliates operating in the American market. They are enterprises from many different countries, and there can be little doubt, that similar patterns exist for FDI affiliates operating in other markets, even though hard evidence will have to come forth in the future. What becomes visible here through the multilateral lacework of affiliate trading connections is the truly fundamental function played by FDI in the globalization process. One can only marvel at the intricate patterns emerging from the data. Of particular interest is the confirmation, that trade with the parent country of these subsidiaries is not necessarily the only, nor even the most important, link they use to access supply sources or markets for their goods.

III. FDI-RELATED TRADE OF FRANCE

Fortunately, France is one of the countries that very closely monitors inward FDI's role in the French economy, and regularly publishes the findings. This has resulted in useful time series of information concerning the impact on the manufacturing sector's production, employment, gross product, and foreign trade. Data for other sectors like services and basic industries are absent, as is any such information for French outward FDI except for 1993 only.

For the novice in international accounting statistics it should be pointed out that when French statistics labeled "industries" appear, this is not an all-inclusive reference to all industrial sectors like in U.S. statistics or those from other countries. In the French dictionary the term industry refers strictly to manufacturing. This nomenclature, by the way, affects also Euro-statistics, which are commonly divided into three categories: primary, industry (manufacturing!), and services sectors. One has to be careful to separate the components to make them comparable. All of which only serves to remind the reader that international statistics are still not totally harmonized.

Trade data connected with inward French FDI are more abundant than for outward FDI enterprises, for which import and export data could only be found for one year, 1993. As a curiosity, export coverage for foreign companies in France is also more comprehensive than for imports. (Table 5.11) It would afford valuable insight into the country's trade balances, if both were available in more detail.

IIIa. Trade Connected with French Inward FDI

Data published by French authorities show that exports by foreign companies doing business in France have increased from 28% in 1977 to 36% of total merchandise exports in 1993. Imports by the same firms have decreased from 43% to only 32% of total French imports during that same time span, but by exceeding exports in volume they produce a sizable trade deficit. These figures are generally in line with the total ownership and output relationships displayed by foreigners in the French manufacturing sector. (Table 5.8)

Quite valuable is a breakdown of imports by foreign enterprises for 1993. The picture looks familiar and is reminiscent of data published for internal U.S. FDI. Here it was found that foreign affiliates rely to 75% (Table 7.5) on intra-affiliate imports, almost identical to the French situation with 72%.

Furthermore, imports from affiliates consist to 81% of finished product ready for resale, and only 19% for further processing. Again very close to the U.S. situation with 75% described in Table 7.8. Imports from non-affiliated suppliers show exactly the reverse picture with only

EXHIBIT 2.

Total 1993 Imports*	380	100%	
1. By Manufacturing Affiliates	201	53	
Intra-affiliate	118	31	100%
For resale	65	17	55
Further processing	53	14	45
Other suppliers	83	22	100%
For resale	6	2	7
Further processing	77	20	93
2. By Trade Affiliates	179	47	100%
Intra-affiliate	155	41	87
Other suppliers	24	6	13
3. Total Intra-Affiliate Imports	273	72	100%
For resale	220	58	81
Further processing	53	14	19
4. FDI Imports from Non-affiliates	107	28	100%
For resale	30	8	28
Further processing	77	20	72

*in Ffrs billion. (Source: *Industrie française et mondialisation*, SESSI 1998, p. 81).

28% for resale and 72% for further processing. This makes sense, because buying from third parties in finished form is not only expensive, it also hurts the bottom line. Buying in finished form from affiliates on the other hand is prudent, since it helps the bottom line. Not necessarily the affiliate's, but definitely the corporation's. Especially, if these sales go through tax advantaged distribution channels. (Exhibit 2)

What these data cannot convey is the split between imports from suppliers in the parent country, which normally include parent companies and unrelated business partners, and suppliers in other geographic locations. Without consideration of such a possibility, one might be tempted to assume that most or even all affiliate imports originate from the paternal country. It seems like a logical consequence of direct investment strategies, but reality is more complicated than that. Actual data published on this subject present somewhat of a surprise, because it now becomes obvious, how much affiliates import from third countries, be it from affiliate or non-affiliate organizations. (Table 7.10)

In the American example discussed above wide differences were pointed out in how investors use their affiliates for exports from parent organizations. Foreigners did so for a markedly higher degree than American firms. That observation is confirmed by French data on this subject as demonstrated in Table 7.10.

The difference between American and German FDI companies operating in France is striking. German affiliates established in France source more than 68% of their imports from their home country, with 85% of all affiliate-related imports furnished from there, and 50% of all imports from unrelated suppliers.

By comparison, only 22% of American company imports into France originate in North America. Also, only 29% of all purchases from affiliate organizations come from that region, and an even lower 18% from non-affiliated suppliers.

Equally striking is the difference between the import reliance on affiliate and non-affiliate sources between French, German, and American companies. The split between the two supplier categories is a strong ratio of 23:77 in favor of third parties in the case of French companies, a less pronounced but still clear 40:60 split in favor of non-related business partners for American companies, while German companies prefer affiliates over non-affiliates by a marginal factor of 53:47. All in all, a beautiful illustration of the advanced, yet differentiated, state of globalization of the world economy.

Table 7.10.   1993 French FDI Imports By Affiliate Status and Geographic Origin—Percentages

Origin of Imports	French Companies		German Companies		American Companies	
	Affiliates	Other	Affiliates	Other	Affiliates	Other
Germany	8.9	21.6	84.8	50.2	21.1	19.1
Belgium-Luxembourg	13.1	6.7	2.5	4.1	8.4	10.7
Italy	5.3	11.6	1.4	8.1	7.9	5.2
Netherlands	1.9	2.1	0.6	4.7	3.1	2.5
UK	6.4	7.7	1.7	4.2	14.5	10.8
Rest of Europe	43.6	13.7	6.7	9.5	11.2	12.6
Japan	2.0	3.0	0.5	3.4	3.3	2.7
U.S.A. & Canada	5.0	17.0	0.7	5.9	28.9	17.9
Eastern Europe	4.0	2.2	0	1.2	0.2	1.9
Asia	1.7	4.0	0.3	5.7	1.0	7.5
Other	8.1	10.4	0.8	2.1	0.6	9.1
Total	100	100	100	100	100	100
Ffrs billion	41.0	139.7	15.0	13.3	56.9	84.9

(Source: *Industrie française et mondialisation*, SESSI 1998, p. 80).

IIIb. Trade Connected with French Outward FDI

Information here is characteristically less plentiful than for inward FDI. One reason is the previously stated general preoccupation with developments relating to inward FDI activities. They get more attention, because of potential political and financial implications connected with the influx of large foreign capital interests. Relics of the mercantilist past, which was actually less concerned with FDI but all the more so with foreign trade as the key to increasing national riches and power.

Such mentality is not uniquely French. It is mirrored in the detailed trade statistics maintained by practically all countries, which dwell on the minutest specks of information. The lack of a similar fastidiousness on the FDI side only proves the lack of understanding as far as its role is concerned, and more basically it reveals, how shallow the concept of globalization still is and, despite its ubiquitous appearance in public pronouncements, how little it has penetrated human minds.

As an illustration of the weak appreciation of any or all aspects relating to FDI beyond mere capital, trade, and income flows, the following facts may be cited. The U.S. is the only nation that has produced a comprehensive statistical history for inward and outward FDI, and its impact on the country over a period of at least five decades. Americans made good use of annual BOP statistics coupled with periodic surveys, in order to gain a clear insight into FDI's economic impact on all nations touched by its outward FDI, but also the effect of foreign inroads into her own. In this vein American statistics cover all major macro-economic indicators relating to FDI, even including foreign trade by American affiliates abroad, something no other country apparently tracks to this day.

In the case of France, there is much useful information on the development of inward FDI, but the first comprehensive survey on the country's outward FDI was produced only in 1994. Germany probably ranks right behind the U.S. for the scope of facts produced beyond mere BOP flows and the span of time covered. But there is no coverage of foreign trade relating to inward and outward FDI anywhere. Japan and Sweden are reported to have started only recently to investigate their FDI situation in greater detail. But this is only four countries out of 28 OECD nations with a proven record of statistical interest and concrete, yet only partial measurements of such a vital aspect for their economic fortunes.

The volume of French exports reported varies greatly depending on whether airbus data are included or not. This may seem strange, but it must be remembered that Airbus is a consortium of French, German, and Italian capital interests. After this brief explanation of France's national trade statistics, in general, here are 1993 data relating to trade between France and French-owned enterprises abroad. All data are in Ffrs. billion.

The data collected so far reveal a curiosity. On the export side French-owned enterprises ship less to their foreign affiliates than foreign enterprises do ship from France to their clientele located outside the country. The actual figures are F191 billion against F287 billion for 1993. Surprising actually, since foreigners employed only 737,000 people in France compared to 979,000 people employed by French affiliates abroad in 1993. (SESSI 1998, pp. 69, 76/79)

The same can be said about the import side, where French companies import less in volume than foreign-owned affiliates. But while foreigners import more than they export they contribute only red figures for the French trade balance, exactly the opposite is true for the French companies with a positive trade balance in 1993. A recast of the situation found in the U.S. case.

EXHIBIT 3.

Total 1993 Exports*	457	100%	
1. To manufacturing affiliates	100	22	100%
For resale	56	12	56
Further processing	45	10	45
2. To trade affiliates	91	20	100%
3. Total intra-affiliate exports	191	.42	100%
For resale	146	32	76
Further processing	34	7	18
Other	11	3	5
4. Sales to third parties**	266	58	
Total 1993 Imports	181	100%	
For resale	28	15	
Further processing	153	85	
5. Total intra-affiliate imports	45	25	

*in Ffrs billion. **includes airbus (Source: Adapted from: *Industrie française et mondialisation*, SESSI 1998, p. 73–82).

When looking at the finishing status of traded merchandise, foreign companies in France import 81% of their intra-affiliate imports ready for resale, but this figures shrinks to only 28% for imports from non-affiliate suppliers. (Exhibit 2) French-owned companies, on the other hand, ship 76% in finished form to their affiliates, and closer to 100% to non-affiliates. (Exhibit 3) On the import side, about 85% of their imports require further processing. This is again very similar to the situation found for the U.S. inward FDI trade situation, where intra-affiliate trade is predominantly at a high level of finishing, whereas non-affiliate trade is just·the opposite, requiring a great deal of further processing before it is ready for sale to the market.

Another parallel exists in that U.S. parent exports to affiliates account for between 40–50% of their total exports, very much like the 42% for French companies. But while 40–50% of parent imports stem from affiliates in the American case, only 25% French company imports originate from them, if data for only one year reflect the actual situation accurately.

As far as the role of parent trade for affiliate business is concerned, it is not very significant in the U.S. case. According to Table 7.6 around 4% of affiliate sales were made to parents, but a higher 12% was furnished by them. In the French case, the 1993 estimate pegs affiliate imports from parents at 25% of their business, twice the level for U.S. companies. The 5% of their business stemming from parent purchases, on the other hand, is remarkably close to the American situation.

A final comment relates to the weight of FDI-generated trade for both countries. 80–90% of total U.S. merchandise exports are related to both inward and outward FDI, and about 75% of the country's imports. For France the FDI share is around 70% on the export side, and about 50% for imports according to Table 7.11. Despite the evidence presented here, it is reasonable to assume that total French data related to FDI trade, if they were available, might be closer to the U.S. situation. What French statistics measure is only trade connected with manufacturing establishments. It represents, therefore, the absolute minimum FDI penetration in the country's foreign trade picture. If statistics were available for service industries, such as wholesale and retail operations owned by foreigners like in the U.S. case, it could change the picture dramatically.

Table 7.11.   French Merchandise Trade—Ffrs 000

Year	Total	Outward FDI*	%	Inward FDI*	%	All Other	%
				EXPORTS			
1980	490,600	260,347	53.0	103,129	21.0	127,124	25.9
1981	576,700	301,527	52.3	122,751	21.3	152,422	26.4
1982	633,100	335,738	53.0	142,629	22.6	154,733	24.4
1983	723,100	379,950	52.6	156,459	21.6	186,691	25.8
1984	850,900	431,544	50.7	175,892	20.7	243,464	28.6
1985	906,900	408,010	45.0	158,979	17.5	339,911	37.5
1986	863,500	N/A	-	N/A	-	-	-
1987	888,900	440,004	49.5	188,133	21.1	260,763	29.3
1988	997,700	490,005	49.1	213,391	21.3	294,304	29.5
1989	1,143,200	539,102	47.2	244,266	21.3	359,832	31.5
1990	1,177,200	N/A	-	N/A	-	-	-
1991	1,221,400	560,294	45.9	276,733	22.7	384,373	31.5
1992	1,248,800	571,583	45.8	289,190	23.2	388,027	31.1
1993	1,190,500	520,345	43.7	287,205	24.1	382,950	32.2
1994/95	-	N/A	-	N/A	-	-	-
1996	1,479,900	618,293	41.8	412,174	27.9	449,433	30.4
				IMPORTS			
1977	346,400	99,471	28.7	74,717	21.6	172,212	49.7
1993	1,149,100	181,000	15.8	380,000	33.1	588,100	51.2

*manufacturing enterprises only (Sources: *l'implantation étrangère dans l'industrie*, various issues. *Importations/Exportations et Filiales Françaises de Firmes Multinationales*, STISI, Publication No. 10, pp. 67, 71).

SUMMARY

According to UN estimates FDI affiliates have generated between 27% and 32% of world exports between 1983 and 1995, data which corroborate the above findings. (UNCTAD, *World Investment Report, 1998 Trends and Determinants*, p. 6) FDI activities are truly a very important contributor to global trade and, in turn, the output of global GDP, especially when the role of the relevant parent organizations is included in the picture.

As mentioned before, FDI trade accounts for a much higher share in world trade, than FDI-generated gross product does in world GDP. Adopting the affiliate 30% share in world trade as a realistic portrayal of their position, it contrasts sharply with their 6–7% share in the generation of global GDP discussed further on.

From the American and French example it becomes evident, how FDI dominates the trade picture of both countries, if inward and outward FDI trade shares are combined. It also becomes clear how outward FDI in both cases is a country's main export channel with a positive influence on the trade balance, because they export more than they import. The picture changes significantly for inward FDI-related trade. Again in both cases, we find a similarity in that these foreigners dominate the country's total imports, and with a decidedly negative impact for the balance of trade. In other words, they are the main cause for the crushing deficits in the

U.S., while in the French case their deficits cannot upset the overall positive trade balance for the country.

It is not known to what degree this same situation applies to other nations. For European countries with a very high FDI basis world-wide, and even higher trade shares in the production of their GNPs than found for the U.S., it is conceivable that FDI accounts for very high shares in their foreign trade. This should apply to outward and inward direct investments as well.

Japan must be assumed to be an exception. Not only is its inward FDI almost insignificant by comparison with other developed nations, and thus cannot produce trade shares of the magnitude described here. It can also be assumed that the highly cartelized structure of Japan's industry does not allow much room for independent Japanese companies to get involved in foreign trade. It could very well be that in this case FDI controls close to 100% of the foreign trade, with foreigners holding only minuscule shares in both imports and exports.

The above discussion provides further important insight. Affiliate companies are capital-controlled extensions of their parents, whose nationality they share, especially where majority-owned enterprises are concerned. Their triple functions include production for local consumption, importing from parent groups and unrelated foreigners, and exporting to the same parties.

Stated differently, retaining their parent nationality would significantly affect the trading position of that country. Not giving credit in this manner, on the other hand, means the role of the investor nation in global trade is understated, while that of the host nation is exaggerated.

Another point to make concerns the strategic differences in which FDI-associated trade channels are being employed by U.S. and foreign companies. For U.S. outward FDI companies, essentially parent-affiliate combinations, trade plays a rather limited role of around 8% each for exports and imports in the total affiliate business volume. Materials provided by parents and ready for resale without further processing account for less than 5% of affiliate sales.

Foreigners, here mainly Europeans, are using their U.S. subsidiaries more actively as channels for their own exports. Affiliate imports reach around 15% of their sales which practically doubles the share shown for U.S. outward affiliates. The share of imports ready for resale stands above 10% of affiliate sales. In terms of actual dollars this translates into the fact that sales of finished merchandise ready for resale abroad stood at $62 billion for outward U.S. FDI in 1994 compared to $177 billion for inward FDI firms creating another imbalance in its own right, with important consequences for the nation's output of value-added, not to mention the disastrous impact of these foreign enterprises on the U.S. trade balance.

Total U.S. merchandise exports to American affiliates abroad, even though only about 27% of total U.S. exports and 8% of affiliate sales support an outward affiliate sales volume that is three times larger than all U.S. exports put together. In a similar fashion, U.S. inward FDI interests generate annual sales that amount again to three times the level of all U.S. exports and more than double the volume of all U.S. imports.

Such relationships between trade and affiliate sales volumes highlight the fact that while FDI involves a very high percentage of international trade, its true economic impact from the globalization point-of-view stems from the much larger sales volumes, which ultimately determine their market shares in foreign nations and the world market as such.

The key importance of the relationships between affiliate trade and other commercial activities lies in the relative growth patterns of outward vs. inward business volumes. FDI implies national control over business and markets beyond national boundaries, in short the global

market. The fact that foreign owned FDI enterprises located in the U.S., or France for that matter, have gained so much ground on their local counterparts operating abroad has implications
for the competitive position of both nations in the global economy. After all, only two decades
ago foreign sales in the U.S. through FDI operations stood at 38% of like U.S. sales abroad,
$194 vs $507 billion (1977). By 1997 sales by foreigners in the U.S. had reached 87% of the
comparable U.S. FDI business volume abroad. (Table 5.1) Unfortunately, similar statistics do
not exist for France. But even here, foreign manufacturing establishments had a business volume of Ffrs. 860 billion in France compared to the French volume of 770 billion through its
overseas affiliates in 1993.

It is relationships like these that determine and document a nation's true competitiveness.
But, it is not merely the measure of comparable business transactions that counts. This is only
a symptom of underlying relative strength. What really counts is the related payoff in income
accruing to nations in this friendly, but highly competitive tug-of-war, a topic to be addressed
in the next chapter.

Chapter Eight

National BOP Flows of FDI-Related Income

INTRODUCTION

In view of the paucity of solid, uniform, and comprehensive information seen in the previous chapter it is difficult to establish the true economic role of global FDI. Beyond only partial bits of information for less than a handful of countries there are, however, three time series that may be employed in developing indirect, but reasonable estimates of FDI's actual global dimension. Two of them were analyzed before under the topics of direct investment fund flows, and related position estimates.

Now, a third subject can be added in the form of income streams flowing from all those investment activities. All of them are financial measuring sticks imbedded in the BOP of nations, available for reasonable time periods, and enjoying a growing degree of standardization under the guiding hand of several international organizations. Data covering FDI fund flows and stock estimates measuring financial size and weight are rather meaningless for the assessment of operating results produced, because that is just not what they measure. Income, on the other hand, is perfectly suited for this purpose, because it is a fairly direct measure of business results generated by FDI. In this respect it approaches the informative quality of sales, from which it is derived, and allows definitive conclusions to be drawn about the actual competitiveness at work.

All data appearing in this section stem from IMF publications, which have traced individual country data for decades. Their biggest advantage lies in the fact that they have been converted into the U.S. dollar, thus rendering them directly comparable. In order to get maximum value out of the information available it is necessary to discuss a few basic accounting principles involved in producing it. In the discussion of FDI fund flows and position estimates in Chapter 3, it was pointed out that all information covering that subject need to be approached with extra caution, because it may not have been generated on the basis of fully compatible accounting principles. Important concerns about the validity of the material related to the questions of what is actually covered by the data, and how was it measured. Do all pieces of information provided by national statistical services, seemingly so equal on the surface, really fit together as a homogeneous representation of global FDI? The problem in the equation was the uneven coverage of reinvested funds, as discussed in detail.

The already familiar problem surfaces here again. Countries follow different accounting practices in measuring FDI income, or worse yet, have none at all. From the material surveyed one gets the impression that separate tracing of FDI statistics is often not a high priority item on the list of BOP statisticians. This opinion is substantiated by the often erratic nature of investment details for many countries surveyed, particularly where reinvestments are concerned.

FDI-related income may thus be defined as actual in- and outflows of earnings to investors, exclusive of reinvestments, which are fairly easy to monitor by central banks, because they are all subject to reporting requirements. Or they may include both but, so far, not uniformly for all countries. The real difficulty here stems from the fact that reinvested earnings, a non-flow item, may not be subject to formal central bank monitoring, in which case they can be established only by sheer estimates, or with the voluntary help and support of the firms undertaking the reinvestments. In either case completeness of information is not guaranteed.

Two prime examples for the real situation are furnished by Belgium and Switzerland. In the first case, FDI and portfolio income flows are not separated until 1995, while for Switzerland there is an unbroken record for FDI-related reinvestment credits and debits, which is only a partial piece of information on the subject. There is also an unbroken record for other FDI income credits, but nothing for income debits (outflows) until 1998. This "other FDI income" category is the more important one. It always exceeds reinvestments by a substantial margin and should, because reinvested earnings can only be provided from this "other income." In a related vein Japan did not furnish any reinvestment information, either under the heading of capital or earning flows, until 1996.

All of this, of course, affects the historic evolution of BOP flows as summarized below and explains the often major discrepancies evident in the time series. The gradual progress in uniform information furnished by the various countries, and economically important ones at that, leads to often significant adjustments in the relative position experienced by major economies. How much of the general decline in America's income share, for instance, vis-a-vis Europe and Japan can be ascribed to actual changes in competitive positions, and how much is merely due to the evolving accounting accuracy?

Of the three BOP series mentioned, FDI related income appears to be the most valuable, realistic, and meaningful indicator for the assessment of national competitive positions. Countries are thus very interested in getting accurate readings on the actual flows in and out of the country for a better projection of their potential effect on exchange rates, the economy, the nation's credit rating, political implications, etc. One must assume that great care has been exercised in generating the most accurate data on the subject of actual fund flows. The same cannot be said about reinvestments for the reasons stated above. Historically, many countries could not even monitor reinvestments, simply because their BOP was not designed to keep track of them, since such funds are a matter of internal capital formation covered by a different statistical service. Even now it is obvious, how many BOP statisticians still find it difficult to treat reinvestments as part of the income from FDI operations, a fact that will later be found to be a major factor for confusion.

Keeping track of reinvested funds is definitely a legitimate undertaking. Their inclusion in the income picture is a necessary step for the evaluation of the total return on investments. This is the reason behind the efforts of the IMF and other organizations to get more details on a permanent basis from member countries, information that was so much neglected in the past.

FDI income data from OECD nations presented in the following analysis follow an increasingly uniform collection process, but that does not make them immune to the impact of variable currency valuations aside from all other factors mentioned. The yen, for example, went up from Y227/$1 (1980) to Y94/$1 (1995) and back down to Y140/$1 in the middle of 1998. In a similar fashion, the German mark oscillated between DM 1.81/$1 in 1980 to DM 2.94 in 1985 reversing to around DM 1.70 in late 1998. Valuation swings of the dollar have shaped international data to such extent, that databases expressed in national currencies are hardly recognizable any more, and may actually show totally atypical trends after their conversion.

There are other minor concerns. The OECD, for instance, as the roof organization of the developed nations counting 28 countries among its members at this moment, while the IMF recognizes only 23. When it comes to the conversion of financial data for those nations the use of exchange rates among the agencies also seems to vary, leading to noticeable distortions in the databases. Some of these transient factors become visible only when going from summary tables published by these roof organizations to individual country statistics.

The income streams generated by portfolio and FDI investments, government transfers, etc. are separated neatly in the BOP statistics of OECD nations. In many cases they even provide details for many or all of the following items: dividends, interests, royalties and license fees, management and technical assistance fees, and increasingly also reinvestments, management and technical assistance fees, and increasingly also reinvestments.

Reinvestment information deserves a few explanations, because the values shown may change from negative to positive amounts in the tables, which can lead to difficulties in their interpretation. It is best to start by pointing out, that all BOP statistics are maintained on a double-entry system. That is to say that a credit in one account has to be balanced by a debit entry in another. Concretely spoken, a country leaving part of its earnings from FDI operations in another economy is reinvesting, which adds to its FDI position. Accounting for this fact involves two separate flows entries by the capital exporter: income inflows in the current account (+), and capital outflows in the capital account (−). Let us assume that a U.S. company reinvests $100 million in a country, which is equivalent to a regular capital transfer, because it enhances the U.S. FDI position. It would thus lead to these two entries in the U.S. BOP: a positive entry of $100 million in the U.S. income account (inflow), and a simultaneous, but negative entry of the same amount in the U.S. capital account (outflow).

This is necessary to keep the BOP in balance as the term implies. Conversely, if a foreign company reinvests $100 million in the U.S. the bookkeeping works in the opposite manner: a negative entry in the U.S. income part of the current account, and a positive entry in the capital account, because the reinvestment is again like a capital transfer from abroad. Always look for the way the money flows: an outflow is negative and an inflow is positive. The bewildering aspect for many students is the fact that a capital outflow is a negative entry (−) for the country, but leads to positive growth (+) in its outward FDI position.

The cross-currents of inward and outward fund flows sketched here for a number of the world's leading economies reveals much about a specific country's competitive strength in the international economy. If inflows consistently and substantially exceed a country's outflows, then this country is broadening its earnings base abroad faster than foreigners do their's in the country. Positive flow balances are indicators of a superior competitive strategy at work. Negative balances are indicators to the contrary, the country suffers from a competitive weakness, evidenced by a net drain of liquidity to foreign owners of productive and financial resources, which may cause persistent pressures on its currency.

Unfortunately, there seems to be no smooth correlation between the development of FDI position and related income flows. In the buildup phase of FDI stock it would be unrealistic to expect income streams running at maximum levels. Even at more mature stages of FDI commitment and activity, normal economic cycles run their course, legal changes demand profit policy adjustments, etc., all independent of amounts invested, but definitely leaving their mark on earning flows generated. In addition, once funds leave the economy where they originated, they become exposed to the vagaries of the exchange market with unpredictable outcome.

DEVELOPMENT OF BOP INVESTMENT INCOME FLOWS IN OECD COUNTRIES

Two major forces are driving international income flows. They are portfolio and foreign direct investment accounts, that is capital accounts, held by a country abroad, or conversely by foreigners within a country. The income produced by either party's assets or commercial activities leads to opposite income flows in the BOP, and their net position determines that country's character as either a creditor or a debtor nation.

The master bookkeeping job for all these flows, aside from the maintenance of statistics by the single nation in their own currency, falls into the domain of the IMF. To the great relief of the student of such macro-economic income streams, the organization offers individual as well as aggregate statistics converted into the U.S. dollar for convenience and comparability.

Available time series are displayed in different configurations to crystallize the main points of interest for this study. In order to give an impression of the flow magnitudes involved, the summary tables at this point are maintained in their original division of credit and debit flows. They show total national income flows from investments for three categories: total income from all investments (covering portfolio and FDI income), and separately its FDI subcomponents of reinvested earnings and other FDI income, which excludes reinvestments. Needless to say the numbers involved are impressive, ranging from mere millions into billions, and even trillions, of dollars depending on what is being measured.

GLOBAL INCOME FLOWS FROM ALL INVESTMENTS

Income flows in this section cover payments associated with investment statistics maintained by international organizations, mainly the World Bank and IMF, national governments, and the private sector. They represent a summary view of returns on investments undertaken by direct and portfolio investors which latter includes the public sector. As a matter of curiosity, published data show global debit flows exceeding credit flows for most years and aggregate time periods, where they should more or less balance each other, because a debt payment should result in an income credit of approximately the same amount.

OECD nations monopolize credit flows with around 85–90% of the total, even though with a clearly declining tendency. That is not surprising. Earlier it was seen how the OECD produces 80% of the world's GDP. The group is the source of global wealth, the main provider of capital for investment, and consequently the main beneficiary from global income flows. It is also a nice illustration of the 80/20 rule which says that 80% of the results come from 20% of the resources committed. Generally, this holds true throughout the business and financial world.

On the debit side of the flow ledger OECD's share is slightly lower reaching between 80–85%. Expressed in actual dollars this leads to the conclusion that developing countries, which benefit from major injections of development capital from OECD, carry a disproportionately heavy burden by repaying practically twice as much as they receive from assets of their own. They display the typical symptoms of debtor nations with high and mounting payment deficits. In the 1980s their net income outflows amounted to $290 billion, and tripled to $869 billion in the nineties. (Tables 8.1 & 8.2)

Getting only 11% of international income receipts, but paying close to 20% of all debits, leaves the urgent prospect of default for many of these debtors. A recurring subject at G8 meetings with a growing consensus, that the problem may have to be solved by debt forgiveness on a massive scale. An inevitable event, so it seems, especially in view of the lending practices, and remedial prescriptions for economic restructuring imposed through austerity measures by international lending institutions, which have materially contributed to their insolvency.

Among OECD members, America's share in global flows of income credits shows a general decline between 1980–1992, a very pronounced share erosion in the early 1990s, and a sharp recovery beginning with 1993. But throughout the whole period, there has been a substantial and perennial surplus.

Europe displays only minimal gains in its share of credit and debit flows flowing in both directions. Noteworthy is the fact that the area's income flows reach three times those of the U.S. which is remarkable in view of the practically equal weight of both economic blocs. These figures show the Europeans to be more active lenders and borrowers.

Japan is the real powerhouse when it comes to profiting from international investments. In terms of income earned, it reaches two thirds of U.S. flows in the 1990s, and one-third of the European level. Its share in global credit flows surged from 4% to 18% between 1980 and 1995, but then going into a steep decline which cut its peak shares by about 50%. This is partly explainable with the strong appreciation of the yen since 1992. On the debit side the country followed a similar trend pattern by growing from 4% to 13% in the 1980 to 1995 period and then falling back to between 2–3%, yielding a sustained and very comfortable surplus situation. (Tables 8.1 and 8.2)

OECD debit flows have slightly exceeded credit flows for much of the time, a phenomenon that causes little concern as much of the differences are quite small in comparison to the overall volumes in question. The U.S. trend reflects an overall surplus situation, but one that is feeling a pronounced squeeze in percentage terms. For the 1980s there was a positive credit balance in the amount of $218 billion, which grew to only $237 billion in the nineties. Considering the fact that income statistics are biased in favor of US outward FDI, is this an indication of an actual reversal of the US position in the world economy?

Measured on equal terms, Europe shows a persistent deficit which also seems to accelerate. For the 1980s the shortfall in credit flows amounted to $41 billion, but in the 1990–99 period it jumped to $215 billion. Much of this money actually flows into U.S. coffers, due to the 50% of their outward position being invested here.

Japan is in a unique position with a credit surplus ballooning from $85 billion in the 1980s to $428 billion in the 1990s. But even here are signs of a slowdown. Between 1996 and 1999

Table 8.1.   World Total Investment Income Credits—$billion

Year	Total	U. S. A.	%	Europe	%	Japan	%	OECD	%	Other
1980	279.6	72.6	26.0	147.9	52.8	11.3	4.1	244.4	87.3	35.2
1981	296.8	86.7	29.2	183.4	61.8	16.0	5.4	300.9	NMF	NMF
1982	321.3	86.3	26.9	184.1	57.3	18.5	5.8	309.8	96.6	11.5
1983	316.2	85.3	27.0	154.9	49.1	15.8	5.0	268.9	85.1	47.3
1984	361.8	104.9	29.0	164.2	45.3	19.0	5.2	305.9	84.5	55.9
1985	358.6	93.7	26.1	165.9	46.2	22.3	6.2	297.7	83.0	60.9
1986	409.0	92.1	22.5	190.0	45.5	29.3	7.2	325.0	79.5	84.0
1987	479.2	100.9	21.1	226.3	47.2	49.4	10.3	392.9	82.0	86.3
1988	550.7	129.2	23.4	278.4	50.5	75.1	13.6	504.1	91.4	46.6
1989	680.3	152.7	22.5	348.6	63.3	102.2	15.0	626.6	92.2	53.7
1980-9	4,053.5	1,004.4	24.8	2,043.7	50.4	358.9	8.9	3,576.2	88.2	477.3
1990	823.7	163.5	19.9	465.5	56.6	122.6	14.9	776.8	94.3	46.9
1991	856.0	141.4	16.5	498.0	58.2	140.9	16.5	802.9	93.8	53.1
1992	891.8	131.1	14.7	508.2	57.0	142.3	15.6	798.3	89.5	93.5
1993	891.1	132.7	14.9	504.3	56.6	147.1	16.5	799.0	89.7	92.1
1994	893.5	163.9	18.5	454.9	50.9	154.3	17.2	793.0	88.7	100.5
1995	1,061.3	209.8	19.8	509.1	48.0	191.3	18.0	934.8	88.1	126.5
1996	1,013.7	224.1	22.1	521.0	51.4	112.2	11.1	882.4	87.0	131.3
1997	1,067.5	258.8	24.2	526.8	49.3	111.5	10.4	928.1	86.9	139.4
1998	1,161.9	257.5	22.2	588.5	50.6	100.0	8.6	974.7	83.9	187.2
1999	1,201.0	288.3	24.0	597.4	49.7	91.7	7.6	1,006.9	83.8	194.1
1990-9	9,861.5	1,971.1	20.0	5,173.7	52.5	1,316.1	13.3	8,827.5	89.5	1,034.0
2000	1,386.9	350.7	25.3	680.7	49.1	96.9	7.0	1,163.8	83.9	223.1
2001	1,305.2	281.4	21.0	680.9	52.2	102.9	7.9	1,095.9	84.0	209.3

(Sources: see Table 8.2).

Table 8.2. World Total Investment Income Debits—$billion

Year	Total	U. S.	%	Europe	%	Japan	%	OECD	%	Other
1980	244.5	43.1	17.6	128.3	52.5	10.5	4.3	215.2	88.0	29.3
1981	319.0	54.3	17.0	187.7	58.8	16.8	5.3	302.3	94.7	16.7
1982	357.1	57.1	16.0	195.6	54.8	16.9	4.7	312.7	87.7	44.4
1983	346.5	54.5	15.7	162.7	47.0	12.8	3.7	270.6	78.1	75.9
1984	403.9	74.9	18.5	169.2	41.8	14.8	3.7	306.9	76.0	97.0
1985	407.3	73.9	18.2	175.1	43.0	15.6	3.8	311.1	76.4	96.2
1986	446.6	80.0	17.9	197.6	44.2	19.9	4.5	342.4	76.5	104.2
1987	530.6	92.2	17.4	233.7	44.1	33.1	6.2	409.7	77.2	120.9
1988	600.9	116.7	19.5	288.3	47.9	54.5	9.1	518.9	86.4	82.0
1989	731.6	139.7	19.1	347.2	47.4	79.3	10.8	631.1	86.2	100.5
1980-9	4,388.0	786.4	17.9	2,085.4	47.5	274.2	6.2	3,620.9	82.5	767.1
1990	882.3	141.5	16.1	484.2	54.9	100.2	11.3	793.6	90.0	88.7
1991	915.7	119.9	13.1	524.8	57.3	115.0	12.6	822.9	89.8	92.8
1992	952.3	105.5	11.1	543.9	57.1	105.9	11.1	802.7	84.3	149.6
1993	946.3	105.1	11.7	530.9	56.1	105.8	11.2	787.8	83.3	158.5
1994	955.8	142.8	15.0	474.6	49.7	113.4	11.9	785.8	82.2	170.0
1995	1,131.9	180.6	16.0	533.5	47.2	146.3	12.9	926.0	81.8	205.9
1996	1,087.2	195.5	18.0	546.9	50.3	58.7	5.4	867.8	79.9	219.4
1997	1,122.7	233.7	20.8	535.6	47.7	53.3	4.7	893.2	79.5	229.5
1998	1,244.8	244.8	19.7	601.7	48.3	45.4	3.6	954.5	76.7	290.3
1999	1,276.8	264.4	20.7	612.9	48.0	34.2	2.7	977.9	76.6	298.9
1990-9	10,515.8	1,733.8	16.5	5,389.0	51.2	878.2	8.3	8,612.2	81.9	1,903.6
2000	1,447.7	323.0	22.3	682.2	47.1	36.5	2.5	1,110.7	76.7	337.0
2001	1,376.2	260.9	19.0	703.6	51.1	33.6	2.4	1,059.9	77.0	316.3

Includes reinvested FDI earnings, other FDI income, other investment income, labor and property income. (Sources: IMF, *Balance of Payments Statistics Yearbook*, various issues).

receipts as well as disbursements fell precipitously from the record highs reached in 1996. (Tables 8.1 and 8.2)

GLOBAL INCOME FLOWS FROM FOREIGN DIRECT INVESTMENTS

Narrowing down the discussion to FDI income flows, which is part of the total income stream from overseas investments outlined above, requires the elimination of returns on portfolio and government investments.

In order to convey an impression of each separate income category, data published by the IMF for 1999 (Exhibit 4) highlight the importance of direct investments in the global income constellation. Surprisingly strong are reinvested earnings in relation to remitted earnings, the actual BOP flows. Was it the need to finance old and new projects with retained earnings, the attempt to avoid heavy exchange expenses, or tax considerations that kept these funds abroad?

In line with the customary BOP accounting practices, there is a separate entry for funds flowing to owners of inward (debits) or outward FDI positions (credits). Actually the credit/debit entries are two sides of the same coin, with debits of one country becoming the credits of another, or more likely, more than one other. FDI income comes in the form of dividend and interest payments—the actual BOP flows—on the capital in place and reinvestments. The latter give rise to specific problems, which will be addressed below. For now, it may be helpful to see how the information is collected by the IMF under these two headings:

a. reinvested earnings
b. other direct investment income

All information is maintained on a dollar basis, which is a tremendous advantage for the analysis of the material. Who else but an international organization could produce such time series involving thousands and thousands of individual country data, maintained in their own currency, and translate them year-by-year at proper exchange rates into the U.S. dollar for immediate comparability?

The following analysis of IMF information covers the selective groupings of the original, except for Table 8.11, which summarizes the net income picture for some important countries resulting from the relative in- and outflows of income.

EXHIBIT 4.

Total Investment Income Credit	*$1,386,881**	*100.0%*
FDI total	*375,524*	*27.1*
Reinvested earnings	185,654	13.4
Other	189,870	13.7
International Organizations	35,745	2.5
All Other	975,612	70.3

*2000 data. (millions of dollars). (Source: IMF: BOP Statistics Yearbook 2002, Part 2, Table B-13)

Share fluctuations shown in all tables may be influenced by many diverse factors like exchange rates, improved statistical data collection methods, the gradual inclusion of reinvested profits for European countries and Japan, etc. What becomes visible now, is specific information about several different inputs. Income as credits (inflows) or debits (outflows), by specific country or area, over two decades, and by type of income like actual BOP fund flows (headed: "other direct investment income"), and more sketchy non-flows (headed: "reinvested earnings"). Even though the latter do not actually take place, they still serve a useful function by furnishing a more complete picture of all earnings derived from FDI-related business operations for individual nations captured in Tables 8.3 and 8.4.

FDI INCOME FLOWS

While the OECD holds a fairly constant share in overall global investment income of around 90% in the 1990s. (Table 8.1), it dominates global income flows generated by FDI activities with a much higher share reaching close to 100%. (Table 8.3) On the debit side its FDI flow share is quite steady, but much less prominent, reaching only about 71% through most of the 1990s. (Table 8.4) A sharp drop from the 83% share seen in OECD's aggregate debit flows registered in global income flows. (Table 8.2)

In turn, this translates into the very one-sided flow picture for the developing world, which gets less than 3% of all FDI credit flows, but has to produce 29% of the larger debit flows. In terms of actual dollars this imbalance translates into debit flows six times larger than corresponding credit flows, evidence once more of the tremendous FDI tax on the aspirations of these emerging economies. (Tables 8.3 and 8.4)

Overall, FDI-generated income as part of the total OECD income credit streams amounted to 17% in the 1980s and 21% in the 1990s (Tables 8.1 and 8.3), indicative of a relatively small, but highly dynamic, role for FDI in the development of the global economy.

On the credit side of the total FDI income picture (Table 8.3) the U.S. reigns in first place until 1996, when it ceded that position to Europe. Europe's and Japan's shares are on the upswing here, while that of the U.S. is declining. Not necessarily a sign of untoward competitive factors, but more likely the consequence of less vigorous outward FDI activities on America's part as evidenced by similar share developments in the respective FDI positions discussed in chapter 3. (Table 3.8)

What poses a major problem in this context is the obvious misalignment of income flows and also shares relative to other FDI indicators developed for these countries. Why, for instance, should the U.S. with a reported 25–30% position share in global FDI, receive a much higher 40–50% share in the global income credit stream generated by these very same FDI organizations? In the same vein, how can it be, that Europe with an outward investment position twice that of the U.S. (Table 3.8) generates an income stream only matching that of the U.S. at best? Or the UK, representing 26% of the European outward position, generating almost one-half the European income credit volume. Japan's 12% investment stock reaping only 6% of the respective world income associated with FDI in general can be explained by the late inclusion of reinvestment flows. (Table 8.5 and 8.6)

What conclusions have to be drawn from these apparent inconsistencies? Are some countries' industries run by better business people, may different accounting methods be at work,

Table 8.3.   Total World FDI Income Credits—$billion

Year	Total	U. S. A.	%	Europe	%	Japan	%	OECD	%	Other
1980	45.9	28.6	62.3	13.8	30.1	1.0	2.2	43.4	94.6	2.5
1981	45.0	27.6	61.3	12.6	28.0	1.2	2.7	41.4	92.0	3.6
1982	35.4	19.3	54.5	11.3	31.9	1.4	4.0	32.2	91.0	3.2
1983	47.5	26.9	56.6	15.1	31.8	2.0	4.2	44.0	92.6	3.5
1984	53.6	30.0	56.0	18.1	33.8	2.2	4.1	50.3	93.8	3.3
1985	50.5	28.3	56.0	15.9	31.5	2.5	5.0	46.7	92.5	3.8
1986	59.4	30.8	51.9	21.1	35.5	2.7	4.5	51.3	86.4	8.1
1987	79.2	38.1	48.1	30.8	38.9	3.6	4.5	78.0	98.5	1.2
1988	104.0	52.0	50.0	40.5	38.9	3.7	3.6	102.9	98.9	1.1
1989	115.6	55.3	47.8	48.0	41.5	4.6	4.0	114.1	98.7	1.5
1980-9	636.1	336.9	53.0	227.2	35.7	24.9	3.9	604.3	95.0	31.8
1990	120.7	58.7	48.6	49.2	40.8	4.8	4.0	118.6	98.3	2.1
1991	107.9	52.2	48.4	44.0	40.8	6.4	5.9	105.8	98.1	2.1
1992	118.8	58.0	48.7	46.1	38.7	7.9	6.6	116.0	97.5	2.8
1993	134.7	67.2	49.9	50.6	37.8	8.3	6.1	131.4	97.0	3.5
1994	171.1	77.3	45.2	71.0	41.5	9.7	5.7	167.3	98.2	3.8
1995	206.5	95.3	46.2	87.4	42.3	9.4	4.6	202.0	97.8	4.5
1996	237.2	102.5	43.2	103.5	43.6	14.7	6.2	231.6	97.6	6.0
1997	267.8	115.3	43.1	115.6	43.2	16.1	6.0	262.2	97.9	5.6
1998	275.1	104.0	37.8	126.5	46.0	12.4	4.5	255.2	92.8	19.9
1999	324.0	128.4	39.6	153.0	47.2	6.1	1.9	312.3	96.4	11.7
1990-9	1,963.8	858.9	43.7	846.6	43.1	95.8	4.9	1,907.8	97.1	56.0
2000	375.6	149.7	39.8	172.9	46.0	8.3	2.2	348.7	92.8	26.9
2001	341.7	126.0	36.8	156.1	45.6	16.8	4.9	313.7	91.8	28.0

Table 8.4. Total World FDI Income Debits—$billion

Year	Total	U. S.	%	Europe	%	Japan	%	OECD	%	Other
1980	43.3	6.6	15.2	13.4	30.9	0.4	0.9	20.4	47.1	22.9
1981	46.5	5.8	12.5	11.8	25.4	0.5	1.1	18.1	38.9	28.4
1982	41.2	2.8	6.8	12.6	30.6	0.5	1.2	15.9	38.6	25.3
1983	43.0	5.6	13.0	14.2	33.0	0.7	1.6	20.5	47.7	22.5
1984	46.8	9.2	19,7	15.5	33.1	0.8	1.7	25.5	54.5	21.3
1985	44.8	6.1	13.6	17.6	39.3	0.8	1.8	24.5	54.7	20.3
1986	46.9	7.1	15.1	20.1	42.9	1.3	2.8	28.5	60.8	18.4
1987	61.5	7.4	12.0	28.4	46.2	1.6	2.6	48.0	78.0	13.5
1988	80.9	11.7	14.5	36.5	45.1	2.0	2.5	65.7	81.2	15.2
1989	80.8	6.57	8.0	38.0	47.0	2.3	2.8	60.7	75.1	20.1
1980-9	535.7	68.8	12.8	208.1	38.8	10.9	2.0	327.8	61.2	207.9
1990	77.8	2.8	3.6	39.8	51.2	2.3	3.0	55.5	71.3	22.3
1991	62.5	-3.5	-	34.5	55.2	2.1	3.4	39.4	63.0	23.1
1992	74.7	3.3	0.4	38.4	51.2	1.9	2.5	51.2	68.3	23.5
1993	88.7	7.9	8.9	40.5	46.1	1.8	2.0	61.4	68.5	27.3
1994	117.2	22.2	19.0	45.2	38.6	1.9	1.6	85.2	72.6	32.0
1995	161.9	30.3	18.7	66.7	41.1	2.5	1.5	118.4	73.1	43.5
1996	179.0	33.1	18.5	74.7	41.7	3.6	2.0	131.0	73.2	48.0
1997	203.4	43.0	21.1	76.6	37.7	4.0	2.0	146.6	72.1	56.8
1998	236.0	38.4	16.3	81.9	34.7	2.4	1.0	157.6	66.8	78.4
1999	277.7	53.4	19.2	115.1	41.3	2.3	0.8	192.0	69.1	85.7
1990-9	1,478.9	252.6	17.1	608.5	41.1	24.8	1.7	1,039.2	70.3	439.7
2000	336.8	60.8	18.1	139.8	41.5	2.6	0.8	227.0	67.4	109.8
2001	290.4	23.4	8.1	128.1	44.1	4.1	1.4	185.1	63.7	105.3

Note: includes actual income flows and reinvestments shown separately in the next two tables

Chapter Eight

Table 8.5.   World Reinvested Earnings Credit—$billion

Year	Total	U. S. A.	%	Europe	%	Japan	%	OECD	%	Other
1980	18.1	13.1	72.8	4.8	26.7	N/A		17.9	98.9	.2
1981	15.6	11.4	73.1	3.9	25.0	-		15.3	98.1	.3
1982	4.3	1.1	25.6	2.8	65.1	-		4.1	95.3	.4
1983	19.7	13.5	68.5	5.7	28.9	-		19.2	97.5	.5
1984	28.7	17.2	59.9	11.1	38.3	-		28.3	98.6	.4
1985	22.6	14.1	62.4	8.0	35.4	-		22.1	97.8	.5
1986	19.9	8.4	42.2	10.7	53.8	-		19.1	96.0	.8
1987	36.8	15.9	43.2	18.3	49.7	-		36.8	99.9	.1
1988	35.6	11.6	32.6	23.5	66.0	-		35.4	99.4	.1
1989	40.2	11.9	29.6	25.6	63.7	-		40.0	99.5	.2
1980-9	241.5	118.2	48.9	114.4	47.3	-	-	238.2	98.6	3.4
1990	45.8	20.4	44.5	22.9	50.0	-		45.5	99.3	.3
1991	33.6	17.0	50.6	16.7	49.7	-		33.5	99.7	.1
1992	32.8	22.4	68.3	9.2	28.0	-		32.6	99.4	.2
1993	54.5	36.7	67.3	16.2	29.7	-		54.0	99.1	.5
1994	67.4	31.0	46.0	30.6	45.4	-		66.8	99.1	.6
1995	97.2	53.9	55.5	36.9	38.0	-		96.6	99.4	.6
1996	111.5	54.7	49.1	48.5	43.5	2.3	2.1	110.7	99.3	.8
1997	123.1	58.0	47.1	51.1	41.5	5.2	4.2	122.0	99.1	1.1
1998	98.8	44.2	44.7	39.5	40.0	2.9	2.8	91.9	93.0	6.9
1999	166.5	75.5	45.3	77.1	46.3	.5	.3	158.5	95.2	8.0
1990-9	831.2	413.8	49.8	348.7	42.0	10.9	1.3	812.1	97.7	19.1
2000	185.7	101.2	54.5	67.3	36.2	-1.8	-	174.3	93.9	11.4
2001	145.1	79.7	54.9	38.7	26.1	6.9	4.8	132.4	91.2	12.7

Table 8.6.   World Reinvested Earnings Debits—$billion

Year	Total	U. S.	%	Europe	%	Japan	%	OECD	%	Other
1980	10.9	3.9	35.8	3.7	33.9	N/A		7.6	69.7	3.3
1981	7.8	2.5	32.1	1.8	23.1	-		4.3	55.1	3.5
1982	2.4	-2.2	-	1.7	70.8	-		-.5	-	2.9
1983	5.0	.1	2.0	3.0	60.0	-		3.1	62.0	1.9
1984	10.2	2.9	28.4	5.0	49.0	-		7.9	77.5	2.3
1985	7.0	-1.4	-	5.6	80.0	-		4.2	60.0	2.8
1986	6.3	-.8	-	3.9	61.9	-		3.1	49.2	3.2
1987	16.1	-.8	-	8.6	53.4	-		13.7	85.1	2.5
1988	14.2	.7	4.9	6.1	43.0	-		11.7	82.4	2.5
1989	11.6	-8.7	-	11.8	101.7	-		8.1	69.8	3.5
1980-9	91.5	-5.2	-	51.2	56.0	-		63.2	69.1	28.4
1990	-5.1	-14.7	288.2	6.7	-	-		-7.9	133.9	2.8
1991	-12.4	-19.5	157.3	5.6	-	-		-16.1	129.8	3.7
1992	- 5.2	-10.5	394.2	2.4	-	-		-9.3	178.8	4.1
1993	7.1	-7.1	-	6.4	90.1	-		2.7	38.0	4.4
1994	24.0	4.9	20.4	4.6	19.2	-		16.8	70.0	7.2
1995	38.4	8.4	21.9	12.1	31.5	-		30.8	80.2	7.6
1996	43.5	8.5	19.5	18.4	42.2	.7	1.6	36.0	82.8	7.5
1997	65.1	15.0	23.0	20.0	30.7	.4	0.6	45.6	70.0	19.5
1998	61.2	2.8	4.6	9.3	15.2	-.2	-	34.3	55.0	26.9
1999	83.8	4.1	4.9	40.4	48.2	-1.1	-	52.4	62.5	31.4
1990-9	300.4	13.6	4.5	125.9	41.9	-.2	-	185.3	61.7	115.1
2000	119.7	6.5	5.4	51.5	43.0	-.1	-	70.8	59.1	48.9
2001	62.3	-19.7	-	25.2	40.4	1.5	2.4	25.1	40.3	37.2

(Sources: IMF: *Balance of Payments Statistics Yearbook, Part 2*, Tables C-6, C-9, B-14, various issues.).

or superior profit strategies concerning the income distribution between domestic and international operations via transfer pricing, exchange rate fluctuations, creative accounting, or any other factors?

In order to approach an obvious problem in a constructive fashion, a closer look needs to be taken at the two components of FDI income separately: the flows actually taking place and the part dealing with reinvested earnings mentioned above. This step yields an immediate improvement in the percentage configuration found for the "other FDI income," the actual fund flows registered in national BOPs. The distribution of these data more closely matches, as should be expected, the FDI position distribution established in Table 3.8. America now accounts for a lower 39% income share in the nineties, much closer to its position share of 25–30%. Europe's 38% income share for the period 1990–99 is now equal to that of the U.S. for the same period, even though not double as the ratio for the FDI stock distribution suggests, and Japan's ratios are also closer to each other as they should. (Table 8.7)

The relatively lower income shares, compared to position data, for Europe and Japan can be attributed to a general decline of the dollar in the 1990/97 period, which inflates foreign incomes in terms of dollars, and deflates income for countries with stronger currencies. A particular case in point is FDI income transmitted from the U.S., which must be shrinking for these nations after translation into their own currencies. A very reassuring finding, inasmuch as it builds confidence in the reliability of FDI measuring methods employed in the two related areas of position and income. At the same time, this is a reminder of previous observations that investment positions and income flows do not necessarily have to go in tandem. Both are impacted by totally independent factors.

The absence of similar, if only fairly close correlations for reinvestment income and investment stock, and more cannot be expected here, leaves the time series developed for reinvestments under a big question mark. Closer inspection of the data reveals that the perplexing distortions alluded to above, definitely originate here. To quote the American example again, it does not make much sense for the U.S. to account for 50% of global reinvestment volume (Table 8.5), when they account for only 27% of the global FDI stock. This is only possible, of course, if some countries do not reinvest their foreign earnings at all.

Not a very likely situation, as it would be quite uneconomical considering the exchange cost involved in two capital transfers, one for the repatriation of the earnings and the other for exporting investment funds. For that reason alone it would make little sense for Europe with an investment base double that of the U.S., to reinvest only half of their overseas earnings. The whole scenario leaves little or no doubt that the accounting process in this area is in need of improvement.

Here is not the place to give technical advice on what needs to be done, but the subject has very practical and intriguing implications. Assuming for the moment, that American reinvestments are portrayed correctly, and that other investors follow similar reinvestment policies and practices, even though they are not reflected in published documents, global reinvestments should be three to four times their presently documented level, in accordance with all other ratios uncovered earlier. If this hypothesis can be proven to be correct, it would have two direct and important consequences. For one, it would bolster income from FDI by no less than 50% in absolute dollar terms, and its share of total global income, after the necessary adjustments, would certainly be higher than the 27% shown in Exhibit 4.

Table 8.7.   World Other Foreign Direct Investment Income Credits—$billion

Year	Total	U. S. A.	%	Europe	%	Japan	%	OECD	%	Other
1980	27.8	15.5	55.8	9.0	32.4	1.0	3.6	25.5	91.7	2.3
1981	29.4	16.2	55.1	8.7	29.6	1.2	4.1	26.1	88.8	3.3
1982	31.1	18.2	58.5	8.5	27.3	1.4	4.5	28.1	90.4	3.0
1983	27.8	13.4	48.2	9.4	33.8	2.0	7.2	24.8	89.2	3.0
1984	24.9	12.8	51.4	7.0	28.1	2.2	8.8	22.0	88.4	2.9
1985	27.9	14.2	50.1	7.9	28.3	2.5	9.0	24.6	88.2	3.3
1986	39.5	22.4	56.7	10.4	26.3	2.7	6.8	32.2	81.5	7.3
1987	42.4	22.2	52.4	12.5	29.5	3.6	8.5	41.2	97.2	1.2
1988	68.4	40.4	59.1	17.0	24.9	3.7	5.4	67.5	98.7	.8
1989	75.4	43.4	57.6	22.4	29.7	4.6	6.1	74.1	98.3	1.3
1980-9	395.0	218.7	55.3	112.8	28.6	24.9	6.3	366.1	92.7	28.4
1990	74.9	38.3	51.1	26.6	35.1	4.8	6.4	73.1	97.6	1.8
1991	74.3	35.2	47.4	26.7	36.7	6.4	8.6	72.3	97.3	2.0
1992	86.0	35.6	41.4	36.9	42.6	7.9	9.2	83.4	97.0	2.6
1993	80.2	30.5	38.0	34.4	42.5	8.3	10.3	77.4	96.3	2.8
1994	103.7	46.3	44.5	40.4	38.5	9.7	9.3	100.5	97.1	3.2
1995	109.3	41.4	37.9	50.5	46.2	9.4	8.6	105.4	96.4	3.9
1996	125.7	47.8	38.0	55.0	43.8	12.4	9.9	120.9	96.2	4.8
1997	144.7	57.3	39.6	64.5	44.6	10.9	7.5	140.2	96.9	4.5
1998	176.3	59.8	33.9	87.0	49.3	9.5	5.4	163.3	92.6	13.0
1999	157.5	52.9	33.6	75.9	48.2	5.6	3.6	142.7	90.6	14.8
1990-9	1,132.6	445.1	39.3	497.9	43.9	79.3	7.0	1,095.7	95.3	53.4
2000	189.9	48.5	25.5	105.6	55.6	10.1	5.3	174.4	91.8	15.5
2001	196.6	46.3	23.6	117.4	59.7	9.9	5.0	181.3	92.2	15.3

*exclude reinvestment credits.

Thoughts of this nature may actually not be totally out of place. The U.S. reinvested 48% of her FDI earnings in the nineties, Europeans only 39%, and Japan an even smaller 22% for four years shown. Are these real relationships, or are accounting differences at work here? (Tables 8.3 and 8.5)

FDI INCOME'S ROLE IN TOTAL BOP INCOME FLOWS

FDI-related income is an integral part of total income received from global investments, and with significant differences for countries. It has to do with a country's overall command over financial, technical, and manpower resources, domestic investment opportunities against those abroad, differences in the historic growth of industrial structures and, as such, the competitiveness of nations.

An interesting picture emerges from the comparison of the investment stock, and the FDI investment income flows for selected nations. It allows the calculation of a return on funds invested and, by adding the total investment income information, the role of FDI in the country's generation of income streams from overseas investments. (Table 8.9)

As far as the return on the FDI position is concerned, the marked differences in levels from 4–14%, with a global average of 7.7%, raise questions similar to those posed before on the validity of the information provided by the data in general. Any return on FDI stocks of less than 10%, even after taxes as given here, would seem unacceptable from a business point of view. Putting those FDI funds into a bank would bring better returns with a lot less risk. In the case of Belgium-Luxembourg the rate is that low, because reinvestment information is not furnished. If included, it would certainly raise the rate. But the returns, inclusive of reinvestments, for France, Germany and Japan also seem unduly low.

Turning to the role of FDI income in the countries' overall investment income is enlightening for two reasons. One is the high rates for the U.S., the Netherlands and the UK, which may be due to their prominence in the petroleum trade. The other point is the enormous income amounts flowing from total foreign investments in terms of dollars for the Netherlands in relation to their direct neighbors France and Germany with incomparably larger populations and economies. The same could be said about the UK which shows FDI income to be 3.5 times larger than that of France and Germany, both of which are larger measured in terms of national GDP.

In a little different vein, Table 8.10 offers a rank list for countries leading with high FDI-related income flows in absolute terms. The first striking impression of those credit and debit data, is their often remarkably wide disparity. As we are dealing with leading industrial nations, the levels involved would have to be high, and not only for inflows, but also for outflows. After all, these are the economies that have the capacity to invest large amounts abroad and, at the same time, are very attractive targets for large foreign investments in their industries.

One would assume, that a country's rank order be determined by the relative size of its economy against all others, like a big national economy, defined in the traditional sense, automatically reaching a high position in the income credit streams produced. But the Table 8.10 proves otherwise. Surprising is the performance of such countries as Belgium/Luxembourg, Sweden, Switzerland, and Canada in comparison to much larger economies like Germany and France. Even Japan's position again appears to be relatively modest considering its overall economic weight in the world community.

Table 8.8.   World Other Foreign Direct Investment Income Debits—$billion

Year	Total	U. S. A.	%	Europe	%	Japan	%	OECD	%	Other
1980	32.4	2.7	8.3	9.7	29.9	.4	1.2	12.8	39.5	19.6
1981	38.7	3.3	8.5	10.0	25.8	.5	1.3	13.8	35.7	24.9
1982	38.8	5.0	12.9	10.9	28.1	.5	1.3	16.4	42.3	22.4
1983	38.0	5.5	14.5	11.2	29.5	.7	1.8	17.4	45.8	20.6
1984	36.6	6.3	17.2	10.5	28.7	.8	2.2	17.6	48.1	19.0
1985	37.8	7.5	19.8	12.0	31.7	.8	2.1	20.3	53.7	17.5
1986	40.6	7.9	19.5	16.2	39.9	1.3	3.2	25.4	62.6	15.2
1987	45.4	8.2	18.1	19.8	43.6	1.6	3.5	34.3	75.6	11.1
1988	66.7	11.0	16.5	30.4	45.6	2.0	3.0	54.0	81.0	12.7
1989	69.2	15.2	22.0	26.2	37.9	2.3	3.3	52.6	76.0	16.6
1980-9	444.2	72.6	16.3	156.9	35.3	10.9	2.5	264.6	59.6	179.6
1990	82.9	17.5	21.1	31.1	39.9	2.3	2.8	63.4	76.5	19.5
1991	74.9	16.0	21.4	26.0	38.6	2.1	2.8	55.5	74.1	19.4
1992	79.9	13.8	17.3	36.0	45.1	1.9	2.4	60.5	75.7	19.4
1993	81.6	15.0	18.4	34.1	41.8	1.8	2.2	58.7	72.0	22.9
1994	93.2	17.3	18.6	40.6	43.6	1.9	2.0	68.4	73.4	24.8
1995	123.5	21.9	17.7	54.6	44.2	2.5	1.9	87.6	70.9	35.9
1996	135.5	24.6	18.2	56.3	41.5	2.9	2.0	95.0	70.1	40.5
1997	138.3	28.0	20.2	56.6	40.9	3.6	2.5	101.0	73.0	37.3
1998	174.8	35.6	20.4	72.6	41.5	2.6	1.5	123.3	70.5	51.5
1999	193.9	49.3	25.4	74.7	38.5	3.4	1.8	140.5	72.5	53.4
1990-9	1,178.5	239.0	20.3	482.6	40.9	25.0	2.1	853.9	72.4	324.6
2000	217.1	54.3	25.0	88.3	40.7	2.7	1.2	156.2	71.9	60.9
2001	228.1	43.1	18.9	102.9	45.1	2.6	1.1	160.0	70.2	68.1

Excludes reinvestment debits (Sources: IMF: *Balance of Payments Statistics Yearbook, Part 2*, Tables C-7, C-10, B-15 various issues.)

Table 8.9.   FDI Income Flows Benchmark Comparisons by Country*—$million

Country	FDI Stock	FDI Income	% Return	All Investment Income	FDI Income %**
USA	1,130,789	128,460	11.4	288,340	44.5
France	279,847	14,832	5.3	56,326	26.3
Germany	394,220	14,732	3.7	82,321	17.9
Netherlands	257,130	16,809	6.5	42,871	39.2
Sweden	101,701	11,221	11.0	19,602	57.2
Switzerland	192,494	23,254	12.1	49,030	47.6
UK	651,002	53,434	8.2	161,544	33.1
Japan	248,786	6,107	2.4	91,699	6.7
WORLD	3,541,382	323,993	7.7	1,201,039	27.0

*1999 data. **see Table 8.12 for more details. (Sources: OECD, *International Direct Investments Statistics Yearbook*, 2001. IMF, *Balance of Payments Statistics Yearbook*, 2002).

Both the credit and debit information shown may be a fair approximation of the real picture. On the credit side, the countries shown represent 96% of all fund flows recorded by the IMF for 1999. A slightly larger number of countries on the debit side, however, account for only 86% of relevant total fund flows. This makes sense, because of the large flows from developing nations in this account. But, the important question remains, to what degree the database used here is influenced by the sporadic inclusion of reinvestments, which are definitely not treated uniformly in all cases.

THE NET FLOW EFFECT OF FDI INCOME BY COUNTRY

IMF statistics permit other important conclusions to be drawn about the effects of FDI income flows for the economies of individual nations. For instance, by netting the income in- and out-flows for major countries one can pinpoint those that maintain steady positive or negative balances in their accounts, while others oscillate between both.

The information on balances represents an important indicator for two separate aspects of national economies: first, it is a reliable measure of a nation's industrial competitiveness in the global market and, second, it reveals the extent of "foreign" ownership within a national economy. Current surpluses mark a nation's industry as a respectable global competitor that actively and successfully pursues foreign market opportunities more vigorously than outsiders do within the country. They are, at the same time, the real winners as far as global market shares

Table 8.10. FDI Income Flows by Major OECD Country*—$million

	Rank	1990	%	Rank	1995	%	Rank	1999	%
					CREDIT FLOWS				
Total OECD		$114,163	100		$201,929	100		$301,155	100
U.S.A.	1	58,740	51	1	95,280	43	2	128,460	43
Europe	2	50,094	44	2	87,338	43	1	153,030	51
UK	3	28,060	25	3	39,059	19	3	53,434	18
Netherlands	4	6,372	6	4	13,454	7	5	16,809	6
Germany	5	5,770	5	6	9,220	5	7	14,732	5
Sweden	7	3,690	3	8	7,244	4	8	11,221	4
Switzerland	8	2,829	2	9	5,590	3	4	23,254	8
France	9	2,270	2	10	2,228	1	6	15,914	5
Japan	-	N/A	-	5	9,401	5	10	6,107	2
Canada	6	3,890	3	7	7,321	4	9	10,066	3

*includes reinvestments where available

are concerned, as well as the drivers of globalization. Current deficits, of course, say exactly the opposite.

The amounts involved can be impressive. Especially for smaller economies, whose national wealth depends to a large degree on economic activities in foreign markets unlike for larger economies. From the data it seems that smaller countries can be major beneficiaries of FDI. If they have developed their competitive skills well, they benefit most from their use in outside markets, while the economic size of their home market acts as a protective barrier against serious outside competition within. Sweden and Switzerland may be cited as two prime examples for this argument.

Looking at net figures reveals some interesting facts that were not immediately visible from a glance at national income in- and outflows separately. It is somewhat of a shock to find, for instance, that Europe with a larger FDI outward position than the U.S. derives a smaller net income. Even more perplexing is the fact that the U.S. derives a net income from their FDI activities that is larger than that for the rest of the world put together. (Table 8.11) Probing into the data more deeply makes this scenario appear reasonable. It has to do with U.S. FDI, which grew longer and stronger relative to the rest of the world for historic reasons, and whose position was only gradually counterbalanced by the growth of inward FDI in the U.S. as discussed before.

The U.S. situation may actually also be overstated, as has been said previously. According to official records, quite a few American parent companies and their subsidiaries included in U.S. outward FDI statistics are in reality foreign controlled as per this quote cited before:

"although MOFA'S and U.S. parents are under the control of one or more U.S. parents, in some cases the U.S. parent is, in turn, under the control of a foreign parent company; in 1997, U.S. par-

Table 8.11. Net FDI Income Flows by Major OECD Country*—$billion

	DEBIT FLOWS								
Total OECD		$58,504	100		$118,397	100		$192,895	100
U.S.A.	8	2,870	5	2	30,330	26	2	53,450	28
Europe	1	42,717	73	1	82,985	70	1	115,110	60
UK	2	12,600	22	3	21,818	18	3	27,449	14
Netherlands	3	7,091	12	8	6,084	5	6	10,890	6
Germany	4	6,280	11	7	6,345	5	9	8,110	4
Ireland	7	4,350	7	5	8,334	7	4	22,834	12
Finland	9	2,770	5	14	1,022	1	13	2,404	1
France	10	2,720	5	11	2,905	2	12	5,773	3
Spain	11	2,455	4	15	933	1	15	469	-
Switzerland	13	1,286	2	16	698	1	8	8,279	4
Norway	14	798	1	12	2,072	2	7	10,435	5
Sweden	15	473	1	9	4,315	4	11	7,553	4
Japan	-	N/A		12	2,544	2	14	2,321	1
Canada	5	5,730	10	4	10,283	9	5	13,971	7
Mexico	12	2,304	4	10	4,259	4	13	4,213	2
Australia	6	4,488	8	6	8,234	7	10	7,718	4

*+indicates credits, −indicates debits. Note: includes reinvestments

ents that were ultimately controlled by foreign parents accounted for 11 percent of all U.S. parents and for 8 percent of their gross product." (SOCB, July 1999, p. 11)

Of course, this statement applies to all the other facets of these companies, such as employment, sales, assets, earnings, etc. and, finally, the income streams recorded for these enterprises in the U.S. BOP. Applying the strict principle of national capital control over FDI activities, as advocated here, could thus lead to a 8–10% lower estimate to reflect the true American position in the global context.

The important factor to see here is that the balance between inward and outward FDI income flows for individual countries, or areas of the world, does not necessarily and automatically leave countries with an income surplus.

Small countries, in particular, may experience two exactly opposite income consequences from FDI. Those with the right combination of skilled, low-cost labor, under-employment, tax incentives, access and proximity to larger market potentials, stable governments and exchange rates, etc., but no important overseas investments, may derive huge economic benefits from attracting inward FDI. The flip side of the coin is that foreign investors can overwhelm existing local industries, or prevent them from developing and spawning important FDI organizations of their own in the world market. These economies are dependent on the continued presence and interest of foreign business organizations. Prime examples are Ireland, Belgium-Luxembourg, Spain, Australia, Mexico, etc. They are prime candidates for protracted income deficits.

Other small nations may see a totally different effect. If they are highly developed, have special skills, full employment, and highly advanced social systems, plus sizable direct investments abroad, their market size may protect them from significant inroads by foreigners. They can take tremendous advantage of their talents in foreign economies via FDI operations, but need not worry about undue dependence on foreign business powers at home. Case in point is Switzerland.

The situations described offer two opposite and very different perspectives. Foreign direct investments are wonderful for the local economy, employment, personal income, and tax collections, where internal development potential lies dormant, or cannot be adequately tackled with internal resources. But this comes at the price of often gravely negative consequences for the country's BOP, perhaps its sovereignty. Ireland with a population of only 3.7 million people holds the distinctive first place among all OECD nations with a net disbursement of $20 billion to foreign capital owners alone in 1999, an amount estimated at 15% of the national GDP. It is an enormous feat for such small economy. The U.S., by comparison, with a population of around 270 million only disburses an amount roughly three times the Irish volume to the owners of direct investments in America. (Table 8.4)

Switzerland, on the other hand, as the prime example for the highly developed and competitive small economy, is blessed by perennial income surpluses. Here, the combination of economic size and competitive skills guarantees economic and political independence and growing prosperity.

Table 8.11 offers a convenient way to characterize national economies as creditor (net inflow) or debtor nations (net outflow) with respect to their FDI situations. OECD as a whole is easily established as a creditor organization, with permanently positive inflows. The same applies to the U.S., Europe, and Japan. But there is a surprising number of countries that show equally permanent net outflows, indicating a FDI deficit or much higher inward FDI positions than outward commitments.

Ireland has been mentioned, but the list includes also Canada, Mexico, Belgium, Spain, Norway, Australia, and New Zealand. What they have in common, is the lack of critical economic mass to grow their own industries, meaning it is more convenient and economical to let foreign capital and technology develop whatever resources the country offers. Norway is a typical example. Development of its oil resources could not have been accomplished efficiently through local resources.

Similarly, the primary sector mixed with industrial projects offered strong incentives for inward FDI in Australia, Canada, Ireland, Spain, and New Zealand. The same, however, cannot be said for Mexico, which reserves its oil industry for Mexican business interests, but invites foreign capital to develop other industries.

FDI, of course, is only one form of investment that leads to national income streams, positive or negative. It is also not necessarily the largest income factor appearing in the BOP of all nations, as proven by previous information, which is abstracted in Table 8.12.

OECD as a whole derived 16% of its total income credits from direct investments in the 1980s and 19% in the nineties. The U.S. displays much higher shares with 34% and 44% of overall investment incomes in the two decades. Europe reached 11% and 14%, while Japan shows an atypically low yet steady 6–7%, mainly because the country did not include reinvestments until 1996.

As an exception, the UK (24%) and the Netherlands (33%) break away from the European averages, with ratios closer to the U.S. situation. Finding reasonable explanations for the enormous differences is more difficult than making the observation of their existence. One contributing factor could be seen in the heavy engagement of these countries in the energy sector. However, France with its own globe-spanning oil industry does not support this theory, with its FDI income reaching only 9% of total income.

One irrefutable fact is brought home by the above collection of BOP flows of all nations listed. FDI plays a larger and larger role for the generation of national income from foreign business activities, supporting the hypothesis advanced earlier that FDI has been the real motor of economic globalization so far. Expressed differently, the private sector served as the dynamic executor of global development and integration policies spawned by governments and international organizations.

Table 8.12. FDI Income as % of Total Investment Income Credits by Major OECD Country*

	1990	1991	1992	1993	1994	1995	1996	1997	1998	1999
OECD	15.3	13.2	14.5	16.6	21.2	26.1	23.5	25.4	24.1	26.4
U.S.A	35.8	36.9	44.3	51.1	47.3	45.5	46.2	45.1	41.5	43.4
Canada	25.8	22.8	28.7	31.1	43.5	38.8	41.8	44.9	43.7	47.3
Europe	10.6	8.8	9.1	10.2	14.1	17.8	20.2	22.3	22.0	23.5
Belg/Lux.	-	-	-	-	-	9.0	8.0	7.6	6.3	7.0
France	4.1	3.7	4.6	4.5	16.1	5.2	17.1	19.8	17.8	14.3
Germany	8.8	7.6	6.1	5.0	8.3	11.5	18.5	19.1	20.0	16.9
Ireland	12.0	9.2	9.1	9.0	13.9	18.7	14.7	14.4	14.4	13.9
Italy	1.4	2.5	1.7	1.1	4.2	4.6	2.7	3.0	3.5	5.4
Netherlands	24.3	25.4	27.3	28.7	36.3	41.2	39.6	44.5	32.7	36.3
Spain	-	0.3	0.2	0.8	0.4	0.7	0.3	0.3	0.9	0.8
Sweden	38.1	27.0	13.7	22.7	47.1	48.9	42.9	49.1	54.9	57.2
UK	17.7	15.0	20.5	24.2	28.8	27.7	30.4	30.2	29.5	31.2
EU - 15	10.8	8.7	9.1	9.6	15.2	17.4	19.7	21.9	20.6	22.3
Norway	2.2	4.7	-13.7	-1.9	16.3	20.7	26.2	23.0	19.7	27.8
Switzerland	9.9	8.7	8.3	21.1	20.9	18.4	24.8	28.1	39.8	46.3
Japan	3.9	4.5	5.5	5.6	6.3	4.9	6.5	7.2	5.9	3.2
Australia	23.5	16.7	33.5	48.3	59.4	57.2	63.4	62.5	59.0	62.9
New Zealand	42.4	NMF	NMF	40.4	35.4	65.1	N/A	N/A	0.9	NMF

*Note: includes reinvestments

Chapter Nine

FDI and Globalization

INTRODUCTION

Given the level of attention accorded globalization, one would expect to find detailed documentation on its scope, development, and actual impact on the global economy. But, the exact opposite is true. Pertinent information on the subject is very fragmented, deals mainly with only partial aspects like capital and income flows, but not sales, value added, employment data, foreign trade, etc., with the exception of, literally, less than a handful of countries. This is amazing for several reasons. First of all, economic globalization as characterized by FDI is financed predominantly by developed nations, which are also the main recipients of FDI investments, technology transfers, competitive managerial skills, etc. What they have in common are well developed statistical services in general, but just not for the coverage of FDI activities. The whole subject complex seems to suffer from the proverbial out-of-sight out-of-mind syndrome. After all, the prevailing notion is still that inward FDI is an integral part of the domestic economy, with adequate statistical coverage, and outward FDI is not of any practical statistical concern of the exporting nation except for the capital streams it produces.

Such reasoning produces extensive financial statistics on flows of FDI capital, income, and maybe even stocks in relative abundance from international organizations or countries themselves, all of which have one major drawback. They only measure investments, a declaration of economic intent, but not their operational results, which could be related to national production and commercial processes, a major disconnect for businesspeople and researchers alike. Without specific information on just this point it is very difficult, to accurately judge the actual impact of FDI activities on the globalization of national economies plus the world economy itself

Ideally, there should be solid annual data for overseas business operations by investor and host countries like sales, number of employees, employee compensation, output of gross product, its key component the annual operating income, foreign trade volumes, etc. All of them relate to commercial activities that would not only show the dimensions of GlobalFDI.com, but could be tied conveniently to similar macro-economic output information available in sufficient measure for OECD economies.

Actually, reliance on financial data alone as provided by national and international organizations is apt to produce distorted impressions about FDI's role in the global economy. Investment trends cannot automatically be equated with economic performance, or even advances in competitive market position by these enterprises as is so often and automatically assumed.

In reality, direct investments are subject to regular business cycles, competitive strategies, legal and political developments, and the law of diminishing returns, that is to say it takes more and more capital to produce the same volume of sales, output of gross product, and related profits.

Also, FDI turns out to be only one of several important globalization forces, a multi-trillion commercial enterprise that is heavily influenced by political, cultural, and other factors, which do not leave all that much room for independent action. It is hard to tell, for instance, whether FDI is strictly an opportunistic participant in international growth and development, or a true and clear-cut contributor to it. Both possibilities are supported by previous discussions. On one side it has more of a displacement effect on already existing production capacity, without necessarily a net additive economic effect, as evidenced by the fact that 80% of all FDI funds are invested in other developed areas. On the other, only the remaining 20% of FDI funds flowing into developing nations may be considered to be a true development motor, as there is not much in the way of productive capacity that might be displaced.

The absence of standardized, direct, and coherent statistical information on FDI, however, does not mean that everything is lost. Nobody has ever seen a black hole, but astronomers still can describe this natural phenomenon, making it visible to the human mind. Similarly, the understanding of macro-economic physiology allows the construction of a global FDI outline by analogy with a comfortable degree of acceptability. Proceeding from known facts and using them as building blocks, it is possible to reconstruct the rest of the building so it becomes visible in, at least, a rough outline.

Three avenues offer themselves for the undertaking. Capital flows and stock building are two leading financial indicators of strategic intent for FDI protagonists, the bricks and mortar aspect so to speak. The third input, aggregate income flows from FDI activities presented in Chapter 8, provide an equally unbroken record, and strong evidence of strategic effect. All are widely available BOP components, which can be used in the reconstruction of the missing links. The basic hypothesis is, of course, that the economies of the developed world, on which the discussion has centered so far, employ a fairly standard pattern of economic behavior, can adapt quickly to competitive changes, and enjoy unrestricted access to the latest technology. Drawing on America's FDI experience becomes invaluable for the reconstruction job in our context. After all, the U.S. engagement in global FDI exceeds that of any other nation, carries a substantial weight from all evidence published, and is well documented. Yet, the construction of a global FDI model is strictly hypothetical, and rests on a number of additional and very specific assumptions:

a. All FDI enterprises use the combination of land, labor, capital, management, and technology as productive inputs in fairly similar ratios for a given industry, or industrial aggregates.
b. FDI searches for profit opportunities at least equal, if not superior, to those found in the home country.
c. Direct investors use the latest and most powerful combination of production factors in pursuing overseas business opportunities.
d. FDI technology and management skills are superior to those of local competition not engaging in FDI, but fairly equal to those of their FDI competitors. At today's diffusion rates the latest technology offers only temporary advantages.

e. Taken as a whole global FDI operates under fairly equal input/output ratios. Thus, income depends on amounts of capital invested, number of people employed, sales produced, gross product generated, etc

f. These ratios are completely measurable for American outward FDI over a period of decades, and may be used as a reference for FDI members from other nations. Partial pieces of such information exist for other nations, notably France and Germany, and may be used in a similar manner as cross-references.

g. Statistics available from national or supranational organizations are now collected and made available in a fairly standardized fashion, which makes them comparable within acceptable limits. This applies more to their expression in national currencies than after their translation into dollars as commonly practiced. It adds to the transparency of global dimensions, yet inevitable leads to trend distortions from exchange rate fluctuations, which have to be expected and accepted.

i. The aggregate picture of global FDI emanating from this reconstruction effort has an acceptable margin of error. While it cannot be 100% accurate, it has a strong probability of being representative.

I. U.S. FDI AS THE CORNERSTONE OF GLOBAL FDI

A. U.S. Outward FDI

Having spelled out major caveats, a first attempt can be made at estimating the size and economic weight of global FDI by anchoring such exercise on the well-documented role of American FDI, both inward and outward.

According to UNCTAD, America's share in global outward FDI may be estimated at about 25%, if measured in terms of position or stock accumulated by the late nineties. (Table 3.3) Another benchmark is set by the flows of FDI income, where the U.S. seems to hold a share in the vicinity of 35%, if measured in terms of actual BOP flows, exclusive of reinvested earnings, for the same period. (Table 8.7)

The income figure does not match up well with the position level. But it is technically enhanced by two factors, which may not exist for other nations. A recent WTO decision (February 23, 2000), against the tax-sheltered accumulation of profits from American Foreign Sales Corporations (FSCs) in tax havens located in American overseas territories divulges, how existing tax American laws may lead to artificially high income levels overseas. The income thus sheltered was estimated to reach around $5 billion a year or about 12% of the official income flows. The FSCs may not be the only tax advantage offered American businesses engaged in international commerce or FDI, which makes it a reasonable assumption that income without those incentives would be closer to 28% than 35% of global income figures related to U.S. FDI. Either way, these U.S. shares are significant as a sampling size, reliably measured, and thus helpful in establishing a reasonably firm base for estimating the economic weight of global FDI along two macro-economic standards in wide use.

The second factor bearing on these statistics stems from the accounting practices guiding the valuation of international transactions in the American BOP. To quote:

"For U.S. direct investment abroad, the following major items appear in the U.S. international transactions accounts: direct investment capital outflows, direct investment income, direct investment royalties and license fees, and other direct investment services.

Two adjustments are made to the data before they are entered into the U.S. international accounts and the national income and product accounts, but these adjustments are made only at the global level; the data required to make them for the countries and industries are not available. The data from the benchmark survey are adjusted from a fiscal year basis to a calendar year basis.

In addition, income and capital outflows are adjusted to ensure that depreciation charges reflect current-period prices and to more closely align income earned in a given period with charges against income in the same period, as required by economic accounting principles.

The adjustment is accomplished in a three-step process. First, a capital consumption adjustment is made to convert depreciation charges from a historical-cost basis to a current- or replacement-cost basis. Second, earnings are raised by the amount of the charges for depletion of natural resources, because these charges are not treated as production costs in the national income and product accounts. Third, expenses for mineral exploration and development are reallocated across periods to ensure that they are written off over their economic lives rather than all at once." (1994 Benchmark Survey, p. M-20).

It is difficult to assess the impact of two different accounting practices on the discussion here. But it could be a partial explanation of the much higher 35% U.S. share in FDI income flows reported by the IMF, and an even more incredible 54% reinvestment share, than would be expected from its 25% share in the global FDI stock position.

Assuming America's role in global FDI to be realistically portrayed by this 25% share in the global FDI stock position, it puts projected global FDI dimensions at 35.6 million people employed with an annual GDP of around $2.6 trillion in 1999. Such numbers suggest global FDI to be roughly equivalent to one fourth each of the industrial economies of the U.S. and Western Europe, equal to that of Germany, or half the Japanese economy. In other words, FDI is probably the fourth largest economy in the world after the U.S., Japan, and Germany.

This projection was derived from 1999 data for U.S. total nonbank affiliate employment of 8.9 million people worldwide, producing an estimated GDP of $660 billion based on adjusted Mofa GDP figures of $561 billion for that year, and an assumed 85% Mofa share in overall U.S. FDI based on Exhibit 5.

The estimate implies a 1999 gross product output of $73,000 per employee for our hypothetical FDI economy. A figure that is open to a quick cross-validation from different angles. The 1999 GP/Mofa employee for U.S. outward FDI reached $75,100, practically identical to

EXHIBIT 5.

	Mofa % Share of Total U.S. FDI			
	1982	*1989*	*1994*	*1999*
Assets	44	54	63	87
Sales	71	75	79	85
Employees	74	76	79	84
Investment position	88	89	90	86
Income	88	89	90	81

(Sources: Benchmark Survey 1982, p. 27; ibid., 1989, p. M-25; ibid., 1994, p. M-27. SOCB, March 2002, pp. 24–54).

the per capita output of U.S. inward affiliates with $76,300 documented for that same year. (Table 5.1) The differences in output levels of GP can be attributed to variances in the weight carried by specific national factors involved in the generation of GDP. In the U.S. situation, employee compensation accounts for two-thirds of the GP/capita produced by U.S. parent companies, with profit type components a distant second at around 15% of the total. These two accounts outweigh the combined net interest, indirect business taxes, and capital consumption allowances by a factor of 4:1.

GP/capita produced by the subsidiaries of these parents, on the other hand, is not only is higher than that of parental employees in actual dollar terms, it is also structured very differently with employee compensation at 40%, profit-type returns and indirect business taxes at 25–27% each, and the rest at less than 10%. (Hackmann, 1997, pp. 328–30)

Furthermore, data collected elsewhere allow the calculation of the per capita output of industrial GDP for OECD countries serving as another quick cross-reference for the above findings. Coupling data in Table 2.1 and Table 2.2 allows total OECD's per capita industrial GDP for 1999 to be established at $71,300 per employee. The comparatively higher figures for U.S. outward and inward FDI is quite reasonable in view of the significantly lower cost and high productivity profile of typical cutting-edge companies. The higher output of GDP/capita found for U.S. and other companies documented here has been assumed to be FDI specific, and thus most likely applicable to FDI operations from all countries.

Putting all the different pieces of this approach together allows the conclusion that by the end of the twentieth century all FDI enterprises put together accounted for roughly 10% of the world's industrial GDP, and only a more modest 8% of overall global GDP.(Tables 1.1 and 2.1).

B. U.S. Inward FDI

Using a different approach, information available for America's inward FDI can also be helpful in measuring global FDI. Data collected in Table 3.4 indicate a global inward FDI position reaching $5.1 trillion for 1999. This must be considered a sort of minimum figure because, as explained before, many countries do not routinely include reinvestments in their position estimates. According to U.S. statistics, cumulative inward FDI stock stood at $956 billion during that year, or 18.7% of the total. (Tables 3.4 and 5.1) These foreign companies employed 6.0 million Americans producing a GDP of $457.7 billion, or $76,300 per capita as mentioned above.

Projecting these numbers yields a global FDI employment of 32.1 million people and a GDP of $2.4 trillion. Both figures are about 10% below the estimates reached by the first method of calculation, but do not necessarily invalidate them. The U.S. employment situation can perhaps be explained with foreigners employing more productive and skilled people, using more modern equipment and, finally, creating relatively less value added due to less upgrading needed for imports with a higher finishing status in the U.S. than vice-versa. In view of this information, global FDI employment should fall into a relatively narrow range of 32–35 million people, producing about $2.4–2.6 trillion of GDP in the late nineties. These projections again differ from UNCTAD estimates of $3.0 trillion in global FDI output of gross product for 1999. (UNCTAD 2000, p. 4) See also Exhibit 6.

II. IMF INFORMATION

A. FDI Income Flows and GDP

Similar reconstructive accounting can be undertaken by using other avenues to projecting the GDP for global FDI. GDP is synergistically and directly determined by all the following factors, which are available partially or in total for some countries: investment stock, assets, number of people employed, sales, productivity, etc. The combination of such productive resources results in operating income, regardless of how it is measured exactly, which allows the underlying determinants, like sales and GDP, to be estimated on the basis of correlations unearthed in available statistics.

One of the strongest indicators of GDP volume exists in the income streams documented by BOP data as discussed in Chapter 8. After all income is an integral part of the value added process. Statistics on such national income flows are maintained in domestic currencies, and translations into dollars by the IMF. The latter come in two different versions. One measures actual BOP income flows directly attributable to FDI under the heading "other FDI income credits or debits," and the second relates to a more hypothetical flow labeled "FDI reinvestment credits or debits." The first is composed of transfers in the form of dividends and interests to parent organizations, while the second refers to parent claims against funds earned by their affiliates, which are treated by some nations as hypothetical fund flows in international accounting, but never cross international boundaries like the first.

The difficulties arising from reinvestments being treated as fund flows in national BOPs were amply discussed before. The main detractor here is that not all reporting nations follow universally accepted accounting standards. This leads to inconsistencies in reporting across a wide range of nations and, unavoidably, major distortions as a consequence. Another problem stems from the uneven nature of reinvested earnings, which depend on the need for investments and the earnings available to finance them, which in turn result from quite variable economic conditions of international markets. Also, in contrast to actually measured cross-border flows, reinvested funds are often only estimates, if the spotty information on this subject is a reliable indicator. As a result, total flows defined in line with the U.S. practice, do not display the same smooth consistency of actual income flows appearing in the national BOPs. Results may be further influenced significantly by constantly fluctuating exchange rates.

In the U.S. case income figures combine actual BOP flows plus reinvestments derived from all FDI affiliates, while GDP data refer strictly and only to Mofas. In order to make both series compatible, the data need to be adjusted to include minority-held affiliates. In the benchmark years 1982, 1989, 1994, and 1999 Mofa net income accounted for 81–90% of all FDI related income produced. (Exhibit 5)

By analogy, it may be assumed that increasing Mofa GP by 10% across the board to account for the minority-held companies should establish a reasonable estimate for the total GP production by America's outward FDI. Such estimate in turn can now be tied to total income flows reported in the U.S. BOP in order to establish a meaningful correlation between the two measures. Making these adjustments results in GDP levels averaging 6x reported income volumes including reinvestments, and 12x actual flows excluding the latter.

The 12,626 foreign affiliates (OECD 1996) operating in the U.S. provide a somewhat different picture. In the 1994–96 period, and after the introduction of a new definition of perti-

nent BOP flows, income flows excluding reinvested earnings translate into an income multiplier of roughly 17 times to reach documented GDP. If reinvested earnings are included the picture turns inconclusive, because the data were heavily impacted by losses, which led to total
income reported of less than actual fund outflows. These problems seem to have been overcome by 1996, when total income begins to exceed the volumes reported for reinvestments.
Now, income/GDP multipliers reach 15 times for 1996 and 9x for 1997. These discrepancies
could be a result of the accounting principles applied to the American BOP cited above. It may
also be assumed that the special estimates for depletion and other allowances playing an infla-
tionary role in U.S. outward FDI income do not carry the same weight for inward FDI companies, which are not engaged to the same degree in primary industries.

Another interesting, yet somewhat confusing, piece of information is provided by similar
data covering Germany's FDI situation. It has to be remembered that in this case GDP estimates were developed from published sales for outward and inward subsidiaries. Measuring
these estimates against and actual income flows portrayed by IMF statistics, shows a GDP/in-
come ratio of 12–33:1 for the 1994–96 period in the case of inward FDI, and an even higher
multiplier averaging 26 times for outward FDI between 1990 and 1996.

Such bizarre statistics do not necessarily invalidate the approach nor the results produced.
But they lead to the conclusion, that income-based projections of global FDI GDP have to be
approached with extreme caution as they do not lead to clear and reliable correlations. Ob-
serving such aberrations leaves the researcher with little but a painful experience and the inability to reconcile the differences.

Discrepancies of this magnitude may result from quite inconsistent measuring and weighing
processes, that often seem to plague international data series, plus aberrations from exchange
rate fluctuations, loss situations, estimates, under- or over-reporting, taxation, etc. That such
factors may play a role here, is shown by a quick reference to two sets of data used before. According to Table 3.3, America's outward FDI stock stood at around 25% of global FDI in the
1990s, while on the income side America's share averages 45% of global FDI income. (Table
8.3). Obviously, this is a very unlikely scenario and, therefore, a statistical mismatch.

Adopting, for argument's sake, an arbitrary multiplier of 10 times, that seems to come close
to the U.S. experience, and applying it to global FDI income reported by the IMF points once
again to a global FDI GDP of around $2.9 trillion, which comes close to UNCTAD estimate
reported above.

B. FDI Position and GDP

Another attempt to gauge global FDI promises to be more satisfactory, simply because it appears to yield less erratic results. The rational premise for this approach is provided by the assumption, that there should be some reasonable relationship between the FDI funds invested
and the GDP output achieved by such investments. After all, investments are undertaken to
yield economic results.

Capital invested in FDI projects, in particular, merely amounts to a declaration of strategic
intent, which after a lapse of time should lead to predictable and visible responses in FDI employment, sales, profits, BOP income streams and, of course, output of value added. In other
words both investment and resulting output should display some meaningful evidence of correlation.

Again, published evidence of such correlation is available, but due to the sporadic nature of GDP output in particular, permits only very general observations and conclusions. There is a fairly consistent and unbroken record of estimated FDI positions for most countries in the world and particularly for OECD nations, which were discussed in Chapter 3. As far as the GDP produced by these investments is concerned, however, only the U.S. shows a fully developed time series.

Germany does not provide any GDP data per se, neither for inward nor outward FDI, but offers an equally unbroken record of data for sales, employment, and assets, which allow to the reconstruction of fairly acceptable GDP estimates between 1980 and 1997. France is a third country providing inward FDI employment, sales, and GDP data for a number of years, but only for the manufacturing industry.

In addition there are some cross-reference possibilities coming from macro-economic data furnished by the IMF, UNCTAD, the OECD, and Eurostat. Putting all the information together, and approaching it with a good dose of critical evaluation and skepticism, leads to defensible conclusions.

The first interesting point that emerges is, that FDI stock and output of value added do not develop in a straightforward and lock-step fashion. According to American and German information investment stock movements are subject to the law of diminishing returns. That is to say, the growth in the output of GDP unexpectedly trails the pace of investments over time. Whether this applies universally is hard to determine without more detailed information from other economies. What the information seems to convey is that the generation of value-added is dependent on more and more capital-intensive processes, which is a familiar thought. It is borne out by quickly increasing per capita output of gross product, where it is documented, and comparable per capita concentration of investment stock. This finding is further supported by UNCTAD research, which shows FDI assets to grow faster than its related GDP. (Exhibit 6).

The statistical backdrop for this observation might, of course, be affected by the steady improvement of accounting for reinvestments discussed earlier, which would solely affect the FDI position and not the output of GDP. U.S. data, however, do not suggest reinvestments to be a factor in the divergent trends between position and GDP, because the U.S. FDI accounting has always included reinvestments.

Exhibit 6.

Year	GDP/Asset Ratio*	GDP/Stock Ratio**	Global FDI GDP Estimate		Percent of Global GDP	
			Own	UNCTAD	Own	UNCTAD
1980	30.3% (1)	108%	$567	—	5.2	—
1985	26.5	95%	654	$604	5.3	4.9
1990	24.7	85%	1,400	1,419	6.7	6.7
1995	18.2	75%	2,100	1,833	7.2	6.3
1996	18.0	73%	2,300	2,026	7.7	6.8
1997	18.7	71%	2,500	2,286	8.4	7.8
1998	18.3	69%	2,800	2,677	9.5	9.1
1999	17.2	67%	3,200	3,045	10.4	9.9

Global FDI GDP Estimates 1980–1999

$billion Adapted from Tables 1.1 & 3.3. *UNCTAD, World Investment Report, various issues. **Estimates were derived from U.S. and German FDI data relationships. (1)1982 data.

Data for the U.S. and Germany—estimates here—alike portray an astounding similarity, when measuring the development patterns between investment stock and GDP. In the early eighties both countries recorded GDP levels in excess of position figures, which then gradually reversed their respective weights until GDP had dropped into the range of 65–70% of stock levels by the mid-1990s. A remarkable coincidence, which even when its very hypothetical nature for universal application is allowed, may be used to draw a very cautious and tentative global GDP picture over a period of almost two decades.

Such estimates match previous projections of global FDI GDP quite closely, lending additional support to the likelihood of being realistic. Not only do these hypothetical data permit to gauge the growth rate of GDP against funds invested, but also FDI's importance in the output of global value-added.

FDI's share in total global GDP with its 10% share at the end of the period investigated amounts to a surprisingly modest achievement, and may be summarized for the period 1980–99 as follows: investment stock grew nine-fold, value added value less than six-fold, and share in global GDP only two-fold during the period. Not only a solid confirmation of the law of diminishing returns at work, but also an important reminder to not automatically equate growth in capital flows and investment position with similar gains in output and market shares. FDI, after all, is only a modest growth factor in a dynamically expanding world.

Another benchmark can be established by comparing the above estimate for people employed by FDI enterprises against total OECD industrial employment. The U.S. employs 63% its FDI labor force in OECD countries, and Germany 65%. Assuming global FDI employment to reach 33 million people, of which 65% or 21.5 million are working in the OECD, indicates a 7–8% FDI penetration of OECD's industrial labor force, and perhaps double that level for industries in developing nations. Still, another indication of FDI's only limited role in the global economic context.

III. GLOBAL FDI AND INTERNATIONAL TRADE

Having now a phantom outline of FDI's position in the global output of goods and services, it is tempting to explore its place in global trade. Again, and for the same reasons, a new process of analogy is required. Now, a much wider scope of research has to be employed, because there are additional dimensions to international trade not found in the analysis of economic output alone.

Foreign trade involving FDI operations needs to be looked at from the perspective of: 1) the country's concurrent duality as FDI donor or host, and 2) the trading activities of such country's outward affiliates beyond the parents' national boundaries. How much more complicated this sort of research can become, compared to the value-added calculation, is demonstrated by the need to cover import and export activities of businesses engaged in inward and outward FDI for a given nation, or FDI-affiliated foreign trade in the broadest sense, plus the much narrower import and export activities of outward affiliates for the same nation, where they exist. This particular aspect is vital for assessing the full national ownership of international trade, as such affiliates represent physical extensions of national capital control and ownership into foreign territories.

In its widest application, this touches on trading activities by parent organizations with their foreign affiliates but also unrelated foreigners, both for exports and imports, plus affiliate trade with unrelated business partners in all countries including the parent country and, in addition, their trade with other affiliates of the same parent company. The crux of the matter is, that most nations have absolutely no information on any of these subjects. The only exception, and only by degree, is the U.S. Here we find a fairly complete record of trading activities for both inward (foreign) and outward American businesses (parents and un-affiliated U.S. parties) related to FDI, and a fragmented sort of evidence for U.S. outward FDI affiliates discussed in Chapter 7.

Supplementing this body of evidence are OECD data for some of their member countries, but limited to the manufacturing sector alone, which makes it difficult to gauge the total impact of FDI on the global trade in goods and services. The information flows from the first known attempt by an international organization to tackle the much needed, comprehensive, and practical research in this area. A big step forward, yet disappointing in a way, because with the single exception of the U.S. again, the fragmented data for a handful of countries and the total absence of FDI trade statistics even for major economies, attests to the low level of interest paid to such a vital area by the majority of nations.

Still, even these glaring shortfalls in detailed information cannot hide the exponentially larger weight carried by FDI companies in the trade area. Whereas their role in the world's output of value-added is still no higher than 10%, it must reach into solidly into the 80–90% range of global trade.

Once again it becomes necessary to draw heavily on American FDI's trade experience discussed in Chapters 6 and 7, and summarized for both outward and inward FDI partners in Table 9.1. It shows that almost 90% of U.S. exports are accounted for by inward and outward FDI operations. On the import side FDI's role is reduced, but still dominates with a 70% share. A deceptive figure, because it represents a smaller share of a much larger trade volume, and is actual cause of the country's perennial, and rapidly growing, trade deficits.

The data perfectly illustrate the dual purpose of FDI as production and trading organizations. Outward FDI displays a decided export orientation, with export volume always exceeding import volume, and thus producing a favorable balance-of-trade effect for the home economy. Inward FDI plays the reverse role with a decided emphasis on imports, which exceed their exports by almost double in the U.S. case. In a broader context, this allows the general conclusion that outward FDI normally has a positive effect on a country's BOP, and inward FDI just the opposite.

These relationships reveal the intimate and changeable liaison between trade and FDI in general, with trade leading FDI development up to a point, and then apparently becoming dependent on the success of the FDI ventures in foreign markets. In other words, outward affiliates are primarily used as export conduits for a variety of suppliers, including parents and others, from the parent country. Seen from the host country, these very same but now inward subsidiaries, serve automatically and predominantly as import channels, with a reduced role in the country's exports. This trading relationship touches on the important volume of FDI trade taking place between related business organizations, the so-called intra-firm trade. American FDI parents ship roughly 40% of their overall exports to affiliates around the world, and import about an identical share of their total imports from them. Such family trade translates into shares of about 25% of total U.S. merchandise exports, and 17% for imports.

It must be emphasized, that these are shares based on the invoice volume of intra-firm transactions. As most, if not all, of such trade is conducted at price levels different from similar trade with

Table 9.1.   FDI Share in U.S. Foreign Merchandise Trade

	U.S. Outward FDI		U.S. Inward FDI		Total FDI Trade Share	
	Exports	Imports	Exports	Imports	Exports	Imports
1990	62%	43%	24%	37%	86%	80%
1991	62	43	23	37	85	80
1992	61	41	24	34	85	75
1993	60	39	23	34	83	73
1994	69	38	24	35	93	73
1995	65	39	23	34	88	73
1996	67	40	23	32	90	72
1997	65	40	21	31	86	71
1998	65	39	22	32	87	71
1999	63	37	22	32	85	69

(Source: Table 6.1)

unrelated customers, the so-called transfer pricing mechanism, it can be assumed that these shares are likely to be understated. That is to say, if this trade among FDI-affiliated organizations were expressed in physical volume shares, it would most likely be significantly higher.

For American inward FDI organizations the picture changes dramatically. In general, they export close to 50% of their foreign shipments to parent groups, and import between 70–80% from them. A much closer parent-affiliate relationship than is visible for U.S. outward FDI. Intra-firm trade values are also affected by the different finishing stages of merchandise traded, as was discussed in Chapter 7.

The parent/subsidiary role in America's trade picture presents a statistical curiosity insofar as it draws attention to the fact that many of the officially designated American parents are actually foreign owned. The exact degree of ownership, whether minority- or majority-held capital shares, is not entirely clear. But there is a clear reference to the fact, that trade labeled "trade with foreigners" by U.S. parent organizations includes trade with their own foreign parent organizations. This trade is significant for three reasons: from the dollar volumes involved, the real extent of trade taking place between all affiliated companies and, finally, also the potential effect these data may have on the true ownership of America's foreign trade as discussed here. In the most extreme case, full conversion of the trade involved could lead to the conclusion that much more of America's foreign trade is already in the hands of foreign business interests than official accounting intimates. To cite only 1997 figures, outward FDI exports would be reduced from 65% to 55% of total U.S. exports, and their import share would experience an even more severe reduction from 40% currently to only 30%. Conversely, foreign-controlled exports would rise from 22% to 32%, and imports from 32% in 1996 to 42%. This accounting problem surfaced before in the discussion of the actual size of America's FDI position in the global system. Could it be overstated substantially? (See Tables 7.1, 7.3, for details).

Data available elsewhere furnish additional, but very fragmented insights into FDI-related trade for a handful of other nations. With the exception of Japan, they reveal roles for inward FDI companies resembling the U.S. situation.

Canada shows that over 50% of merchandise exports are shipped by foreign companies active in the country. In the manufacturing sector that share reaches between 49–54%. A surprisingly high percentage figure at first glance, but in view of the very strong 80% plus position of U.S. companies in this trade, quite plausible. While not covered, trade related to Canada's outward FDI organizations probably pushes all FDI trade close to 100% of all Canadian foreign transactions.

Finland reports significantly lower involvement of foreign-owned companies in the country's export sector, with figures barely reaching 10%. But it can be assumed that still close to 100% of all exports are made by FDI-related companies, with a dominant role falling to outward FDI companies.

Significantly higher shares in merchandise exports are reported for foreign companies located in France, with shares reaching into the 35% range for members of the manufacturing industry, and closer to 22% for all industries. Once more it must be assumed, that overall FDI shares in the export sector reach into the 80–90% range in view of the country's strong engagement in foreign markets, with a reported total FDI employment of close to a million foreign workers. Also, intra-company exports by French parents to their foreign affiliates alone accounted for 24% of all exports in 1993. Adding parent exports to unrelated foreigners would raise their share substantially.

Information is given for only one year on the import side, where foreigners seem to hold a share in the 31% range based on parent shipments alone. French parent imports from affiliates in the vicinity of only 6% (1993) of all merchandise imports appear very small. Once more, these figures do not preclude all FDI-related imports from reaching into the 70–90% range.

Truly stellar trade shares for foreign investors are reported for Ireland. Around 80% of merchandise exports are in the hands of inward investors, and about 75% of like imports. With such penetration rates the country's name could justifiably be changed to Hireland, as its industry is practically entirely hired out to foreign business interests.

Japan registers a 3% foreign-controlled share of her exports, and a more significant 11% share in her imports. Most of this trade is among affiliated organizations: 50% for exports, and 70% for imports. In view of the country's leading export position, it is reasonable to assume that the lion's share of all foreign trade is in the hands of Japanese parent organizations.

In the case of Mexico it can be assumed that around 50% of its foreign trade is transacted by foreign organizations, led by American companies with about 70% of total FDI-related exports and imports.

The Netherlands are represented with data for 1996 only. Here a fairly uniform 35% of all external trade, imports and exports, is held by foreigners. A similar situation is found in Sweden, where foreigners control 25% of merchandise exports and an even higher 40% of imports.

Despite the very sketchy picture, it is probably reasonable to assume that global FDI, including parent organizations, dominates international trade with shares reaching into the

80–90% range, a position that is almost ten times larger than its share in global GDP. In the context of foreign trade FDI definitely rules the globe. UNCTAD estimates for affiliate trade seem to confirm this conclusion. According to the World Investment Reports of 1998 (p. 5) and 2000 (p. 4) affiliate exports reach between 35–40% of global merchandise exports, a figure established by more or less the same analogy used here.

NATIONAL CONTROL OVER THE GLOBAL ECONOMY AND TRADE VIA FDI

The ultimate conclusions to be drawn from the discussion of FDI's aggregate role in the global output of GDP and trade concern the national shares in the total picture. It has been the central theme of all analytical efforts expended so far to question the continued use of the traditional concept that geography truly represents national positions in a global economic context. It was postulated from the outset that by adhering to tradition rightful credit may be denied to national movers and shakers in the globalization process.

Bringing all facts in support of such hypothesis to the surface, can only develop and deepen the understanding of the actual competitive forces generated by national industries, and identify the real winners in the rush for global market shares. Size of national economies in a geographical sense is only the result of history. It cannot disclose meaningful information for national capital ownership and control exerted through FDI firms beyond the confines of their home countries.

Relevant data for America's position in global trade point out, how significantly the picture changes once geographically defined U.S. trade has been transformed into trade defined by the proposed capital control hypothesis. The formula now changes from the exclusive use of official U.S. exports in the conventional sense, to first identifying the real U.S. controlled portion of exports from the continental U.S., by eliminating exports controlled by foreign enterprises. The revised volume is then combined with exports from U.S.- controlled subsidiaries located in foreign markets to capture the true impact of American industry on world trade.

The results of this step-wise transformation are laid down in Table 9.2, and what an eye-opener they turn out to be. If measured in the traditional, that is geographical sense, U.S. merchandise exports are shown to hold a 12% share in global exports. Adjusting for foreign control over these exports reduces the actual U.S. owned share from American shores in world trade by roughly three percentage points to around 9%. By adding exports from majority-controlled U.S. subsidiaries operating in foreign economies, however, the real American share in global trade jumps to 19% for most of the 1990s, and even 22% in 1999, thus practically doubling U.S.-based exports from rightfully "American" enterprises.

The fact that subsidiary exports are almost as big as total unadjusted U.S. exports registered in the official BOP figures, and definitely larger than exports from truly American owned domestic enterprises alone, is another jolting realization. It suddenly turns the spotlight on the true importance of the country's FDI business operations. As minority-held companies are not included here, the real American share in worldwide exports could realistically be pegged at

Table 9.2. America's True Share In Global Merchandise Trade—($billion)

	1990	1991	1992	1993	1994	1995	1996	1999
1. Global Merchandise Exports								
$ Total	3,405.0	3,501.4	3,743.2	3,744.1	4,260.0	5,106.8	5,268.0	5,554.4
2. Official U.S. Merchandise Exports								
$ Total	392.9	421.8	448.2	465.1	512.6	584.7	625.1	702.1
% of Global	11.5	12.1	12.0	12.4	12.0	11.5	11.9	12.6
3. Inward FDI Merchandise Exports								
$ Total	92.3	96.9	103.9	106.6	120.7	135.2	140.9	153.6
%of	2.7	2.8	2.8	2.9	2.8	2.6	2.7	2.8

(*continued*)

Table 9.2.   America's True Share In Global Merchandise Trade—($billion) (*continued*)

3. U.S. Capital Controlled Domestic Merchandise Exports*							
$ Total	300.6	324.9	344.3	358.5	391.9	449.5	484.2	548.5
% of Global	8.8	9.3	9.2	9.6	9.2	8.8	9.2	9.9
4. U.S. Outward FDI Affiliate Merchandise Exports**							
$ Total	346.3	365.3	382.9	387.4	424.3	N/A	N/A	688.9
% of Global	10.2	10.4	10.3	10.3	10.0	-	-	12.1
5. U.S. Capital Controlled Global Merchandise Exports							
$ Total	646.9	690.2	727.2	745.9	816.2	N/A	N/A	1,237.4
% of Global	19.0	19.7	19.4	19.9	19.2	-	-	22.3

*Official exports less exports by foreign-owned enterprises in the U.S. **Mofas only (Source: U.S. trade statistics: Table 6.1 World merchandise exports: *International Financial Statistics Yearbook 1999*, p.129, IMF).

21–24%. Pretty close to the share America holds in the conventionally defined global output of GDP.

The next significant realization is that redefining America's true position in world trade leads to an automatic and major realignment of trade shares for all other nations. Unfortunately, none of these details are available for any other country. If they were, they would allow more accurate insights into the global trade position of many countries. Taking Ireland and Japan as two extreme cases can illustrate this point, even though actual and complete data are nonexistent. Ireland's exports, for instance, are about 75% controlled by outsiders, which would reduce the country's standing in world exports by a very significant margin because, in addition to the sharp reduction of Irish-owned domestic exports, the small outward FDI engagement could only add little to her global trade position.

Japan, on the other hand, with very little foreign control over her domestic exports—about 3%—has a very solid foundation for the Japanese-owned share in global exports from her domestic exports alone. Adding to this exports generated by Japanese affiliates throughout the world can only expand their stature significantly. Even though actual data cannot be furnished there is a possibility to estimate their affiliates' contribution in a very roundabout, yet plausible, way. In 1996/7 Japan held 36% of its outward FDI position in the U.S. Assuming similar trade patterns for the Japanese affiliates located outside the U.S. would balloon the $52.5 billion in exports shown for their affiliates in the U.S. in 1997 to no less than $146 billion worldwide.

Continental Japan's merchandise exports reached $400 billion for that year. Adjusted for the foreign factor, this turns into $388 billion of bona-fide Japanese exports from the island, a figure that expands by 38%, when adding the estimated affiliate exports.

In other words, the true Japanese share in global exports now rises from 9.4% based on domestic exports alone to 12.5%. Putting that figure into sharper focus is the fact that this volume represents close to two-thirds of the comparable U.S. position in global trade. Not bad for a country whose GDP stands at a very similar 62% level relative to the U.S., and being produced by a population less than half—47%—that of the U.S. Going one step further, the combined shares of both countries now account for 35% of world trade against only 25% before, leaving even less room for other nations.

A final glimpse of FDI's role in world trade can be generated by a different scenario. Foreigners controlled 23% of U.S. exports in the 1990s and 30% of her imports. Important figures, inasmuch as they can also be used as the basis for roughly estimating the global dimension of all FDI trade generated by affiliate organization alone.

With U.S. internal FDI amounting to roughly 20% of the global FDI position in the 1990s, and assuming similar trade patterns for the other 80% of these firms located in other parts of the world, admittedly always very iffy, would yield a global trade volume for non-U.S. FDI companies in the neighborhood of $750 billion for 1998, calculated on their U.S. export volume of $151 billion in that year. Adding to this exports by American subsidiaries exports raises this estimate to $1.1 trillion or a total FDI share of 22% of global merchandise exports. (Tables 7.4 and 7.8)

But, as pointed out before, inward FDI firms are more important for their import than export function. Their $290 billion import volume into the U.S. market would point to a global import volume of about $1.5 trillion for these non-American affiliates. Adding an estimated $500 billion imported by American affiliates, or at least more than the $400 billion exports shown in Table 9.2, raises all affiliate imports across the world to no less than $1.8—2.0 trillion. Such a volume indicates, that FDI affiliates alone appear to control between 35–40% of all world trade, a level that does not even include their parent organizations. This projection corroborates the UNCTAD findings mentioned earlier.

Unlike for the U.S. situation these FDI trade volumes cannot be redistributed by their true nationality, meaning that 75% of the affiliate trade volume is still in search of a proper national identity from the capital control point-of view.

Turning now to estimates for national shares in the world's output of GDP, they should follow similar calculation methods. Starting with a country's domestic GDP in the conventional sense, adding the gross product of its outward FDI affiliates, but deducting the gross product produced by foreign FDI within its boundaries, should produce reasonable approximations of the real situation.

Identification of gains and losses of a nation's share in global GDP is easier after the discussion in Chapter 3 than attaching real numbers to these relative positions. But, by employing relationships uncovered in previous cases, this may realistically portray true national shares in the global output of value added.

Table 9.3 identifies two groups of countries: those that increase their national share in global GDP by having a positive net outward stock position, and those that lose share, as defined in the traditional geographical interpretation, because their net FDI position is negative due to inward stocks exceeding their outward investments. These findings are supported by the discussion of the relative BOP income streams in Chapter 8. Calculating national shares in global output of GDP based on capital control over productive resources can materially change a country's share in the list, and more pronounced for small nations with a relatively large FDI impact than for larger ones. Switzerland, for instance, now shows a national GDP that is 33% larger than previously assumed, Sweden gains 10%, while Irish-controlled GDP shrinks by 20%. The U.S. position gains, as that of Europe, the EU, and Japan, but NAFTA's position is diminished under the influence of Mexico with no traceable outward FDI compared to the inward position.

The American position trend is approaching a precarious breaking point with inward FDI threatening to outstrip the country's outward stock according to Table 3.6. Considering that a an estimated 15% of all U.S. outward FDI is under foreign ownership and control according to official disclosures, the country may already have passed this important threshold.

MIRAGE STATISTICS

Looking at statistical evidence from so many different sources inevitably leads to critical observations about the nature of the information provided. What measures reality and stands up under cross-examination, what is based on solid assumptions and rational projections, and does the use of the same nomenclature assure full comparability for international sets of data? The following deals mainly with American statistical practices, that are country specific, but not necessarily country exclusive. In other words, all statistical evidence, regardless of geographic or organizational provenance, should be approached with a healthy dose of skepticism and careful analysis. American statistics are, of course, of special interest to the outside world which sees its economic and political fortunes largely depending on the health of the American economy. Thus, official U.S. pronouncements carry a lot of weight in influencing global psychology.

Table 9.3. **Estimated Real National Shares In Global Output of GDP in 1999 ($billion)**

	Official		Net FDI	Regression	Net FDI	Revised	
World	$30,876	100.0		GDP is		30,876	100.0
				estimated to			
U.S.A	9,237	29.9	44,177	uniformly	29.6	9,267	30.0
NAFTA	10,035	33.5	47,258	reach 67% of	31.7	10,067	32.6
W. Europe	9,112	29.5	817,718	net FDI	547.9	9,660	31.3
EU	8,506	27.5	684,309	position	458.5	8,965	29.0
Japan	4,347	14.1	253,975	(for an	170.2	4,517	14.6
Germany	2,112	6.8	195,313	explanation	130.9	2,243	7.3
UK	1,443	4.7	269,543	refer to	180.6	1,624	5.0
France	1,432	4.6	116,038	Exhibit 6 on	77.7	1,510	4.9
Italy	1,171	3.8	60,375	page 138)	40.5	1,212	3.9
Canada	635	2.1	12,081		8.1	643	2.1
Netherlands	394	1.3	91,162		61.1	455	1.5
Switzerland	259	0.8	126,354		84.7	344	1.1
Sweden	241	0.8	36,949		24.8	266	0.9
Mexico	483	1.6	-9,000e		-6.0	477	1.5
Korea	407	1.3	-5,566		–3.7	403	1.3
Australia	407	1.3	-63,334		–42.4	365	1.2
Austria	210	0.7	-5,841		–3.9	206	0.7
Ireland	93	0.3	-28,873		–19.3	74	0.2

Americans like big numbers. They also like numbers that support the appearance of growth, prosperity, and leadership, which leads to the selection and presentation of positive information, while negatives are de-emphasized or suppressed. As this writer once heard in a business session "if you see a problem with this company, you are the problem," a very persuasive argument as it implied consequences for the person's job security.

The scandals of corporate America reported in the recent past are well documented, and were met with professions of official indignation and promises of corrective action. That spawned the Sarbanes-Oxley Act holding corporate CEOs responsible for truthful disclosures in financial statements, but deceptive practices seem to continue. Financial statements require careful reading, especially of the small print which may shed more light on the true situation than the big numbers up front. According to a study released by Pricewaterhouse Coopers on 3,623 companies in July 2003, 37% of the companies surveyed reported some fraud in the last two years, up from 29% two years earlier. Also, the bigger the company, the higher the rate of fraud. The legislation has also caused hundreds of companies to voluntarily delist from the stock markets rather than comply with the Act. (Lynn Carpenter, Publisher, *Fleet Street Letter*, 10/2/2003).

"Pro-forma, projected, estimated profits, and goodwill" statements provided by Wall Street sources are suspect of being wishful thinking, if not outright fabrications. Sales/income data may be deliberately overstated per se, or by understating expenses. Pension plan shortfalls, or separation package provisions for top executives, the golden parachutes, for instance, have thus often been excluded from mention. Statements about profit improvements are deliberately vague. Do they refer to estimates, or prior period actual numbers? Are they due to better business conditions, slashing of costs and expenses, or revised accounting methods? On balance, optimistic company and industry forecasts may clash with the actual development of official industry profits, which have declined steadily for so many years as a percentage of GDP.

Even government statistics deserve diligent scrutiny. Some of the issues were addressed in the foregoing analysis, like the BOP entries concerning reinvestments. It is not known, whether the figures are actual company representations, simply estimates, projections of assumptions and past trends, or the like. Further, at what exchange rate were they converted from local currencies? Whatever their nature, the inclusion of non-flow items in the U.S. BOP current and capital account tends to magnify American statistics in relation to those of countries not following this practice.

Official unemployment statistics are beset with question marks, especially if they are "seasonally adjusted." Basically, they are estimates based on surveys, not actual counts like in other countries. Often they are deliberate estimates subject to revision and adjustment in later accounting periods, when their original impact is long forgotten. The practice of understating actual job losses for a given month and later making substantial upward revisions, tends to leave the impression of a job situation much better than exists in reality. As a practical example, official job losses were reported by the BLS (Bureau of Labor Statistics) as 17,000 and 30,000 for May and June of 2003. The follow-up report from the same BLS revised these figures to 70,000 and 72,000 respectively, more than double the first volume of payroll reductions.

Reported job losses raise another inconsistency. First-time unemployment claims have hovered at over 400,000 per week for the last 25 and more weeks. Manufacturing has shed workers for fully 40 months straight up to December of 2003, in sharp contrast to the job losses reported officially at less than 100,000 per month. It calls the real numbers of the unemployed and the related unemployment rate into serious question.

Official unemployment data report an actual rate of around 5.9% at the end of 2003. This is based on the official definition of unemployment, which was revised by the BLS in January of 2003 to include revised "population controls" in their household survey. Table A-12—Alternative Measures of Labor Underutilization—states Atotal unemployed, as a percent of the civilian labor force (official unemployment rate) dropped to 5.9%, while "total unemployed, plus discouraged workers, plus all other marginally attached workers, as a percent of the civilian labor force, stayed the same at 6.6%." If one adds to these categories underemployed, "part-time employees forced by economic reasons," then the unemployment rate actually jumped from 9.5% to 9.7 %. In the BLS explanation: "marginally attached workers are persons who currently are neither working nor looking for work, but indicate that they want and are available for a job and have looked for work sometime in the recent past." They include another category "discouraged workers" who have given job-related reasons, like totally unsuitable jobs, for not looking anymore.

Another peculiarity of BLS accounting are the estimates of new jobs created. The assumption is that in periods of improving business, as predicted by the government, people normally open new businesses. The prediction alone leads government statisticians to automatically add 30,000 — 50,000 "pro-forma" workers to the work force. Most likely it reflects wishful thinking, but not necessarily reality. These imaginary data are later revised away without mention in the monthly job loss statistics, which are better than they should be to begin with. (Richebächer, 9/28/03). Estimates are the miracle working in employment, consumer debt, GDP, and government deficit projections.

The hedonic value added inflator used for computers in the calculation of the country's GDP growth has been mentioned. Simply put computer investments are not calculated on the basis of their nominal value added (cost/price based) in the production/selling chain, as is the international norm, but on the increase of their computing power since 1995/96. This calculation requires computer output to be stated in terms of physical units (the real GDP) times market prices times the growth factor in computing power. The consequence of this arbitrary decision is a significant growth spurt in GDP output, where in reality it slowed down once the computing enhancement factor is removed. Computers, by the official measure, advanced from 15% of the annual GDP output to 78.5% between 1996 and 1999.

The practical impact of the computer legend is illustrated by the discussion of second quarter GDP figures for 2003. Official computer spending of $38.4 billion faced a real expense of only $6 billion. The $32 billion difference is sheer "hedonic" fiction, and for a single quarter only. The official second quarter 3.1% increase in GDP output would thus shrink to only 1.7%, most of it came from war spending. (U.S. News & World Report, September 22, 2003, p.86)

The cumulative effect of this hedonic adjustment on Information Technology (IT) spending has been estimated for the period 2000 — 2003 by V. Anatha Nageswaran writing for the Business Times (Singapore), in October 2003. According to his calculations, the nominal value of investment in computers and peripherals stood at $95.7 billion at the end of the second quarter 2000. Exactly three years later, at the end of the second quarter 2003, the figure had dropped to $82.6 billion, a 13.7% reduction. Statisticians at the Bureau of Economic Analysis turned these data into a 43.5% increase from $249.2 billion to $357.5 billion, a difference of no less than $121.4 billion. During this same period the U.S. GDP displayed a cumulative growth of 4.6%, leading him to conclude that, without the IT inflation the economic output *"would have stagnated at best or contracted at worst."*

This leads to another issue. Fed Chairman Alan Greenspan is convinced that labor productivity increases will eventually cure the deficit mentality of America. There is no question about productivity gains, currently at an annual rate of 6.8% for the first half of 2003. But how did they come about? Plausible explanations range from job losses, a 25% reduction in plant utilization, and shifting the work load to remaining workers. Net fixed industrial investments are unlikely contributors. They are declining with dwindling profits. Here, the computer story comes in. Its claimed productivity enhancement provides the superficial cover for the productivity myth.

In a similar vein, government statisticians garnish reality with hypothetical, wishful, but surreal constructs appearing under "imputed" valuations. The savings rate, for example, is enhanced by the assumption that rising real estate valuations lead to "imputed income" for the owner, which may be added to savings as if it were real.

Finally, the BLS calculates the inflation rate according to this formula. In 1990 it introduced an enhanced seasonal adjustment procedure called "Intervention Analysis Seasonal Adjustment" for its Consumer Price Index (CPI), which is intended to eliminate extreme price volatility of index components: "extreme values and/or sharp movements which might distort the seasonal pattern are estimated and removed from the data prior to calculation of seasonal factors." (Cornerstone Investment Services, 9/27/03)

Also, growth rates are stated in various ways, which becomes another source of artificial impressions. American quarterly growth rates are stated at annualized rates. For instance, if the actual rate was 0.2% year-over-year for the same quarter, or against the previous quarter, as is the international standard, American figures are multiplied by 4 to get the quarterly figure at an annualized rate of 0.8%, without necessarily making a mention of it. If the hedonic price deflator is added in the American case, the result can be dramatically higher GDP projections. Government statisticians begin to look more like economic beauticians.

There is no telling how wide-spread American macro-economic accounting has been adopted. But it seems to have reached also Japan where a 3.9% spurt in real GDP (a physical volume measure) was reported for the second quarter of 2003, at the same time that the U.S. GDP expanded by 3.3%. This figure clashes with the report of the Bank of Japan, which says unequivocally for the same quarter: "economic activity still continues to be virtually flat as a whole . . . private consumption continues to be weak, housing investment remains sluggish, and public investment is declining. Net exports are virtually flat. Industrial production continues to be basically level in response to these developments in final demand, and corporate profits are on a moderate uptrend." (*Japanese Phantom Growth*, Richebächer, 12/12/03).

A Financial Times report seized on this discrepancy, reporting one economist's comment about the government "using deliberately manipulated statistics," using in particular an "incorrect measure of deflation." This led to an official response by Japan's Department of National Accounts, whose director explained to the FT that the "basic price statistics used in Japan's GDP deflators, such as the consumer price index and corporate goods price index, adopt the hedonic (sic!) method to track price changes accompanying quality improvement in goods," which he defended as a common international practice. He also used the annualized growth projection for the quarter, which can be deceptive through its magnification of reality. Without both elements, the quarterly growth stated in the traditional way amounted to only 0.3% or 1.2% at the annual rate.

Marveling at the differences in statistical practices among nations, and the U.S. and Japan are probably not alone, makes one wonder how real our perception of the world actually is.

Chapter Ten

Evaluating Globalization

"Have I therefore become your enemy by telling you the truth?"

Galatians 4:16.

Modern globalization is a product of the Western world, born from interwoven forces of economic and political expansionism. According to the foregoing discussion, globalization's impact on the world economy after half a century of running its course has been rather modest. Most noteworthy among its achievements are greatly reduced trade and investment barriers resulting in annual trade volumes in the trillions of dollars, plus freely flowing capital streams reaching cumulative and aggregate positions comparable in volume to the trade figures. But, despite these impressive numbers, private sector efforts to build and secure a strong position in the world economy via direct investments have yielded no more than a 10% share in the output of global GDP. This refers to globalization efforts by all developed economies combined, leaving much smaller shares for individual countries. Even the U.S., as the largest single competitor for market share, and the originator of the globalization movement, cannot claim more than a 1.8% share in global GDP from its direct investment enterprises. In view of the enormous resources committed and the high level of attention they receive in professional and media discussions, a rather sobering result, which should help to correct the often critically evaluated role of the multinationals.

The main reason for this rather average achievement is the fact that 80% of the investments are concentrated in industrialized nations, a highly competitive environment in which to fight for successful pursuit of commercial advantage. Local production resources were often sophisticated enough to rapidly meet these imported challenges, which blunted their impact. Also, foreign investments do not necessarily produce additive effects for the recipient economy. Rather, they often serve a displacement function, regardless of whether they are of the greenfield or acquisition type.

As far as the economic benefits for global enterprises are concerned, they do not seem to produce spectacular results either. Even though exact measurements are difficult to establish due to the wide spectrum of profit strategies pursued, plus the still rather poor documentation of all relevant factors, it is probably fair to state that profitability in general does not decisively differ from levels commonly seen in similar domestic endeavors. College textbooks note correctly that elevated profit expectations have a major influence on business decisions to engage in foreign ventures, and the perceived risks associated here make this a legitimate decision instrument, but experience shows that average results are the norm. In the defense of truth it must be noted that exchange rate developments play a heavy role here, and they are largely beyond the control of FDI managers.

From a macro-economic point-of-view, the rather light share of FDI in the output of global GDP raises the question what FDI's real contribution to the development of the global economy has been so far. For developed economies, the 80% in the equation, the ratio between outward and inward investment position of 1.3:1 suggests a much weaker economic impact than for the developing nations with a completely reversed ratio of 1:2.9. In this latter constellation lies the major benefit of important net capital inflows for these nations, but also the main arguments for opponents of globalization, the overshadowing presence of foreign companies in the fledgling economies. Yet, even for the developed part of the world, individual nations have to weigh the net impact resulting from the existence of outward versus inward FDI, which may have off-setting effects for their economy, their balance of payments, and their national independence.

The impact of direct investments on world trade is different. FDI-related enterprises account for 70–80%, or even more, of the global trade volume. Thus, they are the motor behind its rapid expansion owing to the logistical needs of their expanding global network of plants and service facilities. At the same time, an indicator of the rapidly growing cultural diffusion process set in motion, and the main reason for all demonstrations of resistance to, even outright rejection of foreign interests affecting the livelihood of companies, industries, even whole nations in one form or another. What does the future hold? Will global economic integration continue as in the past, does it promise to accelerate, or could it even face an unthinkable slowdown? What is certain is that the process will remain in place in some form, but subject to changes that are, already, becoming quite visible.

FREE TRADE, INVESTMENT, AND GLOBALIZATION

One of the basic credos of the globalization movement is the 200 year old concept of free trade, first expounded by Adam Smith and David Ricardo. They correctly saw how regional differences in the natural endowment of production factors could increase the welfare of both areas, if the division of labor and concentration on production of goods with a natural output advantage and free trade were introduced. The theory's basic premise is indisputable, even though it appears narrow and inflexible by today's understanding of international economic relations. Where the free traders saw a fixed natural advantage, influenced by pre-industrial production methods and a working gold standard of exchange as the basis for free trade, our understanding of international commerce realizes that trade advantages can be created by modern production processes, application of new technologies, availability of mobile capital and credit, better education, modern transportation modes, relative levels of wages, and flexible exchange rates. Modern trade exists less by virtue of natural factor endowment, as seen then, and more on cost calculations derived from an almost infinite choice of factor combinations by hard-nosed business managers. Theory and practice have become more differentiated, fluid, and thus more realistic. While the nature of production and exchange has changed, the basic premise of the free traders, namely increased welfare for all of mankind stands unshaken.

But, while the global economy as a whole benefits from liberalized trade, capital transfer, and fixed investments, the pursuit of low-cost production and higher profits from trade do not always translate into unquestionable benefits for all parties involved as postulated by the advocates of free trade.

A major issue at the moment for the U.S. is the loss of employment and shrinking incomes as the consequence of "out sourcing," that is the relocation of American factories in low-cost regions of the world.

An estimated 3 million American workers have already lost their jobs and livelihood since early 2001, mostly in the textile and other manufacturing industries. Permanent losses, at that, from shifting jobs to Far Eastern competitors in China, Japan, Taiwan, Korea, etc. that are also the main contributors to America's huge trade deficits, in themselves a testimony to America's declining competitiveness.

Official data and private think-tank projections reveal the extent of this new industrial revolution. By early 2004, 450 U.S. companies had settled in China, employing 250,000 people. Wal-Mart sources more than $10 billion worth of merchandise from there, making it one of the largest trading partners for the nation, which contributes the major portion of the U.S. trade deficit together with its neighbor Japan. While China provides a new manufacturing base for the U.S., India promises to become its counterpart for service and research jobs emigrating from America in large numbers in such industries as biotech, banking, insurances, software development, and telecommunications. India's allure is its large base of highly educated, young and eager, but low-paid labor.

A December 2003 article in Business Week revealed that GE Capital Services employs 16,000 Indian Information technology workers, Intel 1,700, IBM Global Services will have 10,000 there by 2005, and Oracle 6,000. The list includes also Microsoft, EDC, Texas Instrument, and J.P. Morgan Chase. This is only part of the estimated 500,000 service jobs gone abroad so far.

The exodus promises to accelerate. It was estimated by the Gartner Research firm that 1 in 10 U.S. technology jobs will go overseas by the end of 2004. Another projection by Forrester Research sees 3 million white collar jobs going to places like India over the next 15 years. With it will go $136 billion in wages mostly in the Information Technology sector of the economy. The Haas School of Business, finally, sees as many as 14 million positions being outsourced, affecting no less than 11% of America's workforce. Regardless of which figure comes closer to the true situation, it taxes the imagination to find Government officials seeing this as a normal development with the potential to enrich the American economy. While it may be true for the companies involved, it cannot convince people looking for such type of employment to see it in the same light. Not to speak of the long-term impact on the country's educational system and human resource development.

The Bureau of Labor reported in February of 2004, how the average salary of American workers has dropped from $44,570 in 2001 to only $35,410 in early 2003, a drop of 41%. This corroborates a study by the Economic Policy Institute that shows that between 1973 and 1998, real hourly waged fell for the bottom 60% of the U.S. workforce.

The same office released its 10–year projections of America's job growth on February 11, 2004, with details by industry and occupation. The sobering assessment predicts the bulk of job growth to come from low-paid service jobs, most of which do not even require a college education. Conspicuously absent are the high-tech and knowledge jobs promised to make up for the loss of production jobs to foreigners. Occupations in the production sector rank among those with the lowest growth. It taxes the imagination how the erosion of America's production and knowledge base can be called beneficial for the country in the long run. Is this what the "The Race ToThe Bottom" looks like as described by the book with this ominous title? (Tonelson, 2000)

Hollowing out an existing production base through job exports not only weakens a nation's capacity to export and earning the funds for imports, but produces persistent trade imbalances and erosion of its currency, as experienced by the U.S. right now. Where it involves transfer of technology and capital to set up and maintain these cheap supply sources, it inevitably is detrimental to domestic investments, employment opportunities, standards of living, and social programs. It is important to note here, that the jobs lost are always the high income jobs, where rationalization moves result in the biggest payback. The displaced workers, if they can find work at all, are forced to take lower paying jobs. In only two short years, between November 2001 and November 2003, the U.S. has lost 1.3 million manufacturing jobs, 272,000 in information services, and 93,000 in professional/technical services, all above average wage sectors. Jobs were added in administrative, and accommodations/food services, lower paying sectors. In real terms the declining sectors paid $16.92/hr. compared to $14.65/hr. in the expanding sectors. (Economic Policy Institute, November 2003).

The result is a reduction of household income from actually declining real wages since 2001 at a time when interest income from savings has been reduced by over $30 billion in 2003 alone due to the low-interest policy of the Fed system, a hardship experience for retirees who counted on sizable proceeds from their nest eggs.

Similar developments appear in Europe whose high unemployment rate indicates related causes. Especially worrisome are high unemployment rates among young people in the major economies, and industry reluctance to draft apprentices, a common European on-the-job training program. Industries there relocate production facilities to low-wage countries, but often within other European countries like Ireland, Spain, and Portugal, that is to say within its own boundaries. This practice partially explains the drive to expand the EU eastward into Central Europe, where 10 developing nations with huge pools of unemployed or under-employed workers are just waiting to join the community in 2004. But again, the redirected money flows to be expected are largely contained within the European family.

While the adherence to free trade and investment may be a sound policy from a purely theoretical and macro-global aspect, it definitely leaves big question marks for the advanced economies.

A basic one is, whether living standards of the developing nations are rapidly rising to the level of the developed nations, and to the mutual benefit of both, or whether the industrialized nations sink rapidly to the level of the export nations, the hypothetical "race to the bottom." Closely connected to this one is, what options do nations have to mitigate or even reverse some of the negative effects of total freedom for corporate decision making. Are they totally helpless, even irrelevant, in managing their economic fortunes? (R. Went, 2000)

Superficially, the situation promises only advantages for the future suppliers of goods and services to the top tier economies which, opportunistically, have formed the AGroup of 20," a new international alliance aiming at maintaining their currencies cheap, forming their own trade bloc in competition with already established ones, achieving independence from the powerful nations, and using their export surpluses as the main source of development capital.

Freely flowing investments into production plants, together with massive transfer of technology and know-how from the industrial nations will jump-start their economic development with the latest in equipment, swell their employment ranks, and rapidly growing export earnings feed the process. It raises incomes, tax bases, and creates sustainable prosperity like in China right now. The group lists Brazil, China, and S. Africa among its members. If their cohesion can be maintained in view of their wide geographic dispersion and different development levels, they might become a force to reckon with, assuming the developed world will always support free trade.

But even for the newly industrializing nations, the free flow of investments and trade can quickly turn into a short-lived, though pleasant experience, as some of these competing countries are now finding out. In the pursuit of ever higher profits, businesses from the rich countries will always seek the lowest cost combinations offered on the globe. They have no lasting commitment to any single producer or supplier, often invest little of their own money there, and can move on when it seems convenient. Mexico, for example, is now losing employment to Far Eastern producers, dashing its hopes for lasting benefits to be derived from the NAFTA agreement. The same is true for European nations, which see their favored investment status for a while turning into bitter disappointment. Portugal, another example, is seeing an exodus of firms that only recently built plants there with big subsidies from the EU (taxpayers), to relocate in Hungary and Poland, because they offer more favorable economic terms. What they leave behind are empty factories, with little chance of maintaining employment for lack of capital and customers.

As long as cost differences in production factors exist, or can be contrived, this roller-coaster game will continue with multinationals playing one business partner against another. The only real winners are international companies, it seems, which operate totally independent of outside control and regulations. Their slash and burn tactics give many of them a bad name as employers under slave-labor like conditions, child labor, starvation wages, lack of hygienic and safety installations, and no social programs for their workers. These excesses are reminiscent of early capitalism and have led to charges of government corruption for tolerating such inhuman employment practices.

While such practices may reflect good business acumen, they will by necessity and ultimately raise once more the above question, whether such independent behavior will be acceptable by all concerned. In other words, will business function as a servant to the benefit of society, or its master with potentially corruptive effect. The answer will decide the future of nation states, and the continued existence of programs for the protection of human welfare. The question is already on the table. How, for instance, are the U.S. and Europe going to deal with the sad examples of corporate governance, the shocking display of total irresponsibility and lack of respect for legal and ethical codes from Enron to Parmalat to Yukos?

Another question is, whether the term globalization is truly justified by developments that have taken place over a period of decades. The first step in that direction was undertaken by the Europeans and their gradual evolution to presently the EU of 15, and 25 by 2004. By all appearances, this is a regional form of economic integration, and not a global development. The same can be said about NAFTA. Plans to expand it from the three nation market to all of the Western Hemisphere, the FTAA, is also not global in scope. Then there are the ASEAN countries, which are definitely a regional organization. Another regional market could be in the formation stage by the Muslim nations, which have introduced a common gold currency, the gold dinar.

For the moment globalization seems too distant a concept to take it seriously. It may become a viable end stage, if, and only if, regional formations prove to become stable stepping stones in that direction.

ECONOMIC SLOWDOWN

Another important development could be s slowing world economy, or more specifically, in the developed economies. If Kontradieff's theory of business cycles still has merits, the last 50 years of uninterrupted growth in the global economy could turn into 50 years of decline or stagnation, at best, as he predicted. Raising prospects for such event are sheer blasphemy, of course, yet the frantic efforts in all countries to stimulate private consumption, business investment, exports, and getting control over rising unemployment through interest and tax cuts plus pumping vast amounts of liquidity into their economies, are all unmistakable indications how concerned governments and central banks are of the potential for experiencing the dreaded three successive stages of economic slowdowns: recession, deflation, and depression.

Contributing factors to a likely and prolonged decline are seen in the following developments. 1. The global overcapacity in manufactured goods, which leads to crushing competition among industrialized and lately also developing nations; 2. falling prices, profits, and real investments because of disappearing pricing power of businesses; 3. high and rising levels of unemployment everywhere; 4. rising business and consumer bankruptcies; 5. deflation of asset values in many sectors, especially equity markets; 6. trade wars fought via subsidies and currency devaluations; 7. corporate mergers leading to major reductions in white- and blue collar workforces; 8. rising long-term interest rates that will decimate interest sensitive sectors and business expansion in general. 9. perverse valuation bubbles coexisting with the generally weak economic conditions that seem poised to add more capital destruction and malaise coming from their inevitable implosion.

Japan is setting an ominous example. It has already seen 14 years of a deflationary cycle following the incredible buildup of economic bubbles in consumption, equity markets, and real estate valuations. So far, no turnaround is in sight. The unsettling part in their experience is the obvious ineffectiveness of government and central bank actions directed at reversing the economic misfortunes for this once vibrant nation. Instead of giving tax cuts early to fire up slack consumption, the government enacted huge public works programs. Unfortunately, consumers were not responding to any of the stimulation efforts, exhortations, and incentives. Rather than increasing spending, they increased savings to bolster income flows from their pension plans hit hard by the low interest policies. A counterproductive move under such circumstances. As a consequence, business investments slumped, unemployment soared to a still low 5.5% by comparison with other industrial countries, but high for a nation that once adhered to the principle of lifetime employment; and by waiting for always better prices, which is typical for a deflationary scenario Japanese consumers did their level best to exacerbate the decline. Yet, despite the weak domestic economy Japan has been able to maintain its traditional trade surpluses.

An accommodating banking system set the bubble economy in motion by financing real estate even at the height of astronomical valuations. It now faces financial devastation after the 80% decline in values over the last decade. Mocking the real estate mania, the Nikkei soared to 39,000 and above, more than 100 times earnings, only to collapse to 25% of its former level. Now banks are criticized for not taking the necessary steps to clean their balance sheets of uncollectible debt and stop extending loans to practically defunct businesses, as they were advised by foreign experts. Interest rates have been reduced to practically zero, but even the most favorable borrowing conditions in a lifetime could not trigger loan demand by consumers or business in view of the soft domestic economy.

It appears now that all the good advice given to no avail by outsiders to the country may face a similar test in other economies as well. The irony of it all is that economic matters are neither natural nor divine phenomena. They simply are the product of human aspirations, toils, and philosophies that politicians and economic experts alike are conspicuously incapable of managing, regulating, directing, manipulating, or controlling for sustained prosperity.

The industrial sector of the U.S. economy is presently in a phase of protracted weakness that thirteen interest rate cuts by the Federal Reserve between 2001 and mid-2003 plus massive liquidity expansion of $5.7 trillion (more than half of the annual U.S. GDP) have been unable to reverse. The surge in credit creation has effectively increased GDP by only $823 billion, meaning it takes very high levels of credit to produce effectively measurable results for the output of GDP. Actually, it takes more and more credit to produce the same effect on the output of GDP, because credit expansion is vulnerable to the law of diminishing returns under contracting business conditions. Thus, during the period 1991to mid-1993 it took $2.20 in debt to get $1 increase in GDP. Now, in the fourth year of the new millennium, it takes about $7 in new debt to have the same effect. A shocking revelation, as the Federal Reserve's stimulus policy dwells almost exclusively on money and credit expansion to turn the feared deflation into reflation, even inflation. (Richebächer, 2003).

The country has the lowest savings rate of all developed nations, and has managed to build credit debt from a level equivalent to 130% of GDP in the fifties, to 150% in the seventies, to no less than 295% by 2003. The last time it reached this level was back in 1929, when debt peaked at 264% of GDP.

Also, between 2000 and 2002 the federal budget has gone from a $295 billion surplus to a $257 billion deficit. For 2003 this deficit is expected to explode further to 500 billion or more. In combination with the trade deficit of practically equal proportions it should add between $1–1.5 trillion to the nation's debt mountain. The situation puts conventional economic thinking on its head, because such credit excesses should be followed by inflation, high interest rates, and a falling dollar, but exactly the opposite is true.

Interest rate cuts have reduced the Federal Reserve rate to exactly 1% by mid-2003, and 30–year mortgage rates are at a twenty-nine year low of 4.5–5.5% depending on whether fixed or variable rate contracts are involved. Inflation has been kept at bay with low industrial capacity utilization, the industry's inability to raise prices, the obstinate pursuit of free trade and a flood of cheap imports, mainly from China, plus the liberal availability of foreign capital transfers discussed below. As a result profits of non-financial institutions have fallen since 1997, when they amounted to 6% of GDP, to 4.3% in 2000, and 3% in 2003. The profit carnage caused fixed investment in the business sector, so vital for economic recovery and expansion, to all but dry up.

Unemployment is at a 9-year high, and climbing even after three years of steady job cuts. Output in manufacturing has fallen steadily for two years as a result of the U.S. recession, companies moving production abroad, cheap import and slack exports. The economy is obviously stalling out as evidenced also by the official unemployment rate of 5.9% at the end of 2003. Actually, it could be 50% higher by some estimates, if the peculiarities of employment tracking by the Bureau of Labor Statistics are taken into account. (See Chapter 9 for details).

Americans are stretched with $1.97 trillion in credit card and consumer debt on their hands, and 1.6 million personal bankruptcies per year attest to their plight. This does not include mortgage debt of $9 trillion. At the end of 2003 consumer debt reaches $6,600 per each person, yet people keep borrowing to pay their mounting bills in the belief that wealth creation from their high-tech, financial, and real estate investments will finance their excesses. Consumer debt is rising at a 5.1% annual rate in an economy that officially grows only by 1.4%. The Federal Reserve estimated in 2000, already, that the total debt load of the average household exceeded its annual income. After the tech crash a new financing source was discovered. Low interest rates led to a boom in home refinancing to extract the equity bonus, the difference between the old mortgage debt and the home's estimated market value which banks readily financed. Conclusion: consumers are living on borrowed time, they are getting poorer. Mortgage debt in the 1950s amounted to 15% of a home's value today it has reached 57%. Actually, the figure is 80%, if people with a clear title to their property are removed from consideration.

In the five years before 2003 the country's overall debt—consumers, industry, public sector—has grown 52%. The 2003 growth rate is estimated at 7.7%, which will force the total debt load up to $41 billion from the present $31 billion in the next four years, if this rate is sustained. Serving such a $31 trillion behemoth of debt may be possible for a while given a healthy economy and a regimen of low interest rates, expanding consumption, and stable employment. It is totally unthinkable in a period of weak business conditions, and the moment of truth approaches with rising long-term interest rates despite the easy money policy of the Fed.

The federal government shows $6.4 trillion in accumulated debts, requiring annual interest payments of about $2 billion. That debt figure could easily double within the next ten years according to the non-partisan Congressional Budget Office. But government figures exclude trillions in agency and off-budget debt, which makes the real public debt load incalculable. Corporate debt adds only a rather modest $4 trillion to the overall picture.

Annual trade deficits have been escalating for three decades, and the trend is still up. Reaching about 5% of annual GDP at the moment, it is considered a dangerous level for the stability of any currency. That applies specifically to the dollar, whose purchasing power has declined by 70% since 1970 under the burden of perennial budget shortfalls within the country, and whose exchange rate has declined by 30% recently against the Euro as of late. Serving as the monetary and reserve standard of the world for so long, the situation poses a dilemma for the country. A lower dollar would slow imports, while increasing the likelihood for more exports and lowering the trade imbalance, which would benefit America's labor situation, income levels, and investments, if local consumption could be stimulated fast enough. But it would also cause a jump in inflation and higher interest rates, a threat to economic recovery.

Maintaining a strong dollar, on the other hand, guarantees a continuation of the present situation, characterized by massive and rising trade deficits, job transfers to foreign workers, reduction of income and investments at home, and further reduction in sales of domestically produced goods. It is estimated that, already, up to one half of all manufactured goods sold in the U.S. are imported.

A weaker dollar could pose an even larger problem by endangering the international financial system. Foreign investors have helped to finance America's budget deficits and consumer frenzy for so long, by parking their trade deficit receipts in the U.S. Their belief in the dollar as a safe haven for their investments may come to an end in view of lower stock valuations on Wall Street, a collapsing bond market, plus allegations of massive corruption in corporate and financial circles, very low interest rates, and a sliding dollar, which in combination have produced billions in losses for them already.

It would amount to a catastrophe for the U.S. economy and public finances, if foreigners would effectively stop accepting dollars in payment for their exports, refrain from further investments, or even repatriate their funds. Local capital markets would be totally incapable of balancing such a loss, as America has forgotten how to save.

It could also turn into a tragic loss of capital for foreign creditors, who willingly transferred their savings into American assets, in their unshakable belief in the dollars gold-like quality. A strong dollar policy attracted these foreign investments even at insignificant returns on their capital, a weak dollar would not lighten the nominal debt load of the U.S., but it would surely lead to grave reductions for the wealth of other nations. Sustained dollar weakness as the result of a new orientation of American fiscal and monetary policy, begin to serve as growing incentives for international investors to look at alternatives in the Euro, the yen, perhaps even the Chinese renminbi in the future, and the nemesis of all mismanaged paper currencies, gold.

Europe parallels the American situation in some ways, except for higher unemployment rates and lack of comparable consumer credit excesses. Yet, it begins to display early symptoms of a Japanese-style deflation with people cutting back on unnecessary expenses in the face of reductions in employment and increasing cost sharing of private citizen to maintain the accustomed social safety net. Also, falling tax revenues begin to inflate public deficits beyond the guidelines of the Maastricht agreement.

INCREASED INDUSTRIAL CAPACITY, CREDITS, AND DEBTS

Greed, managerial self-aggrandizement, and the curse of cut-throat competition drive the free enterprise system everywhere into excessive generation of production capacity for goods and services exacerbated by relocating domestic industries in developing countries, and deeper economic cycles. The result is fierce global competition, downward pressure on prices and profits, and deliberate interference with free trade principles.

Practically unlimited availability of credit is the main motor behind the development in national economies, especially the U.S., where short-term interest rates have been driven down to the lowest levels in 45 years by the Fed. The policy aims at further inflating America's private consumption, roughly two-thirds of U.S. GDP, and preventing dreaded deflation at all costs.

The results are visible in declining savings rates, expanding deficits for federal, state, and municipal budgets, and rapidly rising indebtedness of consumers, industry, and the public sector. But the deliberate bloating of the "want component" in the behavior model of consumer needs and wants has also produced historically high bankruptcy cases for wage earners in a shrinking employment environment. The situation reminds very much of doping a racehorse to make it run faster and longer until it ultimately collapses and expires.

The consumption and investment bubbles created for the U.S. economy spilled over into many parts of the world economy, thanks to the unchecked imports of the world's largest consumer market. Almost unlimited credit was ushered in with the formation of the IMF by the Bretton Woods agreement after World War II, which established the dollar as the only reserve currency with an exchange rate at $35 per ounce of gold. This vestigial gold standard had to be abandoned by President Nixon in 1971, when dollar earnings accumulating in foreign central banks from America's investment flows and trade deficits were offered in exchange for gold, particularly by France in the late sixties. Continuation of the arrangement could have depleted U.S. gold reserves, or led to an upward adjustment of the gold price, effectively a politically unacceptable dollar devaluation.

Nixon's step removed all restraints on national as well as international credit generation by fully and absolutely substituting the U.S. dollar for the precious metal as the universal medium of exchange, macro-economic accounting denominator, and reserve asset at the same time. An arrangement openly embraced by central banks, governments, and international businesses, because of its facilitating convenience. The world needed the dollar and America's perennial and growing trade deficits assured a growing supply of the currency. As dollar reserves stacked up worldwide, so did liquidity in all economies that accepted the dollar at face value, financing economic booms wherever they went ashore.

With the gold exchange option removed, a new phenomenon began to surface. It appeared in the form of a financial vortex, a money machine of epic proportions. Expanding trade deficits over a period of three decades kept dollars cascading into the world market, only to be returned by foreigners trusting in the currency's enduring value and omnipotence. Not only did foreigners willingly finance U.S. trade deficit for so long, they also kept buying public and private debt instruments thereby fueling the country's ballooning internal and external debts.

Foreign capital thus assumed the role normally reserved for domestic savings, which gradually disappeared, giving the country a sense of unlimited wealth creation. This feeling was intensified through accommodating monetary and credit policies of the Federal Reserve leading not only to ample liquidity, but also a general debt and deficit mentality throughout the country. The end results are an artificially high standard of living and excessive asset valuations in stocks, real estate, and artificially low interest rates like those in the Japan of the eighties.

But, it inevitably turned the country from a comfortable position of being the largest creditor nation into the world's largest debtor in the course of one and a half decades. In 1980 the U.S. had a favorable net external investment position of $361 billion, its zenith. By 2002 it was reversed into a $2.6 trillion deficit. Foreigners at this moment have claims against the U.S. amounting to $9.1 trillion compared to $6.4 trillion in foreign assets for the U.S. Foreign claims of this magnitude amount to no less than 61% of total international debt positions according to the Bank for International Settlements (BIS), the central guardian bank in Switzerland. America's net foreign liabilities reach about one third of the country's annual GDP. At such levels, the deficits should begin to cast a shadow on the dollar's appearance of invincibility, normally evidenced by rising interest charges for perceived higher risks associated with capital transfers, and exchange rate adjustments. Both are beginning to surface, which foreshadows interest rate hikes, a weaker dollar, and the end of America's standard of living from rising prices and the collapse of the debt pyramid in its wake.

It follows simply from the law of supply and demand. Commodities in unlimited supply lose value over time, and in order to foster the impression of a stable dollar, central banks around the world were persuaded to sell reserves of gold in their vaults, the only possible barometer of the dollar's real value. Even the IMF reduced its gold holdings by 36 million ounces between 1999 and 2002. By shedding gold reserves no longer needed for exchange reserve purposes, the gold price was kept artificially depressed reinforcing the impression of dollar strength, even though the dollar supplies began to rapidly outstrip gold holdings. An interesting side show concerning alleged manipulations of the gold price is offered by a pending antitrust law suit filed by Blanchard & Co., a New Orleans coin and bullion dealer, against Barrick Gold and J.P. Morgan Chase claiming a conspiracy to control the gold price. Barrick's claim of immunity from suit as an agent of central banks in the implementation of their gold policies, was denied by the court. Former President George Bush Sr. is an ex-member of Barrick's board. It should be noted at this point that, historically, all paper currencies have lost value against gold, and it stands to reason that the imbalance between reserve dollars and the yellow metal will ultimately be corrected, powerful intervention not withstanding.

The flip-side of such exuberant credit creation and artificially high standards of living is, of course, increased vulnerability to economic downturns, erosion of asset values, and potential bankruptcy, both public and private. It also means potential loss of all belongings for the average consumer, the paraphernalia of his good life, and a formerly solid credit rating, the basis for future loans. Consumers today do not understand that easy credit can deteriorate into bitter dependency and financial enslavement for a life-time, because they do not see debt as their guaranteed companion unlike savings, jobs, or income. Seen in this light, what they saw as the economic miracle of all times, may very well turn out to be a crushing illusion of epic proportions, a mirage produced with smoke and mirrors by experts in deluding the masses.

All these developments shed a different light on the term "globalization." Free trade and international capital movements have, undoubtedly, benefited the world economy. But the dollar standard provided America with a special economic windfall bonus estimated to be equivalent to an additional 1.5–2% of America's GDP, because it did not force the country to play by traditional trade rules whereby a country finances its imports with earnings from exports in order to keep trade accounts in balance. The country owned and controlled the source of unlimited purchasing power permitting, for as long as the dollar was accepted without question, the country to continue building the "New Era" or "New World Order," the supremacy of America in a tolerant world.

Probably unintended at first, it has all the makings of a clever perpetuum mobile for wealth creation at this moment. Buy foreign goods and services, pay in dollars, and get them back as capital imports to cover the many trade and budget deficits, which domestic savings would be totally unable to handle. Just make sure to increase imports to keep the wheels lubricated for ever more of the same. But, it leads not only to grave distortion of global trade, production, and capital allocation, it also impoverishes the American working class which is displaced by cheap foreign imports, and threatens foreign creditors with catastrophic loss of capital once the money machine comes to a grinding halt. It is their capital, after all, which finances U.S. government waste and expensive military campaigns, both of them historic loss operations. First signs appear in the war against Iraq, which cannot be won and stretches America's financial blanket to the point where the country has to ask for help from all nations of the world.

A recent report from the New Economics Foundation in London sees it this way: *"Globalization was triggered by elected politicians, and central bankers, in both the U.S. and the U.K. In the post-Vietnam war era, led by Richard Nixon and later Ronald Reagan, these politicians sought ways to avoid making the "structural adjustments" necessary to the American economy if debts incurred by foreign wars were to be repaid by U.S. taxpayers. Rather, these politicians preferred to disband the existing system of paying off debts by exchanging gold, and opening up capital markets, so that the U.S. could borrow to pay off its debts. This new arrangement also allowed them to print the money in which they paid off those debts (unlike poor countries which have to repay debts in foreign currencies like dollars or sterling). British politicians and central bankers were only too happy to act as U.S. intermediaries in the capital markets. Together they constructed a new financial architecture that effectively obliges central banks of both rich and poor countries to lend to the U.S. by buying U.S. Treasury bills (debt).*

It is U.S. treasury bills that have now effectively become the world's reserve currency—where once that reserve currency was neutral (gold). . . . It is this international financial system that makes the U.S. administration so arrogant in its refusal to "adjust" its economy by cutting spending and paying its way. . . . It is this financial system, which makes the U.S. financiers so confident that the rest of the world will continue to finance their nation's extravagant spending binge."

Adds David Goldman, head of debt research at Bank of America Securities: *"America is at little risk for the foreseeable future, simply because the world's capital has nowhere else to go."* (Wall Street Journal, 13 August, 2003).

Goldman may be correct in summing up the history of the last three or four decades from the American perspective. It explains the nonchalant attitude towards the country's perennial twin deficits in external trade and government budgets, the explosive growth in consumer and corporate indebtedness, the appearance of excessive investments and valuations in real estate and financial assets, all without the cover of domestic savings, only the trusting willingness of foreigners to invest their savings at low interest rates to keep the hollow standard of living afloat. It is estimated that 80% of the world's savings have gone to feeding the voracious appetite for capital of 5% of its total population.

It also shows in the demands for foreign financial and manpower assistance in the Iraq theater. What choice do countries have, for instance, that run all the great trade surpluses with the U.S. If they want to continue their lucrative export business, and prevent their holdings of dollars from collapsing in value, they better send them back to where they came from to finance more export business. The Euro, the yen, and gold could be, and promise to be increasingly so, an investment alternative, but likely only at the expense of thriving exports to the U.S. or, in the worst case, direct military intervention.

The positive aspect here lies in the fact that the U.S. are a solid credit risk, always able to repay their foreign debts denominated in dollars, and Fed. Governor Ben S. Bernanke has reassured the world that America's hi-tech printing presses can furnish unlimited supplies of those on demand, at any time.

The British source concludes in its ground-breaking economic analysis "Real World Economic Outlook" released on September 1, 2003, that excessive credit creation throughout the developed nations has led to ballooning financial assets far in excess of underlying real assets, in turn creating the price inflation for stocks, real estate, and a total financial asset bubble reaching 10 times the volume of national outputs of GDP. It also found that Japan's economic collapse was triggered by just about that ratio. It started when total financial assets exceeded GDP by a margin of 9:1.

In other words, the exploding financial sectors brought to life by central banks and public policies turned their interests from building the production base of their economies for guaranteed future prosperity to asset inflation and outright speculation. Economic wealth creation directly through financial and real estate markets instead of indirect wealth creation by production of tangible goods. This was the credo of the much-touted "New Era."

Evidence to the latter is furnished by two very different developments. The Chinese chief economist Wang Jian (2003) observed that 80% of all global money transactions before 1970 related to the production of material goods. But, only five years after the collapse of the Bretton Woods agreement, Nixon's closing of the gold window in 1971 and the introduction of the dollar reserve standard, only 20% of all money transactions related to the production and marketing of tangible goods. According to his latest estimate the ratio has declined to a mere 0.7% by 1997. (2003). He virtually confirms the conclusions of the British study cited above.

This period coincides roughly with the emergence of the global derivatives market, the multi-stage credit creation on the basis of real underlying or assumed assets, estimated at $140 trillion, or four times the global GDP. (BIS, September 2003). For the U.S. it was marked by the 1985–2000 period, when the output of material goods grew by 50%, but the money supply increased threefold or six times faster. This credit bubble was twice threatened with collapse. The first major blow came with the S&L debacle in 1989, a $250 billion bankruptcy which had to be shouldered by the American taxpayer. The second arose after the sudden implosion of the infamous LTCM, a U.S. arbitrage fund with thousands of derivative contracts amounting to more than $1 trillion worth of exposure in 1998. Actual losses sustained reached $4.5 billion, but that was enough to threaten the very foundations the world's financial system, and only the quick assembly of an international rescue team by Mr. Greenspan himself averted the worst. The crisis coincided with the Russian bond default, and the Asian currency crisis allegedly triggered by Mr. Soros, and generous credit expansion by the Fed to shore up investor confidence. The most famous fatality after LTCM was Enron, which collapsed in 2001 under a mountain of derivatives, leading to investor losses 16 times larger than those for LTCM. Still, the derivatives market is alive and strong, with a total volume estimated to reach $180 trillion, five times the size of the whole world economy. Examples of the credit escalator range from the sale of bundled mortgages by banks to specialized financial institutions like Fannie Mae and Freddie Mac, thus freeing up new funds for further lending by the selling bank, to the Pentagon's proposal to create a "futures market" on terrorism, through which investors could bet on likely scenarios like Middle Eastern events, terrorist attacks, even assassinations.

Fannie Mae, Freddy Mac, plus twelve regional Federal Home Loan Banks (FHLB) could all become the next links in this disaster chain. They are government-sponsored enterprises (GSEs), a unique hybrid of private company and federal agency. They were set up, originally, under Congressional charter to afford low-cost mortgages to low- and middle income Americans by promoting a stable secondary mortgage market for banks and other lenders to assure a constant supply of funds to home buyers. This charter provides special circumstances like exemption from regulatory oversight and reserve requirements commonly employed in the private banking sector, a special line of credit from the U.S. Treasury, government subsidies, exemption from state and local income taxes as well as SEC registration requirements. In addition both Fannie May and Freddie Mac could access up to $2.25 billion each from the Treasury in case of emergencies, while the FHLB system has a similar credit line of about $4 billion. In combination these special arrangements have created an aura of assumed, even though not explicitly stated, government guarantees for their liabilities.

Apparently, both have disappointed the purpose of their original charter, and now are seen as a major danger to the financial health of the nation, and indeed beyond. Uncontrolled assumption of debts beyond huge government subsidies, only one third of which is serving the primary mortgage lenders, the banks, in violation of charter commitments, another third is being invested in assets serving the shareholders, again in violation of the charter, and huge exposure to hedge fund operations, commonly called derivatives, have turned these organizations into gambling casinos with money—creating powers alongside the Fed system with monumental risks for taxpayers.

A first inkling of the stakes involved is presented by the reported loss in shareholder equity of $10.6 billion at Fannie Mae in the third quarter of 2001, and FHLB losses of $9 and $7 million in Atlanta and Pittsburgh, and more ominously $200 million in New York in the third quarter of 2003.

How far things got out of control is illustrated by the 2003 accounting scandal reported at Freddie Mac, involving understated earnings of $4.5 billion back to 2000. It caused the dismissal of Freddie's chief operating officer David Glenn "with cause," imposition of a $125,000 fine and loss of a $13 million severance package.

The three GSEs have a more than $2 trillion in combined debts outstanding, much of it accumulated in the low interest, high credit generation atmosphere since September 11, 2001. A study released by the IMF put the total GSE debt at $5.6 trillion as of End of March 2003, $2.4 trillion in directly issued securities plus $3.2 trillion in mortgage-backed securities. Putting these figures into perspective is the fact that they amount to 161% of all outstanding U.S. treasury securities and more than half of the annual GDP. Any reversal in interest rates, mortgage payments, and stock market valuations, slowdown in foreign investments in the U.S. or worse yet, a significant repatriation of funds precipitated by a falling dollar, the deepening quagmire in the Middle East, rising unemployment, falling incomes, and a host of other possibilities could suddenly capsize the GSEs under an avalanche of defaults.

The consequences would be unmanageable in view of the amounts involved, and devastating not only for the U.S. But it is not beyond the realm of the possible. Ominously, one indicator of the creditworthiness of U.S. government obligations is showing signs of weakness. The Morgan Stanley Government Income Trust, which holds about 42% of its assets in GSE securities, 30% in U.S. Treasuries, and 28% in short-term bonds, is beginning to show rising yields in late 2003, a measure of higher perceived investor risks. Even Mr. Greenspan begins to worry and warns of potential disaster for the financial system from the unrestrained behavior of these mortgage financiers.

Credit inflation led to overemphasis on financial assets, considered a quick, novel, and acceptable shortcut to sustainable wealth creation in the new era according to the interest groups promoting them, have de-facto led to a drop in real investment rates as a share of GDP throughout the G7 countries from the eighties to the nineties, and continued to fall in the second half of the last decade against the first half. The only exception were the U.S., where data were artificially inflated by about 10% on the basis of the "hedonic" price calculation for the computer industry, that was mentioned before. Productivity growth was cut in half as a consequence of lagging investments from annual 2.5% rates in the early seventies to 1.2% in the 1990s. At the same time unemployment in major countries has steadily edged up, and real earnings of employees, as a share of GDP, have fallen in the last three decades.

NEW TECHNOLOGIES

Another sign of coming times for the industrialized world is the absence of major technological advances comparable to those appearing after World War II. New industries which promise to have a mega-impact on production, investment, employment, personal income and consumption even remotely similar to that of automotive, electronics, transportation, telecommunications, medical techniques and devices, major pharmaceutical products for humans and animals, etc. are nowhere on the horizon. There could be one exception, hydrogen-based technology and other renewable energy sources, if the entrenched oil interests allow it to reach the market. There may be others as seminal concepts, but they are definitely far from being available to propel mankind to ever-loftier levels of living standards. There will be new products and processes, of course. Progress has followed mankind since Adam and Eve, but the question is whether they add net new economic activities, or turn only into mere replacements for already existing technology. What is needed are new industries of a magnitude to handle inter-stellar travel and building resorts on the moon.

DEMOGRAPHICS OF AGING

Even more imminent and foreboding are demographic changes affecting all industrialized economies. Their populations are growing older, want to retire earlier, enjoy a higher life expectancy, and thus represent a growing segment in the overall population. With birth rates falling this, obviously, poses a particular set of problems not seen before. The crux lies in the growing demands on retirement and health care plans. So far, both have been unfunded in all countries. Expenses were covered by taxing the incomes of the working population. But, with the latter declining percentage-wise, and unable to meet the needs of the older generation and their own standard of life simultaneously, something has to give. The handwriting is on the wall. Public pension and health care plans face a major liquidity crisis due to exploding disbursements, falling worker contributions and tax revenues. This leaves a choice between rising deficits, cuts in social services, or maintaining them at the expense of other programs.

America has opted for a split solution as far as Federal programs are concerned. Medicare, Medicaid, and unemployment benefits will be expanded as a government commitment made by President Bush. Higher taxes could afford this luxury, were it not for the fact that the same government has enacted a tax reduction program that makes this step politically unacceptable, exactly at a time when revenues are shrinking from weaker economic conditions. Thus revenues for the first 10 months of the 2003 federal budget were down by 3.9%, at the same time that expenditures soared by 7.1% in connection with exploding social services and the very costly Iraq campaign. It is expected to create a deficit of at least $500 billion for the full year, and a total of $5.8 trillion over the next few years, practically doubling the presently accumulated federal debt of $6 trillion.

But political expediency is winning over fiscal prudence, and the sure-to-follow twin deficits in trade and the federal budgets will be addressed in the usual fashion. Low interest rates for as long as possible, printing new money supplies, purchases of financial assets by the Federal Reserve, and financing by foreign private investors and their central banks like in the past. The latter seem to have little choice in the matter, if they want to avoid serious implications for their own economies as discussed above.

Balancing the budget requires the adoption of new definitions for long-term liabilities under public programs. The problem of an aging population for the Social Security Trust Fund is well known. The trust would be defunct under present income and expenditure projections by 2017, forcing reductions in payments to pensioners. One way to solve the problem is a gradual increase in the age at which retirees become eligible for payment. Right now it is either 62 (reduced benefits) or 65 (full benefits), but will rise to 65 to 67, and then 67 to 70 by the year 2029 under a proposal by President Bush. People will have to work five more years before they can draw a pension. Also, by the year 2017, Social Security payments will be calculated on an annuitized, that is actuarial table, basis rather than as a fixed payment scheme, which will reduce these payments by an estimated 50%.

In American budget practice, many established and known government agencies are not financed via the official budget, but are kept under a different system of bookkeeping, which serves to understate total government liabilities by a substantial margin, to the tune of 50% by some estimates.

Europe for its part, and because EU guidelines demand new deficits not to exceed 3% of GDP, has opted for slashing funds allocated as a vast number of subsidies to industry, agriculture, public services, and consumers. Germany faces a declining economy in real terms, slumping tax revenues, higher costs of social services, development of the former East Germany, and rising defense expenditures, all adding up to deficits exceeding the Maastricht guidelines. France, having similar problems, warned its workers of changes in mandatory retirement laws and other labor legislation, which led to a strike. Under discussion in the frantic search for ways to alleviate budget shortfalls are reductions in social services for pensions, health care, privatization of public property, reduction in the private and public labor force, longer work weeks and later retirement, etc.

Germany facing a "war among the generations" seriously discusses cutting socialized pension payments by 10% per year beginning with age 75. The U.S. is proposing legislation to make overtime pay illegal for eight million workers. Desperate efforts to plug budget holes which often are contradictory and of little or no economic sense. Drastic adjustments in sensitive areas of social contracts always carry the danger of a political backlash and civil disobedience.

As gerontocide is not accepted, at least for now, this can mean only one thing. It amounts to robbing senior citizens of their nest eggs accumulated for their golden years. The old generation produced the economic miracles of the past half century, but now is expected to accept a lower standard of living than they were looking forward to and, ultimately, a lower standard of living for everyone, because major wealth transfer from the older to the younger generation, as seen in the past, will become less and less possible.

The speed of the palpable decline depends not only on reduced levels of coverage and payout, but also interest rates. The low interest response to the looming economic crisis in America, Japan, and Europe at this moment has already had a devastating effect on retirees with their life savings in fixed income plans, bank accounts, or CDs. It could turn even worse, if after being forced to dip into the principal, inflation were to return in the aftermath of massive reflation policies everywhere.

Facing a largely synchronized environment, all industrialized nations are confronted by very similar problems at the same time. That makes it more than likely they will harmonize their responses by pulling the whole register of conventional and also unconventional means, because there is no one with actual experience to handle potential declines of this magnitude. The collapse of the world economy in the twenties and thirties of the last century, is only a distant memory, and the present political leadership as well as economists have practically only known prosperous times, which spawned their carelessness when it came to public spending. There will be much confusion, trials and errors, in the scramble for a secure footing and getting back on track. This becomes very obvious from central bank policies across the world which are under the strong influence and guidance of the U.S. Federal Reserve Board. It is also a regular point on the agendas of the periodic G8 meetings. Has the developed world reached the pinnacle of prosperity, and a living standard that it cannot maintain?

SOCIO-DEMOGRAPHIC CHANGES

A totally different problem arises from declining populations in the developed countries. UN estimates predict that Europe's population is going to decrease by 90 million people in the next 50 years, because of fertility rates are consistently falling below the natural rate of reproduction with 2.1 children per woman. Other areas of the world are predicted to follow the European example, even some developing nations, affecting no fewer than 34 countries by 2050. The reason for the developments are seen in the high use of contraceptives, higher levels of education and career opportunities for women, and thus less years devoted to child-rearing. Not only will this exacerbate the problems facing retirees, it could also cause major waves of migration from less developed regions to fill the void. For the EU it is estimated that just to maintain the ratio of workers to support the retirees at present levels would require net immigration of about three million persons a year between 2000 and 2050.

In contrast, the U.S. population is expected to expand by 40% until 2050, but 80% of that growth will come from present immigrants, their descendants, and new waves of immigration. In the 1990s the U.S. took in the largest number of immigrants in one decade ever. 33 million of its present 280 million people are foreign-born. Extending current trends, America's population could reach between 440–550 million by the middle of the century, surpassing Europe's population, and could reach almost 50% of China's where birth rates are falling fast under the influence of the one-child-per-family policy and rising affluence. (Economist, 9/4/2003).

This in itself should cause major demographic, social, and political adjustments, even clashes between totally different ethnic groups, which could very well disrupt the stable conditions of those nations affected. In America, it is associated with the growth of the Hispanic population and other minorities. Non-white Americans may be outnumbered as early as 2020 for the first time in the country's history. In Europe, there is a major influx of North Africans, Middle Easterners, Eastern Europeans, and Asians. Whether they can be accommodated without significant concessions by the indigenous residents remains to be seen.

Major shifts from the high population pressure centers to the areas suffering from population deflation might actually be a blessing in disguise for the normally wealthier nations. Having older people leave in larger numbers than natural replacement brings back into the economy can only cause a real estate crisis of major and enduring proportions. The demand for rental property, new or even old houses, will necessarily dwindle away, leading to a dramatic erosion of real estate values unless, of course, more liberal immigration policies are being drafted to fill the yawning population holes.

WORLD TRADE

Less conspicuous are massive schemes to manage the so-called free trade by means of massive exchange rate manipulations distorting the world's financial markets and trade patterns. Nobody wants their exports to suffer because of a strong currency. Asian countries have actively intervened in currency markets to keep the dollar up relative to their currencies. Japan bought around $190 billion in 2003, with another $900 billion allocated for 2004, to keep the yen low and exports to the American market and their trade surplus up. China has fixed the renminbi at CNY8.28:$1for the very same purpose. Part of both countries' surplus dollars is reinvested in American assets, in effect covering one third of the U.S. trade deficit in 2003.

China's fixed rate creates the specter of even more competitive Chinese export pressures on America and Europe suffering from already weak economic activity. Both would prefer a free Chinese currency floating up to relieve their trade balances and domestic employment pressures. Even the president of the Swiss National Bank recently declared his readiness to weaken the franc "if the strong franc hurts our exports." The gyrations of the Euro against the dollar from strong to weak and back again, similarly for the yen, the switch from a strong to a weak dollar policy in the U.S. for the dual purpose of getting more competitive clout in world trade, and allowing a more liberal credit policy at home, are indications of tactics to gain economic advantage.

A similar game was played before and during the Great Depression, then described as "beggar-thy-neighbor" policies, which ended in the total collapse of world trade. The willingness to tamper with currency values, in fact amounting to a deliberate debasement of national monies, is beginning to show in rising commodity prices as investors flee from paper currencies to hard assets.

In response to the dwindling dollar value, and concerns over not getting a fair price for their natural resources, Moslem countries have recently introduced the Gold Dinar, a functional gold currency and a deliberate strategy to depose the dollar standard reigning over world trade and global finances for the last half century or so. If successful, the end of the dollar era would cause painful adjustments on a global scale, financially and implicitly economically. It could very well blow away most of the wealth accumulated since World War II in the industrialized nations.

The list of currency woes is expanding. One of the reasons for the Iraq war is said to be Saddam Hussein's decision to invoice his oil exports in Euros, an outright challenge to the dollar's role in the global commodity markets. The effect on the U.S. economy would be incalculable, if that had been permitted to set an example for other oil exporters, who seem to discuss this step among themselves. Pertemina, the Indonesian oil conglomerate, let it be known recently, that they were considering this move. A very touchy situation for several reasons. Not taking this step would deprive oil exporters of potentially larger purchasing power from a declining dollar. Taking it might provoke American intervention a la Iraq. But, even for America, the question poses a dilemma. Forcing the retention of the dollar as the global lead currency would only expose America's industry to the fluctuations in the price for crude, which presently promises to be down for the intermediate term in view of the weak world economy and renewed Iraqi supplies.

For other countries this would amount to a welcome double subsidy bolstering their competitiveness in world markets from the twin effects of stable or declining oil prices and a falling dollar in the short run. Long-term and with demand for oil from a recovering world economy rising, a weak dollar would still cushion America's competition from the effects of rising energy prices, while broad siding the U.S.

Oil is a political and economic time bomb as shown by events unfolding once again in Iraq and beyond. Anglo-American interests are trying hard to monopolize oil production in the Middle East, estimated at 66% of global crude reserves plus that of the Central Asian oil fields, estimated at another 20% of world crude reserves, while keeping Russian oil interests at bay. It may also be seen as a determined effort to preserve the dollar over the Euro as the standard world currency.

The war against terrorism in Afghanistan was and still is connected with plans to build a pipeline from Central Asia through Afghanistan to the Indian Ocean. As realization of this project is very iffy due to the tenacious resistance of Taliban and alQaeda forces plus a number of unpredictable warlords ruling vast parts of the country, another project dealing with the construction of a huge pipeline between Baku on the Caspian Sea and Ceyhan on the Mediterranean is in the works. It will be financed with the help of the World Bank and the European Development Bank, which have committed $500 million each to the project, that will ultimately link Central Asian oil to Western markets.

But the pipeline needs to cross Georgia on its way from Azerbaijan to Turkey and the Mediterranean. Here former President Sheverdnaze wanted to get Russian oil interests to join the project, a move strenuously opposed by the Western consortium. As a result of the conflict, Sheverdnaze, became a casualty of the power struggle between East and West. He was reportedly toppled with the help of Western oil money and replaced by the new president Mikhail Saakashvili, a U.S. trained lawyer, who opposed the Russian energy plans for Georgia. (SchNEWS, issue 433, December 5, 2003, quoting the director of the 'Liberty Institute' of Georgia). It makes him the second implant of America's oil policy after Hamid Karzai, president of Afghanistan and a former employee of Unocal, a Halliburton subsidiary, which negotiated with the previous regime to build an oil/gas pipeline connecting the Central Asian energy fields with loading facilities in the Indian Ocean.

In view of all this wrangling, maybe the time has come for seriously searching for suitable alternative energy sources without oil's terribly disruptive potential for political, economic, environmental, and human upheaval. Among others, hydrogen technology has advanced to the commercialization stage. It is the ideal replacement candidate for oil, a 'democratic' product for being available to everyone, offers absolute independence from external meddling, besides being environmentally friendly.

Then, there is the perennial problem of barriers to free trade. Europe and America both subsidize agricultural exports with billions of dollars every year, making it difficult for countries with natural cost advantages to compete. The unwillingness to make concessions in their policy was the reason for the collapse of the WTO meeting in Cancun, Mexico, in the fall of 2003. Add higher tariffs on U.S. steel, which were rescinded recently, rejection of hormone laced or genetically modified animal and plant products by Europe and others, and the possibilities for retaliatory policies are enhanced, and not minimized, as they should, if one were to believe the lip service rendered on behalf of free trade.

An interesting perspective comes from the Chinese side which, for obvious reasons, is vitally interested in the geo-political implications of the Anglo-American attempt to get a stranglehold on the world's oil resources under the guise of fighting international terrorism, the fate of the dollar and possible alternative reserve currencies, as well as new realignments among present and former political and military alliances.

According to Mr. Wang Jian the Chinese expect to see 'a world in three' within about 15 years, led by the West Pacific Economic Zone as the largest trade area including China, Taiwan, Hong Kong, Japan, South Korea, and the Russian Far East with a population of 1.7 billion people and a GDP of $25 trillion. It will be followed by the expanded EU with a population of 500 million, and a GDP of $21 trillion. The third bloc consists of NAFTA with 400 million people and a GDP of $19 trillion. Importantly, he sees the role of the U.S. in the world economy gradually diminishing with their influence declining in Europe, not becoming significant in the Western Pacific, and increasingly limited to the Western hemisphere. He also makes a strong point that the Western Pacific Economic Zone is considered to remain relatively free of American influence, staking out China's special interest sphere without saying so directly. Also, "*the evolving tendency of the world's economic situation after the Cold War is probably that regionalization is stronger than globalization.*"

Interesting is the fact that he makes no mention of Russia as a whole, only the Eastern part of it. Does he see it eventually merging with Europe? This question has relevance from a different angle as Mr. Wang foresees a serious confrontation, maybe even armed conflict, between the U.S. and Europe over the Euro. His prediction is based on the observation of the falling U.S. stock market due to vast outflows of foreign capital, and the sharp decline of the dollar against the Euro. This is a major challenge to U.S. economic interests, because it might prevent the influx of capital that is needed for a continuation of foreign financing of the country's internal and external deficits. America is thus interested in destabilizing or even destroying the Euro. For this purpose the U.S. first launched the war in Kosovo, which did not produce the desired effect. Now, the oil card is being played. The EU depends on oil imports for 60% of its energy needs, the U.S. only to 20%. Pushing up the world price through a protracted war in Iraq, would thus impact the EU much stronger, weakening the Euro, Europe in general, plunge its trade into deficits, and destroy the attractiveness of the Euro for foreign investors. Hopefully, they would be persuaded to return to the dollar. (http://www.atimes.com/atimes/printN .html and http://www.rayeslemmens.com/).

A most interesting scenario, but it does not take into account that the rising Euro, even if not used as the billing currency, will neutralize higher oil prices to some degree. In addition, Europe is not totally dependent on American-controlled oil, because it is linked to Russia's vast oil and gas reserves that are flowing freely into Western Europe at this moment. The blockade of Russian energy by Western oil interests practically ties the two areas even closer together. Also, there is no assurance that America can effectively control oil supplies from the Middle East and Central Asia due to the instability of both regions engendered by the war against Iraq.

GOVERNMENT EXPANSION

The poor record of authorities in the developed nations in managing their economic affairs in good times, without contemplating and providing for eventual bad times, makes them politically liable for broken social promises, disillusionment, desperation, and potential social upheavals. It is also a sobering lesson for all democratic constituents to beware of putting so much blind trust in their governments, instead of exercising their constitutionally granted rights to control them. Now, everybody will pay for the public excesses encouraged or tolerated by their timid negligence.

One thing is absolutely certain. The government octopus keeps growing, which means more taxes, regimentation, erosion of individual liberties and living standards manifested by increasing demands for "politically correct" behavior. This is very clearly spelled out by the "Tax Freedom Day," celebrated in many countries. In the U.S., the average taxpayer had to work until January 30 to pay for all applying taxes in 1913. In 1964, that date had advanced to April 13, and in 2003 to April 19, after going as high as April 30 in 2000. By 2003 these taxpayers had to work 109 days to pay the government which, incidentally, is more than the 105 days required to cover basic necessities of food, shelter, and clothing combined. Seen differently, the effective tax burden in America has advanced from 5.7% on national income in 1990, to 33% in 2000.

Compared to other countries this is not even bad. In England the famous day has rapidly advanced from May 23 in 1993, to June 2 in 2003, and is projected to march ahead to June 9 in 2005. For Euro taxpayers there are no better news in store. June 13 is the estimated cut-off date to meet all tax obligations here in 2003. Whether these dates will be the utmost limit taxpayers will be willing to tolerate is hard to tell. But, with actual tax burdens for individuals reaching the 50% level or above, the cracking point may be close. America's revolution was triggered by an estimated tax liability to the British crown of only 3%, after all.

The miracle economies after World War II were founded first on rebuilding ravaged countries, the liberalization of world trade, international aid programs, the appearance of totally new industries, prodigious social programs, liberal credit policies, all adding up to rapidly increasing wealth and consumption without much government interference. With the boom conditions behind us, the demand creation factors have given way to demand maintenance, slowly growing or even stagnant consumption patterns that leave consumers, industry, and governments with often unmanageable levels of debt and mounting deficits. Fertile grounds for government meddling in order to control the imbalances For the U.S. there is the added burden of huge deficits in foreign trade and the federal budget from the war on terrorism which, by the way, could easily infect other countries, if they make the American war their own, and thus become drawn into a messy confrontation with terror organizations.

DEFLATION

The enormous credit expansion, initiated by the Fed in the U.S. to fend off the possibility of recession, has spilled over into the world economy driven by America's trade deficits, has led to the formation of industrial capacities outstripping world demand in developing nations, the appearance of bubbles in asset valuations from financial assets, to real estate, and raw materials. Yet, these signs of economic exuberance in some sectors cannot hide the underlying facts of stagnant to declining demand, consumer prices, profits, and employment, the typical attributes of deflation in the industrialized nations. They are evident worldwide in industries like wireless and telecommunications, semiconductors, electronics, business software, automobiles, airlines, and tourism.

Stock markets around the world are in danger of implosion from shrinking business profits, a $180 trillion derivatives sword overhanging the global financial system, expanding social welfare programs, government waste, etc. This is a fact, that even temporary appearances to the contrary, from artificially pumped up equity valuations far beyond historical norms and other assets cannot make disappear.

A negative wealth effect is in the making that bodes poorly for consumption and investments. The 80% fall in Japan's real estate from all-time highs could spread to similar bubbles visible in the U.S. and Europe. Deflation's inevitable companions are dropping investments and employment. Unemployment in Europe exceeds 10%, and is also climbing in the U.S. beyond the official, and likely understated, 6% mark.

The key to battling the deflationary spiral is not the consumer alone, usually the central focus of attention and remedial action. Normal economic growth depends on two factors: consumption and business investments. If companies do not invest, expand revenues, profits, and employment, consumer income declines. Consumers do not employ people, nor do they pay wages, salaries, and business taxes. Industry does. With business investment in a dead spot, the circular flow of production, income, saving and investment, and consumption is interrupted. How to jumpstart the deadlock in economic activity, and prevent further deflation is the key question.

Contributing to the malaise is the indiscriminate pursuit of free trade and foreign investment, which has become the bible of all politicians. It has caused a global overcapacity in the manufacturing sector, severe competition from developing countries with their inherent cost advantages like China, the decline in competitiveness for manufacturing in developed countries leading to outsourcing and abandonment of domestic output and rising unemployment. A sort of self-evisceration because the production industries are more important to national income than service industries with much lower wage rates and per-capita income. The inevitable outcome, unfortunately, seems to be a sinking standard of living for the industrialized world, lower consumption, production, and investment where more is needed, falling profits, and more deflation.

In support of this scenario it is estimated, that middle-income couples in the U.S. have added 20 weeks of work, equal to 5 additional months, over the 30–year period 1970–2000 just to maintain their way of the expected good life. More and more of this extra work is needed to run ahead of the rising flood of debt at their heels, despite all the reported productivity gains. Americans paid about $63 billion in credit card interests in 2000, and late fee payments to lender banks increased from $1.7 billion in 1996 to $7.3 billion in 2002. (Elliott Wave, November 2003). Clearly, the extra efforts lead only to growing consumer illiquidity. No wonder then, that at the end of September 2003 personal bankruptcies had climbed by 7.8% year-over-year to an all-time high of 1.63 million according to a report from the Administrative Office of the U.S. Courts. Ultimately, these are so-called misery indices for the wealthiest society in history.

CONCLUSION

The present situation is strongly reminiscent of the period between World War I and II, when the world economy went into a severe slump accompanied by rising tariff barriers, outright trade warfare, currency devaluations, bilateral trade agreements, and virtual cessation of international investment. The many uncertainties facing the world of today forebode poorly for a continuation of the rapid expansion in global investments, both direct and portfolio, trade, and the straight continuation of economic globalization seen so far. A major slowdown here is almost a certainty for the Western economies, but the same may not be true for the fast developing giants of Asia. They are well on their way to becoming the next centers of global economic activity. China, India, and other nations of Asia show economic growth rates of which Western nations can only dream at this moment.

China is now the fourth largest industrial nation behind the U.S., Germany and Japan. It has the capacity to furnish the rest of the world with practically any type of manufactured item they choose, and at prices that are already threatening industries in America and Europe. According to the Wall Street Journal China's market shares in worldwide sales of the consumer durables reach: 50% of all cameras; 35% of television sets; 30% of air conditioners; 25% of washing machines; 22% of refrigerators; and 70% of metal cigarette lighters. $40% of all microwave ovens sold in Europe originate here. It is already the world's largest manufacturer of textiles, garments, footwear, steel, refrigerators, TVs, radios, toys, office products, and motorcycles. No wonder then, that the country was the third largest exporter after the U.S. and Germany in 2002, and could take the number two spot in the near future.

That is why calls are heard for China to adjust the presently fixed exchange rate of their currency by letting it float freely in financial markets, which would mean an upward move to the relief of the developed world. India has become a choice supplier for software development and communication facilities at very low costs as mentioned before. That is why American banks, credit card companies and others are transferring statistical, marketing, and billing services there in growing numbers.

In both cases the technical know how and facilities at their disposal are equivalent to the best the developed world has to offer. Their ascent begins under the most favorable conditions, with the latest in technology and almost unlimited investment capital at their disposal. In combination with huge populations, young and eager to acquire the necessary professional skills and higher standards of living, they will turn into economic, military, and political power houses to rival the developed world.

Either country alone has more population than all industrialized nations put together and given their comparatively high internal growth rates plus foreign trade advantages they are bound to overtake the West including Japan in the not-so-distant future.

That fact is hidden by a statistical veil measuring their output of GDP at prevailing official IMF exchange rates. Switching to purchasing power parity comparisons (PPP) drives home the fact how quickly they are closing the gap between themselves and the industrialized world. China is believed to only weigh in at one tenth the U.S. GDP by the first method of calculation, where in reality it may already reach 50%, or even more. According to the World Bank's estimate on the PPP basis (all data in $trillions), China produced a Gross National Income of $5.2; India $2.9; the U.S. $9.8; Japan $3.2; and the EMU $7.3 in 2001. Even more telling are the annual growth rates of China with 7–8% and India's 5–6%, which is 5–7 times the rates of important industrial nations. (2003 World Development Indicators, World Bank)

To get an impression of the forces propelling China, one only needs to take a look at the dynamic transformation of Shanghai, which will host the Olympic games in 2008, and Beijing at this moment. The pace of real estate developments is breathtaking, as are the ultra-modern industrial park complexes sprouting up all over the country. China has, already, become the fourth largest automotive market in the world. Vehicle sales have grown by 80% to 4 million in 2003 against a 60% increase in 2002. Just watching evening news casts demonstrates how rapidly city traffic there has graduated from pedestrian and bicycle to automobiles. Further attesting to the advanced stage of the country's technological capability is the launch of China's first manned space mission in October of 2003.

Looking at the world through PPP-corrected lenses that is by eliminating the price level distortions introduced by official exchange rates, one is quickly forced to take note of a dramatic change in the world map of real economic output. Of the World Bank's total global GNI estimate (all data in $ trillions) for 2001 amounting to $45.2; the U.S. and Canada provided $10.8 (23.8%); Western Europe $7.3 (16.2%); Southern Asia from Pakistan to Indonesia and the Philippines $10.2 (22.5%); Japan and Korea $4.0 (8.8%); Latin America $3.6 (8.0%); and the rest of the world 20.7%.

This puts all Asian economies solidly into first place with a combined 31.3% share. With the exception of Japan and Korea these are countries that will have to increasingly address the expectations of their stirring populations. By necessity that will lead to expanded trade and investment activities among themselves and the rest of the world, which are so closely linked as was shown in the preceding discussion. The West better prepare for a globalization boomerang from that part of the world. It is an indisputable fact that the developing world as a whole already has a higher economic output than the so-called industrialized nations, but it will be East Asia that forces a realignment of the world's power structure, politically, economically, and militarily.

A recent study adds bold projections through 2050 to these outlines of realistic economic power shifts affecting the so-called developed world. The study is based on exchange-rate-dependent GDP estimates,which affects their relative economic weight at this moment and, of course, the time frame of their dynamics. According to the study, the GDP of major economies will develop between 2002 and 2050 as follows; all data in US$ billion.

	2002	2050
USA	10,446	35,165
Western Europe*	5,824	12,594
Japan	4,358	6,673
China	1,252	44,453
India	469	27,803

*France, Germany, Italy, and UK only. (Source: Goldman Sachs, 2003)

There is other tangible evidence of the dynamics driving this area. The World Trade Center in New York was the monumental symbol of America's economic prowess. It was the tallest building in the world for a long time with 415 and 417 m, but had to yield that distinction to the Petronas twin towers (452 m) in Kuala Lumpur before it melted down in the September 11 attack. In turn, the Malaysian wonder was beaten by the Taipei 101 (508m) tower within a handful of years, which claims to be totally safe from typhoons and earthquakes in one of the world's most active tremor zones. It may not enjoy the spotlight of attention for too long, though, as the Chinese are planning to build an even taller building—The Shanghai World Financial Center—for the 2008 Olympics to be held in that metropolis.

Not to be outdone by all that competition, New York plans to rebuild the World Trade Center site with a memorial and tower to reach 1,776 feet (583 m) tall, including a 91m spire. Why this particular footage? Because the number reflects the year of the Declaration of Independence and it makes the structure the number one again in the world.

How significant these competitive rivalries will turn out to be in the long term, at least, they are peaceful and thus welcome. But they cannot hide the fact that other areas of the world besides the industrialized nations are catching up rapidly. Are we looking at the decline of the so-called developed world, both relatively and absolutely speaking? It would fulfill the prophecy of the German historian and philosopher Oswald Spengler, who not only foresaw the "Decline of the West" in two volumes published under this title in the late 1920s, but correctly predicted the rise of Asia, the "yellow peril" in his words, to cause the West's fall from power.

Epilogue: Globalization in Conflict

"The state is likewise nothing but the guarantor of all exploitation, to the profit of a small number of prosperous and privileged persons, and to the loss of the popular masses. In order to assure the welfare, prosperity, and privileges of some, it uses everyone's collective strength and collective labor, to the detriment of everyone's human rights. In such a set-up, the minority plays the role of the hammer, and the majority that of the anvil."

Mikhail Bakunin,
Three Lectures to Swiss members of the Communist International, May 1871.

"The fact is that the average man's love of liberty is nine-tenths imaginary, exactly like his love of sense, justice, and truth. He is not actually happy when free; he is uncomfortable, a bit alarmed, and intolerably lonely. Liberty is not a thing for the great masses of men. It is the exclusive possession of a small and disreputable minority, like knowledge, courage, and honor. It takes a special sort of man to understand and enjoy liberty—and he is usually an outlaw in democratic societies."

H.L. Mencken, Baltimore Evening Sun, February 12, 1923.

Globalization can be evaluated along different dimensions. Only its economic aspect has been chosen for discussion in the preceding study: the global role of private enterprise as a familiar and controversial contributor to the process. Its mark on the integration of the global economy was found to be rather modest if taken as a group, and even much less so when considering the contributions of individual national enterprises as potential purveyors of national interests, as public discussions would have it.

Compared to other globalization factors, foreign direct investments complete with their financing, production, and trading activities look not only small, they are also relatively benign with their principal focus on profits to be gained from visible and controllable commercial activities rather than hard-fisted political tactics.

In this latter aspect, they are definitely outflanked by other globalization forces that might collectively be grouped under the term geopolitics, less transparent strategies designed to gain influence, power, and profits by any means including, but not limited to, ideological inroads, military campaigns, trade sanctions, subversion, financial manipulations in the broadest sense, deception, disinformation, etc. to further the goals of a person or a group blinded by greed and delusions of grandeur. Support for their cause is usually solicited by hiding their true intentions under the cloak of moral and emotional appeals, or precious national interests whose protection becomes a patriotic duty. The past overflows with examples of such power plays, all pretending to cure the real or contrived evils of this world. Now, the world is facing a new political ground swell that embraces all-to-familiar aspects and arguments in a new guise.

THE NEW AMERICAN CENTURY

Every epoch in human history had its proprietary vision of the ideal society, or Weltanschauung, imbedding the political credo and mission of powerful movers and shakers in their quest for shaping the world in their image. Accordingly, dominant dogmas pursued secular or spiritual aspirations, territorial expansion or seclusion, political power for an elite or the masses, Machiavellian despotism, totalitarianism, capitalism or socialism. Whatever the delusion du jour, it always went hand-in-hand with an obsession of its leaders to imprint their visions by means of peaceful persuasion on the greatest possible number of blind followers, or by force on unwilling subjects.

The compulsion to search for new vistas has, not surprisingly, produced two major and fundamentally opposed contemporary visions, blueprints for a remodeled world, and thus on a collision course. One, oriental in origin, is the fervent Islamic fundamentalism, the politico-religious force inspired by the strict interpretation of prophet Mohammed's teachings laid down in the Koran, which demand full submission to the word of Allah in a Muslim's daily life, and conversion of the infidels to Islam. This would technically cover the rest of humanity, but is primarily directed at the Western world that harbors the rival Christian faith and heretic dogmas like capitalism, communism, and the worship of utterly decadent lifestyles according to their values. America evokes a particularly strong enemy image, because it magnifies all the undesirable Western traits and tries to spread the American way of life via political or military interventionism. A splendid example of cultural clash. Osama bin Laden deliberately speaks of the West as the crusaders, the arch enemies of the budding Islamic faith 1300 years ago, when he refers to America's military presence in the sacred lands of Mohammed. By using a familiar and compelling analogy for all devout Muslims, he is fanning anti-western sentiments among one billion or more followers of the faith.

The other, Anglo-American in origin, and thus particularly offensive to Muslims because of both nations' imperialist history in the cradle of Islam, the oil-rich Middle East, posits a mundane dogma without any transcendental, philosophical, or humanistic embellishments, simply offering the "New Era" or "New World Order."

By no means a widely understood, accepted or inspiring ideology with a global appeal, and the capacity to evoke the fire of enthusiasm or widespread popular support the lifeblood of any grandiose idea. Actually, just the opposite may be true. A doctrine for a very small, elitist, but very determined inner circle of several hundred people, at the most, with a fervent nationalistic bent. But what they lack in numbers, they make up by sitting at the controls over huge military and economic resources.

Proponents are made up of American academics, statesmen, politicians, business and military leaders, and media moguls, backing an agenda that clearly blends elements of pragmatism, capitalism, socialism, and unbridled national power politics. The credo and mission of this exclusive club is global hegemony.

The power brokers setting the course for the new world order draw their inspiration from the deeply ingrained dogma of America's uniqueness among all nations since colonial days which entitles, even demands, the nation to assume a leadership role in the world. This idea is nurtured and expanded by a number of little known, and to outsiders almost obscure American think tanks and strategy incubators. In combination, and closely networked with America's mainstream political powers, they represent the spiritual fountain from which the new order flows, so to speak.

The oldest is the *Council on Foreign Relations* (CFR), located in New York, and entirely comprised of U.S. citizens. Founded with Rockefeller backing in 1921 as the American branch of the British Royal Institute on International Affairs (RIIA) which in turn was the brainchild of the British financier Cecil Rhodes and devoted to the reunification of the US and the British Empire. Its key meetings are strictly confidential and absolutely off the record. Its quarterly journal "Foreign Affairs" plus regular meetings and seminars reveal a glimpse of its luminaries and parts of their agenda for the new world.

The second, the *American Enterprise Institute for Public Policy Research*, (AEI) founded 1943 in Washington, DC, (http://www.aei.org) is dedicated to preserving and strengthening the foundations of freedom, government, private enterprise, cultural and political institutions, a strong foreign policy and national defense.

The third, the *Trilateral Commission* (TC), was organized by David Rockefeller in 1973. It holds regular annual meetings that are not open to the public and independent media, but may conduct periodic seminars that are less exclusive. Membership is limited to the elite from the US, Canada, Western Europe and Japan numbering in the hundreds. The TC issues periodic reports labeled "Triangle Papers." David Rockefeller has served as the organization's perennial chairman since its founding days.

The TC has been called the Child of Bilderberg, alluding to a fourth power group in this constellation that is European in origin, possibly even at the Vatican's initiative, and comprised of two thirds European and one third American membership. The Bilderberg Group was named after the Dutch hotel of the same name in Oosterbeek, Holland, where the first meeting was convened under the auspices of Price Bernhard of the Netherlands in May of 1954. Super-secret and heavily guarded annual meetings are attended by about 115 participants, one third from government and politics, the rest from industry, finance, education, and the media, predominantly from NATO members. Lately, some Russian and Eastern European delegates has been observed. The events are never made public, nor are agendas or final communiqués for that matter.

The chairmanship has always been held by European dignitaries, with a predominance of English citizens. Meetings are usually rotated among European locations, with a sprinkling of U.S. and Canadian venues. American participation dates back to the Eisenhower administration. From the start, this group was heavily influenced by the Rockefeller family, the Standard Oil competition to Prince Bernhard's Royal Dutch Petroleum. The Bilderberg Group has been characterized as a flexible and informal international leadership forum in which different viewpoints can be expressed freely to deepen mutual understanding in an atmosphere of total privacy. According to former participants no resolutions are proposed, no votes taken and no policy statements made.

This may be the case, yet the consultations may still serve a broad-based strategy diffusion purpose for the new world order movement. This, at least, is more or less suggested by the observation that its meetings always take place ahead of the Group of Eight, or G-8, summits, and in close geographic proximity to each other. It may be inferred that the Bilderbergers act as soft-glove implementation facilitators for the heads of state representing the core of the developed world. From there, policies may also filter down to other states and international facilitator agencies like the UN, the World Bank, the IMF, OECD, etc. for coordinated action. (Nexus Magazine, Volume 3,#1 Dec '95-Jan.'96; Google, Bilderberg).

The fifth element in this emerging world government is named "Project For The New American Century," (PNAC), which emerges as a very determined American action plan to assume world leadership. It presents a sharply polarized alternative to the rather low-key and broad-based attempts at world union by mutual consent envisioned by the Bilderbergers, and embodied in the UN. A non-profit, educational organization closely associated with the neo-conservative movement, whose membership includes many of the important actors in the present G. W. Bush administration.

By historic standards, the dogma is in its infancy, and like a child it is certain to grow a lot. Its foundation was laid with the initial publication of the "Defense Planning Guidance" by Paul Wolfowitz, now Deputy Secretary of Defense in the Bush Administration, in 1992, which later evolved into the 'Bush Doctrine.' The PNAC's "Statement of Principles" appeared on June 3, 1997 advocating America's global leadership. Among its signatories appear names like Jeb Bush, the brother of President G.W. Bush, Dick Cheney, Dan Quayle, Donald Rumsfeld, and Paul Wolfowitz. Its key mission unequivocally states that America is "*to shape a new century favorable to American principles and interests.*" (http://www.newamericancentury.org/).

The actual proposals advanced in their publications range from the ouster of Saddam Hussein (1998!) to "*discouraging advanced industrial nations from challenging our leadership or even aspiring to a larger or global role*" according to the Guardian Weekly of London, March 20-26, 2003, p. 11. This statement echoes the New York Times explanation of the Wolfowitz Doctrine stating America's political and military mission to: "*ensure that no rival superpower be allowed to emerge. With its focus on this concept of benevolent domination by one power, the Pentagon document articulates the clearest rejection to date of collective internationalism.*" Such semi-official statement amounts to a premature obituary for the UN which, after all, was the brainchild of post World War II American foreign policy.

Consistent with these new principles is America's frantic preoccupation with potential adversaries ranging from Russia, China, to Iran, Iraq, Syria, and North Korea. The latest ruminations of this nationalistic interest group can be viewed on their website, and in publications like *Commentary, National Review, New Republic, The Public Interest, The New York Post, The Wall Street Journal, and Weekly Standard.*

Piecing the various sources together reveals a master plan for a new world that is purely Anglo-American in origin, outlook, and leadership. The British heritage in this constellation cannot be overlooked, as many similarities to the British Empire's policies can be established A well drafted model plan for world domination under the motto to spread "American Greatness," built on purely quantitative calculation in military and economic terms, advocacy of military adventurism and intervention as a justified tool of foreign policy, cultural hubris, a healthy disregard for a potential backlash and, thus, of explosive conflict potential.

A recent broadcast on National Public Radio brought the new ideology down to a neat common denominator. The statement made by a contender for the 2004 presidential election declared that *"to survive in today's world you have to dominate it."* A modernized and supercharged rebirth of America's Manifest Destiny, the nineteenth century doctrine declaring it to be the destiny of Anglo-Saxon nations, notably the U.S., to dominate the entire Western hemisphere. Yesterday it was directed at America's neighbors, today at the whole world.

The new version of this historic dogma guiding present-day American foreign policy is tightly woven into the nation's unshakeable belief in its own uniqueness and superiority. It was Alexis de Tocqueville, the astute and critical observer of the young nation almost 200 years ago, who coined the phrase "American exceptionalism," the defining difference between the American nation and the rest of the world, which forms the basis for its moral claim to world leadership.

It is the sum total of America's physical attributes, values, morals, institutions, traditions, and beliefs which make the country so attractive to outsiders at one moment, and strange, even scary, the next. It is the often stark black-white contrast of what makes up the "American way-of-life" that leads to these opposing reactions. The co-existence of old traditions and ultra-liberal ideas, advocacy of lofty human principles and naked worship of materialism, benevolence and unbridled greed, generous tolerance and iron-fisted displays of dominance, open-mindedness and rigid dogmatism, worship of democratic equality and glaring social injustice.

Many of these sharp contrasts are admired by the outside world as expressions of a youthful and dynamic nation. Others receive more sober evaluations and even outright question marks. The judicial common law and jury system, driven by almost a million lawyers, more than the outside world has combined, appears subjective and unpredictable in comparison to the code law system practiced by the majority of nations. Similarly, the civil rights agenda, the conformist pressures for politically correct thinking and behavior, multi-culturalism, etc. are bewildering to nations with centuries of societal evolvement, but still tolerant of differing viewpoints, languages and ethnic affiliations. One peculiar American trait is, unquestionably, the "not-invented-here-syndrome," which prevents the adoption of the clearly advantageous metric system over the less convenient measures for length, weight, volume, area, temperature, dry measures, even time, etc. A country full of such puzzling cross-currents is seen as still in search of a stable identity by the outside world, a view that will weigh heavily in responding to America's present compulsion to imprint itself on the world. (*"A nation apart. A survey of America."* The Economist, November 8,2003. Lipset, 1996)

This historic package is strongly evident in numerous policy statements by President Bush. In his 9/11 memorial service at the Washington National Cathedral he says *"Our responsibility to history is already clear: to answer these attacks and the world of evil."* In the 2002 State of the Union address he calls the war against terrorism a broad-based moral obligation: *"History has called America and our allies to action."* A more refined vision comes from his graduation speech to the cadets at West Point that same year where he advanced the new policy of preemptive attacks against terrorists and *"unbalanced dictators"* in this form: *"Our security will require all Americans to be forward-looking and resolute, to be ready for preemptive action when necessary to defend our liberty and to defend our lives."*

This statement signals a clear break with the former foreign policy principle of containment, that guided the cold war period, and introduction of the new position justifying a first strike. It makes America and American interests the sole arbiter for situations triggering the preemption principle: *"The moral truth is the same in every culture, in every time, and in every place. America will call evil by its name."* In the January 2003 State of the Union address and the February speech to the National Religious Broadcasters convention, President Bush was even more deliberate about America's fundamental responsibilities to the world by declaring: *"We must also remember our calling as a blessed country to make this world better . . . to help the afflicted, and defend the peace, and confound the designs of evil men."*

Furthermore, America's advocacy of freedom is not just a special interest of America, because freedom is not *"America's gift to the world. It is God's gift to humanity."* Peacemaking, and defeat of global terrorism, is the core demand of this policy: *"we are called . . . to lead the world to peace."* It justifies the employment of America's superior military power anywhere and anytime in the world.

Humanistic, even messianic principles combine with strong religious undercurrents which are noteworthy for a country that advocates a clear division of matters of state and the church. President Bush claims to be reborn Christian and obviously sees himself and the country as tools of divine providence, not unlike Osama bin Laden on the other side of an epochal conflict that is just starting to become more intense. More ominously, he sees the world as a polarized division between the good and the bad—*"the axis of evil."* (Tony Carnes, 2003).

Disagreement with America's claim to absolute supremacy is not to be taken lightly. The statement: *"who is not with us, is against us"* is a serious and intentional warning, an outright threat, even to friends and allies who seem to be wavering in their unconditional support for the American position. Its best interpretation allows the conclusion that critics and potential rivals of the American dogma will be excommunicated from the trusted inner circle. Could they also join the ranks of declared terrorist targets?

The anecdotal pronouncements show nascent attempts at formulating a major change for America's foreign policy. They build up as time passes and flow coherently together in what has become known as the "Bush Doctrine." A lengthy 33-page document that outlines the change in strategy and by intended target as discussed below. By all appearances it is not the final document, but rather the cornerstone for America's intended leadership role in the world.

Vestigial evidence to that effect comes from attempts to shed all entangling alliances that might infringe on its independence in conducting global policies. Earlier references to "allies" in the fight against terrorism have disappeared from public statements after the disappointing support from assumed allies in backing America's war against Iraq. The term "allies" has given way to "coalition," emphasizing the temporary nature of a military alliance excluding formerly important friends of the U.S. with the exception of England.

The present situation reveals a deepening rift in the Western camp. The U.S. insistence on having the uncontested command over the war against terrorism, the demand for troops and financial support from other nations to be under American high command, the punitive exclusion of nations not supporting the Iraq campaign from sharing in Iraq's reconstruction budgeted in the amount of $87 billion of U.S. taxpayer money, U.S. calls for forgiveness of $120 billion in Iraqi debt owed mainly to those European nations opposing the war, are demonstrations of America's resolve to exercise its leadership claim.

So far, increasing American pressure has met with stiffening resistance by those countries favoring participation in an international force under the auspices of the UN, and not America. They stand ready to make concessions on their sovereignty by accepting a supra-national leadership as the credible demonstration of common rather than merely national interests. The tension is threatening to shatter the primus inter pares image that America so carefully cultivated, and that was accepted by the free world aspiring to be unified by consensus rather than dictate.

Making a connection between America's history and the neo-conservative policies advocated by the Bush government is not totally absurd in view of America's 200-year old foreign policy record. It is a history of territorial expansion and influence-building by means of land purchases, trade, coercive diplomacy and, more importantly, by military intervention and conquest. Without the latter, the U.S. would not exist in their present form, and certainly enjoy only a much less significant geopolitical prominence. Much of her national territory was gained by one or the other strategy from England, France, Russia, and Mexico. The Spanish-American war led to more territorial gains and influence in the Caribbean, the Western Hemisphere, and even across the Pacific region. Admiral Perry's black ships entering Tokyo harbor in 1853 to force Japan into free trade and opening its closed society to the outside world is but one more example of long-standing U.S. foreign policy. But it was World War II that took America from a regional power to uncontested leader of the free world, which practically puts America now into the position to impose her will on the rest.

This is summed up by the insightful remark made by Admiral Stansfield Turner, former head of the CIA, to a British reporter during the Iraq campaign: *"Our power is so great, and so unlikely to be challenged for many, many years, that you have to go back to Rome for any kind of parallel. It is a misnomer to speak of the United States as being merely a super-power. We're a super-duper power, and I don't know that the world has seen one of those before."*

But this window of opportunity to reach for world hegemony will not stay open forever. The nation's insular existence, which offered excellent protection in the past, is no longer the comfortable asset it once was. The arsenal of sophisticated weapons of mass destruction, nuclear, biological, or otherwise plus technology for intercontinental precision-guided missiles is spreading to a growing number of nations. Terrorist organizations can bridge the oceanic moat with ease, and cross the country's highly permeable boundaries in the same manner.

America is tangibly and visibly pursuing a new globalization agenda, aiming at world hegemony, by suddenly flashing the military supremacy card. The penetration of the world economy via foreign investments has not led to a sufficiently dominant position anywhere, which would allow the realization of its global leadership ambitions through economic or diplomatic influence alone. This is clear from the discussion of economic globalization in the preceding pages. Adopting the military option promises faster and more assured results, as long as practically all assets are in the country's favor. The largest single economy, the strongest military the world has ever seen with a strategically dispersed military presence in about 130 countries, permanent bases in 40, all developed economies as still-allies, a well developed intelligence system covering friends and foes alike via networks of satellites, ground interception, spy organizations, and commanding influence over all major international organizations.

It is hard to imagine, how such constellation of overwhelming options at the disposal of U.S. leaders could be much enhanced, just as it equally hard to imagine that it will not be employed given the combative frame of mind of the present neo-conservative leadership.

So, what is in store for America and the world, if the neo-conservative doctrine survives the Bush era? For an appreciation of its agenda two core documents need to be scrutinized more closely: the Patriot Act and the Bush Doctrine.

The Patriot Act was passed by Congress in response to the attacks of September 11, 2001, and was signed into law by President Bush on October 26, 2001, hardly six weeks after the terrorists struck. The hasty passage of a major piece of legislation could be explained with the overwhelming catastrophe hitting the country out of the blue, and the need for a legal framework to prevent a recurrence. On the other hand, it creates the impression that the legislation had been under preparation for some time, just waiting for an opportune time to be brought forth.

Patriot is an abbreviation and stands for Uniting and Strengthening America by Providing Appropriate Tools Required to Intercept and Obstruct Terrorism. The Act gives federal officials greater authority to track and intercept communications, both for law enforcement and (foreign) intelligence gathering purposes. It vests the Secretary of the Treasury with regulatory powers to combat corruption of U.S. financial institutions for foreign money laundering purposes. It seeks to further close America's borders to foreign terrorists and detain and remove those within our borders. It creates new crimes, new penalties, and new procedural efficiencies for use against domestic and international terrorists. (CRS, The Library of Congress, April 18, 2002). The legislation is broad and changes immigration laws, tightens controls on money laundering, and greatly expands the legal use of electronic surveillance without specific judicial authorization. These latter devices were specifically excluded from electronic eavesdropping by previous legislation without a court order and proof of a probable cause.

The Center for Constitutional Rights (CCR) has found many provisions of the Act to violate Constitutional rights, the laws of the United States, and international and humanitarian law, both within the U.S. and in the detention camp at Guantanamo Bay, Cuba. Enough reason for the constitutional watchdog organization to file seven lawsuits directly challenging the new law. The charges are that the Bush Administration, the Justice Department, and Congress have enacted a series of Executive Orders, agency regulations, and laws undermining civil liberties, the checks and balances that are essential to the structure of a democratic government, and indeed, democracy itself. As a result, the war on terror is largely being conducted by Executive fiat, seriously compromising constitutional guarantees for both citizens and non-citizens alike.

Additionally, the center claims, government actions have been shrouded in a cloak of secrecy that is incompatible with democratic government. Hundreds of non-citizen have been rounded up and detained, many for months, in violation of constitutional protections, judicial authority and INS policy. The government has repeatedly resisted requests for information regarding the detainees by loved ones, lawyers and the press; it has denied detainees access to legal representatives; and has conducted its hearings in secret, in some cases denying the very existence of such hearings. In a democracy, the actions of the government must be transparent or our ability to vote on policies and the people who create those policies becomes meaningless.

Perhaps the most disturbing aspect of the government's actions has been its attack on the Bill of Rights, the very cornerstone of our American democracy. The War on Terror has seriously compromised the First, Fourth, Fifth, and Sixth Amendment rights of citizens and non-citizens alike. From the Patriot Act's over-broad definition of domestic terrorism, to the FBI's new powers of search and surveillance, to the indefinite detention of both citizens and non-citizens without formal charges, the principles of free speech, due process, and equal protection under the law have been seriously undermined.

Finally, the United States' actions with regard to prisoners held at Camp Delta at the Guantanamo Bay naval station have been in direct violation of the Geneva Conventions. These prisoners are being held as "unlawful combatants," a term that has no meaning in international law.

The government's disregard for international law can only serve to encourage other nations to act likewise and undermine the very "War of Terrorism it seeks to fight." (www.ccr-ny.org/v2/, 10/20/2003).

Among other detractors of the Patriot Act are 152 communities, including several major cities and three states, that have now passed resolutions denouncing the Patriot Act as an assault on civil liberties. They have been joined by members of Congress introducing legislation to invalidate or mitigate some of the more offensive violations of the Act. (www.slate.msn .com/id/20887984/).

The abovementioned Bush Doctrine, promulgated in the first National Security Strategy, Chapter V, in September 2002 enshrines the President's right to preemptive warfare, without explicit declaration of hostile action by Congress, the traditional and constitutional source of such pronouncement. The idea of America's right to preemptive warfare is not new. It was first mentioned at the start of the cold war, when Russia's possession of nuclear capabilities led to a revision of U.S. foreign policy vis-a-vis a former ally. But rather than opting for preemption, the policy revision aimed at containment.

The Bush Doctrine represents a significant expansion of the right to self-defense laid down in Article 51 of the UN Charter, which allows immediate defensive measures by any nation under acute attack, and before the UN Security Council can take measures necessary to maintain international peace and security. President Bush, in his June 1 West Point speech, clearly addresses the rationale for his right to act preemptively by pointing to the potentially devastating nature of modern terrorist attacks with weapons of mass destruction: "*If we wait for threats to fully materialize, we will have waited too long.*"

What makes the doctrine so noteworthy, nonetheless, is its unilateral declaration without any attempt at coordination with the UN to begin with and its rapid implementation before any conclusive evidence as to the seriousness of Iraq's alleged threat could be furnished by UN investigators deployed there.

This haste proved to be unfortunate for the Anglo-American coalition campaign launched against Iraq in 2003. Invoking the necessity of such step on the alleged existence of weapons of mass destruction (WMD) that could be mobilized within minutes against America by Saddam Hussein, and his conspiratorial partnership in al Qaeda's global terrorist organization turned into a great embarrassment for the Bush administration for several reasons.

After the conclusion of first round of hostilities, coalition forces could not produce any evidence of such weapons of mass destruction, any Iraq link to al Qaeda, nor any purchase of nuclear raw materials by Saddam Hussein from Africa, thus invalidating the primary reasons put forth in favor of urgent military intervention. It amounts to a moral victory for all parties calling on America and the UK to give the UN initiative more time before unleashing the war on Iraq, and a justification for their subsequent refusal to support the coalition with money and military units.

The absence of a united international front now leaves the coalition isolated and fully responsible for an action that seems baseless by hindsight. In addition, the coalition's inability to bring the campaign to a successful conclusion, notwithstanding the eventual capture of Saddam Hussein, begins to unravel the image of superior military might, the cornerstone of America's new strategy. At this moment, at least, the coalition is incapable of controlling Iraq. America's angry denouncements of allies distancing themselves from a war without UN approval, have aggravated its own position by causing alienation of formerly solid friends and supporters. This alone could well force the U.S. into a painful reassessment of its future role in the world community.

What seemed to be the needed ounce of prevention at the moment, now has turned into a very costly pound of cure. The guerilla war that was sparked by the intervention promises to be long-lasting, expensive, and without promise of stability, peace, or the effective establishment of democratic political structures in the region. It may be assumed that this ill-fated, unilateral campaign actually served to strengthen America's opposition, while weakening old alliances.

The list of declared U.S. targets are terrorist organizations with an assumed global reach, weak states that harbor and assist such terrorist organizations, and rogue states. The latter are states that "*brutalize their own people and squander their national resources for the personal gain of the rulers; display no regard for international law, threaten their neighbors, and callously violate international treaties to which they are party; are determined to acquire weapons of mass destruction, along with other advanced military technology, to be used as threats or offensively to achieve the aggressive designs of these regimes; to sponsor terrorism around the globe; and reject human values and hate the United States and everything it stands for.*" (Jeffrey Record, 2003).

Neo-conservatives are political zealots of the sort found in Islamic fundamentalism. As such they claim and endorse the following positions as part of their constitutional credo: "*Permanent revolution, violent as well as intellectual. Redrawing the map of the Middle East, if necessary by force. Preemptive war as a justified means to reach desired ends. Acceptance of the welfare state, huge central government, and deficits. Endorsement of an American empire. Suppression of the truth is acceptable if it benefits the state. A centrist government is deemed beneficial for society. The fate of society should rest in the hands of the elite, that is not responsible for sharing the master plan with those it governs. Neutrality in foreign affairs is ill-advised. Imperialism, if progressive in nature, is appropriate. America's ideals can be imposed on others by force. Military superiority is not restricted to national defense alone. 9-11 resulted from the lack of foreign entanglements, not from too many. They dislike and despise libertarians, the guardians of the constitution. Endorsement of violations of civil liberties, and unconditional support for Israel.*" (Quoted from a speech given by the Hon. Ron Paul of Texas to the House of Representatives on July 10, 2003).

A rough and raw cocktail of "Realpolitik" mixed with key ingredients from worldly philosophies like Machiavellianism, Marxism, national socialism, fascism, and utilitarian morals. Add to this strong, almost religious, references to America's historic mission in the world, plus the declared readiness to move against any assumed threat, not necessarily imminent but out into the future, and the world looks at the highest moral, yet utterly scary, authority on this globe.

The events surrounding the first, and especially the second war against Iraq are ominous confirmation for many of these points. The decade-long embargo with catastrophic consequences for the civilian population, for instance, and the ruthlessness of a preemptive war on false premises, and over the objections of allied nations, are glaring examples. Secretary of Defense Ronald Rumsfeld promised the campaign to spread "*shock and awe*" in the world, amounting to the use of deliberate and unchecked brutality, which is no surprise in view of the government's adopted policies. What is of great concern outside the Anglo-American coalition is the dismissive treatment of the UN, NATO, and friendly allies that were urging restraint on the Anglo-American war plans until all the threats allegedly posed by the Saddam Hussein regime could be confirmed through UN investigators. None of this mattered, because Iraq has been a target of the neo-conservatives for some time. As has been Afghanistan and the oil-rich nations on the southern flank of Russia all the way from Central Asia to Turkey where American military outpost have been effectively established. The next targets are already marked: Iran, Syria, and North Korea.

America is already facing the real fallout of its foreign policy reorientation. Stretching its military and financial resources to the breaking point is one consequence that contributed to the downfall of all former empires from antiquity to modern times. The Iraq campaign has already exploded the federal deficit, practically doubling the anticipated costs of the war, and in view of Iraq's destroyed infrastructure and economy promises to turn into a bottomless pit. It addition, it becomes clear, that without the support of other nations and the UN, America's unquestioned military superiority is neutralized by unconventional guerilla warfare and terrorism. The same situation that defeated the U.S. in Vietnam, France in North Africa, and Russia in its centuries old struggle with the Chechens, and their ill-fated campaign against Afghanistan.

Events may lead the U.S. to revise its independent stance in world politics. Campaigns in the Balkans, Afghanistan, and Iraq have not produced solid and convincing results for America's global ambitions. If anything, they have demonstrated a need to draw the full support of international alliances, which are becoming increasingly alarmed about America reaching unilateral foreign policy decisions, but expecting the full backing of allies with the necessary resources to serve American aims. The present situation is not only straining relations within old alliances. It is most likely to lead to major changes in mutual commitments, perhaps even totally new political alignments, in order to moderate the incalculable consequences stemming from decisions and actions set in motion by Anglo-American power politics.

One such major change is already taking place in the U.S.- European constellation. The Europeans, as part of their 25-nation Constitutional Project to be completed by May 2004, are establishing their own continental army to eventually replace American troops in Europe and probably NATO itself. Another sign is the French-German-Russian triple entente formed in opposition to the Iraq campaign in the Security Council, and a joint statement declaring their refusal to any military commitment or further financial contributions there as demanded by the U.S. Even Turkey demonstrates independence by first declining free passage to the U.S. air force over its territory, and later backtracking on their promise to send troops to Iraq

There can be little doubt that the hawkish neo-conservatives are a fateful development for America and the world, because their platform runs squarely against the constitutional intent and legacy the founding fathers had in mind for the fledgling nation. They envisioned America to be a constitutional republic governed by laws protecting liberty and private property alone. They had explicitly warned against making it a democracy, totally anathema to them, as it meant centralized power, control by arbitrary majority opinion, and serving the purposes of elitist interests. The word democracy appears nowhere in the constitution, nor the Declaration of Independence for that reason. James Madison, the creator of the constitution, put it this way: "*Democracies have ever been spectacles of turbulence and contention; have ever been found incompatible with personal security or the rights of property; and have in general been as short in their lives as they have been violent in their death.*"

In view of these sentiments, America's present political system is definitely not in line with the country's constitutional intent and historic mission. Not only that, its expressed goal of exporting democracy to all the world, and setting itself up as the new world government, is seen by critics as a violation of national rights to self-determination. Ironically, why should the form of state the founding fathers declared unfit for the budding American nation now become the ideal government for the rest of the world? The other cornerstone of the constitution's vision and mission was the desire to curb government in size and responsibilities. Less, and not more, government for an independent America was considered a fundamental virtue of a system protecting civil rights and liberties. Nothing was ever said about making it a model for the rest of the world.

Quite to the contrary, they wanted no foreign adventurism. George Washington had warned against foreign entanglements, advice that was repeated in President John Quincy Adams' prophetical address on the 4th of July, 1821. America, he said: *"goes not abroad in search of monsters to destroy. She is the well-wisher to freedom and independence of all. She is the champion and vindicator only of her own. . . . She well knows that by once enlisting under other banners than her own, were they even the banners of foreign independence, she would involve herself beyond the power of extrication, in all the wars of interest and intrigue, or individual avarice, envy, and ambition, which assume the colors and usurp the standard of freedom. The fundamental maxims of her policy would insensibly change from liberty to force. . . . She might become the dictatress of the world. She would be no longer the ruler of her own spirit."*

How meaningful these words ring after President George Bush's state of the union address in January 2002, where he thundered against the *"axis of evil,"* and his declared intent to wipe out international terrorism in the protection of America's best interest. Unquestionably, an unqualified pursuit of the neo-conservative agenda as outlined above, would deeply influence the world's perception of, and reaction to, America's role for the globalization process of the future. For the moment, the alternatives seem to boil down to voluntary or imposed submission to America's "New World Order," or standing up for a world community based on majority consensus along the UN model, exactly what America now wants to prevent, because it would run squarely against the country's leadership ambitions.

America's vision of the future is exclusive. It has to be the American way, or confrontation. The National Security Advisor Condoleeza Rice declared *"American values to be the organizing principle of the world."* (CNBC article of 6/2/03). Richard Maybury in his Early Warning Report of July 2003 had this to add: *"The new International Strategy says that Washington will build the 'infrastructure of democracy' all over the world. Only by making the whole world democratic, they can claim they eliminate terrorism."* This was in response to an observation made by Thomas Carothers in the Jan/Feb 2003 issue of 'Foreign Affairs': "US officials and policy experts have increasingly come to believe that it is precisely the lack of democracy in many of these (Islamic) countries that helps breed Islamic extremism."

Missing this point amounts to a potentially catastrophic miscalculation. Richard Maybury continues: "This desire to force the whole world into a U.S.-led democratic matrix is expressed in a new phrase used by U.S. policy gurus: 'disconnectedness defines danger.' If you are not part of the U.S.-led global community, then you are a threat. This is a restatement of a line Bush has often used 'you are either with us or with the terrorists.' Both these lines are, in effect, declarations of serious consequences for anyone who does not join the U.S. Empire."

In short, the New International Strategy is designed to impose American-style democracy, financial structures, legal systems, and culture on the Middle Eastern states; on Islamic states in general; on "former" Communist states; and ultimately on most of the Third World. This new doctrine (supported by Bush officials Rumsfeld, Cheney, and Wolfowitz) is an important part of the "nation building" which America is presently attempting in Afghanistan and Iraq. (The McAlvany Intelligence Advisor, October 2003).

It is very much in evidence in Iraq, where the Shiite majority is prohibited from forming an Islamic state, like in Iran, under Islamic law—the sharia of the Koran. Centuries of cultural heritage blotted out by foreign fiat. So much for a practical demonstration of democratic self-determination.

This plan for the iron-fisted imposition of the New World Order can only lead to confrontation on a broad front beyond Iraq. It is already visible in the non-support of the Iraqi campaign by assumed allied nations, and intensifying campaigns of terrorism, the only effective response to overwhelming acts of aggression and interference from the outside.

Now, it turns out that strategies of preemptive strikes against any chosen adversary are incompatible with allies who strive for independence in a system of democratic consultations and decision-making. It amounts to a rejection of U.S. plans to set the marching order for a bunch of vassal states by dictating the terms of cooperation and compliance. But, unfortunately, America has become impervious to even well-meaning advice from friends and allies, and totally ignores popular movements questioning any form of globalization, which might threaten the realization of its ambitions.

The ad hoc pronouncements by the US President are not mere slips of the tongue. They are integral parts and evidence of a new foreign policy agenda, which manifests itself in the unilateral rejection of many international treaties, most of which were initiated by America itself, like the nuclear non-proliferation treaty which was rejected to pave the way for the development of tactical mini-nukes, the bans on nuclear testing, use of land mines, biological warfare, reduction of ICBMs, the Kyoto agreement, and lately the rejection of the International Criminal Court ratified by the UN. They are bona-fide evidence of America's inflexible determination to act as the world's supreme leader.

The list could easily be extended to include the abandonment of long-standing American policies like the sacrifice of the holy grail of free trade by unexpectedly imposing duties on U.S. steel imports, or granting major farm welfare concessions which are all considered illegal protectionism under WTO rules. In a similar vein are the trade frictions with the EU over bananas, hormone-laced beef, genetically modified grains and animals, etc., and the frequent threats of retaliatory duties to force compliance with U.S. trade plans. Trade spats which can probably be resolved without doing lasting damage to once very close and friendly relationship but still evidence of gnawing frictions.

More important than these domestic squabbles are signs of slowing direct investment activities, a declining world economy, probably aided by growing political uncertainty, which in combination do not bode well for the economic globalization movement initiated by the developed world. For the moment, at least, it seems that the old world order is still very much alive, and consolidating in face of the determined American push for the New World Order.

Is America to become another example in history destined to validate the observation made by the British historian Alexander Tyler in 1787 who wrote "A democracy cannot exist as a permanent form of government. It can only exist until the voters discover that they can vote themselves largess from the public treasury. From that moment on, the majority always votes for the candidates promising the most benefits from the public treasury, with the result that a democracy always collapses over loose fiscal policy, and is always followed by a dictatorship. The average age of the world's greatest civilization has been two hundred years."

Hopefully, the burning desire for world leadership will not lead the Bush administration, or its successors for that matter, into the globalization trap that became the fate of King Croesus of Lydia in 550 BC. He wanted to conquer Persia—a curious parallel to President Bush's declared target of Iran 2,500 years later!—the arch enemy of his universe, and asked the Oracle of Delphi about his chances of winning. The reply by the Pythia was unequivocal. If he crossed a river "Croesus will destroy a great empire." Unfortunately, it turned out to be his own.

APPENDICES

Exhibits and Tables

EXHIBITS

TABLES

INDUSTRY CLASSIFICATION IN U.S. FDI BENCHMARK SURVEYS

Census Years	1950	1957	1966	1977	1982	1989	1994
ALL INDUSTRIES	X	X	X	X	X	X	X
Agriculture, Forestry, Fisheries	X	X	X				
Agricultural production				x			
Forestry				x			
Fisheries				x			
Agricultural services				x			
Agriculture, forestry, fisheries combined				x			
Mining	X	X	X	X			
Metal Mining				x			
Iron	x	x	x	x			
Copper, Lead, Zinc, Gold, & Silver	x	x	x	x			
Bauxite, Other Ores, & Services	x	x	x	x			
Coal & Other Nonmetallic Minerals	x	x	x	x			
Petroleum	X	X	X	X	X	X	X
Oil and gas extraction		x	x	x	x	x	x
Crude petroleum extraction (no refining) and natural gas			x	x	x	x	x
Oil and gas field services		x	x	x	x	x	x
Petroleum and coal products				x	x	x	x
Integrated petroleum refining & extraction		x	x	x	x	x	x
Petroleum refining without extraction		x	x	x	x		x
Petroleum and coal products, nec.				x	x	x	x
Petroleum wholesale trade		x	x	x	x	x	x
Other		x	x	x	x	x	x
Petroleum tanker operations							x
Petroleum and natural gas pipeline							x
Petroleum storage for hire							x
Gasoline service stations							x
Manufacturing	X	X	X	X	X	X	X
Food and kindred products	x	x	x	x	x	x	x
Grain mill and bakery products			x	x	x	x	x
Grain mill products							x
Bakery products							x
Beverages				x	x	x	x
Other				x	x	x	x
Meat products							x
Dairy products							x
Preserved fruits and vegetables							x
Other food and kindred products							x

INDUSTRY CLASSIFICATION IN U.S. FDI BENCHMARK SURVEYS
(*continued*)

Census Years	1950	1957	1966	1977	1982	1989	1994
Paper and allied products	X	X	X				
Chemicals and allied products	X	X	X	X	X	X	X
Industrial chemicals and synthetics			X	X	X	X	X
Drugs			X	X	X	X	X
Soap, cleaners, and toilet goods			X	X	X	X	X
Agricultural chemicals			X	X	X	X	X
Other			X	X	X	X	X
Rubber & Miscellaneous plastic products	X	X	X				
Primary and Fabricated Metals	X	X	X	X	X	X	X
Primary metal industries			X	X	X	X	X
Ferrous				X	X	X	X
Nonferrous				X	X	X	X
Fabricated Metal Products			X	X	X	X	X
Metal cans, forgings, and stampings							X
Cutlery, hand tools, and screw products							X
Heating and plumbing equipment and structural metal products							X
Fabricated metal products nec., ordnance, and services							X
Industrial machinery and equipment	X	X	X	X	X	X	X
Farm and garden machinery			X	X	X	X	X
Construction, mining, materials handling machinery				X	X	X	X
Computer and office equipment			X	X	X	X	X
Other			X	X	X	X	X
Engines and turbines							X
Metalworking machinery							X
Special industry machinery							X
General industry machinery and equipment							X
Refrigeration and service industry machinery							X
Industrial machinery and equipment nec							X
Electronic and other electric equipment		X	X	X	X	X	X
Household appliances			X	X	X	X	X
Radio, TV, and communication equipment.				X	X	X	X
Household audio and video, and communications equipment							X
Electronic components and accessories			X	X	X	X	X
Other			X	X	X	X	X
Transportation equipment	X	X	X	X	X	X	X
Motor vehicles and equipment			X	X	X	X	X

INDUSTRY CLASSIFICATION IN U.S. FDI BENCHMARK SURVEYS

Census Years	1950	1957	1966	1977	1982	1989	1994
Other			x	x	x	x	x
Other manufacturing	x	x	x	x	x	x	x
Tobacco products			x	x	x	x	x
Textile products and apparel			x	x	x	x	x
Textile mill product							x
Apparel and other textile products							x
Lumber, wood, furniture, and fixtures				x	x	x	x	x
Lumber and wood products							x
Furniture and fixtures							x
Paper and allied products				x	x	x	x
Pulp, paper, and board mills							x
Other paper and allied products							x
Printing and publishing				x	x	x	x
Newspapers							x
Miscellaneous publishing							x
Commercial printing and services							x
Rubber products				x	x	x	x
Miscellaneous plastics products				x	x	x	x
Glass products			x	x	x	x	x
Stone, clay, and other nonmetallic mineral products				x	x	x	x	x
Instruments and related products			x	x	x	x	x
Measuring, scientific, and optical instruments							x
Medical instruments, supplies, and ophthalmic goods							x
Photographic equipment and supplies							x
Other				x	x	x	x	x
Leather and leather products							x
Miscellaneous manufacturing industries							x
Transportation, Communication, Public Utilities	X	X	X				
Water transportation	x	x	x				
Communication	x	x	x				
Other	x	x	x				
Trade	X	X	X	X	X	X	X
Wholesale trade	x	x	x	x	x	x	x
Durable goods					x	x	x	x
Motor vehicles and equipment							x
Lumber and construction materials							x
Professional and commercial equipment and supplies							x
Metals and minerals							x

INDUSTRY CLASSIFICATION IN U.S. FDI BENCHMARK SURVEYS

Census Years	1950	1957	1966	1977	1982	1989	1994
Electrical goods							x
Hardware, plumbing, and heating equipment, and supplies							x
Machinery, equipment and supplies, nec							x
Nondurable goods				x	x	x	x
Paper and paper products							x
Drugs, proprietaries, and sundries							x
Apparel, piece goods, and notions							x
Groceries and related products							x
Farm product raw materials							x
Nondurable goods, nec							x
Retail	x	x	x	x			
Depository Institutions							X
Banks							x
Savings institutions and credit unions							x
Banking				X	X	X	
Finance, Insurance, Real Estate				X	X	X	
Banking	x	x	x				
Finance, except depository institutions		x	x	x	x	x	x
Business franchising							x
Other							x
Insurance	x	x	x	x	x	x	x
Life insurance							x
Accident and health insurance							x
Other							x
Real Estate				x	x	x	x
Holding Companies	x	x	x	x	x	x	x
Nonbusiness entities						x	
Services					X	X	X
Hotels and other lodging places					x	x	x
Business Services					x	x	x
Advertising					x	x	x
Management, consulting, and PR services				x			
Equipment rental (ex. automotive and computers)				x	x	x	
Computer and data processing services					x	x	x
Computer processing and data preparation services						x	
Information retrieval services							x
Computer related services, nec							x

INDUSTRY CLASSIFICATION IN U.S. FDI BENCHMARK SURVEYS

Census Years	*1950*	*1957*	*1966*	*1977*	*1982*	*1989*	*1994*
Business services, nec							x
Services to buildings							x
Personnel supply services							x
Other					x	x	x
Automotive rental and leasing						x	x
Motion pictures, including TV tape and film					x	x	x
Health services					x	x	x
Engineering, architectural, and surveying services					x	x	x
Management and public relations services						x	x
Other services					x	x	x
Automotive parking, repair, and other services							x
Miscellaneous repair services							x
Amusement and recreation services							x
Legal services							x
Educational services							x
Accounting, auditing, and bookkeeping services							x
Research, development, and testing services							x
Other services provided on a commercial basis							x
Other Industries	X	X	X	X	X	X	X
Agriculture, forestry, and fishing				x	x	x	x
Agricultural production—crops							x
Agricultural production—livestock							x
Agricultural services							x
Forestry							x
Fishing, hunting, and trapping							x
Mining					x	x	x
Metal mining					x	x	x
Iron ores							x
Copper, lead, zinc, gold, and silver ores							x
Other metallic ores							x
Metal mining services							x
Nonmetallic minerals					x	x	x
Coal							x
Coal mining services							x
Nonmetallic minerals, except fuels							x
Nonmetallic minerals services,							

INDUSTRY CLASSIFICATION IN U.S. FDI BENCHMARK SURVEYS

Census Years	1950	1957	1966	1977	1982	1989	1994
Construction		X	X	X	X	X	X
Transport., communication., and public utilities						X	X
Transportation						X	X
Railroads							X
Water transportation							X
Transportation by air							X
Pipeline, except petroleum and natural gas							X
Passenger transportation arrangement							X
Transportation and related services, nec							X
Communication and public utilities						X	
Communication							X
Telephone and telegraph communications							X
Other communications services							X
Electric, gas, and sanitary services							X
Retail trade					X	X	X
General merchandise stores							X
Food stores							X
Apparel and accessory stores							X
Eating and drinking places							X
Retail trade, nec							X
Real estate	X	X	X				
Hotels		X	X				
Advertising, related business services		X	X				
Motion pictures	X	X	X				
Services				X			
Other	X	X	X				
Unspecified							X

Sources: 1950 census, p. 45. 1957 census, p. 94. 1966 census, pp. 13–17. 1977 census, p. 33. 1982 census, p. 37. 1989 census, p. 4. 1994 census, pp. M-13 to M-15).

Glossary

Affiliate. see Foreign Affiliate.

AIE. American Enterprise Institute for Public Policy Research.

AL QAEDA. "The Base." A Muslim activist movement founded by Osama bin Laden

ARM'S-LENGTH PRICING. Intracorporate prices set at level of prices charged to unrelated parties under similar circumstances. See also transfer pricing.

ASIA. Includes Japan and Middle East, but excludes Turkey.

BEA. Bureau of Economic Analysis, part of the U.S. DOC.

BENCHMARK SURVEY. Periodic census taken of U.S. FDI companies. The study includes those for 1950, 1957, 1966, 1977, 1982, 1989, and 1994.

BLS. Bureau of Labor Statistics (USA).

BOP. Balance of Payments.

BOT. Balance of Trade.

Branch. Consists of operations or activities in one location that a person in a second location conducts in its own name, rather than through an entity incorporated in the first location. (1982 benchmark survey, p. 4).

BRANCH EARNINGS. Income or profits earned by a branch operation.

CCA. Capital Consumption Allowance.

CCR. Center for Constitutional Rights. www.ccr-nv.org

CFR. Council on Foreign Relations.

CPI. Competitive Power Index. Measures share in national or industrial gross product achieved by foreign direct investors.

CRS. Congressional Research Service. http://www.loc.gov/crsinfo/whatscrs.html

DEBT CAPITAL. Intercompany loans. See interests and intercompany debt.

DERIVATIVES. Financial transactions whose value depends on the underlying value of an asset. Financial derivatives include: forward contracts, futures contracts, swaps, and options. Employed to manage business and financial risks stemming from uncontrollable market forces. Considered very risky themselves, because of changeable nature and value of primary asset.

DIRECT INVESTMENT (U.S. Definition). Implies that a person in one country has a lasting interest in, and a degree of influence over the management of, a business enterprise in another country. For the U.S., ownership or control by a single person of 10% or more of an enterprise's voting securities, or the equivalent, is considered evidence of such a lasting interest or degree of influence over management. Thus U.S. direct investment abroad is the ownership or control, directly or indirectly, by one U.S. person of 10% or more of the voting securities of an incorporated foreign business enterprise or an equivalent interest in an unincorporated foreign business enterprise. "Person" is broadly defined to include any individual, branch, partnership, associated group, association, estate, trust, corporation or other organization (whether or not organized under the laws of any State), and any government (including a foreign government, the U.S. Government, a State or local government, and any agency, corporation or financial institution, or other entity or instrumentality thereof, including a government-sponsored agency). This definition treats an associated group as a single person. (Excerpt from 1989 benchmark survey, p. M-4).

DISTRIBUTED EARNINGS. Funds remitted for the use of equity capital, dividends. Interests are not included here.

DIVIDEND. Income on equity investment.

DOC. U.S. Department of Commerce.

EARNINGS. Affiliate income after foreign corporate income taxes, but before distribution and related withholding charges. They are income to the U.S. parent, whether they are reinvested or distributed/remitted to the parent.

ECHELON. America's Secret Global Surveillance Network.

EEA. European Economic Area. Agreement between the European Community (EC) and The European Free Trade Area (EFTA) to form a single market of 19 countries in 1991.

EEC. European Economic Community. Predecessor of EC and EU. Established 1957 by Treaty of Rome.

EC. European Community, the successor of the EEC. 1965.

EFTA. European Free Trade Area. 1960.

EQUITY CAPITAL. Ownership capital. In its net form determined by increases minus decreases in parental fund flows. See dividends.

EU. European Union presently comprising 15 nations in Western Europe.

EUROPE (OECD). Includes Western Europe, Czech Republic, Hungary, Poland, Turkey, excludes other Eastern Europe.

EUROSTAT. Office for Official Publications of the European Communities, L-2985, Luxembourg.

FISCAL YEAR. Data for foreign affiliates and U.S. parents were required to be reported on a fiscal year basis. The 1989 fiscal year was defined as the affiliate's or parent's financial reporting year that ended in the calendar year 1989. The fiscal year data from the benchmark survey are not comparable with the calendar year estimates of transactions between foreign affiliates and their U.S. parents that appear in the U.S. balance of payments accounts or the with the calendar year estimates of the U.S. direct investment position abroad on a historical cost basis. (1989 benchmark survey, p. M-7).

FHLB. Federal Home Loan Bank, a Federal Government mortgage institution.

FOREIGN AFFILIATE. A foreign business enterprise in which there is U.S. direct investment —that is, it is a foreign business enterprise that is directly or indirectly owned or controlled by one U.S. person to the extent of 10% or more of the voting securities for an incorporated business enterprise or an equivalent interest for an unincorporated business enterprise. The affiliate is called a foreign affiliate to denote that it is located outside the U.S. (although the direct investment interest in it is owned by a U.S. person. A business enterprise, and therefore an affiliate, may be either incorporated or unincorporated. Unincorporated business enterprises include branches and partnerships. (1989 benchmark survey, p. M-6).

FDI. Foreign Direct Investment.

FOREIGN DIRECT INVESTMENT. See also Direct Investment. It comes in two variants: outward and inward direct investments. Outward (foreign) direct investments are a record of the investments made abroad by a capital exporting nation. Inward (foreign) direct investments are the record of foreign capital invested in the recipient nation. The measurements of FDI do not follow a universal standard. Some nations measure only actual capital flows to arrive at cumulative investment stock estimates at historical costs. Others combine capital flows with reinvestments to arrive at cumulative stock estimates at historical costs. A third approach combines flows and reinvestments with valuation adjustments of the existing stock. The latest version establishes stock estimates also on the basis of current costs (replacement costs) or market value in addition to the historic cost method, essentially the present U.S. practice.

FTAA. Free Trade Area of the Americas. Successor to the North American Free Trade Area or NAFTA. Will incorporate all countries between Alaska and Argentina.

GAAP. Generally Accepted Accounting Principles for the U.S.

GATT. General Agreement on Tariffs and Trade. Now called WTO.

GDP. Gross Domestic Product.

The GDP is equal to the total of the gross expenditure on the final uses of the domestic supply of goods and services valued at purchasers' values less imports of goods and services valued c.i.f., or the sum of the compensation of employees, consumption of fixed capital, operating surplus and indirect taxes, net, of resident producers and import duties. (OECD).

GNP. Gross National Product Adding Net Factor Income/Payments (-) Abroad To GDP produces Gross National Income (GNI), formerly known as Gross National Product (GNP). (IMF).

GNI. Gross National Income. See GNP.

GROSS DOMESTIC PRODUCT. see GDP.

GROSS NATIONAL PRODUCT. see GNP.

GSP. Generalized System of Preferences.

GSE. Government-sponsored enterprise. Private enterprise under government charter to serve public service needs. Enjoys special privileges like preferential tax treatment, access to government subsidies or emergency credit lines from the U.S. Treasury, etc. Even though not actually a government organization, it is assumed to have government guarantees in case of economic hardship, which provides a higher credit rating and lower borrowing costs.

HEDONIC. concerned with the production of pleasure, sensation of subjective pleasure or advantage. Hedonic valuations are used by U.S. government accountants to establish the GDP contributions from computer investments in the economy. This basis is not the actual value added by computers as the accepted way of calculating the GDP contribution, but the computing power measured in terms of 1996 prices for equivalent computing equipment. In the second quarter of 2003 this position was thus overstated by a factor of 6.4 times: $38.4 billion against really $6 billion spent.

IIP. International Investment Position (of the U.S.)

IMF. International Monetary Fund. Organization set up to assist nations with BOP difficulties in order to maintain relatively stable exchange rates. Now, and together with the World Bank, also engaged in the management of third world debt problems.

INCOME. The term is exclusively used 1.) for the U.S. parent share in affiliate profits after foreign income taxes and withholding taxes on distributed earnings in this study, including reinvested funds. 2.) It may also appear in U.S. government publications, including FDI benchmark surveys, in reference to income statements of U.S. parents where it reflects total revenues consisting of sales, income from equity investments, capital gains/losses, and all other. 3.) Its use by other government or international organization statistics refers strictly to actual BOP flows of profits remitted to parent organizations, exclusive of reinvestments, unless indicated otherwise.

INDIRECT TAXES. Includes production royalty payments plus taxes other than income and payroll taxes minus subsidies received.

INDUSTRY. In most cases refers to commercial organizations active in the three industrial areas of primary, manufacturing, and service production. In some instances, French and Eurostat statistics, the term refers only to the manufacturing sector.

INS. Immigration and Naturalization Service of the U.S.

INTERCOMPANY DEBT. Outstanding loan volume from parents to affiliates. Net positions are affected by increases in U.S. parents' receivables less increases in U.S. parents' payables. An increase in U.S. parents' payables is a decrease in intercompany debt and, thus, a capital inflow in the U.S. BOP, and vice versa.

INTEREST. Income on debt capital. Usually quoted net of withholding taxes. Term may also be used to denote general capital participation.

INWARD FDI.   see Foreign Direct Investment.

LATIN AMERICA. In U.S. statistics covers continental republics south of U.S. and island nations in Caribbean. Other nations employ term exclusively for continental republics from Mexico to Argentina.

LDC. Less Developed Countries.

MANUFACTURING INDUSTRIES. For detailed definition in U.S. statistics, and changes over time, see section: "Industry Classification in Benchmark Surveys" in the Appendix.

ME. Middle East.

MOFA. Majority-owned foreign affiliate.

NAFTA. North American Free Trade Area. Includes the U.S., Canada, and Mexico. Plans are drafted to extend the agreement to rest of the Americas.

N/A. Not available.

NET FLOWS. Any fund flows netted for payments coming in less payments going out.

NIL. not significant, not measurable.

NMF. no meaningful figure.

OCEANIA. Australia and New Zealand.

OECD. Organization for Economic Cooperation and Development. Presently consists of 29 nations considered to have achieved a high degree of industrial development. Organization offers complete coverage of detailed economic statistics for member nations: http://www .oecd.org/std/gdp.htm

OTHER DIRECT INVESTMENT SERVICES. Charges for the use of tangible property,and film and television tape rentals. Both receipts and payments are net of (foreign or U.S.) withholding taxes.

OUTWARD FDI. see Foreign Direct Investment.

PARENT. A U.S. person who has direct investment—that is, a 10 percent or more direct or indirect ownership interest—in a foreign business enterprise. Although the U.S. government may have equity investments in a foreign business enterprise, such investment is not covered by BEA's direct investment surveys. (1989 benchmark survey, p. M-5).

PETROLEUM INDUSTRY. Includes extractive and processing activities in the American accounting system. For details see next section: "Industry Classification in Benchmark Surveys." Other countries include this industry in energy sector.

PNAC. Project For The New American Century. http://www.newamericancentury.org/

PRODUCTION ROYALTIES. Depletion charges levied by some oil-producing nations. Included under Indirect Taxes.

PROFITS. A term normally avoided in all government publications dealing with FDI. Instead such terms as income, earnings, reinvested earnings, etc. are used.

REINVESTED EARNINGS. That part of affiliate earnings not distributed to parent organization.

REINVESTMENTS. same as Reinvested Earnings.

RETAINED EARNINGS. same as Reinvested Earnings.

RIIA. British Royal Institute on International Affairs.

ROYALTIES AND LICENSE FEES. Receipts by U.S. parents from, less payments by U.S. parents to, their foreign affiliates of royalties, license fees, and other fees for the use or sale of intangible property or rights, such as patents, industrial processes, trademarks, copyrights, franchises, designs, know-how, formulas, techniques, manufacturing rights, and other intangible assets or proprietary rights. Both receipts and payments are net of (foreign or U.S.) withholding taxes. Net can also imply parent receipts minus parent payments in some cases. (1982 benchmark survey, p. 25).

SERVICE INDUSTRIES. For a listing of the various industries included in the American system of industrial classification, and their changes over time, see next section "Industry Classification in U.S. FDI Benchmark Surveys". May differ for other countries.

SERVICE CHARGES. Consist of fees for services-such as management, professional, or technical services-rendered between U.S. parents and their foreign affiliates, whether in the form of sales of services or reimbursements. (1982 benchmark survey, p. 25).

SOCB. Survey Of Current Business. Monthly publication of the U.S. Department of Commerce.

SUBSIDIARY. same as Foreign Affiliate.

TC. Trilateral Commission.

TRADE INDUSTRY. Normally includes wholesale and retail operations. But may be restricted to wholesale only where indicated.

TRANSFER PRICE. Pricing of goods and services exchanged in intra-corporate transactions. See also arm's- length pricing.

TRIANGLE TRANSACTION. Physical business transaction between customers in two countries is invoiced through a third where the profit is made. Normally involves tax sanctuaries.

TRIMS. Trade Related Investment Measures (GATT/WTO).

TRIPS. Trade Related Aspects of Intellectual Property Rights (GATT/WTO).

UK. United Kingdom.

UNCTAD. UN Council on Trade and Development.

VALUATION ADJUSTMENTS. U.S. FDI position estimates include translation adjustments for foreign currency fluctuations against the dollar affecting translation of affiliate assets, liabilities, revenues and expenses, other capital gains or losses, and other.

VALUE MEASURES. 000 = thousands; mil. = million; bil. = billion.

VAT. Value Added Tax.

WITHHOLDING TAX. Tax on funds remitted like dividends, interests, royalties, license fees, other service fees, etc.

WMD. weapons of mass destruction.

WORLD BANK. The International Bank for Reconstruction and Development. Originally set up to provide development capital for the participants in World War II. Today it provides essentially the same services to developing nations.

WTO. World Trade Organization—formerly GATT. Main purpose is now to provide protection of industrial property rights and settlement of trade disputes. For a complete summary of agenda access: http://www.wto.org/legal/ursum_wp.htm

Bibliography

Arnold, David. *"The Mirage of Global Markets."* (Pearson Education, Inc. Financial Times Prentice Hall; Upper Saddle River, N.J. 2004).

Bank for International Settlements (BIS), Basel, Switzerland. http://www.bis.org/

Barlow, M. *"The Multilateral Agreement on Investment and the Threat to American Freedom."* (Stoddart Publishing, 1998. Out of business).

Bonner, William & Addison Wiggins. *"Financial Reckoning Day."* (John Wiley & Sons, Inc., Hoboken, NJ, 2003)

Boyd. G. and J.H. Dunning. *"Structural Change and Cooperation in the Global Economy."* (Edward Elgar Publishing, Northampton, MA, 1999).

Boyd, G. (Editor). *"The Struggle for World Markets. Competition and Cooperation Between NAFTA and the European Union."* (Edward Elgar Publishing, Northampton, MA, 1998).

Brewer, T.L. and G. Boyd. *"Globalizing America. The USA in World Integration."* (Edward Elgar Publishing, Northampton, MA, 2000).

Carnes, Tony. *"The Bush Doctrine."* (Christianity Today Magazine, 8/20/2003. http://www.christianitytoday.com/ct/2003/005/3.38.html).

Caulfield, C. *"Masters of Illusion: The World Bank and the Poverty of Nations."* (Marion Wood/Henry Holt, New York,1996).

Cavanagh, John, et al. *"Alternatives to Economic Globalization."* (Barrett-Koehler Publishers, Inc, San Francisco, CA, 2002).

Chossudovsky, M. *"The Globalization of Poverty: Impacts of IMF and World Bank Reforms."* (Common Courage Press, Monroe, ME, 2000).

Council on Competitiveness. 1401 H Street, N.W., Suite 650, Washington, D.C. 20005. Tel: 202-682-4292 or Fax: 202-682-5150. E-mail: http://compete.org/main.htm

Danaher, K. and R.Burbach. (Editors). *"Globalize This!: The Battle Against The World Trade Organization."* (Common Courage Press, Monroe, ME, 2000).

De Tocqueville, Alexis. *"Democracy in America."* Volume I, 1835. Volume II, 1840.

Economic Report of the President, (United States Printing Office, Washington, DC, February 1995 & 1997). www.bea.doc.gov/bea/pubs.htm

Economic Policy Institute. (1660 L Street, NW. Suite 1200, Washington, DC 20036). http://www.lights.com/epi/

Elliott Wave International. http://www.elliottwave.com/

EUROPEAN UNION—Brussels, Belgium, or Delegation of the European Commission, 2300 M. Street, NW, Washingto, DC 20037-1434. (http://www.eurunion.org).

European Commission—3 Dag Hammarskjold Plaza, 305 East 47th Street, New York, NY 10017
  —*Eurecom*, Monthly Bulletin of EU Economic and Financial News, various issues. http://www
    .eurunion.org/news/index.htm
  —*Employment in Europe 1999*
  —*Structure and Activity of Industry, Community total*, various issues
Eurostat—Office for Official Publications of the European Communities, L-2985, Luxembourg
  —*National accounts, ESA*, various issues
  —*Employment and Unemployment Aggregates*, various issues
Fingleton, Eamonn. *"Unsustainable: How Economic Dogma is Destroying American Prosperity."* (Nation Books, New York, 2003).

FRANCE
  Ministère de l'Economie, des Finances et de l'Industrie,Direction Générale des Stratégies Industrielles, (SESSI), Service des Statistiques Industrielles, 20, Av de Ségur, 75353 Paris 07 SP, France
  —*Industrie française et mondialization,* Edition 1998
  Ministère de l'Industrie, de la Poste et des Télécommunications Direction Générale des Stratégies Industrielles, (SESSI), Service des Statistiques Industrielles, 20, Av de Ségur, 75353 Paris 07 SP, France—*les échanges intragroupes dans la mondialisation industrielle, premiers résultats 1993*
  —*l'implantation etrangere dans l'industrie,* edition 1997
  Ministère De L'Industrie, Direction Générale des Stratégies Industrielles (stisi), 85, boulevard du Montparnasse, 75006 Paris, France
  —*Importations, Exportations et Filiales Francaises des Firmes Multinationales, 1977*
  Ministère De L'Industrie Et De La Recherche (sessi), 85, boulevard du Montparnasse, 75006 Paris, France
  —*9 ans d'implantation étrangère dand l'industrie 1er janvier 1973- 1er janvier 1981*
  Ministère Du Redéploiement Industriel Et Du Commerce Extérieur, Traits Fondamentaux Du Système Industriel Français, Direction Generale De L'Industrie—SESSI, 85, boulevard du Montparnasse, 75270 Paris Cedex 06
  —*L'Implantation Etrangere Dans L'Industrie Au 1er Janvier 1984*
  —*L'Implantation Etrangere Dans L'Industrie Au 1er Janvier, 1974–82.*
Fleet Street Letter, 808 St. Paul Street, Baltimore, MD 21202. www.Fleetstreetltr.com
Freedom Alliance, 400 West Service Road, P.O. Box 16119, Washington, DC 20041-61619. E-mail: www.freedomalliance.org
Gábor, H. *"Integration Through Foreign Direct Investment."* (Edward Edgar Publishing, Northampton, MA, 2000).

GERMANY
Deutsche Bundesbank, Wilhelm-Epstein-Strasse 14, 60431 Frankfurt am Main
Die Kapitalverflechtung mit dem Ausland
  Sonderdruck aus: Monatsberichte der Deutschen Bundesbank
  Nr. 4, April 1984 (1976 bis 1982)
  Nr. 4, April 1989 (1981 bis 1987)
  Statistische Sonderveröffentlichung 10
  —1991–93, Mai 1995
  —1992–94, Mai 1996
  —1994–98, Mai 2000
Die Entwicklung der Kapitalverflechtung der Unternehmen mit dem Ausland von 1976 bis 1985 Sonderdruck aus: Monatsberichte der Deutschen Bundesbank, März 1987, S. 21
  —1983 bis 1989, April 1991, Nr. 4
  —1987 bis 1989, April 1991, S. 28
  —*1989 bis 1991,* April 1993

—1991 bis 1993, Mai 1995, Nr 5

—1993 bis 1995, Mai 1997, Nr. 5

Die Zahlungsbilanz der Bundesrepublik Deutschland mit dem Ausland 1971 bis 1983. Beilage zu: "*Statistische Beihefte zu den Monatsberichten der Deutschen Bundesbank*", Reihe 3, *Zahlungsbilanzstatistik Nr. 7*, Juli 1984

—April 1991, Nr. 4 (1983 bis 1989)

—*Zahlungbilanz nach Regionen, Juli 1994*

—*Kapitalerträge (einschliesslich reinvestierter Gewinne)* 1970 bis 1993

—*Technologische Dienstleistungen in der Zahlungsbilanz, 1982–93*, Mai 1994

Goldman Sachs. "*Dreaming with BRICS. The Path to 2050.*" (Global Economics Paper No: 99, October 1, 2003. 1 New York Plaza, 47th floor, New York, NY1000). https://www.gs.com

Griffin, Edward. "*The Creature From Jeckyll Island.*" (American Media Publishing, West Desmoines, IA, 1998).

Hackmann, R. "*U.S. Trade, Foreign Direct Investments, and Global Competitiveness.*" (International Business Press, an imprint of The Haworth Press, Inc., New York & London, 1997).

Harvard Business Review. "*It's Time to Retire Retirement.*" March 2004.

Hertz, Noreena. "*The Silent Takeover: Global Capitalism and the Death of Democracy.*" (The Free Press, New York,2001).

Human Events, The National Conservative Weekly (1 Massachusetts Avenue, N.W., Washington, D.C. 20001).

Huntington, Samuel P. "*The West Unique, Not Universal.*" (Foreign Affairs, November/December 1996, Vol. 75, No. 6). 28–46. "*The Clash of Civilization and the Remaking of World Order.*" (Touchstone, Rockefeller Center, 1230 Avenue of the Americas, New York, NY 10020. Simon and Schuster, 1996).

IMD (WCY) P.O. Box 915, CH-1001 Lausanne, Switzerland. Fax: 41-21-618 02 04. E-mail: http://www.imd.ch/wey//approach/summary.html

World Competitiveness Yearbook, various issues

INTERNATIONAL MONETARY FUND (IMF), Washington, DC.

—*Balance of Payments Statistics Yearbook*, various issues

—*International Financial Statistics Yearbook*, various issues

Levitt, Theodore. "*The Globalization of Markets.*" (Harvard Business Review, May-June, 1983) 92–96.

Lipset, Seymour Martin. "American Exceptionalism: A Double-Edged Sword." (W.W. Norton & Co., Inc, 500 Fifth Avenue, New York, NY 10110).

Lowenstein, Roger. "*When Genius Failed: The Rise and Fall of Long-Term Capital Management.*" (Random House, New York, 2000).

MacArthur, R. John. "*The Selling of Free Trade: NAFTA, Washington, and the Subversion of American Democracy.*" (Hill and Wang, New York, 2000).

Martin, H-P. and H. Schumann. "*The Global Trap: Globalization and the Assault on Prosperity and Democracy.*" (Zed Books Ltd., London & New York, 1998).

Mohr, Jakki. "*Marketing of High-Technology Products and Innovations.*" (Prentice Hall Inc., Upper Saddle River, New Jersey, 2001).

Møller, J. Ø. "*The End of Internationalism. Or World Governance?*" (Praeger Publishers, Greenwood Publishing Group, Inc., 88 Post Road West, P.O. Box 5007, Westport, CT 06881-5007, 2000).

Mourdoukoutas, P. "*The Global Corporation.*" (Quorum Books, Greenwood Publishing Group, Inc., 88 Post Road West, P.O. Box 5007, Westport, CT 06881-5007, 2000).

Nader, Ralph, et al. "*The Case Against Free Trade.*" (Earth Island Press, San Francisco, CA, 1993).

New American Century, see PNAC

New Economics Foundation. 3 Jonathan Street, London, SE11 5NH, UK. http://www.neweconomics.org/. Telephone: 020 7820 6300. Fax: 020 7820 6301.

Nexus Magazine, PO Box 30, Mapleton Qld 4560, Australia. editor@nexusmagazine.com

OECD 2, rue Andre-Pascal, 75775 Paris Cedex 16, France
   INTERNATIONAL DIRECT INVESTMENT STATISTICS YEARBOOK 1993
   INTERNATIONAL DIRECT INVESTMENT STATISTICS YEARBOOK 1996
   INTERNATIONAL DIRECT INVESTMENT STATISTICS YEARBOOK 1998
   MAIN ECONOMIC INDICATORS, various issues
   NATIONAL ACCOUNTS, Main Aggregates, Volume I, 1988–99, 2001
   NATIONAL ACCOUNTS, Main Aggregates, Volume I, 1960–96, 1998
   NATIONAL ACCOUNTS, Detailed Tables, Volume II, 1988–98, 2000
   NATIONAL ACCOUNTS, Detailed Tables, Volume II, 1982–94, 1996
   Measuring Globalization, the Role of Multinationals in OECD Economies, 1999 Edition

PNAC   *"Project For The New American Century."* 1150 17th Street NW, Suite 510, Washington, DC 20036. Tel: (202) 293 4983. See: http://www.newamericancentury.org

Poole, Patrick S. *"ECHELON: America's Secret Global Surveillance Network."* (Free Congress Foundation, U.S.A. 1999/2000).

Porter, Michael E et al. *"The Global Competitiveness Report 2000."* (Oxford University Press, 198 Madison Avenue, New York, NY 10016, 2000).

Rao, C. P. *"Globalization and its Managerial Implications."* (Quorum Books, Greenwood Publishing Group, Inc., 88 Post Road West, P.O. Box 5007, Westport, CT 06881-5007, 2000).

Record, Jeffrey. *"The Bush Doctrine and War with Iraq."* (Parameters, U.S. Army War College Quarterly, Spring 2003).
   http://carlisle-www.army.mil/usawc/Parameters/03spring/record.htm.

Richardson, M. *"Globalization and International Trade Liberalization."* (Edward Elgar Publishing, Northampton, MA, 2000).

Richebächer, Kurt. "The Richebaecher Letter." (Agora Publishing, Inc., P.O. Box 1936, Baltimore, MD 21203. Tel: (203) 699 2921. dailyreckoning@agora-inc.com).

Robertson, James O. *"American Myth, American Reality."* (Hill and Wang, New York, 1982).

Saari, D. J. *"Global Corporations and Sovereign Nations. Collision or Cooperation?"* (Quorum Books, Greenwood Publishing Group, Inc., 88 Post Road West, P.O. Box 5007, Westport, CT 06881-5007, 1999).

Schaeffer, R. K. *"Understanding Globalization: The Social Consequences of Political, Economic, and Environmental Change."* (Rowman & Lilleefield Publishing, Boston, 1997).

SchNEWS. PO Box 2600 Brighton, BN2 2DX, England. http://www.schnews.org.uk/

Spengler, Oswald. *"The Decline of the West."* (Oxford University Press, 198 Madison Avenue, New York, NY 10016, 1991).

Sullivan, J. J. *"The Future of Corporate Globalization. From The Extended Order to The Global Village."* (Quorum Books, Greenwood Publishing Group, Inc., 88 Post Road West, P.O. Box 5007, Westport, CT 06881-5007, 2002).

The McAlvany Intelligence Advisor. P.O.Box 84904, Phoenix, AZ 85071-9965

Tonelson, Alan. *"The Race to the Bottom."* (Westview Press, Boulder, CO, 2000).

UNITED STATES OF AMERICA
U.S. DEPARTMENT OF COMMERCE, Washington, DC
U.S. OUTWARD FDI DATA
Survey of Current Business
U.S. Direct Investment Abroad: Detail for Historical-Cost Position and Related Capital and Income Flows
   1977–90, August 1991, 81–107
   1982–88, August 1992, 116–144
   1990, August 1991, 81–107
   1991, August 1992, 116–144

1992, July 1993, 88–124
1993, August 1994, 127–161
1994, August 1995, 88–116
1995, September 1996, 98–128
1996, September 1997, 119–148
1997, October 1998, 117–155

U.S. Direct Investment Abroad: 1989 Benchmark Survey Results October 1991, 29–55
Direct Investment Positions on a Historical-Cost Basis, 1993: June 1994, 72–78

U.S. Multinational Companies: Operations in . . .

1984, September 1986, 27–39
1985, June 1987, 26–45
1986, June 1988, 85–96
1987, June 1989, 37–39
1988, June 1990, 31–44
1990, August 1992, 60–78
1991, July 1993, 40–58
1992, June 1994, 42–62
1993, June 1995, 31–51
1994, December 1996, 11–37
1995, October 1997, 44–68
1996, September 1998, 47–73
1997, July 1999, 8–35
1998, July 2000, 26–45

Employment and Employee Compensation of U.S. Multinational Companies in 1977 February 1982, 37–49

Gross Product of U.S. Multinational Companies, 1977–91, February 1994, 42–63

Benchmark Surveys

U.S. Direct Investment Abroad

1977 Benchmark Survey, April 1981.
1982 Benchmark Survey Data. December 1985.
1989 Benchmark Survey, Final Results. October 1992.
1994 Benchmark Survey, Final Results. May 1998.

INWARD FDI DATA

U.S. Department of Commerce, *Economics and Statistics Administration, Bureau of Economic Analysis:* www.bea.doc.gov/bea/pubs.htm

Benchmark Surveys

FOREIGN DIRECT INVESTMENT IN THE UNITED STATES

— *1980 Benchmark Survey,* October 1983
— *Selected Data 1950–79,* December 1984
— *Operations of United States Affiliates, 1977–80,* 1985
— *1987 BENCHMARK SURVEY, PRELIMINARY RESULTS,* July 1989
— *1987 Benchmark Survey, Final Results,* August 1990
— *1992 BENCHMARK SURVEY, PRELIMINARY RESULTS,* August 1994
— *1992 Benchmark Survey, Final Results,* September 1995

International Direct Investment, Studies by the Bureau of Economic Analysis, March 1999

Economic and Statistics Administration, Office of the Chief Economist

FOREIGN DIRECT INVESTMENT IN THE UNITED STATES, An Update, Review and Analysis of Current Developments, August 1991

Ibid., June 1993

Ibid., January 1995
Ibid., September 1997
SURVEY OF CURRENT BUSINESS (SOCB)
Foreign Direct Investment in the United States: Detail for Historical-Cost Position and Related Capital and Income Flows
1980, August 1981, 40–51
1981, August 1982, 30–41
1982, August 1983, 31–41
1983, October 1984, 26–48
1984, August 1985, 47–66
1987, August 1988, 69–83
1988, August 1989, 47–61
1990, August 1991, 47–79
1991, August 1992, 87–115
1992, July 1993, 59–87
1993, August 1994, 98–126
1994, August 1995, 53–87
1996, September 1997, 75–118
1997, September 1998, 74–110

Balance of Payments and Direct Investment Position Estimates, 1980–86, December 1990
U.S. Affiliates of Foreign Companies: Operations in . . .
1981, November 1983, 19–34
1982, December 1984, 28–47
1983, November 1985, 36–50
1984, October 1986, 31–45
1986, May 1988, 59–75
1987, July 1989, 116–140 (1987 Benchmark Survey Results)
1988, July 1990, 127–143
1989, July 1991, 72–92
1990, May 1992, 45–68
1991, May 1993, 89–112
1998, August 2000, 141–158

Foreign Direct Investment in the United States, Affiliate Operations in . . .
1992 Benchmark Survey Results, July 1994, pp. 154–186
1993, May 1995, 57–81
1994, July 1996, 102–130
1995, June 1997, 42–69
1996, June 1998, 39–67

Foreign Direct Investment in the United States, Preliminary Results from the 1997 Benchmark Survey
August 1999, 21–54
STATISTICAL ABSTRACT OF THE UNITED STATES, various issues
The Economist, 111 West 57th Street New York, NY 10019-2211
"*The case for globalization.*" September 23–29, 2000
"*Euroshambles.*" September 16–22, 2000
The Guardian Weekly, 75 Farringdon Rd, London EC1M3HQ, UK
UNITED NATIONS, New York and Geneva. E-mail: www.un.org/
Human Development Report 2003
Statistical Yearbook, various issues

World Investment Report, UNCTAD, various issues

Yearbook of National Accounts Statistics, various issues

von Weizsäcker, C.C. *"Logik der Globalisierung."* (Vandenhoek & Ruprecht, Göttingen, Germany, 1999).

Wang Jian. *"War: Greenback's Attempt to Stifle Euro."* http://www.atimes.com November 2003.

— *"US-China-EU: An Exercise in Asymmetry."* http://www.rayeslemmens.com November 2003. (Mr. Wang is Secretary General of the Economic Planning Commission, Beijing, and Vice-president of the China Society of Macro-Economics).

Went, Robert, Peter Drucker, Tony Smith, Robert Wentz: *"Globalization: Neoliberal Challenge, Radical Responses."* (Pluto Press, 345 Archway Road, London N6 5AA, UK, 2000). pluto@plutobooks.com

WORLD BANK, Washington, D.C., 1994 & 1995.

World Development Indicators, various issues

World Tables, various issues

WORLD PRESS REVIEW, (The Stanley Foundation, 700 Broadway, New York, NY 10003).